MW00324224

THE MEMOIRS OF
BARON VON MÜFFLING

THE MEMOIRS OF
BARON VON MÜFFLING

A PRUSSIAN OFFICER
IN THE NAPOLEONIC WARS

Baron Carl von Müffling

Introduction by Peter Hofschröer

Frontline Books

The Memoirs of Baron von Müffling

A Greenhill Book

Published in 1997 by Greenhill Books, Lionel Leventhal Limited
www.greenhillbooks.com

This edition published in 2015 by

Frontline Books
an imprint of Pen & Sword Books Ltd,
47 Church Street, Barnsley, S. Yorkshire, S70 2AS
For more information on our books, please visit
www.frontline-books.com, email info@frontline-books.com
or write to us at the above address.

This edition © Lionel Leventhal Ltd, 1997
Introduction © Peter Hofschröer, 1997

ISBN: 978-1-84832-827-3

Publishing History
The Memoirs of Baron von Müffling was first published in 1853 as *Passages From My
Life, together with Memoirs of the Campaign of 1813 and 1814* (Richard Bentley,
London), a revised and edited translation of the original German, *Aus meinem Leben*,
first published in 1851. It is now reproduced exactly as the original edition, complete
and unabridged, with the addition of an Introduction by Peter Hofschröer.

CIP data records for this title are available from the British Library

Printed and bound by CPI Group (UK) Ltd, Croydon, CR0 4YY

INTRODUCTION

MÜFFLING'S CAREER

Philipp Friedrich Carl Ferdinand Freiherr (Baron) von
Müffling was born on 12 June 1775 in Halle, a town near
Leipzig which had been under Brandenburg-Prussian
rule since 1680. His father, born into the Saxon minor
nobility, was a veteran of the Seven Years and the Revolutionary Wars, and was severely wounded at Jena in
1806. The young Müffling, as was normal practice in the
military families of the period, joined the Prussian army
as an adolescent 'Gefreiterkorporal' in 1788. He was fortunate to be enlisted in one of the newly founded fusilier
battalions, élite formations whose officers were later to
provide many of the more skilled and able senior leaders
of the Prussian army. One could describe the fusilier
battalions as the nursery of the general staff; indeed,
Müffling came to be one of the most respected and able
staff officers in the Prussian army.

Müffling rose through the ranks from 1793 to 1795,
participating in the battles in the Palatinate as a 2nd
Lieutenant in the Fusilier Battalion von Schenck. He
described his earlier years in the army as having taught
him very little. However, in the years immediately after
the Peace of Basle of 1795, he started to show a propensity for cartography which was to play a significant role
in his later life. In 1803, Müffling transferred to a new
line regiment, the Infantry Regiment Wartensleben

(No. 59). This regiment was based in the fortress of Erfurt, and its commander described Müffling as a 'particularly distinguished, talented and industrious officer'.[1] A year later, he received his first post in the general staff, the beginning of a most successful career. Significantly, in 1805, he received an appointment to Blücher's staff, although at the beginning of the ill-fated Campaign of 1806 he was attached to Hohenlohe's retinue, and delegated to the staff of Duke Charles August of Weimar's Corps. In the course of the retreat from Jena, Müffling came across Blücher's forces and was taken prisoner along with the old war horse at Ratkau. Once peace was agreed, he joined the Duke of Weimar's government as a civil servant. Here he remained until the outbreak of the Wars of Liberation at the beginning of 1813.

On 26 April 1813, urged by Scharnhorst, the famous reformer and staff officer, Müffling returned to the Prussian army with the rank of lieutenant-colonel. Lehmann, Scharnhorst's biographer, describes Müffling as 'sober, mathematical, basically of the old school, and unfortunately also vain and selfish'.[2] Scharnhorst, however, valued his energy and ability to grasp matters easily. At first, Müffling got on well with Gneisenau, another of the leading reformers of the army, and was particularly befriended by Knesebeck, one of the more conservative senior officers.

In June 1813, Müffling was attached to Blücher's headquarters. A month later, he was promoted to full colonel and appointed senior quartermaster of the Army of Silesia. As such, he had an inside view of the dramatic

---

[1] Priesdorff (ed.), *Soldatisches Führertum* Vol. 3 (Hamburg, no date), p. 309.

[2] Lehmann, *Scharnhorst* Vol. 2 (Leipzig, 1887), p. 600.

events of several major battles, winning an Iron Cross, 2nd Class, at Bautzen, and 1st Class at the Battle on the Katzbach. These were among the first of many awards he was to receive.

Müffling was promoted to major-general at the end of 1813, participating in the invasion of France at the beginning of 1814. After the Battle of Étoges, his relationship with Gneisenau deteriorated. On the whole, Müffling performed well; he was particularly known for his orderliness, his business-like manner, his fluency in French and ability with the pen. However, Gneisenau, in a letter to Clausewitz looking back on certain events in the Campaigns of 1813 and 1814, wrote that: 'Müffling was overconfident in times of good fortune, but became disheartened in times of misfortune. When everything was going well, he wanted to take charge. However, when things were going badly, he became so lethargic that he could not work any more'.[3] His literary skills were recognised by Friedrich Wilhelm III who, on 3 July 1813, ordered him to write an account of that spring's campaign and to keep a record of the forthcoming campaign. This work was later published, and Müffling had the opportunity of setting the record straight, as far as he was concerned, on several matters. He used this opportunity to deal with certain of his critics in the army, a trait that is apparent throughout his writings.

After the fall of Paris, which marked the end of the first phase of the Wars of Liberation, Müffling was awarded the 'Pour le Mérite' with oak-leaves. He became the chief-of-staff of the Russian General Barclay de Tolly before joining General von Kleist as his chief-

---

[3] Priesdorff, op. cit., p. 310.

of-staff with the Prussian Army of the Lower Rhine. He used the short period of peace to pursue an earlier project, the mapping of the Rhineland begun nearly two decades earlier by Le Coq, and assisted by a younger Müffling. This more congenial task was interrupted by Bonaparte's escape from exile on the isle of Elba. Kleist's army was likely to be one of the first to see action in the forthcoming war, and Müffling, as his chief-of-staff, had his best opportunity for fame and glory yet. This was, however, not to be; Blücher replaced Kleist, and Gneisenau replaced Müffling, which did little to help their already poor relationship. Müffling was appointed liaison officer in the Duke of Wellington's headquarters, a task he performed competently, although a politician as astute as Wellington was able to keep the trusting Prussian in the dark on a number of issues, dupe him on others, and finally to use him as the conduit of false information and insincere promises. Müffling later wrote an account of the Waterloo Campaign, another opportunity for him to 'correct' the record. In his researches, it must have become apparent to Müffling how the Duke had managed to fool him on several occasions, but his memories were selective enough not to mention such embarrassing occurrences. Nevertheless, Müffling's contribution to the final victory over the 'Corsican Ogre' was significant, and one could say with some justification that this Prussian was one of the leading personalities that helped to establish a long period of stability and peace in Europe.

The years of peace that followed the decisive victory at Waterloo were enjoyed by Müffling. His abilities and services were recognised by awards from princes and kings from all over Europe. From 1817 to 1820, he continued to map the Rhineland, and his maps were of such a high quality, they were used until the end of the nineteenth century. These maps were of particular importance to the defence of Germany's western border against French aggression, and were highly valued. Müffling also carried out diplomatic missions, but, in 1819, turned down the offer of becoming the Prussian ambassador in London; he would probably have felt most uncomfortable being so close to the Duke of Wellington who had done much to make a fool of him in 1815.

With the task of mapping the Rhineland accomplished, Müffling was, on 11 January 1821, appointed chief of the general staff of the army, one of the most influential positions in Prussia. Here he was again able to provide important services to his nation. His topographical skills were again used, and his method marking the gradients of hills on maps was adopted as a standard which became known as the 'Müffling Method'. He also spoke out in favour of keeping conscription and in support of maintaining the 'Landwehr' (territorial reserves) as an essential part of national defence. While more conservative elements favoured going back to an élitist professional army divorced from the nation as a whole, Müffling took a more progressive line, wanting to maintain the army as the 'school of the nation'. He also carried out a major reorganisation of the general staff, and was closely involved in the training of its officers. He drafted plans of operation in various theatres in which war could break out. Müffling was also a major influence in the training of the entire army, paying attention to all aspects of drill and equipment. In his role as chief of the general staff, Müffling also took an active role in shaping the nature and objectives of the annual autumn manoeuvres. He did much to ensure that the Prussian army would not again make the mistake of complacency, unpreparedness and overconfidence that contributed to the catastrophic defeat in 1806.

Müffling also took over control of the 'Militair-Wochenblatt', making it the organ of the Prussian general staff. This weekly journal attracted many high quality contributions from military authorities and remains even today one of the most significant military periodicals ever produced. Under his guidance, the Prussian general staff started to produce the first of a series of high quality military historical works such as their history of the Seven Years War, published in eight volumes from 1824 to 1847, and illustrated with numerous maps which no doubt Müffling particularly influenced.

Pre-industrial Prussia was a state with limited resources, and government spending cuts were often the order of the day. When, at the end of 1824, the king informed Müffling that his budgets for the general staff were to be reduced, Müffling asked for a transfer. The king refused to move his valued chief from his post at the head of the general staff, increasing Müffling's salary as an attempt at recompense for the cut in his departmental budget. Müffling's dissatisfaction led to him falling ill. By the end of 1827, he had recovered sufficiently to be able to take up his duties again. In 1828, he conducted experiments with shrapnel artillery rounds. The next year, he was sent on a diplomatic mission to the Sultan of the Ottoman Empire in Istanbul. Here, he persuaded the Turks to make peace with the Czar of Russia. Both the Czar and the King of Prussia presented him with awards for his accomplishment. Shortly afterwards, he was finally granted his earlier request for an appointment to a field command, becoming commanding general of the VII Army Corps, based in the Rhineland, where he dealt with an awkward situation in which conscripts were bribing local doctors to issue false medical certificates declaring them unfit for military service. Conscription has always been unpopular, no matter where or when.

Müffling's next major achievement was the introduction of the optical telegraph in 1830. Any improvement to military capabilities in that year of unrest just across the border in France was welcomed; Prussia was always wary of the threat from the west. His corps was placed in a state of readiness, and troops were sent to the border to disarm any insurgents that might cross it. In 1832, his corps was brought up to its war strength as a response to the situation in Belgium, where the French army was expected to intervene. However, the threat of a new European war dissipated, and in January 1833, Müffling's corps was demobilised.

In 1838, Müffling was made Governor of Berlin, the capital of Prussia. His health had deteriorated, and he spent much of his time taking cures. In 1840, he directed the funeral of Friedrich Wilhelm III, and two years later celebrated his fiftieth year of service in the Prussian army. By 1847, his health had become so poor that he retired from service, although he remained colonel-in-chief of the 27th Infantry Regiment, an honour he had received in 1836. He died on 16 January 1851, aged seventy-five years, with the rank of general field marshal.

Müffling was clearly a man of great ability and achievement who accomplished much in his long life of public service. For much of his life, he stood in the shadow of greater men, but when given the opportunity to perform well, he did so, and left a lasting record. His maps of the Rhineland are still used today, although more for decorative and historical purposes; his history of the Waterloo Campaign was reprinted in recent years, and now, at long last, his revealing and informative memoirs are again available. These memoirs are particularly valuable as no others of a senior Prussian officer of this period have been translated into English.

MÜFFLING AND NAPIER'S WATERLOO MYTH

With Müffling's noteworthy record of accomplishment, it is a shame that some writers have failed to fully appreciate his role at Waterloo. The unsubstantiated stories about this fine officer appear to have originated from William Napier, the British historian of the Peninsular War, in his 'Waterloo Letter' written in 1842 and first published in a work of that name in 1891. Napier, at the time of writing, a sick man hallucinating under the narcotics being administered to alleviate his condition, at least has an excuse for his invention.[4] The relevant section of this letter reads:

> He [Wellington] then [at some time after 11 p.m. on 15 June 1815] went into his quarters and found Müffling there, coming from Blücher with the news; he ought to have arrived long before, but the Duke said to me [Napier], 'I cannot tell the world that Blücher picked the fattest man in his army [i.e. Müffling] to ride with an express to me, and that he took thirty hours to go thirty miles'.

---

[4] For details of Napier's condition and its effects, see Bruce, *Life of General Sir William Napier* (London, 1864), p. 198 ff.

Although the above version of these events is in conflict with the record and makes no sense, this has not stopped certain historians from repeating it, although, more fittingly, it has also formed the basis for an episode in Bernard Cornwell's fictional *Sharpe's Waterloo*. As any reader of Müffling's memoirs will see, he had a number of despatch riders at his disposal who carried his messages. Furthermore, Müffling was stationed in Brussels while all the above was going on, so could not have been carrying messages from Zieten in Charleroi to Wellington in Brussels. Also, as a major-general, Müffling was simply too senior an officer to spend his time gallivanting around on a horse somewhere in Belgium. As the French offensive is on record as having started at 4 a.m. on 15 June, then for Napier's story to be true, for Müffling to have taken thirty hours to have brought the message to Brussels at 11 p.m., he would have had to have left with the news of the outbreak of hostilities eleven hours before it happened. Either Müffling was in two places at once and clairvoyant, or Napier's story is totally unfounded. Those historians basing their accounts on Napier's myth would appear to lack common sense, a basic knowledge of military procedures, and even of mathematics. The events as portrayed in the 1970 film *Waterloo* are equally fictional.

MÜFFLING AND THE WATERLOO CAMPAIGN

During the course of researching the Campaign of Waterloo, the writer of this Introduction has had cause to refer to correspondence sent by Müffling to the Prussian army headquarters during the crucial days of the Campaign of 1815 as deposited in the Berlin Archives. In doing so, it has been possible to ascertain the accuracy of certain points in Müffling's memoirs, which were, after all, written some years after these events, and from memory. While the Duke of Wellington first heard of the outbreak of hostilities in a report sent to him about 5 a.m. on 15 June 1815[5] which he received by 9 a.m.,[6] Wellington appears to have kept the news within his headquarters and not informed Müffling.[7] Wellington does not appear to have left a record of his reasons for keeping the Prussian in the dark.

According to Müffling's memoirs, he first heard of the outbreak of hostilities when Zieten, commander of the Prussian I Army Corps which suffered the full brunt of the French assault that day, sent a courier directly to Müffling who arrived in Brussels at 3 p.m. At 7 p.m. that day, after Wellington had issued his orders to his army to concentrate, the Duke had Müffling draft a letter to Blücher on British army note-paper and marked with the British seal, which was carried to the Prussian head-quarters by a British courier, informing Blücher that Wellington would be in a position to support Blücher in force the next day,[8] a promise the Duke, who had just finished drafting certain orders to his army, knew he could not keep. Wellington duped Müffling into pro-viding his commander with false information. When Müffling accompanied the Duke to the front the next morning, Wellington managed to write an important letter to Blücher again making promises he knew he

[5] *Militärisches*, Heft I: Januar 1896 (Leipzig), p. 252.

[6] Gurwood, *Dispatches, etc. of the Duke of Wellington* Vol. 12, p. 473.

[7] Jackson, *Notes and Reminiscences of a Staff Officer* (London, 1903) p. 12, and Public Records Office, London WO37/12, fol. 2, Scovell's papers (both officers on Wellington's staff). Their accounts indicate that the news had reached Brussels before 3 p.m. that day.

[8] Geheimes Staatsarchiv preußischer Kulturbesitz, Berlin, Rep 92, Gneisenau, A 48 fol. 93.

could not keep,[9] and did so in the presence of Müffling without the latter being aware of this. As liaison officer in Wellington's headquarters, it was Müffling's duty to be aware of what was going on, and particularly of matters most relevant to the Prussian army. Wellington kept Müffling in the dark, duped him into sending his commander false information and managed to slip a misleading letter to Blücher under Müffling's nose. Müffling, in later years chief-of-staff with access to the army archives, was in a position to check the records and establish that he had been left in ignorance of these significant items of information. It thus comes as no surprise that he failed to mention these errors on his part in his memoirs.

German historians such as Lettow-Vorbeck[10] and Pflugk-Harttung[11] were rightly critical of those aspects of Müffling's performance in the Waterloo Campaign, and Müffling's failure to mention them. However, this criticism of Müffling, unlike that of other historians, was both warranted and based on documented fact.

Although there is some justification in Lehmann's description of Müffling's vanity and selfishness, as the above incident illustrates, his long record of distinguished service speaks for itself; Müffling was a most able staff officer.

One should not forget that Müffling did much to coordinate the two wings of the Allied forces in the Low Countries in the Campaign of 1815, and thus can be credited as one of the architects of the Allied victory which ensured a period of peace, stability and prosperity

[9] Ollech, *Geschichte des Feldzuges von 1815* (Berlin, 1876), p. 125.

[10] Lettow-Vorbeck, *Napoleons Untergang 1815* (Berlin, 1904), p. 314 ff.

[11] Pflugk-Harttung, *Vorgeschichte der Schlacht bei Belle Alliance – Wellington* (Berlin, 1903), particularly pp. 267–76.

in a war-weary Europe. Müffling's later achievements on the diplomatic front in Russia and Turkey furthered the gains made in 1815 for peace in Europe. His contributions to the military sciences, particularly topography and military literature, likewise left a profound legacy for the use of future generations.

Peter Hofschröer, Rietberg, Germany, 1997.

MÜFFLING'S PUBLICATIONS

Müffling's major works of military history included:

Bemerkungen zu den Grundsätzen der höheren Kriegskunst

Berichte über die Vorgänge bei der Hohenloheschen Armee 1806

Die Geschichte der Armeen unter Wellington und Blücher im Feldzuge 1815

Die Feldzüge der schlesischen Armee unter Feldmarschall Blücher

Napoleons Strategie im Jahre 1813

Works published in the English language included:

History of the Campaign ... in the Year 1815

Sketch of the Battle of Waterloo

His memoirs were originally published in German as *Aus meinem Leben*, and translated into English as *Passages from my Life*.

PREFACE BY THE EDITOR.

THE Baron Von Müffling died at his estate near Erfurt, on the 16th of January, 1851, aged 77. The Work of which the first portion of this Volume is a translation, entitled, "*Aus meinem Leben,*" was published immediately after the decease of the Author, according to his desire. It was reviewed at great length in the *Quarterly Review* for December 1851, and especially recommended as deserving translation.

The concluding part of the original German Work consists of a narrative of a diplomatic mission to Constantinople, with which the Author was intrusted by his sovereign in 1829, and in which he had to play the part of mediator between the Emperor of Russia and the Sultan. He was successful in fixing the terms of peace between these two Powers, and received the cordial thanks of the Emperor Nicholas for his services, with the order of St. Wladimir.

This part of the Work scarcely possesses sufficient interest for English readers, and therefore the Translator has preferred to give the Author's Narrative of the Campaigns of 1813 and 1814, to which, as he states, a great part of the "Passages" is to be considered as a supplement.

The position which Baron Müffling occupied as Quarter-Master-General to the most active of the

German armies, entitles him to the respect of his readers, while the many important facts and interesting anecdotes, previously unknown, must render this Work essential to those who wish to understand the course of events and motives of the actors in those eventful campaigns.*

The English reader will probably turn with especial satisfaction to the unaffected testimony which our Author (a foreigner, and one who in this posthumous Memoir passes his judgment freely on all men and actions which come before him) bears not only to the military skill, but to the moral qualities—the straightforwardness and singleness of mind of the great Chief this country has lately lost. Sent to the head-quarters of the English army with a caution against its General, which to Englishmen must appear of the strangest character, Müffling soon found out the truth. At the close of the campaign the impression made on his mind by the character of the English General is forcibly evidenced by the remark, that he set a higher value on the good word of the Duke of Wellington than on the honours bestowed on him by the Regent of England.

PH. J. YORKE.

LONDON, JAN. 1853.

* To give a notion of the scale of operations, and consequent amount of casualties, in the campaign of 1813, we lay before our readers the following numbers. Those for the battle of Leipsic are taken from Wolzogen's Estimate (Q. R.). The British, from the "Companion to the Almanac for 1853 :"—

Number of killed and wounded on both sides, at the battle of Leipsic				80,640
Total British killed and wounded in military actions, from 1793 to 1815 inclusive				85,458

.*. The German mile used in this work is equal to 4 English.

AUTHOR'S PREFACE.

I LEAVE these Memoirs, my dear children, as an inheritance, intended to descend to you and my posterity. They will be a memorial of an ancestor of yours, who, through his official situation, was destined to bear a part in the extraordinary occurrences of a time remarkable for the general importance of its events.

My Memoirs, as a whole, may be in the nature of family property not fitted for publication; but I consider myself bound to leave behind me explanations or corrections relating to particular events of which I was an eye-witness, and to which an European interest attaches.

With this view I have extracted from my Memoirs, under the title of "Passages from my Life," certain sections, which I now hand over to you, as intended for publication. In doing this it was impossible to avoid judging of men and of their relations to each other.

However I carry with me to the grave the consolation that my readers will acknowledge the pains I have taken, in both respects, to keep within the proper limits of history, and how I have consequently avoided assuming the privileges and duties of a biographer.

These Memoirs, which contain the history of my education and life, and set forth the simple position and circumstances of Prussia in which I was involved, are destined to instruct my descendants, not indeed how to steer clear of rocks hidden beneath the surface, but how to bear with calm moderation the shocks which they cause.

My children, as also the readers of these pages, will draw from my Memoirs the conclusion, that during my long life I have been guided by the simple endeavour to do right, and to effect some good; they will perhaps find traces of the satisfaction it has been to me, to see an acknowledgment of this in the testimony of many honourable contemporaries; but it is far from my wish to conceal how often I have myself discovered, in riper years, how much more I might have done, had not my own faults hindered me.

A writer of ability has proposed the question for discussion, in which of two ways the interest of the public is best consulted,—whether more light is thrown on the dark spots and passages of history, by the steady light of general principles, or by what may be called the glimmer of the lantern which each man carries in his own hand?

All those who lay great stress on their conclusions being always preceded by a special contemplation of their own, will declare themselves in favour of the so-called hand-lantern; and all who intend to base their mode of action solely on existing circumstances, to the exclusion of the past and future, will join with them. On the other hand all, who wish to attain their aim without loss of time, will prefer that a light should be shed at once upon their whole path ; and they will be joined by all who are accustomed to follow up steadily a resolution which they have formed, and who meet accidental hindrances only by varying the means which they adopt for the attainment of their object.

The result of the whole suggests the serious question : — Whether the latter class, who guide themselves deliberately, *i. e.* according to principles, —or the former, who draw their conclusions from the perceptions of the moment, *i. e.* who proceed according to circumstances, — rightly comprehend the problem of the practical philosophy of life ?

In my youthful years, I was strongly attracted by these considerations and their consequences ; and the end has been, that I have all my life rejected what I have called the "hand-lantern."

It seemed to me that all who dislike binding themselves by fixed principles, and who prefer, in each particular case, to be guided by circumstances, are exposed to a twofold danger. They either run the risk of becoming useless members of society, by the indecision which results from the constant recurrence of painful subtleties ; or of rendering themselves intolerable in their intercourse with others, by the egotism and arrogance which arises from their being forced by want of time into all sorts of inconsistencies.

Experience moreover taught me, that the habit of acting according to the circumstances of the moment makes characters, otherwise the most open, mistrustful ; and that one soldier will not trust another, if he never knows beforehand how the latter will resolve to act in this or that position.

There was assuredly nothing censurable in my feeling and thinking thus, and guarding carefully against the opposite error; involuntarily, however, and unconsciously, I made the mistake of measuring my fellow-men only by this standard. Consistency gained from year to year additional value in my eyes; so that, without knowing it, I estranged myself from those who, under similar circumstances, had acted differently at different times; and I did this without regarding any brilliant qualities or high rank they might possess, or any influence they might exercise.

Where I found views which my official position obliged me to oppose, I endeavoured clearly to show the reasons which told against them; and as soon as I convinced myself that I was quite understood, I left the decision to my opponents. I did nothing to induce them to accede to my views, because it seemed to me wrong to persuade others, and hurry them on to measures which they did not adopt from conviction. This was an error by which I lost my influence with many a superior, who was used to yield to the art of dialectics or to friendly persuasions, and consequently expected one or the other from me. I could not bring myself to impute to others what I should myself have rejected doing as weak and culpable. If now, in my advanced years, I have to lament this disposition as a consequence of over-exalted notions, I have felt it right to warn my posterity, that they may not through such prejudices fall into similar errors.

Written on my 70th birth-day, 1844.

CONTENTS

CONTENTS

ANALYTICAL INDEX

TO PARTS I. AND II. WITH REFERENCE TO PART III.

SECTION II.

THE CAMPAIGN OF 1814 TO THE FIRST PEACE OF PARIS.

SUPPLEMENT TO PART I.

INDEX TO PART II.

FROM THE FIRST PEACE OF PARIS IN 1814 TO THE SECOND PEACE IN 1815.

INDEX TO PART III.

CAMPAIGN OF 1813.

Section I.

Section II.

Section III.

THE MEMOIRS OF
BARON VON MÜFFLING

PASSAGES FROM MY LIFE
AND WRITINGS.

PART I.

INTRODUCTION.—THE YEARS 1805–1806.—THE CAMPAIGN OF 1813.

INTRODUCTION.

FROM the time when I first began to choose my course of reading, and had to form my own opinion on the matter, I turned with especial predilection to French Memoirs; to speak more correctly, I found no mode of writing so well calculated as memoirs, to bring a section of history clearly before the eyes of the reader.

There are great difficulties in undertaking the duties of an historian, even when they are limited to the uniform progress and uniform treatment of the narrative.

History itself has no claim to such treatment. It is often, during long periods, intolerably dull and tiresome; while the short space of a few years outweighs in importance whole centuries, in instructing posterity, as well as strengthening the mind, which

B

finds in history the most valuable preparation for the development of its powers.

It has always appeared to me too great a demand on the human mind, for an individual who has lived through a remarkable period, to write its history. The higher his position, the more he has himself experienced, and the fuller account he is enabled to give of events; but, on the other hand, in undertaking the task of unfolding occurrences step by step chronologically, he is obliged to receive many statements from others; and inaccuracies, if not untruths and misrepresentations, unavoidably creep in.

Under all circumstances, therefore, truth will generally be found where the author lays before his readers only what he has himself seen, heard, or thought, at the time of the transaction, without troubling himself whether his history be complete and the picture perfected.

These are the principles, the general features, of Memoirs. But as a memoir is not expected to comprise the entire history of any period, as little is it the just province of such a work to aim at giving any complete picture of private life; and a writer who is able to narrate *some* interesting passages of history, must not imagine that he is therefore called upon to unfold his whole life to his readers.

It has always, indeed, struck me (who, in some periods of great international importance, have stood near the central point of political interest), that all which is tedious, and all that ought not to be narrated, must be passed over; but whether I have hit the right medium remains a question which my readers alone can answer.

Frederick II. exercised a very unfavourable in-

fluence on my education. My father,—an officer
of the Seven Years' War, knew that the king's
first demand on all young officers who aimed at a
rapid career, was *fluency in speaking French;* and
upon this my whole education, which was totally
wanting in solid information, was founded.

At that time no other means for training the
understanding existed, than the cultivation of the
dead languages. My father thought this could be
effected just as well by a living language—the
French,—and the argument, it must be acknowledged, was in one point of view correct. He overlooked the fact, however, that the means of teaching
the ancient languages were solid and fundamental,
whereas the teachers of the living languages, particularly French, almost wholly excluded the study of
grammar, assuming that this had already been acquired while learning the ancient languages. To
prove that this assumption was erroneous, could lead
to nothing; for no teacher of modern languages was
sufficiently prepared to teach grammatically. Thus,
in the University of Halle, where I was educated,
there was not a French master capable of teaching
the language *par principes,* or grammatically.

In the years when the first studies should begin,
I was obliged, after the prevailing custom, to enter
the army as an ensign; it is therefore no wonder
that, on my becoming an officer, I had learned
very little. From the year 1792 to 1802, in the
Revolutionary wars on the Rhine, my quarters were
shifted from place to place on the lines of demarcation, without my ever going into garrison. Experience was my sole master in military science: I
had a turn for mathematics, and was therefore

employed from 1798 to 1802 on the Trigonometrical
Survey for Lecoq's Map of Westphalia; and in
1803, after passing an examination I was placed
on the newly-organized General Staff. From this
time, numerous circumstances conspired to favour
my improvement in this branch of the service.

For three years, till 1805, I was employed as
assistant to Herr von Zach, Director of the Seeberg
Observatory. I directed the Thuringian mensuration, and travelled over the central countries of
Germany.

I was appointed to the General Staff Brigade
under Colonel von Scharnhorst, who kindly encouraged my zeal and activity. Scharnhorst had made
Napoleon's mode of warfare, and the means of resist-
ing him, the chief object of his study, and endeavoured accordingly to prepare young men for the
war, then easily to be foreseen, with this dangerous
opponent. The trouble which he took with me was
not thrown away, and when, in the year 1805, the
army was put in motion, I was esteemed by my
comrades, as well as by the superior officers of the
staff, an active, indefatigable officer, well qualified
for his business.

I was thirty years old, Lieutenant Quartermaster
General, healthy, strong, of a happy and contented
disposition. I had married a noble-minded wife,
and three hopeful children enlivened our days,
wnich were devoted to the duties of domestic life.

1805

The General Staff in its new organization had now existed three years.

The Quartermaster General, Lieutenant General von Geusau, was properly so only in name; for, as Inspector of the War Department and Chief of the Engineer Corps, he was an overworked man, who had no time to concern himself about the General Staff. We also knew beforehand that he would not go through the war with us.

Under him were three Lieutenant Quartermasters General, each of whom had a brigade, consisting of staff-officers, captains, and lieutenants, under his orders. The oldest of these, Colonel von Phull, had received his education in the Military Institution of Wurtemberg, then so celebrated, and had acquired the reputation of a great scholar. He was cold, reserved, morose by nature, always bitter, sarcastic and a great egotist. He knew nothing whatever of the life of a soldier or the feeling of a comrade. He did not understand how to deal with men, but repelled every one, and lived isolated. He made an impression on many, but he inspired little confidence, and no affection.

The next in seniority to him was Colonel von Massenbach : he had been brought up in the same Institute as Colonel von Phull, but was of an opposite nature. He was hot-headed, rich in ideas, and full of activity, but of no practical tendency. At the same time he was vehement, dogmatic, restless, and tormented by the peculiar passion for ruling all

around him. Where he met with submission he
showed good-nature, but opposition he could not
tolerate. He valued the art of public speaking
very highly, and was himself well qualified for it,
possessing a sonorous voice, a fine animated eye, and
a high open forehead; but he failed in making an
impression, because the *art* was immediately percep-
tible to his auditor, and the emotion which he strove
to enforce upon others invariably first seized upon
himself.

The third Lieutenant Quartermaster General was
Colonel von Scharnhorst, a thoroughly well-informed
man, who, from the Hanoverian service, in which
he made the campaigns of 1793-4, as officer of the
General Staff, had entered our army as Major. He
had served in all arms, and as teacher and writer he
strove indefatigably to acquire clearness.

By means of the few questions which he used to
put very simply and good-humouredly, he found
out whether a young man, beside his acquirements,
served with zeal and was possessed of presence of
mind. In his judgment of people, he always looked
more to their capacity than to their knowledge, because the former included the practical application
of the latter. A man himself so learned as Scharnhorst might be allowed to express such an opinion.
He has often been reproached with being too deliberate, and hence giving more the impression of a
professor than an officer. There is some truth in
this accusation, since his aim was precisely to appear
such. He did not want fire, but it was subdued and
purified.

There were at that time, in the Prussian army,
from the generals to the ensigns, hot heads without

number; and those who were not so by nature, assumed a passionate, coarse manner, fancying that it belonged to the military profession, and that Frederick II. desired it. It was then a rule inculcated on every young officer, not only to answer in a *determined manner* (as it was called), but to answer *at once*, without reflecting whether the answer were correct or false. It was said that Frederick II. never found fault with a lie *quickly* spoken in reply, but that he had dismissed officers who, on a question put by him, had considered their answer, even when quite right in doing so. This was a bad principle, and it was worthy of Scharnhorst's courage to resist it practically.

If we compare the body of officers of the Prussian army before the year 1802, and in 1813, we shall be obliged to confess that his example was not without effect.

The peace education of the staff officers was entrusted to these three brigadiers, uncontrolled, and each could introduce into it just what he thought proper. The two senior brigadiers laughed at Scharnhorst as a pedantic schoolmaster, and fed their officers with high-flown ideas which they were unable to digest; Scharnhorst alone adopted a well-considered method, to form diligent labourers, able but not conceited journeymen, and sensible masters, who did not fancy themselves capable of doing everything alone.

Until the year 1805, when the army began to be put in motion, I had remained with the third brigade under Scharnhorst. In the new distribution the officers of all three brigades were mixed, and it was then seen how little they had succeeded in introducing into the three brigades of the staff uniform views of the art of war, and still less a uniform mode of conducting the business of this important branch of the service. To us of the third brigade, it seemed as if in the other brigades, much egotism but little practical grasp of the subject had been developed.

I was sent to the army of the Prince of Hohenlohe, assembling in Thuringia, whose head-quarters were at Erfurt. Colonel von Massenbach was appointed Quartermaster General to this army, and I was the senior staff officer under him.

The Prince of Hohenlohe-Ingelfingen was educated in the maxims of the Seven Years' War: he was promoted by Frederick II., and had as early as 1792-4 commanded independent divisions, and finally an independent corps.

Massenbach had been his Quartermaster General. The Prince had much personal ambition; he loved military fame, and had proved himself a brave officer. He was more of a tactician than a strategist, but had been early prevented, by shortness of sight, from superintending the manœuvres of large bodies at drill. In 1805 his fitness for field-service was more than doubtful. He suffered from gout; and just when the command was offered him he had a violent attack, which he tried to check by daily embrocations with opodeldoc. In the morning his quarters smelt of this remedy for his malady, which he nevertheless endeavoured carefully, though in vain, to conceal. Had he clearly examined his bodily condition, and the duties which such an important command enjoined, he ought to have declined it as early as 1805. By this step he would have averted from himself and the army the heavy misfortune which occurred a year later.

The relation between the Prince and Massenbach was of a very peculiar kind. Massenbach influenced and governed the Prince in all his military ideas, yet not without some resistance on his part, which however was confined to keeping up the appearance of independence.

But this did not satisfy Massenbach; he wished for open and manifest subjection, and sought every opportunity of wearying his opponent by vexatious conduct, well knowing that after such provocations the good-natured Prince always, in the end, offered him the hand of reconciliation. In Erfurt I witnessed one of these attempts on the part of Massenbach, which occasioned a comical scene, that would have been entertaining had it not produced discord for a long time.

Massenbach had composed for the Military Society of Berlin, a panegyric on Duke Ferdinand of Brunswick, the victor of Crefeld, Minden, &c. The Prince heard of it, and wished to read it. Massenbach offered to read it aloud, and proposed the critical hour immediately after dinner; Majors von Pirch, von Röder (the Prince's aides-de-camp), and I, were invited to hear it. Massenbach told me in confidence that he intended to avail himself of this opportunity to effect something quite *extraordinary* for the welfare of the army and Prince.

After the death of Duke Ferdinand, the reports

of the Seven Years' War were deposited in the
archives at Berlin, and from these a discovery had
been made (which was little if at all known), that a
Brunswicker named Westphal, who attended the
Duke as secretary in these campaigns, had been at
the same time employed as his confidential strategist.
During the war, Westphal lived in the next room to
the Duke, and conducted his military correspondence, so that he was as accurately informed of all
events and circumstances in the army as the Duke
himself.

When the Allied Army, in pursuance of the
aim of its operations, or in consequence of some
march of the enemy, was obliged to make a movement, the Duke wrote the motive of it on a piece
of paper, and gave it to Westphal in the next room,
who had to write down in the margin what in his
opinion the Allied Army should do in such a con-
tingency.

From this correspondence, it appears not only
that Westphal must have been an unusually gifted
man for this department, but also that the Duke
generally adopted what he proposed, and that he
therefore exercised a great influence on the fortunate
issue of Duke Ferdinand's campaigns.

Massenbach's aim was to be the Westphal of
the Prince of Hohenlohe in the impending campaign; and he considered the reading of his panegyric a favourable opportunity for showing to
the Prince, that by this grand organization the
warlike fame of Duke Ferdinand was more solidly established, than by all the battles he had
won.

My doubts of his succeeding in bringing the

Prince into this opinion, which was quite foreign to him, remained unheeded, and the panegyric, re-touched for this purpose, was read with proper pathos. Massenbach sat opposite the Prince, the candles stood between the two, and I could observe the expression of their respective counte-nances.

The panegyric, which was long in itself, had been considerably lengthened by the additions about the relations of the Duke to his secretary, and we could not conceal from ourselves that it became rather wearisome. The Prince's eyes gradually closed : this Massenbach did not observe. The posture, inconvenient for sleep, occasioned some snoring, but Massenbach read with such fire that he heard nothing. When he came to the passage on the effect of which he had most reckoned, thick drops of perspiration stood on his high forehead, his voice was full of emotion, his eyes filled with tears ; and with the praise of the imperishable fame of his hero, the great moment arrived, when his moistened eye, seeking the approving glances of the Prince, after a side movement of his head, perceived that his chief auditor was sunk in profound slumber. When the Prince woke up at the sudden silence, Massenbach, with a furious look and deep sigh, had already packed up his ponderous discourse, and left the room with some disagreeable remarks.

The Prince, who was at first confused, and after-wards irritable, asked us if we had kept awake ; and when the aides-de-camp replied that respect gives great power of endurance, he complained of the inso-lence of reading such a tedious treatise immediately after dinner.

Massenbach could not forget this scene, so deeply mortifying to his vanity; and contrived, by his behaviour, that the ill-humour between himself and the Prince should be publicly known. When, however, he was summoned to Berlin, to assist at a council of war in the King's presence, the two found that they were necessary to each other: Massenbach, to strengthen his opinion by being able to say that his general saw things in the same light as himself; the Prince, to make the world believe that he had dispatched his Quartermaster General with instructions to this council.

Moreover, Massenbach did not wish to give up his position as Quartermaster General to the Prince. He knew that he could not get on so well with any other General-in-chief, and therefore he attempted in Berlin to bring about the Prince's nomination as Generalissimo. In this however he did not succeed, as the Prince's weakness and vanity were too well known there.

By order of this council of war, a small corps under General von Blücher was collected at Bayreuth (to which I was sent as Lieutenant Quartermaster), in order to watch thence more closely the consequences of the battle of Austerlitz, namely, the occupation of the Principality of Ansbach by Marshal Bernadotte's corps.

It was here that I was first placed under the orders of the man who, eight years later, had the good luck to render such important services to Europe. I here became acquainted with all his good qualities, and learnt to esteem him as the true model of a soldier. In Ansbach I saw the French army, and the lightness of their infantry movements; and I perceived that, without considerable alteration in ours, we must be worsted in a war. All their infantry officers carried knapsacks on their backs, even the chefs de bataillon and adjutants, while our battalions required fifty extra horses. I sent a memorial on the subject to General Rüchel, my patron, who replied,—"My friend, a Prussian nobleman never goes on foot!"

Blücher's corps was withdrawn after the occupation of Hanover; but I was directed to remain with Major-General Count Tauentzien, who commanded the Franconian brigade in Bayreuth until just before the breaking out of hostilities in 1806. I employed my time in drawing up a tableau of the French army, showing the *ordre de bataille* of all the corps according to their regimental numbers. This was necessary, indeed indispensable to us, but was not intended for the commanding officers. The Duke of Brunswick heard of it, and this may perhaps have been the reason of his summoning me near his person, at his head-quarters at Halle.

Here I found the Duke, as Generalissimo, uncertain about the political relations of Prussia with France and England, uncertain about the strength and position of the French corps d'armée in Germany, and without any fixed plan as to what should be done. But he was far from taking upon himself the responsibility of acting according to circumstances; on the contrary, he had determined to lay before the King a plan for his approval.

The Duke of Brunswick enjoyed in his 73rd year a remarkable degree of activity of body and freshness of mind, but he had grown mistrustful and cautious to excess; he wanted simplicity in the management of business, and events had gotten so much in advance of him, that instead of leading he was himself led by them.

He had accepted the command in order to prevent war. I can assert this with confidence, because I heard it more than once from his own lips, when his subordinates had been aggravating the difficulties of his position, or did things behind his back to which he was by no means a party. At times when, in strict confidence, I had suggested to him methods for enforcing and maintaining obedience, he used to vent his ill-humour by describing the peculiarities of all around him in the plainest and bitterest terms. He would call Prince Hohenlohe a vain and weak man, who suffered himself to be governed by Massenbach ; General von Rüchel, a *fanfaron;* Field-Marshal Möllendorf, a dotard ; General von Kalkreuth, a cunning trickster ; and the subordinate generals, in a mass, mere men of routine without talents : winding up with these words : " And it is with such men we are to encounter a Napoleon ! No, the greatest service I can render the King will be to preserve peace for him if I can."

Scharnhorst was appointed the Duke's Quartermaster General, instead of Lieutenant Quartermaster General von Phull, who had been placed in the King's suite because the Duke hated him. The Duke certainly felt an esteem for Scharnhorst, although he had an especial aversion to consult him on military subjects.

The Duke's hope was centred in Lucchesini and Haugwitz, because these men made him believe that war might still be avoided. The answer of Lucchesini still sounds in my ears, when after his

arrival from Paris at the royal head-quarters at
Naumburg, in reply to the Duke's question as to
Napoleon's intentions, he answered: "Sir, he will
never become the aggressor: never! never!"

A gleam of inward satisfaction overspread the
Duke's face at these words. He paid formal court
to both ministers, Lucchesini and Haugwitz, because
he considered them the peace party.

Scharnhorst arrived at head-quarters a month
after me; until then he had been travelling on the
King's business. I wished now to join the Duke of
Weimar's division, to which I belonged by appointment, but Scharnhorst retained me. He had to
overcome the Duke's natural mistrust, which did not
stand in my way. But I was the subaltern, who only
ventured to speak when asked. Scharnhorst had
something methodical in his manner of stating what
he proposed, which was disagreeable to the Duke, who
knew that if he was of a different opinion he could
only end the matter by a distinct and grave reply.

When Scharnhorst made proposals in the spirit of
modern warfare, the Duke started, looked at me with
his large eyes, as if I ought to speak. If I remained
silent, he managed to draw me into the conversation,
and whenever I attempted to place the practical
ideas of Scharnhorst in a still more striking light,
he got out of humour. One morning, when I
accompanied Scharnhorst to the council, he said
to me: "I cannot get on with this singular man,
who is made up of prejudices. I will not peril the
confidence he has in you: do not vote with me in
the important questions upon the decision of war,
that our general may not believe we are continually
plotting to govern him."

The Duke liked, by conferences with some eight or ten persons, to enlighten himself on strategical points, and to these amongst others he invited General von Phull. We had already sat some hours, and much had been said which was useless and incorrect, when the Duke left us to receive a message in the next room. In the interval Phull jumped up with vehemence, and exclaimed : "What good can arise out of such a cursed medley of opinions ? "

In the celebrated conference at Erfurt, on the 5th of October, at which all the Commanding Generals and Quartermasters General were present, as well as Major von Rauch and myself, Massenbach read a long memoir to prove that the army should march off to the left, by Hof and Bayreuth, and there establish a communication with Austria.

There was not a particle of sound sense in this idea. Saxony, encircled by the Erzgebirge, and the Thuringian forest as far as the Hartz, forms a *tête de pont* for the Elbe from Dresden to Magdeburg. We occupied this *tête de pont;* we had resolved not to *begin* hostilities, and Massenbach wanted to lead us out of this *tête de pont* through a needle's eye to Franconia. For what purpose ?

It was not difficult to foresee that Napoleon would permit us to draw quietly towards Nürnberg, and penetrate from the west, without opposition, into Saxony. What then ? Helter-skelter back we should have to go again, not to lose the pass at Hof and the passage across the Elbe ! The whole proposition did not merit an answer.

However, the Duke got into a parley with Massenbach, and on the latter answering him warmly, he asked Scharnhorst : "Colonel, what say you to it ? " Scharnhorst had hitherto made every effort to put the army in motion, not to await the commencement of hostilities by Napoleon, but to break through his armies marching from the borders of Bohemia to form a junction at Frankfort, and force them to a retrograde concentration ; but he had always been put off, and referred to this conference. He now rose and declared : "I certainly cannot agree to the proposition of Colonel von Massenbach ; however, that is of no consequence now ; in war, to act for the best is the main thing ; and one thing is certain, it is best to do *something;* and in default of anything better, this may pass."

This was to the Duke quite an unexpected acquiescence in Massenbach's proposal. He would not set the army in motion, because he hoped that by remaining quiet, peace might still be maintained.

The Duke now asked Field Marshal Möllendorf, Generals Count Kalkreuth, Prince Hohenlohe, Rüchel, and Zastrow, what was to be done ; but they all declared that they knew too little about the enemy to be able to give any opinion.

"How to get information ? "

By detachments which should be sent from Eisenach to Saalfeld through the Thuringian forest. Now this was just what the Duke wanted : he had diverted the attention of his subordinates to other ideas, and could now call upon them for further explanations.

Prince Hohenlohe dictated a plan, of a sheet long, for his corps to proceed in *échelon* through the Thuringian forest, in order at last to advance a couple of squadrons towards Franconia, to the confines of

Coburg and Hildburghausen. The Prince did not
bestow on us a single battalion, nor half a battery;
and the object of the conference was lost, while its
members were exercising their skill in the art of dic-
tating arrangements.

General von Rüchel, who then laid down a plan
of operations for his small corps, went still farther;
he entered into wearisome details, which were not at
all in place, and brought the head of his corps (*one*
squadron) safely to Meiningen, where every place was
barricaded, since the adjoining territory of the King
of Bavaria (who, as a member of the newly instituted
Confederation of the Rhine, belonged to Napoleon's
allies,) was to be looked upon as hostile.

Scharnhorst thanked heaven, when, about midnight, the conference came to an end, as no result
could be expected from such a meeting. No one
who was present at it could deceive himself as to the
issue of the war.

These then were the generals who were to oppose
the youthful Napoleon and his victorious and warlike marshals !

The battles of Jena and Auerstädt, the retreat
and the capitulation of Prenzlau and Lübeck, are
events so well known that I may pass them over here.

For me was reserved the heart-rending meeting
with the Duke on his bed in Brunswick, with bloody
bandages over his sightless orbits, and the equally
melancholy sight of his body on the day of his death
in Ottensen. With deep pain I viewed the remains
of a Prince who, since the Seven Years' War, had
played such an important part in the history of the
world, who possessed many great and excellent qualities, and deserved a better fate.

After the close of the campaign of 1806, I committed to paper the plan of operations of the Prussian-Saxon army; I had the battle-field of Auerstädt surveyed, and marked down the movements of both sides.* Scharnhorst, to whom I sent the work to Königsberg, answered in these words : "I was engaged in writing an account of this battle; but since I have received your plan of it, I have put my own entirely aside,—I can give nothing better."

The object I had in writing my plan of operations, namely, to prove to any unprejudiced person that the Prussian army had not succumbed so disgracefully as the French boasters attempted to represent, and some of our own good-for-nothing countrymen endeavoured to make the world believe, was more nearly attained than I expected.†

I made the retreat with the Duke of Weimar, who, after the dispersion of the Prussian army on this side the Oder, invited me as a companion in misfortune to come to him at Weimar. There he conferred on me the place of a Vice-President. I was too well known to the French as one of their

---

* In order to avoid a conflict with the French police in Germany, I published my work, not under the name my family usually bears, but with the initials of my second name, which are only used in judicial proceedings, C. von W., with the motto, "La critique est aisée, mais l'art est difficile." I have retained this signature also in later writings.

† Among the papers left by General von Clausewitz was found a narrative of the campaign of 1806, cleverly executed, and truthful, but containing sharp and even bitter criticism. At the time of his death a number of the men he censured were still living, and it was deemed advisable to put off the publication. A memoir by Gentz has treated the political part of the short campaign. So far as I could investigate, there is no untruth in it.

greatest enemies, to be able to serve the King materially after the Peace of Tilsit. In 1808, therefore,
I petitioned for my discharge, engaging that, when
ever the King drew his sword again, I would immediately apply to be reinstated.

It was the secret plan of the Duke of Weimar,
to make. his residence, which had hitherto been the
central point for art and science in Germany, now
also the centre of German freedom, as far as circumstances permitted, without drawing on himself
the attention of the French ruler, since so small a
state as the Duchy of Weimar was incapable of
resistance. I was the Duke's only confidant in this
plan, together with his worthy and most intelligent
wife ; and this state of things lasted until the war
broke out again in 1813.

The large literary correspondence kept up in
Weimar with all parts of Germany,—the Duke's
habit of making his chargés-d'affaires, or paid corre-
spondents, send him news from all parts of Europe—
facilitated the news-department.

The hospitality of the Court of Weimar, and the
numerous strangers who were constantly there, gave
opportunities for the dissemination of notions in close
connexion with our object. My part in these doings
was to avoid all that could compromise the princely
pair, and, should a victim be required, to offer myself
to be that victim. Meanwhile I neglected no precaution, and accompanied the Duke yearly on his
excursions to the baths of Teplitz, where, removed
from the burdensome French surveillance, and from
the French police at Erfurt, much could be transacted
more freely and safely than in Weimar.

Thus then, until the time of the burning of the

English colonial wares, Weimar was the central point of German freedom in the true sense of the word. From Weimar, encouragement was extended to the weak, and hatred was fostered against the tyrants; and much was quietly prepared, which, on the breaking out of the war in 1813, showed itself as a genuine German element.

Few, but sure, discreet and influential friends, from all parts of Germany, were informed of the project in view. The Duke had a remarkable talent for concealing, under a jovial exterior bordering on the frivolous, what was passing in his mind, and what he aimed at; so that the French considered him harmless.

At the meeting between the Emperor Alexander and Napoleon at Erfurt, in the autumn of 1808, all who did not belong to the new French system had severe mortifications to experience.

Napoleon evidently endeavoured to gain the Emperor to his ends by marked personal attention, but on the other hand to accustom him to the new relation arising from the Peace of Tilsit. He considered himself as the host, the Emperor as his guest; and he did the honours with scrupulous attention.

The Emperor found every comfort in a house prepared for him. Napoleon kept a daily table, and never neglected to receive him at the foot of his stairs, *en escarpins* with his hat under his arm. His chief attendants, the Prince de Neufchatel, the Grand Maréchal Duroc, the Grand Ecuyer Caulaincourt, the numerous aides-de-camp, the Marshals summoned to this meeting, Soult, Lannes, Oudinot, &c., the Prince de Talleyrand, the Duc de

Bassano, &c., all fêted the Emperor and the Grand Duke Constantine, but with the bearing of grandees.

A part of the French army returned by regiments from Prussia, during the Congress, and were ordered, not undesignedly, upon Erfurt, where Napoleon reviewed them before the gates. They were troops which Napoleon had not seen since the Peace of Tilsit. The Emperor was taken to this parade by Napoleon, who allowed him to ride on his right hand. Arrived on the ground, Napoleon spurred his charger, and galloped along the front of the right wing, without troubling himself about the Emperor, who, mounted on one of Napoleon's horses, had to rush after him like an aide-de-camp. The regiment then formed itself into close column, and Napoleon called out to the officers, "Les braves en avant!" A number of officers, subalterns, and privates stepped forth and formed a large semicircle. Napoleon dismounted; all did the same; he then invited the Emperor and the Grand Duke to come on his right; on his left stood the Prince de Neufchatel, with a tablet in his hand. The semicircle was closed by the Princes present and their suites.

The commandant of the regiment called out by name each individual in succession, and presented him to Napoleon, who inquired where and how he had distinguished himself. This regiment had assisted in determining the fate of the battle of Friedland, and all the rewards to be distributed were for this battle. The men now related their behaviour during the conflict. One had with his own hand killed so many Russians, and made so many prisoners; another had taken a flag; a third a cannon; a fourth had driven a Russian bat-

talion into the water, where it perished. Napoleon
listened to all attentively, and then decreed promotion or the Legion of Honour, which the Prince
de Neufchatel wrote down ; as each person stepped
forward in succession, he repeated the same question,
so that the impression forced itself upon the by-
standers, that it was his intention to embarrass or
torture the Emperor Alexander. All eyes involuntarily turned towards the latter, as he stood beside
Napoleon with the calmest bearing, until the last of
the heroes to be rewarded had vaunted his achievements. The Grand Duke Constantine had withdrawn
from the circle, and was inspecting a battery. The
Russians and Germans naturally viewed Napoleon's
conduct as brutal and revolting ; but, to the honour
of Frenchmen I must observe, that disapprobation
was to be read on many faces around Napoleon.

Immediately after his arrival, Napoleon said to
the Duke of Weimar : "I hear you have a great
quantity of game,—give us a battue." The Duke
bowed, and begged him to fix the day. Napoleon
answered : "I must send to Paris for my guns ;
Duroc will inform you when they arrive, and then
we will arrange the rest."

The Duke knew that I had renewed in Erfurt my
Berlin acquaintance with Duroc, and left all this
arrangement to me. Duroc proposed to me that on
the first day there should be a stag-hunt, then a
dinner in Weimar, after dinner a short concert, concluding with the theatre and a ball. On the following day Napoleon would show the Emperor the
battle-field of Jena, afterwards a déjeûner under the
tent, a hare-hunt, and the journey back to Erfurt.

This project seemed practicable, and Duroc reserved the details till he had received instructions from Napoleon. Now these were to the effect, that not only a list of names for the state dinner was to be handed to me, but at the same time a drawing for the shape of the dining-table, (semicircular, and the outer side of the bow only to be occupied) with the names written down where each person was to sit.

This inconceivable arrogance seemed to me too much to bear patiently. I asked Duroc, whether it was the intention of his master, that *he* should invite the guests to this banquet ? " No, the Duke was still the host; and in our parley, the question was only about the observance of etiquette." I observed, that in this list there were violations of the etiquette to which the Duke was obliged to conform in his residence; according to this plan, for instance, Princess Caroline of Weimar was seated between her mother and the Emperor, and this was not her proper place. Duroc maintained that an unmarried daughter's place was always next her mother: I, on the contrary, asserted, that according to our German, and indeed European, etiquette, a princess who had a court of her own assumed her own place and rank. I further observed, that the Duchess of Würtemberg, a relation of the Emperor Alexander, was on a visit to the Duchess of Weimar, resided in the castle, and had of right a seat at the table; as likewise the Duke of Oldenburg, a near relative of the Emperor Alexander.

Duroc immediately obtained a decision from Napoleon, and brought a new drawing, in which he now assigned his own place to the right of the Duchess of Weimar, that of the Emperor Alexander to her left, between mother and daughter; the Duke of Oldenburg was also admitted on the left wing. Duroc brought word that this arrangement was now unalterable, and that the Duchess of Würtemberg had not the rank to have a seat at that table. It was moreover the intention of his imperial master to do something agreeable to the Duchess, whom he esteemed highly, and for this purpose he had ordered his French actors to play in Weimar. I received this as an especial mark of attention, and made inquiries about the piece, in order to prepare the decorations. Duroc answered: "Talma has already received his instructions."

The Duke would not put up with this arbitrary exclusion of the Duchess of Würtemberg; he had some talk with the Emperor Alexander about it, who however advised peace. The Duchess was for this day to announce herself indisposed.

From Talma I learnt that Napoleon had bespoken for Weimar "La Mort de Cæsar." I could not trust my ears, and asked a second time. They had not dared to give this piece *in France* since Napoleon's elevation: his admirers thought it a grand thing that he caused it to be acted in Weimar.

In allowing it to be acted before Germans, whom he accounted, one and all, sleepy fellows,—and of whom he used to say, "They are content when they have their cabbage-crop in the cellar"—I can see no greatness, but rather something offensive and brutal; and indeed, in the whole range of French tragedies, there was no piece less fit than this one to be given in honour of a lady.

Duroc questioned me as to the police in Weimar. I answered, that we had a police to get the chimneys swept and the streets cleaned, but of a *haute police* we knew nothing. I therefore willingly accepted his proposal to send a brigade of French gensd'armes to Weimar, as it would have been risking too much to make the Duke of Weimar responsible for the safety of a conqueror who had brought such calamities on the peaceable Germans.

Among the number of persons who from curiosity flocked to this hunt at Weimar, were two Prussians who, mounted on good horses, and muffled in cloaks (under which they concealed musketoons), waited for Napoleon near the Webicht (a little wood near Weimar), with the intention of putting an end to his life. He came in an open carriage, but who sat next to him? Prince William of Prussia! The conspirators had agreed to fire on him, though even an intimate friend, of his suite, sitting next him, should run the risk of falling an innocent sacrifice to one of the many scattering balls. When they perceived the brother of their king by Napoleon's side, their arm refused to do its office.

We need not stop to inquire here whether the plan was well arranged, or whether the deed, however immoral and blameable, might find, in a motive of patriotism, some palliation or excuse; this is certain, that Napoleon escaped a great peril by mere chance.

The Prince de Neufchatel, as *Grand Veneur*, questioned me closely beforehand about the mode of beating, and insisted that in the field-beating deep holes should be dug for the shooters. This was done, and the soundness of his reasons was apparent in the course of the day's sport.

Napoleon and the Emperor Alexander stood side by side ; the French marshals on the right and left. When the first hare was started, all the marshals disappeared in their deep holes, and Napoleon fired away indiscriminately at the supports of his empire, at the hares and beaters. After the sport was over, and the guns were packed up, when, in answer to the Prince de Neufchatel's question, I was able to say that we had no wounded, he exclaimed, " Dieu merci !"

Through the intimacy of the Duke of Weimar with the Emperor Alexander, founded on mutual confidence and relationship, the Duke learned that Napoleon urged the Emperor of Russia to give to the marshals present special public marks of his esteem and good will; and that the Emperor resolved, although very unwillingly, to confer orders on those who disregarded money, and to make valuable presents to the avaricious.

From another quarter I learnt that Marshal Lannes had declared that Napoleon was troubling himself uselessly in attempting to draw Russia into his interests; that he would never succeed in making the Emperor Alexander his friend; it was therefore a mistake to withdraw his army from Prussia, and to leave Russia, Austria, and Prussia to themselves, in order to conquer Spain. The answer he received was that Prussia was weak, and the alliance with Russia would prevent her coming to the assistance of Austria, when Napoleon considered it time to pluck her feathers.

Hence we concluded, that Napoleon wished first to silence his Marshals about their mistrust of the Emperor; but from other communications, I was justified in concluding that he had already resolved upon the annihilation of Austria, and only deferred it till after the subjugation of Spain, which he hoped would be accomplished by the middle of the next year.

General Vincent, sent on the part of Austria to Erfurt, was the only one to whom I imparted my discovery, which he received with true diplomatic caution, lamenting my needless distrust. He knew too little of me to venture farther. Indeed, I expected nothing more : my object however was fully attained; I had communicated facts to General Vincent which he could not know, but which he certainly made use of at the right time.

Archduke Charles had written instructions upon the higher operations of war, for the use of the Austrian generals, which were kept secret. I procured a copy of these, and wrote marginal notes in it, solely with a view to draw attention to the dangers which threatened the Austrian army, unless they studied Napoleon's mode of warfare more deeply, and opposed it by better considered methods. Napoleon saw clearly that it was high time to hasten on, by some means or other, the war against Austria. He had discovered at Erfurt, but too well, that Prussia was completely lamed, and that North as well as South Germany were powerless and trembling before him. My apprehensions were realized in the year 1809. In the following years, though we kept up public courage in Weimar, sad experience obliged us to confess that in Germany at large it had sunk considerably, and that the German party yielded continually more and more to the French. The latter became daily more insolent; and when Napoleon at last secretly determined upon the war with Russia, and sent an envoy to Weimar, to watch more closely the Grand Duchess, and the Russian and anti-French party, things went so far that even in Weimar, those of the French party who had hitherto been kept within bounds raised their heads; and the French envoy, M. St. Aignon, had amongst the German inhabitants of the good town of Weimar (mostly servants of the Duke) a fully organized *espionage.*

A melancholy time was this, when every man feared his neighbour, and all feeling of confidence was lost! The well-disposed, but weak and timid, had the bleeding corpse of Palm constantly before their eyes, and hid themselves in their houses, saying *Yes* to everything. Of the strong and unyielding, the greater part went to Spain or Russia, there to continue the war against the suppressor of German freedom.

The Duke and I regarded the war in Russia as decisive for Germany; but we had no great confidence in the power which the Emperor Alexander could oppose to the enormous masses that Napoleon was advancing against Russia. The difference between the *effective* armies of Russia and those upon *paper,* was too well known to us. Meanwhile Napoleon might fall in battle or be carried off by sickness, and the campaign would then fall to the ground of itself.

By circuitous routes through Austria, late but uninterrupted accounts reached Weimar from Russia, by which it appeared that the real state of affairs was very different from what it was represented in the French bulletins. When the burning of Moscow had put an end to all hopes of peace, and at the same time of quiet winter-quarters for Napoleon, we succeeded in raising the spirit of the dejected Germans, and leading them to hope for better times.

The King's proclamation to his people was a

signal for me to apply to be reinstated, and to ascertain his commands whither I was to repair. I sent a trusty messenger to Berlin, and had my note sewn up between the double soles of his shoes. An answer from Scharnhorst, who alone was aware that I had obtained my discharge only for the sake of appearance, informed me that my reinstatement in the army must remain secret until the outbreak of hostilities.

I obtained my *congé* from the Weimar service in due form, in which I had held the office of Member of the Privy Council; and on the 18th of April I arrived in Altenburg, where I found Scharnhorst, as Chief of the General Staff of the army, at the headquarters of General von Blücher.*

The plan to advance in the spring of 1813, with the Russian and Prussian armies, from the marches of Brandenburg and from Silesia, across the Elbe and through Saxony, as far towards the Rhine as Napoleon, after the dispersion of his returning army, would be compelled to allow, originated with Scharnhorst. It was based upon the assurance that all the Germans would rise when Napoleon could no longer protect them, and that their Princes would thus be compelled to renounce the Confederation of the Rhine. The Emperor Alexander, inspired by the idea of becoming the deliverer of Germany, agreed to Scharnhorst's proposition, and conjointly with our King arranged for its execution—after having preceded his armies from Kalisch to Breslau.

* Of our short campaign till the truce, I have published a succinct review: "The Prussian-Russian Campaign in 1813, till the truce of the 5th of June," to which I refer in the following pages.

The Emperor did not foresee the difficulties he would experience from his old General Kutosof, whom he had just proclaimed and rewarded as the saviour of the Russian empire, and whom he had to treat with management in now acting contrary to his judgment and advice. Kutosof considered the Russian war as ended; his desire was to keep the army within the limits of Poland, and to incorporate the Grand Duchy of Warsaw with Russia, as an indemnification for the war, leaving the other European nations to free themselves from Napoleon as Russia had done.

If (in consequence of York's convention) Field-Marshal Kutosof could neither treat Prussia as a conquered country, nor ignore it altogether as a foreign one, he was yet an entire stranger to the views of the Emperor Alexander with respect to the political restoration of his friend the King of Prussia: he would not hear a word of crossing the Elbe; and all Scharnhorst's endeavours to make him more favourably disposed toward Prussia were fruitless. The whole peace party in the Russian army joined with the Field-Marshal, and the Emperor was placed in a difficult position. On my arrival at Altenburg, I found Scharnhorst deeply dejected, for he could not shut his eyes to the consequences of this resistance. Unexpectedly, the death of the obstinate old Marshal occurred on the 28th of April, and the Emperor was thus left free to pursue his own policy.

The accounts which I brought Scharnhorst of the strength of the French army did not agree with his own. He had calculated them at about 40,000 to 50,000 men less than they were; however, this did not much matter. Napoleon would be obliged to fight with a new army, hastily organized; we had for the most part older and more disciplined soldiers. It was therefore for us to try our opponents; but in doing so, we ought to be careful not to attack a force superior to ours. We agreed to be silent about the probable superiority, and placed our confidence in acting vigorously on the offensive, before Napoleon could unite with the Viceroy of Italy and fully develop his strength. In the battle of Lützen, we had to lament that the march to the battle had not taken place a day earlier, and that General von Miloradowitch was not brought up in time,—measures which by some mismanagement were neglected. With respect to the battle itself, I refer to the official accounts, and to the Observations on the Great Operations and Battles, &c., published by me in 1825.

In the battle, I was sent off just as Scharnhorst was brought in wounded. I saw him the evening after the battle for the last time; he considered his wounds of no consequence, and hoped soon to rejoin the army. It is said that he died at Prague, from the effects of mistaken treatment.

General von Gneisenau undertook his duties. Gneisenau, who had justly earned a fair name by his vigorous defence of Colberg, was a worthy successor to the distinguished Scharnhorst, who valued him most highly, although they were of very different natures. Each adhered firmly to his object, but they differed as to the means of attaining it. Scharnhorst examined cautiously step by step, investigated all the details, and left nothing to chance that he could help. Gneisenau passed lightly over all, trusting to his presence of mind and genius. To weigh beforehand all possible contingencies, of which (as he remarked) perhaps only a single one, and that indeed never exactly as presupposed, might occur, gave him *ennui;* conscious that he should be able to help himself when the moment arrived, he assumed that every one possessed the same gift; and in his active mind, he traversed time and space the more readily, as he had a peculiar inclination for any venture that was based on courage. He was aware that courage is no every-day gift, but he fancied it a quality which may be imparted, and that the courageous are able to make others so too. Now here he often fell into a series of illusions: he mistook for courage, ebullitions of feeling which he had called forth; he ascribed to such courage the endurance which belongs only to the deliberate and self-developed quality; he felt himself gifted to call forth noble feelings, great ideas, and to awaken inspiration; he believed himself capable of changing every-day men into men of spirit.

Such a turn of mind, even when acknowledged as an illusion, has something enviable in it; but there is nothing more dangerous for a General than the belief that he can transfer his own strength and energy to others, and that these will execute his will with the same patience and courage as himself.

Gneisenau thus fell into the error of always estimating his own powers too high, and those of his adversary too low. All daring had too great a charm for him, which was not diminished, even when the daring was superfluous. Where an object could be attained by two different ways, he always inclined to the most daring. Chivalrous, noble-minded, and strictly just, he was incapable of shifting on others a fault he had himself committed; he was ever ready to acknowledge the merit of another, though it was difficult for him to give up preconceived opinions,—a difficulty with which men of decided character have at all times had to contend.

Gneisenau wished to continue the management of all the business according to the arrangements Scharnhorst had made; but Scharnhorst had cautiously kept many subjects to himself, which he had not inserted in the reports.

When we had crossed the Elbe on our retreat, I was sent on to Bautzen, to procure from him verbal information upon many points; but on my arrival there, I found that he had set out that morning for Prague.

In Bautzen busy preparations were being made for choosing a strong position for the Grand Army, as it was determined to accept a second battle in that neighbourhood; and here the difference of principles between the Russian and Prussian armies first came clearly to light. In contending with Napoleon, the Russians trusted not only in the system of masses, but also in *lumping* together the whole of their corps and armies into such masses. At Borodino they had stood ten divisions deep, and they considered the not inglorious issue of the battle as the consequence of this disposition.

On the Prussian side such a disposition was considered faulty under all circumstances, but especially when opposed to Napoleon, who, as an artillery officer, with his powerful batteries, knew well how to punish such an error. The Prussians did not require such means, as all our infantry was well practised in rifle and sharp-shooting ; whereas, in the Russian armies only the *Jäger* regiments were riflemen, and the rest of the infantry knew nothing of single fighting. On the other hand, we Prussians laid great stress on protecting all our positions by some barrier in our front, which the enemy could not pass without breaking line : by this means we found an opportunity of attacking our opponents when they were least capable of resistance. Rivers, brooks, marshes, and valleys are the best impediments of this kind. This the Russians did not understand, as in the battle-fields of Russia—the steppes—few such means are found of strengthening their position. On the other hand, the Russians were accustomed to fortify themselves with intrenchments, and to take up their positions accordingly,—a practice which was strange to us, and must remain so, as our men have not the physical strength to march all day, and throw up trenches by night. Besides, on our line of retreat there were so many inequalities of ground, that trenching—which is at best a mere make-shift—could be entirely dispensed with.

When these matters were discussed, it was deemed advisable for us Prussians to conform, as far as possible, without giving up any important principle. We left the Russians to choose the general position, and made our own preparations for its defence.

On the first day of the battle of Bautzen (the 20th of May), when night had put an end to the musketry-fire, Gneisenau summoned me to accompany him to Klein-Burschwitz, where the sovereigns would issue the orders for the following day.

We found there the Generalissimo Count Wittgenstein, and his Chief of the Staff, Lieutenant-
General von Diebitsch. The Emperor appeared
without the King, and expressed his conviction that
Napoleon, who was inferior to us in cavalry, would
attack our left wing with his right on the moun-
tainous ground, and outflank it. I ventured to
express some doubts, and when the Emperor asked
my reasons, I laid before him a plan of our position
on the right, which showed that this quarter was the
favourable point for Napoleon's attack. I stated
that Marshal Ney, with two corps-d'armée, was
already advancing upon our weakest point; and it
was impossible to suppose that Napoleon would
recall him thence toward his centre, to attack the
strongest point of our whole position, namely, the
left wing. I pointed out, that unless we extended
our right wing as far as the windmill-hill at Gleime,
and occupied that height with a strong battery,
Marshal Ney would be before us at Weissenberg,
through which runs the high-road to Görlitz, the
line of retreat for our right wing and centre.

The Emperor did not indeed give up his idea as
to Napoleon's plan of attack, but admitted my reasoning as to the position of our right wing. He asked
the Generalissimo, "How strong is Barclay?" Count
Wittgenstein replied, without reflecting, "15,000
men." The Emperor asked me, "Are these sufficient?" and on my answering in the affirmative,
Barclay received orders at once to occupy the position in question I had indicated.

When we returned to our bivouac on the Kreckwitz heights, it was already daylight; and soon
after Napoleon attacked our left wing on the wooded

heights, as the Emperor had foreseen. About an hour after began the attack of Marshal Ney, who pressed forward with energy by Klix against Barclay, as I had foreseen; and the Emperor became convinced by the hot cannonade at Klix, that at this point the attack was directed in earnest, and that on the left wing, where the Monarchs were, it was only a feigned attack.

One of the Emperor's aides-de-camp brought General von Blücher the order to send me with my plans to Barclay, to inform him of the circumstances of the ground. I found him on the windmill-hill, where a strong battery was just opening its fire. I communicated to him the conversation of the previous evening in Klein-Burschwitz, and said that the Emperor reckoned on his executing his orders, as he had 15,000 combatants. Barclay was silent.

As Ney advanced in close masses between objects which I could overlook on the ground, and measure with the compasses on my plan, I calculated the forces opposed to Barclay at 40,000 men.

The Russian general, Czaplitz, was under cannonade near Gottamelde, but we could not see the force opposed to him. Barclay invited me to come with him into the miller's house, and bolted the door with great formality, although Ney's cannon-balls had already riddled the walls. "You believe," said he, "that I have 15,000 men with me, and the Emperor believes the same. The moment is too important for longer silence; I have just 5,000* men, and you may judge yourself whether I can hold out

---

* The fact that Barclay's force consisted of this small number only was, I believe, never revealed before the publication of this work. General Cathcart gives the number in his table (plate No. 13) as 10,000, and in his text (p. 147) as about 15,000.—Ed.

against the 40,000 who are advancing upon me. I call upon you to repair with the utmost speed to General Blücher, to report to him what you have seen, and bring me reinforcements."

I cannot picture my astonishment! Letting alone the untruth which the Generalissimo had told the Emperor, in stating Barclay's corps to be three-fold stronger than it was, he had thereby wantonly endangered the battle; for as Ney had crossed the Spree, the extension of the battle-field rendered it no longer possible to remedy the mischief. The reinforcements which might be sent to Barclay must at all events arrive too late, for they could only be taken from York or Kleist, who were stationed behind the centre of the army near Litten.

I looked at my watch; in twenty-five minutes Ney would be in possession of the windmill-hill. I galloped back to the Kreckwitz heights, reported the facts, and showed the dangerous position in which we stood. My wish to confide my communication solely in private to the General-in-Chief and Gneisenau, could not be granted, as the custom had been introduced of discussing everything openly, in the hearing of all the officers at head-quarters,—a bad custom.*

* Though I took, later, a great deal of trouble to abolish this custom, I was never able to accomplish this, because Blücher and Gneisenau laid great stress on inspiring by lively sallies all around them with cheerfulness, which spirit, according to Gneisenau's opinion, must spread, when during an action the officers were sent off in all directions. The difference of our views was this,—I maintained, that a General should have no croakers in his suite, who might make others apprehensive or gloomy: Gneisenau, on the other hand, thought it safer to try to improve the "*Trübsals-spritzen*," (*trouble-squirts*), as Blücher used to call them, and liked to see the talents of our own leader employed on this object. I was not against this, but considered it might be done, without its being necessary that all around, even to

During my absence with Barclay, the troops had been moved to the position I had pointed out on the Kreckwitz heights. General Gneisenau, on finding these strong, nay impregnable, was somewhat elated; and Blücher, in his harangues to the battalions, designated the Kreckwitz heights as the Prussian Thermopylæ. All this had just taken place : the sounds of the huzzas caught my ear on the way.

I arrived, knowing nothing of these proceedings, with news which required the most mature deliberation. The sight of my horse, covered with foam, was a signal to all the curious at head-quarters to press close up to Blücher and Gneisenau, the defenders of public discussion ; and under these circumstances I had nothing for it but to say, drily and shortly : "General Barclay cannot hold the windmill-hill of Gleime : he desires a reinforcement, which can neither reach him, nor be spared from our position : he will therefore retire upon the Vogelsberg, behind Baruth, so that the enemy may not reach Weissenberg before us ; but we lose by this the shelter of our right flank, and must take speedy measures." Gneisenau answered, that I placed too little confidence in the bravery of the Russian troops. I explained : "In a quarter of an hour the windmill-hill is in Marshal Ney's hands ; " but in presence of the large assemblage of officers I would neither speak of the 40,000 men I had seen, nor of the 5000 of which Barclay's force consisted.

Gneisenau did not consider my statement worthy

---

the orderly officers, should inquisitively press close to the Commander in Chief, whenever intelligence arrived. Moreover Blücher had a peculiar gift for reducing exaggerated statements to the right track by a bon-mot.

of attention, and Blücher made another inspiriting harangue, which was received with great applause, and had the effect of postponing my proposed measures. When, a little later, I found an opportunity of explaining the circumstances in detail to Gneisenau alone, he fell into a gloomy silence, and put on a show of incredulity.

Barclay's troops, as I had foreseen, were scattered like dust. I had wished to see Preititz occupied, but this measure had been considered unnecessary. I galloped thither, and was received at the entrance with a volley from the enemy; there was nothing now to be done but to employ the reserve, (four battalions of Guards,) to retake that village.

Napoleon advanced against our front under a brisk fire. The Russian artillery assigned us (twenty-four 12-pounders), had engaged at too great a distance, and had exhausted its ammunition; battery after battery therefore dropped off to the rear. On our right flank Ney advanced with a widely extended front against the unoccupied heights, which there was now no question of defending, as our reserve was already engaged.

Our left wing was to have been covered by York and Kleist; but the Sovereigns, on Barclay's proposal, had dispatched Kleist towards Baruth to his assistance. York could not hinder the enemy's raising a battery at Basantwitz, whereby we, on the Kreckwitz heights, were subjected to a cross fire from three sides. It must be considered a piece of extraordinary civility on Ney's part that he contented himself with this cannonade, and did not advance with his whole infantry, in a front of 3000 paces between Pliskowitz and Klein-Bautzen, upon the heights which could not be defended,—a movement which would have cut us off from all means of retreat.

Blücher, with Gneisenau and his staff, remained in the hottest cannonade, quietly beholding what they could not hinder, the process of our being gradually surrounded. No one doubted that, if we remained standing there, we should have to defend ourselves to the last man, or lay down our arms, if the enemy did not attack us, as to break through was quite impossible.

After their recent harangues General Blücher and Gneisenau could not *order* a retreat: the most they could do was to consent to it. When, after a long delay, Ney began at last to ascend the heights, I pulled out my watch, and said to General Blücher, near whom was Gneisenau: "We have still a quarter of an hour, within which time it is possible to get out of this net. Later than this we shall be surrounded. If we do not make use of this time, the cowards among us will surrender,—the brave will die fighting,—but unhappily, without the slightest benefit to their country."

There was a deep silence. Gneisenau was greatly agitated: at last he spoke: "Lieutenant Colonel Müffling is right; and in the present altered circumstances, not only is all bloodshed superfluous, but it is a duty to preserve our forces for a better opportunity." Blücher consented to the retreat, and we just escaped by Gross-Burschwitz.

I confess that during my whole life I have never found anything more difficult than the uttering these few words. One feels a certain scruple in finding fault with a man of courage for being too

courageous; and still more when this has led to
a resolution which has called forth an enthusiastic
hurrah.

Although I saw in the speeches that had been
made, and in the declaration that the Kreckwitz
heights should be Prussia's Thermopylæ, an inconsiderate forestalling of events, and so far an unwar-
ranted misuse of power, yet it required a complete
resignation of my own wishes to the strong warnings
of duty, to act as I did. Gneisenau's behaviour
deserves the highest praise : he was conscious that
he had been over-hasty, a fault which he could not
remedy but by self-compromising inconsistency. He
willingly made this sacrifice of his vanity.

Moreover, now that all the motives of action of
Napoleon, as well as Marshal Ney, are known, we
must acknowledge that the false measures on the
heights of Kreckwitz were in reality highly favourable to us. Had General Blücher abandoned the
heights when Ney, at the head of 40,000 men, had
taken Preititz, Ney would have pressed on to Weissenberg, which, under the circumstances, he would
have reached before us.

By holding these heights, we obliged Napoleon
to lead his reserve against them ; and Ney, on receiving the order to co-operate with him, left Preititz
alone, and advanced with all his forces between Mal-
schwitz and Preititz, upon the Kreckwitz heights,
where he joined Napoleon. Meanwhile, protected
by our reserve cavalry, we had got such a start on
the road to Weissenberg, that the battle was at an
end before Napoleon's and Ney's forces could be
disentangled from each other.

Our abandonment of the Kreckwitz heights met

with severe censure from all around the Sovereigns, in which the Emperor himself in some degree joined. Our King alone, who could not get Count Wittgenstein to shift his left wing toward the centre, when he saw the hostile reserve move from Bautzen against Blücher, fully approved of our retreat.

This movement of the left wing was what the circumstances properly required: if not executed, it was because the Russians, intrenched up to their teeth, would not leave their impregnable position. The pretext for this was easily found. Blücher, they said, with York, Kleist, and Barclay, will hold the right wing, as we the left, for it is not at all certain whether Napoleon will not make the attempt to draw us out of this strong position, in order to wheel round his reserve, and fall upon our left wing with a superior force, after we have diminished the garrison of the trenches, within which we are equal to our opponents.

At last the King resolved to support Blücher with a part of the left wing. It was then too late. The aide-de-camp who brought the news arrived just as we had left the Kreckwitz heights.

After the battle of Bautzen, the Emperor Alexander found himself obliged to confer the chief command of the Russian armies on General Barclay de Tolly. I have never learnt whether this was in consequence of the false report by which Count Wittgenstein had risked the fate of the battle. It was alleged that Count Wittgenstein had bestowed too little care on the internal order of the troops. The convalescent, in marching battalions 1000 strong, led by few officers, arrived by the route along which was placed the line of magazines, out of Poland, in the camps of the army near Bautzen.

Instead of immediately dissolving such a marching battalion, which contained soldiers from all the regiments of the Russian army, and incorporating the men in their old regiments, these battalions were brought as they were into the field of battle at Bautzen, where, unorganized, without superior or subaltern officers, they fought with uncertainty, were irregularly provided, and, if they straggled from their battalion, could not regain their places. Thus on the retreat from Bautzen, large bodies of Russian soldiers, just out of the hospital, still weak, badly armed and clothed, were roaming about; they often did not even know the numbers of their battalions, and when they did, the Russian officers were unable to direct them how to find them again, as such numbers were quite unknown in the Russian army.

General Barclay had been minister of war, and had the reputation of being a good organizer; the Emperor therefore made a good choice in appointing him Commander in Chief. But for us Prussians this nomination was, at the time, anything but agreeable.

Barclay instantly called upon Blücher to adopt, in place of our well-considered and appropriate brigade-dispositions, the Russian plan of position, as at Borodino. He was told, in reply, that the King had prescribed our positions, and therefore the alterations could only be ordered by His Majesty. The King was entreated not to consent to this, and so the matter ended.

Barclay represented to the Emperor that the

disorder was so widely spread, that it would be impossible for him to reorganize the army during operations; and the more so, as they were short of everything, even of ammunition for the artillery. He must therefore make it a condition to lead back the Russian army to Poland, and there reorganize it completely.

This extremely singular condition, at the time of a forced retreat, was wholly unexpected by the Emperor, and a thunderstroke to us. What would become of Prussia, if, after she had entered into the Russian alliance, the Russian army drew back to Poland? And what, in this case, would hinder Napoleon from driving back the Russians, who were anxious to avoid a battle, across the Vistula? Where would Barclay find the rest he sought? The whole project seemed ill-considered; but the Emperor Alexander could not dissuade his general, who wished to continue his retreat through Breslau, from following out his views. This, fortunately, was opposed to the measures that had been concerted with Austria.

The Court of Vienna had not yet completed its preparations, and its declaration of war had been put off until this period. But it was the fundamental condition of such declaration, that the Triple Alliance should begin to act on the offensive; and to render this possible, Austria necessarily desired that the Allied Armies should continue their retreat along the Silesian mountains towards Neisse.

When the Emperor arrived at Jauer, on the retreat from Bautzen, he ordered General Barclay, commanding the Allied Armies, to turn off from the Breslau road, to the right by Schweidnitz,

towards Neisse. In making this deviation to the
right, we placed an ambush at Haynau,* in order to
raise the spirit of the Prussian army, to make Napoleon more cautious in his pursuit, and thus to gain
time. The result was, that Napoleon lost our track
at Liegnitz, and pursued us in the direction of
Breslau.

After the affair of Haynau, I received the King's
order to repair to General Barclay, with the official
charge of providing all that he required for the
Russian army, as far as possible, in Silesia, and
with the secret order to dissuade the General from
the thought of retreating across the Oder. The
following materials were supplied to me for this
purpose :—

The fortress of Schweidnitz had been blown up
by the French after the campaign of 1807, before
their withdrawal from Silesia; and the King had
ordered the Governor of Silesia to restore the walls,
as soon as the news of the retreat on the Beresina
was received. It was therefore assumed that
Schweidnitz was restored.

In the Seven Years' War, Frederick II. had his
famous camp at Bunzelwitz, under protection of
the fortress, and the united Austrian and Russian
armies had not ventured to attack it. It was
therefore assumed that we could occupy the same
encampment, and that Napoleon would likewise not
venture to attack us. We should thereby gain six
weeks' time, which the Court of Vienna required for

* General Cathcart, in his " Commentaries," calls this one of
the most brilliant cavalry affairs of modern days. The French
advanced guard, under General Maison, lost 1500 men and
eleven guns.—TRANS.

completing its preparations. During the battle of Bautzen, I had to convey orders from the Emperor to General Barclay, which the latter executed faithfully in my presence; but he had nevertheless been forced to give way to a superior force. The Emperor, dissatisfied with the issue of Barclay's fight on the windmill-hill of Gleime, censured his conduct; I defended it with all my power, and gave some explanations to the Emperor which fully vindicated Barclay.

I have therefore reason to believe that the Emperor had proposed me especially to the King for this commission. Feeling its importance, I considered at the same time the caution it demanded.

General Barclay received me with the formality peculiar to him, but with openness, and announced to me the inevitable necessity of leaving the scene of war in Silesia with the great Russian army for six weeks. He bitterly lamented that we had quitted the shortest route by Breslau, which would lead him to make great detours, perhaps even to Cracow. I told him that I did not underrate the difficulties of his task, and felt the highest admiration for the improvement which his judicious arrangements had already effected in the eight days he had held the command; nevertheless I could not think that the retreat by Breslau would have been more advantageous to us, as in the great plain from Liegnitz to Breslau, and beyond the Oder to Kalisch, we could not have avoided a battle; whereas the retreat along the mountain-chain afforded constant protection to our left wing, and advantageous positions, in front of which we could always oblige Napoleon to deploy, and could punish every incautious movement on his part. I pointed out the inconvenience of his situation, as he was obliged to follow a circuitous march from Hof, by Schandau, along the Erzgebirge and Sudeten, to the boundaries of an extremely suspicious friend, although not a declared enemy. I then laid the greatest stress—

1. On the reinforcements which awaited us; namely, the whole Silesian Landwehr, which was ordered to assemble, in complete order of battle, at Schweidnitz.
2. On the restored fortress of Schweidnitz, as the central point of many roads.
3. On the celebrated position of Bunzelwitz.

Barclay listened to me quietly: he saw that I shared the views of his Emperor, and did not wish to regard the reorganization of the great Russian army as a matter of no consequence. To his questions about the position at Bunzelwitz, and the state of the fortress of Schweidnitz, I could give no answer, but proposed to go before, and show him both upon the spot.

Arrived at Bunzelwitz, I found an undulating ground, without any impediments (as I already knew from Tempelhof), and, according to our present mode of fighting, not the least adapted for an intrenched camp nor for the strength of the army. I imparted this to General Barclay, who was following me, and hastened forward to Schweidnitz.

Here I found a ruin, i.e., the walls in the same state as when they were blown up. The Governor of Silesia had not put the royal orders into execution.

On inquiring after the Landwehr, no one could

give me any news of it. By chance I learnt that four battalions had arrived at Boyendorf (one mile from Schweidnitz), and that Lieutenant General von Zastrow, to whom the King had given the command of the whole Silesian Landwehr, was just then reviewing these battalions there.

For these fresh troops some 20,000 contract muskets had been purchased in Austria; their completion, however, had been so hurried, that, on examination, it was found the boring of the touch-holes in the barrels had been forgotten. The rest of the arms bespoken were not nearly ready; and the Landwehr battalions for York's corps, being without muskets, were furnished with lances.

Thus all the attempts to support my views with General Barclay came to nothing; and the Landwehr assembled was, in fact, without any arms, since at least four weeks would be necessary to bore the touch-holes in the new muskets. What was to be done? I concealed nothing from General Barclay; and when he positively declared, "Now there is nothing left me, but to go back to Poland," I laid before him the political and military circumstances, as follows: "If we can hold out for the first half of July in the Silesian mountains, protected by the fortresses of Silberberg, Glatz, Neisse, and Cosel, Austria will be ready to declare war. If we retreat across the Oder toward Warsaw, the accession of Austria to the coalition is not to be thought of. If Napoleon pursues us on our retreat as far as the Vistula, or frees his ally, the Grand Duchy of Warsaw, from the Russian armies, then his position is the same as at the outbreak of hostilities in 1812; and it remains to be seen, whether Austria will

E

renew her alliance with him or be able to preserve
her neutrality, as she would doubtless prefer.   But
the first question is : What can the King my master
do, if you draw back to Poland ?   Of the 80,000
men he has under arms in Silesia, about 10,000
are to be thrown into the fortresses, and 70,000 remain available.   If he follows the Russian army with
these forces, all the means of feeding and paying
his army will slip away from him ; we cannot tell
to what this would lead.   The King cannot therefore at all think of following the Russians to Poland.
There remains nothing for us, but to stay behind on
this side the Oder ; and in an entrenched camp at
Neisse, try to bring about the conclusion of the war
in an honourable manner."

General Barclay shrugged his shoulders : " I cannot sacrifice the armies of my Emperor, as they are
not in fighting condition.   In six weeks time I am
here again : the Prussian army must help itself as
well as it can."   I asked, " What prevents your
giving battle ?"— " The want of ammunition."   I
was authorized to provide it ; and referred him, on
the spot, to the depôts of the fortresses of Silberberg
and Glatz.

General Barclay felt the importance of not declining my offer.   If he persisted on his march to
Poland, he separated himself from Prussia, Austria,
and from all Europe.   He disclosed to me that
Napoleon had offered a truce, and that he considered the acceptance of this offer as the only
means to avoid the separation of the two armies.

Although the thought of the conditions Napoleon
would prescribe might excite a shudder, it was plain
that the attempt must be made, as Barclay would

at no events risk a battle with Napoleon, in which we could have engaged with about 130,000 men; and Napoleon, who since his advance from Bautzen had left at least 20,000 marauders behind, could not have opposed us with many more.

Barclay had repeatedly declared to me that the Emperor fully acquiesced in his views; and as consequently all further negotiations with him could lead to nothing, I repaired to the head-quarters of the Sovereigns, in order to inform the King by word of mouth of Barclay's proposed expedient; for I had already announced that he would not give up the winter-quarters in Poland.

I found the King, on my arrival, engaged in his usual deliberations. I went to his Adjutant General, Von dem Knesebeck, whom the King employed as strategist, and whose military opinions were also held in high esteem by the Emperor Alexander. It was General von dem Knesebeck who (after the retreat from Bautzen) recommended the route along the mountain-chain by Schweidnitz, instead of the one by Breslau across the Oder.

General von dem Knesebeck, a friend of my youth, listened to my arguments in favour of concluding the truce proffered by Napoleon, which the Sovereigns had not rejected, but had named commissioners to hear Napoleon's propositions. By the departure of General von Kleist for Neumarkt, this measure had become known in the Prussian army: it was received with great disapprobation, and even occasioned an unseemly excitement. Knesebeck answered: "I have known Barclay from 1806 to 1807: he is firm as a rock, and will be less likely to relinquish his notion of a retreat on Po-

and, as, considered in a purely military point of
view, there is much to say for it.   But if it comes
to this, the alliance with Austria is lost ; as soon as
we cross the Oder, the Viennese Cabinet must per-
sist in maintaining its neutral position.   The conclusion of a truce is now our only safety.   But
we have a new difficulty to overcome before we can
attain this.   The Sovereigns know that the Prussian
army has declared against any truce, and they look
upon this uncalled-for opposition as a proof of fidelity to duty.   They also know well that the whole
Russian army, from the highest to the lowest, longs
for winter-quarters in Warsaw."

In answer to this I observed, that if Barclay
were reconciled to the reorganization of the army in
Silesia, for which he required a period of six weeks,
the Russian army would take up unmurmuringly
with the good quarters there.   But as regards the
Prussian army, I remarked that the agitation arose
from an apprehension that the truce might be merely
the introduction to a shameful peace, which Napoleon, with his well-known cunning, would talk us
into if we once began to treat with him.   In order
to meet the morbid idea, that whoever wished for a
truce must also desire a disadvantageous peace, I
proposed that, on publishing the truce, the King
should at the same time issue a proclamation to his
people to this effect : " No peace !   Prepare for a
contest of life and death."

We sketched out such a proclamation, and took
it to the King, who agreed with us, and went to
the Emperor, taking us with him.   Knesebeck was
spokesman ; the Emperor listened with the deepest
attention.   A report just then arrived from the

Commissioners was favourable to our views. The two generals, Count Schuwalof and Von Kleist, found that they were treated more considerately than hitherto in such conferences; that Napoleon paid attention to their objections, and showed a complying temper. Although they were not yet able to explain the real reason which inclined him to the truce, still they believed they had already discovered that the state of affairs on the Lower Elbe, perhaps an insurrection in the Hanseatic departments and Oldenburg, were the motives for the conclusion of a truce. This circumstance made me think it probable that Napoleon would be particularly complying towards us in Silesia, and the more so if our commissioners were somewhat prolix, while the French commissioners urged a speedy conclusion.

My opinion was supported by a second argument. Breslau had been abandoned, and was garrisoned by French troops. I had expected that Napoleon would immediately remove his head-quarters there with the Guards; but as he remained quiet at Neumarkt, I could only explain this step by supposing that he feared such a solemn taking possession of the capital of Silesia would impede the truce, and consequently that he cared more for its conclusion than for Breslau.

My proposition, therefore, went to require the evacuation of Breslau as an indispensable condition for concluding the truce. The Sovereigns doubted whether this would be attained, nevertheless they consented to the attempt; and so by the firm demeanor of our commissioners, a truce was brought about as much in accordance with our wants as our wishes.

That in concluding this truce Napoleon com-

mitted a grave error, even his greatest admirers
have since admitted. So on the Prussian side, it was
afterwards acknowledged how favourable this truce
was for Prussia ; but on its conclusion it was censured, especially by the members of the Tugendbund
(an alliance of students so called), as unnecessary,
and as a mistake ; nay, it was represented as a
misfortune to the State. I thought myself just as
little called upon as General von dem Knesebeck, to
disclose the secret causes for concluding the truce,
but we did not conceal that we considered its ratifi-
cation an extremely wise measure on the part of the
King. I had many warm disputes on this subject
with General Gneisenau, who, in his excitement, had
dispatched a note containing a bitter censure of the
transaction to the King. The General wanted to
convince me. I opposed him very calmly, but was
determined not to yield, because he spoke as the
head of a party, which had its seat in the army.*

For the continuation of the war after the truce,
when the strength of the Allies was increased, and
the theatre of the war was considerably extended,
it was necessary that the great Powers should not
only act in concert in the distribution of their forces,

---

* As the name of General Baron von dem Knesebeck appears
here for the first time, and the important influence which this
General exerted in the first half of the campaign of 1813 is practically represented, and as this influence likewise continued, after
the accession of Austria, till the second Peace of Paris, it seems to
me advisable in a Supplement to develop the causes of the great
confidence which the three Allied Sovereigns bestowed on him.
For this purpose it is necessary to go back to an earlier period in
the biography of this important man, and to the wars of 1806 and
1812, which, not to interrupt the narrative of the events of the
campaign of 1813, I have done in the Supplement.

but also have a fixed general plan of operations. This was arranged during the truce, at the meeting in Trachenberg, in which the Crown Prince of Sweden, introduced by the Emperor of Russia, played an important part.

The Emperor required his co-operation in settling the relations of Russia with Sweden; and this was a sufficient reason for us to endeavour to satisfy the Crown Prince so far that the Emperor might have confidence in him, and be enabled to employ his forces against Napoleon to the advantage of his Allies, out of the Russian Empire, and to advance to the Rhine without apprehension for his own States. The Crown Prince may have discovered from our proceedings, that the fortunate moment had arrived when he was in a position to make large demands: be this as it may, his influence extended not only over the operations, but over the command of the armies. Together with the command of the Army of the North, the supreme command had naturally fallen to him, over the English, Hanseatic, and North German troops under Walmoden, as well as over the Swedish troops and the corps of Bülow and Winzingerode. But he demanded also the chief command over General Count Tauentzien, whose corps, destined for blockades and sieges, was obliged to remain separated in four distinct divisions, and had quite other interests to look after than those of the Crown Prince of Sweden, who was receiving English subsidies.

But in addition to all this, he demanded also the supreme command of the Silesian army under General Blücher; so that thus he would have commanded from the Danish frontier as far as Bohemia, while the three Sovereigns would have been limited to the left wing in Bohemia.

These demands were too great, and could not be conceded by the Sovereigns. They wished however to see him return satisfied from Trachenberg to Stralsund, and admitted that circumstances might occur to render it necessary for him also to take the command of Count Tauentzien's corps and that of the Silesian army. The Crown Prince returned from Trachenberg satisfied with this acknowledgment. During the meeting at this place the question had been mooted, whether Napoleon could ever be defeated by generals who were strangers to his mode of warfare. These words acquired greater importance when, after the termination of the truce, besides the Crown Prince of Sweden, (formerly Marshal Bernadotte,) as Commander-in-Chief of the army of the North, the two French generals Moreau and Jomini were appointed military advisers at the headquarters of the Sovereigns.

The Russian generals, Wittgenstein, Benningsen, Miloradowitsch, Sacken, Barclay de Tolly, Woronzof, St. Priest, and others, had gained in the wars of 1812 the reputation of being well qualified to command armies; the Prussian generals, York, Kleist, Bülow, Tauentzien, enjoyed, together with Blücher, the confidence of distinguished officers; all these generals were equally wounded by the intelligence that they had not the credit of being able to defeat Napoleon, but that Frenchmen had been chosen for this object. And now, in addition, came the startling behaviour of the Crown Prince of Sweden, who immediately began to grasp at the command over General Count Tauentzien and Blücher, but at the same time kept up very equivocal connections, which were managed by an individual who frequented his head-quarters as a friend. These connections with France and the French army were grounded on the presumption, that the French were weary of Napoleon's rule, and would gladly exchange it for Bernadotte's, if he gave them proofs of forbearance and clemency.

In the reform of the Silesian army, General Gneisenau was appointed the head of its Staff, and I was called to the post of Quartermaster General. I may say, that it was a feeling of duty that animated me in undertaking this important office, with the hope of being useful to my native country by the exertion of all my powers. The General-in-Chief, Blücher, was friendly to me; and since the conflict at Haynau, which I had proposed, and for which I drew up the plan, based on the reconnoissance of Major von Rühle made by my orders, I rose in his favour, because he thought he saw in it that I understood cavalry service. This was an advantage I did not underrate; but I was not placed immediately under him, but under Gneisenau; and with the great difference of our views, the idea that I could gain his entire confidence would have been hopeless. I felt that all I could expect to attain was what my conduct might force from him,—his esteem. But to succeed in this, it was necessary that I should keep aloof from the General-in-Chief, and avoid even the semblance of an intimacy with him, should this at all interfere with the relations between the General-in-Chief and his Chief of the Staff.

On my official announcement consequent on my appointment, I expressed myself openly to General

Gneisenau to this effect, and obtained an equally frank answer. He had wished for Colonel von Clausewitz in my place, who was his personal friend. I could not blame him for this. Moreover, he would not allow that our views of warfare were opposed: he declared that the difference lay rather in my being softer and more doubtful than himself, and that this inclined me to listen to considerations which he disregarded.

In these words he honestly expressed his own views, and I would have subscribed to them, if, instead of "soft and doubtful," as compared to himself, he had designated me as more cautious and less apt to be carried away by impulse.

In the year 1824, under the title, "Contributions to the History of the War, &c.," I published the campaigns of the Silesian army from the Truce to the Peace of Paris, 1814, in which my chief object was to give a true and general picture of events, but to admit no single statement that could not be verified. I had therefore to confine myself to what was found in the reports.

Now, when the heat and passion of the time have died away, and many questions still remain unsolved, of importance to the history of the war, accounts may be supplied of many verbal transactions known to few persons still living beside myself. False conclusions may thus be corrected, and false accusations which have received currency for a period of thirty years will be refuted.

The following, therefore, is to be considered as a supplement to my work, "History of the War, &c.,"* from page 30 of the 2nd edition of 1827.

* Zur Kriegs-Geschichte der Jahre 1813–14. Die Feldzüge

The General-in-Chief rode to York's corps; *
General Gneisenau and I towards Christian's-Höhe,
for the purpose of discovering the enemy's measures,
to assist our further conclusions. We there met
Major von Hiller, who commanded the infantry of
the rear-guard: his battalions were just arriving.
According to his assertion, the enemy must already
be on the plateau, in considerable force. The Commander of the rear-guard, Colonel von Katzler, was
still behind with the cavalry. The rain limited our
horizon to 800 or 1000 paces.

We saw nothing before us; we did not hear a
shot. At last Katzler arrived. On our asking,
"Where is the enemy?" he replied, "Close at my
heels." More he could not tell; for in his inconsiderate hussar manner he had called in all the
flankers. I fell into a warm altercation with him on
the subject, which Gneisenau interrupted by saying:
"The mistake is now made, there is nothing left
for us but to seek the enemy;" and so saying, he
began to move. All the officers followed. Katzler
again wished to go first. I represented to General
Gneisenau, that riding forward in this way could not
gain our object, of finding out whether the enemy
was following with the intention of attacking us.
As the latter had sent out no flankers, it was just
as likely they had retired, as that they were advancing against us in dense and deployed masses.
A single horseman in advance would discover the

der Schlesischen Armee. Bei Mittler in Berlin; 2te Auflage,
1827. This work forms Part III. of the present translation.—ED.

* This relates to the battle on the Katzbach, Part III, p. 317.
To facilitate reference, an Index of Part III. is given at the end.
—ED.

one as easily as the other, but not a large company, which would excite the enemy's attention.

I offered to ride forward alone, if he, General Gneisenau, would remain on this spot with all the officers, and await my return, when the disposition could be issued for the two corps already arrived on the plateau, which was impossible before my return, and in ignorance of what the enemy was doing.

General Gneisenau accepted my proposal, and I rode across the country towards the Kuhbergen. I was mounted on a mouse-coloured horse, and had on a grey cloak, so that in the pouring rain I was not visible at 100 paces. Moreover I took a good plan of the district with me, which I had already learnt by heart. From hence, in the plains towards Klein-Tinz to Jänowitz, not a man was to be seen, nor anything to be heard in the valley towards Ober-Weinberg.

I continued my way along the wooded edge of the valley, and came, by a very circuitous route, to some deeply cut ground before Jänowitz, in the line from Nieder-Weinberg toward the east end of Jänowitz. Here I suddenly saw myself on the prolongation of the line of the front of a deployed body of cavalry, so close to it that I drew back my horse behind a leafy tree, to remain undiscovered. I saw some batteries follow the cavalry on the road from Nieder-Crayn to Jänowitz. I heard behind me cries in French, and saw in the valley of Nieder-Weinberg a column of the enemy's infantry in march, whose head had almost reached the plateau.

I looked at my watch, and retreated slowly to the road from Nieder-Weinberg to Brechtelshof, where I overlooked the line of cavalry in front, and computed it at 3000 horse. I now set spurs to my horse, met General Gneisenau, and reported what I had seen ; and on his sending word to General von Blücher to join us, I made the following proposition : To march at once against the enemy with the two corps of York and Sacken,—York's corps moving between Christians-Höhe and Belawic,* with Sacken's corps feeling his flank, and bringing forward the right shoulder towards Klein-Tinz.

I gave the following reasons for my proposal, watch in hand :—"If General von York sets out immediately, and continues to march uninterruptedly in column, in fifty-one minutes he can reach the point where I saw the hostile column of infantry on the plateau. As they must march through a narrow defile, General von York cannot possibly find more than 10,000 infantry, unless a second column were to come over the Dohna bridge, which I could not see. But this could not well be stronger than the first corps, and consequently General York can manage alone with both, without requiring General Sacken's assistance, who in that case can be employed against any force which may come from the side of Liegnitz. If we secure Schlaupe and Belawic, and keep on the edge of the valley of the Neisse, our operations will be without any danger." General von Gneisenau approved of my proposal, and the Commander-in-Chief adopted it as the order of battle. Officers were immediately dispatched to transmit it verbally.

I had the charge of leading General von York's corps. My plan of action for this column was to this effect : two brigades to advance on to the plain,

* So the place was marked on my above-mentioned plan.

one half-brigade to hold close to the edge of the valley, the other half to occupy Schlaupe and Schlauphof, and to keep up the communication with Langeron's corps : the fourth corps to follow as a reserve, its left wing resting on the edge of the valley.

After this had been agreed to, I rode to meet General von York, who insisted, notwithstanding all my remonstrances, on deploying between Christians-Höhe and Belawic, before he began his further march. I told him that this space would be filled up with two brigades and their batteries ; that his troops would advance in the best order in column ; and that any loss of time would involve him in a harder fight at the point whither I was to lead him. In vain ! he made his troops halt and deploy ; and no other course was left me but to complain, to the General-in-Chief, from whom General York received immediate orders to continue the march in columns, which would instantly restore the line if necessary.

The General deliberated sullenly ; but at last obeyed, though not without signs of anger. I led the left wing of the two brigades towards the Kuhberg, behind which the enemy's cavalry was stationed, with five or six batteries, which were firing at great distances. There was nothing else to be seen of the enemy.

Some of the enemy's infantry appeared unexpectedly on the Kreuzberg, this side the Kuhberg, with some guns, and it became necessary to employ the nearest troops to force them down quickly, which they succeeded in doing. But this occasioned a stoppage in the advance ; and now the episode on the left wing was settled, and I urged the march forward, we found ourselves within range of the enemy's horse artillery. This decided what it was necessary for us to do. First, we must silence these batteries. This might require a cannonade of an hour's duration ; I therefore exhorted Lieutenant-Colonel Schmidt immediately to order up a superior force of artillery (he had above 100 guns), in order to finish with the enemy quickly. This was done; but about this time some of the enemy's cavalry (which must have come from the valley of the Neisse), appeared on our left wing, and a portion as far as Belawic in our rear. This was the signal for a general departure from our previous plan. Our cavalry split into squadrons, who fought singly, and the whole infantry of York's corps stood looking on inactively. The hostile troops who had hitherto shown themselves to York's corps consisted altogether of three broken and five fresh battalions of infantry, along with about 4,000 horse, of which the greater part threatened our front, and thereby placed us wholly on the defensive ; for all command, all co-operation of forces, had ceased.

This state of things, in which the exertions of individuals to bring the masses again into a forward movement were fruitless, might have lasted a quarter of an hour, when suddenly the French cavalry in our front turned their backs on us ; and when our cavalry followed in disorder, they rode off in wild flight. The Russian cavalry, coming from Klein-Tinz, had taken the enemy in flank and rear.

When York's infantry was again set in motion according to its first destination, I thought the serious fighting with the masses of the enemy's infantry would begin ; but, to my great astonishment, along the whole of the plateau, especially from the Kuhberg as far as the road from Jänowitz to the edge of the valley, there were not more than two battalions of infantry, which descended precipitately into the valley of the Neisse together with the cavalry.

With this ended the fighting on the plateau; after which, in the pursuit, we found thirty-two guns, with their carriages, on the road to Nieder-Crayn, which had been driven to the slope of the hill and abandoned.

It was now necessary to take new resolutions, for the firing on the left bank of the Neisse was drawing further and further off towards Jauer, and had already become very faint.

The reports received, while we were fighting, from Count Langeron, that he must give way to superior force, and would not be able to hold his last position on the hill and at Hermannsdorf, had been left unnoticed at my suggestion, for this reason, that he occupied good positions with 130 guns, in which no harm could befall him. My remarks that his messages could produce no alterations in our disposition, and that he must be ordered to stand firm, nevertheless excited the General-in-Chief and Gneisenau beyond measure; and in the parley which was held near Nieder-Crayn, General Langeron was called a miserable poltroon, whom we ought to denounce to the Emperor as deserving to be cashiered. His (cowardly) conduct was contrasted with ours, and without further comment, we by comparison considered ourselves heroes; this was, in a double sense, going much too far. Accordingly here again the hard task fell to me of disturbing inspiriting self-delusions by plain truths, in order to eradicate the consequences of such hallucinations. I therefore made the following remarks :—

"The Silesian army is divided into two portions by the Neisse; the half on the left bank is rather the lesser one.

"The enemy dispatched troops across the Neisse in pursuit of York's rear-guard; he ascended the plateau, and pushed forward against us, without our knowing whether he intended to act also on the offensive on the left bank.

" We had to make up our minds that we should be attacked on the right bank by all the forces at his disposal, and should be infallibly beaten if we allowed him to deploy them. We therefore took the right step in resolving to attack the heads of the enemy's columns, and drive them down again from the ridge. In this we have succeeded; but the enemy has since disclosed his intentions. His main strength is posted on the left bank of the Neisse; there he intends to march to battle, and we on the right bank, with the greater half of the army, have defeated merely *his left-wing patrols.* Thus nothing—nothing at all has yet been done towards deciding the fate of the day.

" Count Langeron may be attacked by a superior force of 30,000 men; if he is beaten, our victory on the right bank vanishes like an insignificant Cossack hurrah.

" If General Langeron were a man quite to be depended on, I would propose to cross the Neisse immediately with all the forces we have at Crayn, Schlauphof, and Schlaupe, to pursue on the right

F

bank those we have defeated ; and on the left, to take the enemy attacking Langeron in the rear.

"This however would be too venturesome so long as we are ignorant of the exact situation of General Langeron on the left bank of the Neisse, and do not know for certain that what he *can* do, he *will* do.* I therefore propose :—

"1. Immediately to clear the defile before us from all the enemy's carriages sticking in it, and to make it passable again.

"2. To cause the reserve brigade of York's corps to advance by Schlauphof to attack the enemy.

"3. To drive the enemy from Nieder-Crayn, and garrison the place strongly with the brigades of infantry nearest to it.

"4. To give to Sacken's corps the charge to as-certain the enemy's strength between Dohna and Liegnitz, and to hold itself in readiness in the middle of the plateau, as a reserve for all further movements. Furthermore, I desire that I may be sent at once with all necessary powers to Count Langeron, but that all fur-ther arrangements be postponed until the delivery of my verbal report on my return."

The preamble to these propositions was received

---

* At the time this proposition was made, we did not know that the enemy's 3rd corps was posted on the Katzbach from Schmachwitz to Liegnitz, and destined to march upon the plateau. We were just as little aware that Charpentier's division had already been on the plateau, and had retreated again across the Katzbach at Dohna, without fighting. It must be admitted that these divisions of the enemy's army were all engaged in the attack on Count Langeron.

with some irritability, but the propositions themselves were sanctioned without opposition.

I expedited orders 1, 2, and 4, myself, and observed that for order 3, an officer must be sent down into the valley of the Neisse, to direct the immediate occupation of Nieder-Crayn, and at the same time to inform General York of the reason of these arrangements.

After this I galloped with some aides-de-camp by Schlaupe* to the hill, where I found General Lan geron engaged in drawing off his troops. With intentional vivacity I called out to him : " Au nom de Dieu, Général, vous battez en retraite, pendant que nous avons remporté une victoire brillante ! Délivré de notre ennemi, nos réserves sont en pleine marche pour passer la Neisse, et pour prendre en revers tout ce que vous avez devant vous."

Generals Prince Czerbatow, Olsuwief, Rudcze witsch, and others, together with Colonel Ende, were at his side, and heard my exclamation.

" Colonel," answered Langeron thoughtfully, " vous êtes mon sauveur ;" and he embraced me. I replied : " Allons, attaquons sur le champ : je resterai avec vous : il me faut être témoin de votre gloire, comme je l'ai été de celle du Général Sacken."

The praise of General Sacken pleased the Rus sian generals greatly. Ende exclaimed : " We have nothing left here but the rear guard ; 100 guns were sent away to the rear long ago."—" Let them all return," I exclaimed, " and let us attack with what we have got!"

---

* As we rode through Schlaupe, fighting had already com menced near this village.

All voted with me, but General Langeron solemnly asked : " Colonel, est ce que vous êtes sûr que le Général en chef ne dispose de mon corps que pour couvrir sa retraite ?"   This was the fixed and firmly rooted idea of Count Langeron, which had misled him into his false measures. I answered: " Je suis sûr, mon Général, que le Général en chef passera la Neisse pour ecraser l'ennemi qui vous attaque ; ainsi il faut tenir ferme ; il faut réparer les erreurs, et intimider les présomptueux, les attaquant tambour battant."

Thereupon the aides-de-camp hastened to bring back to their positions all those who had been sent away ; and when the Prussian reserve-brigade under Colonel von Steinmetz pressed forward by Schlaupe and Schlauphof, fighting and supporting,* all the generals placed themselves at the head of their troops ; and after an energetic, and to the enemy quite unforeseen attack, regained possession of the Weinberg and a part of Hennersdorf.

From this moment the enemy continued to act on the defensive ; and notwithstanding their great. superiority, behaved without energy and irresolutely. They had to form a flank to oppose Steinmetz's brigade. Their strength could be easily overlooked from the hill, and from what we saw, we concluded that when General Langeron collected his whole corps the following morning, he would be quite equal to the enemy.

We agreed that the corps should advance at daybreak either for attack or pursuit. As the day declined, I rode back by Schlaupe, where the water

---

* This may have taken place about six o'clock.

of the raging Neisse not only reached our saddles, but carried away the horses down the stream.

I directed General von Hünerbein, whom I found at Schlaupe, to force Schlauphof; and told him the situation of Langeron's corps, and my arrangements with him. This occurred about eight o'clock; but in consequence of the darkness of the night I did not reach Brechtelshof till after eleven o'clock, where without waiting for me, and against my stipulation, on mere verbal reports of the situation of Langeron's corps, dispositions for the 27th were already issued, which were partly unpractical and partly quite impracticable.

The issuing of the above-mentioned order No. 3 had been forgotten, and Nieder-Crayn was not occupied. When night came on, York's troops remained where they were, lying on the saturated ground, without straw, without wood, wearied out and famished. The rain continued to fall in torrents; and according to the new plan, it was decided that a brigade should set out about two o'clock in the morning, and proceed to Nieder-Crayn, to attempt to cross the Katzbach at Kroitsch. This arrangement was in every respect censurable and ill-considered. It assumed that the enemy, who at nightfall stood with 30,000 or 40,000 men between the Mönchswald and Schlauphof, would have retreated to Goldberg in this dark night; whereas the very contrary ought to have been assumed; that is to say, that before commencing their retreat from Hennersdorf, the enemy would be obliged to secure it; and for this object the most necessary measure was to occupy Nieder-Crayn, which we had neglected to do, as the high road from Hennersdorf to Goldberg passes by it at not quite 3000 paces distance. But in case this had also been neglected by the enemy, or that York's brigade had been able to turn unimpeded towards Kroitsch through Nieder-Crayn, still it might be assumed that the enemy could only retreat in three columns towards Goldberg, and then their left-wing column must march through Nieder-Crayn, where it would fall in with the rear of York's brigade, who, if they found the bridge at Kroitsch destroyed, would be unable to move either forwards or backwards.

Fortunately this very unpractical order was at the same time impracticable, as none of York's scattered brigades could set out at two o'clock. Such impracticable orders have the effect of undermining obedience, and destroying the army's confidence in their commander. My remonstrances, however gentle, were very ill received by General Gneisenau, but still more so when I afterwards pointed out the fact that Horn's brigade received the order to set out at two o'clock, about six,—just four hours too late.

This disposition, which made General von York angry and was the subject of sharp criticism, must be regarded as the introduction to the vexatious correspondence which, during the pursuit, ensued between the Commander-in-Chief and General von York; for the latter would not take upon himself the execution of orders that could not be carried out, and he therefore put questions on every point, to be relieved from the responsibility.

General Blücher had the fixed notion that he had totally beaten the French army, and all that remained was to pursue it warmly, for which the cavalry would suffice. General Gneisenau, to whom I explained that only one-tenth of the army opposed to us had engaged with us on the plateau, and that of the eight battalions (and he had not seen more) five were come back, and three of them even in good order—was obliged to admit to me, that the combat on the plateau could not lead to the supposition that the whole army was defeated ; but he entered into General Blücher's notion, assented to all he wished, and admitted that by this hussar-pursuit Macdonald would reach Dresden *alone*. This was in accordance with the principle laid down by him, that you must always require from men more than they can perform, since in execution invariably less is done than is demanded—a principle which I have always considered as dangerous as it is incorrect.

Our pursuit on the other side of the Katzbach, without any considerable force of infantry and artillery, was imperfect. If these, however, had been brought across the Katzbach, all our strength must have been called out, as the General-in-Chief demanded. The weak and weary might have remained behind to follow afterwards ; they would not be lost to the army.

If, in spite of all this, our imperfect pursuit produced so great a result, it was the consequence of two mistakes in the French army.

The first was this : when the flight began on the plateau, the fugitives were not collected at Nieder-Crayn and led behind the Katzbach at Kroitsch, in which case their flight would have had no influence on the rest of the army, and would have been of no consequence.

The second fault must be laid to Marshal Macdonald's charge, who commanded on the left bank of the Neisse. Until six o'clock, P.M., he continued to act vigorously on the offensive. When about this time he was attacked by Langeron's corps, he defended himself where he stood, although feebly, till seven o'clock, when the sun went down. Whether the resolution to retreat upon Goldberg was a consequence of this attack, may be left in doubt, but yet Macdonald must have said to himself,—" The troops have been, since early in the morning, in active motion ; to-morrow morning the sun will rise about seven, consequently there are eleven hours of night before me, during which interval the enemy, who are just as weary as ourselves, can do me no harm. Which is now the most judicious plan,—to spend these hours in taking food and rest, and then to commence at dawn a retreat of two (German) miles to get behind the Goldberg, or gradually to draw off during the night?" He did not, it seems, foresee that in the latter case the troops must arrive at Goldberg in such a state of exhaustion, that they would no longer be capable of fighting, and must fall into the enemy's hands. General Langeron did, in fact, find the 5th corps in this condition when he overtook it at Goldberg, on the morning of the 27th.

This mistake of overtaxing the human powers had not been foreseen by the Prussian commanders, nor had the disposition for the following day been based upon it ; yet without this mistake the pursuit, as the General-in-Chief had ordered it, would probably have had no result whatever.

Langeron's vigorous attack about six o'clock in the evening of the 26th, was probably the cause of Macdonald's precipitate retreat ; and if Langeron's corps, in consequence, had most share in the dispersion of Macdonald's army, it was a well-deserved reward.

Meanwhile the General-in-Chief and Gneisenau took no further notice of this achievement, and considered the trophies brought in later solely as results of the skirmish on the right bank of the Neisse. They would not admit to me that Macdonald had withdrawn over-hastily during the night,—that at close of day he ought to have ordered his reserve (which had not been engaged in the fight) to fall back three quarters of a (German) mile from the Plinsen ground to the strong position of Prausnitz, and bivouac there, to enable him to lodge his troops there the following morning,—nor that he ought to have waited for daylight, to retreat with order, when his men and horses had recovered their strength. But they maintained that Macdonald's retreat during the night had become unavoidably necessary, in consequence of the discomfiture of his left wing; whence it follows that the dispersion of the enemy's 5th corps was likewise a result of this discomfiture, as had been correctly foreseen, in the orders issued at nine o'clock on the evening of the 26th.

What was done could not be undone ; therefore all that I wanted now, was to avoid impracticable orders for the future, and, instead of increasing the discord between the General-in-Chief and his leaders of corps, to force them to acknowledge that the command of the army must be conducted strictly in accordance with given precepts and the circumstances of the case.

But General von Gneisenau had other objects. He was anxious that the victory on the plateau should be considered by all Europe as a general defeat of the whole of Macdonald's army, because this suited his "electrifying system."

That I was not to be led away to entertain such a view, my temperate statement on the ridge of Nieder-Crayn had already shewn him. He felt uncertain whether I might not be still inclined to declare publicly that the combat on the plateau had been an insignificant encounter, whereas it seemed to him a matter of great importance, on account of some particular circumstances :—namely, it had been a subject of discussion between myself and others, that our Prussian newspapers had admitted accounts of the events of the war up to the truce, which partly gave a distorted picture of occurrences, not unfrequently compromising the army, and partly were of such a nature as to give well-founded cause of dissatisfaction to our Allies. I deemed it quite necessary to remedy this evil, but I considered that in doing so we ought to attend to the following considerations :—

The lively interest which the Prussian nation, from the highest to the lowest, takes in the occurrences of this truly national war, cannot but be gratifying ; and our newspapers only consult the real wants and general wishes of the people, in giving as full accounts of them as they can. Nothing is communicated to them officially ; or if there is, they get the news so late, that fresh events have already thrown the old into the shade.

The newspapers of the three capitals, therefore, admit with pleasure the letters of volunteers, who tell their relations without restraint what they have seen and heard ; while they often unintentionally state the most insignificant as the most important facts, and thereby not only give a very false picture of the situation of the belligerent armies, but, by repeating the disapprobation they may hear expressed against their own or the allied leaders, without any knowledge of the matter or judgment of their own, they become unjust and mischievous. Yet by such inconsiderate communications public opinion is formed, which cannot be rectified afterwards by official articles.

The admission, therefore, of unauthenticated reports from the army by newspaper writers must be prohibited by the Censorship; but at the same time something else must be substituted,—namely, official articles, simple and true; no lying bulletins like Napoleon's. In war *all* cannot be told,—silence must be observed on many points; but what is made known officially ought to be so strictly true, that the sharpest critic may not be able afterwards to point out any untruth.

Reports from the army published on such principles awaken confidence, and are really useful to the Government as well as to the nation. The King entertained the same views. He was satisfied with the temperate statement in the pamphlet which I published "On the Campaign of 1813 till the Truce," and charged me with the drawing up of similar reports of the Silesian army, which were to be sent to him, and, on his approval, to be subsequently printed. I represented to him, that if such reports had to travel to Bohemia and back to Berlin, they would become of so old a date as necessarily to lose much of their interest; and I therefore considered that it would be better to compile the reports from official notices, at the royal head-quarters, from whence they would get much sooner into the newspapers.

The King did not approve of this, but decided that my sketches, sanctioned by the General-in-Chief, should be sent directly from his head-quarters to the principal Prussian newspapers. I was particularly told, that the King expected that these reports should not be wanting in the dignity and tact which our circumstances required.

What I had foreseen,—namely, that these reports would become a source of vexation to me,—began only too soon. General Gneisenau was dissatisfied with the very first report: he found it too cold, measured, and pedantic. The General-in-Chief missed in it the praise of his brave comrades in arms, which, to be just, he could not deny them. To the former, I answered with humility, that I had studied the prose of our official style, that I did not understand how to write differently, and indeed that I did not think any other style would be suitable here.

I represented to the Commander-in-Chief that these reports must be short; that if praise and blame were to be admitted into them, they would not only be very long, but that the Sovereigns might look on such insertions as encroachments on their rights; as these army reports would get into all the newspapers before the statements founded on the reports of the various leaders of corps could reach the head-quarters of the Sovereigns, whose prerogative it is to order rewards and punishments.

All these remonstrances availed nothing. General von Gneisenau adorned my paper with phrases and flowers; General Blücher introduced Prussian names. I was determined, in an affair which concerned the service, not to give way, and declared : " I may be wrong, and this is a question which the King will settle ; meanwhile, in this commission, entrusted to a subordinate officer, who is restricted to writing down simple facts, and is not free either to praise or to censure, I see the surest proof that the King does not wish the army report to be written in a different manner than this first one of mine."

General Gneisenau yielded, not wishing that the affair should be referred to the King for decision. Blücher was quieted when I told him that military achievements, conveying in themselves the highest praise, might be related as facts, and the names of the actors mentioned as a matter of course, without laudatory additions.

This seemed to settle matters for the time, yet each report gave rise to fresh contests of the same nature ; for though my opponents had yielded, I had not convinced them. Gneisenau accused me of viewing all the achievements of the Silesian army as trifles not worth mentioning. Blücher wished to see every well-executed commission mentioned and praised as a warlike exploit. In this continued conflict, Gneisenau felt some apprehension that in the next report I might represent the combat on the plateau as a *Cossack hurrah;* and he strove incessantly to get me to acknowledge its more extensive importance.

What I had said at four o'clock before Nieder-Crayn, was correct as to time and place ; when, in consequence of our victory, and subsequent crossing the Neisse, General Count Langeron began to act on the offensive at six o'clock, the importance of our action was increased; and when Marshal Macdonald by over-hastiness placed his fifth corps hors de combat, this action became the chief cause of the subsequent defeats of the enemy. The difference of our opinions therefore consisted only in this, that I ascribed the great result to three causes:—

1. To our fight upon the plateau.

2. To our passage of the Neisse which immediately followed it, and Colonel Steinmetz's attack.

3. To Count Langeron's attack at six o'clock, P.M.

General Gneisenau indeed disputed the effect of the second and third causes, for no other reason than not wishing to weaken the impression of the first.

Meanwhile he gave himself needless trouble, for when I undertook the duty of stating events concisely and truly, this did not mean that I should go into details, which, if disputed, would be highly dangerous to the good understanding in the army which it was my desire to establish.

Till our arrival before Nieder-Crayn, we had delivered no battle. This designation was first justified when not only the three corps, but their reserves also, had begun to use their muskets. That the Silesian army had delivered a battle, in consequence of which so many prisoners, so many guns, eagles, &c., were brought in, was therefore a fact which could not be disputed, and the army report was complete, as far as its object was concerned, in confining itself to these facts. But if the combat of Langeron's corps, at six o'clock, were ignored, then consistency demanded that the partial fights on the plateau should not be designated as a battle of the Silesian army.

With the third report, written on the night after the battle, the Russians were dissatisfied. Sacken's corps, because much too little had been said of it; and Langeron's, because it had not been mentioned at all.

In the fourth report, the statements of the two Russian generals were printed, because policy demanded that they should be satisfied. This again made General von York extremely discontented, because his statement had not also been printed. General Blücher and Gneisenau inclined always to the discontented party, and I could expect no defence from them.

My experience at this time taught me that it is unpractical to take away from the General in command the charge of drawing up such army reports. If any fear exists of his going too far, he may be kept within bounds by proper instructions. In the advance from the Bober, and the further pursuit of the French army, Gneisenau's ill-humour with me died away, and my propositions for movements and combats constantly met with unqualified approbation as heretofore.

On the 4th of September, when I had again to come forward with the proposal to avoid the battle with Napoleon, the General-in-Chief easily conformed, as we knew for certain, by trustworthy accounts, that we should be attacked by superior forces.

On the 5th, on the Landskrone, I had given out the right moment of departure, in order to cross the Neisse bridges without any serious fighting; but some needless delays in York's corps produced a stoppage on the bridge; and an engagement at a disadvantage became unavoidable, unless the whole body of cavalry of the rear-guard could pass through a ford, for which, on account of its depth, they showed no inclination; but they remained contrary to orders impeding the passage of the bridge by the infantry. In this perplexity I suggested to the General-in-Chief to set the example. Without a moment's hesitation he plunged into the water up to the saddle-bow, with the whole of his staff. All the cavalry was obliged to follow, and, under the protection of a 12-pounder battery, we gained the right bank, without losing a man. A general who thus shares the hardships of the commonest soldier, is followed joyfully, and without a murmur, by his troops.

When, two days after, we again assumed the offensive, with a view to take the King of Naples in flank and rear, everything depended on our concealing from the enemy the flank-march to the left; and General Count Langeron received strict injunctions to allow no fires to be kindled at night in the bivouac at Ostritz, which could be seen from the Landskrone.

Langeron was not aware that Napoleon had gone back to Dresden, and considered the passage of the Neisse at Ostritz an extremely hazardous undertaking. He did not follow the injunction not to allow any fires to be lighted, and thus drew upon himself the suspicion that this fresh instance of disobedience, which deprived us of the fruits of this movement, was not unintentional. He received a well-deserved reprimand, but I had to defend him against the suspicion of any bad intention: as he had received orders to cross at Ostritz the next morning, and could no longer oppose the march, it would have been more than unwise to draw Napoleon's attention to the danger of the course, who would infallibly have availed himself of such a hint to fall upon the Silesian army with all his forces.

In Bautzen, whither General von Blücher removed his head-quarters on the 15th of September, important transactions took place. General Bülow, who had never put any confidence in the Crown Prince of Sweden, watched his machinations at head-quarters; and putting together what incautiously fell from him with what he made known intentionally, the General now possessed himself of the threads of the web. He warned Tauentzien and Blücher, and made a secret agreement with Winzingerode, how far they should obey, and in what cases they must refuse obedience, to avoid irreparable disasters.

It is by bearing in mind these views and agreements, that we may explain General von Bülow's behaviour at Grossbeeren, Dennewitz, and Leipzic; at the conquest of Holland, and on his march to La Fère; also General Winzingerode's advance at Leipzic, and General Count Tauentzien's resistance to an unconditional submission to the orders of the Crown Prince of Sweden. At the same time these views give a complete explanation of General von Blücher's measures, from the time when he arrived at Bautzen with the Silesian army, after the battle on the Katzbach.

After the battle of Dennewitz,* a confidential officer sent by General von Bülow came to head-

---

* Fought on September 26th, between a French army commanded by Marshal Ney, and two corps of the Army of the North, viz., those of General von Bülow and Count Tauentzien, in which the French were defeated.—ED.

quarters, who laid before General Blücher the daily progressive measures which the Crown Prince adopted, to prove to the French army that he acted not only as their countryman, but their friend; and how far he was from wishing to destroy them by his Swedes, or to shed their blood. These proofs were very comprehensive, and of such recent date that they could not yet have reached the royal head-quarters. They decided General von Blücher in taking the resolution to obviate all political high treason by a rapid flank-march to the right; and he persisted in this resolution, even when, almost at the same time, he received orders from the Sovereigns to draw near to them on the left, towards Bohemia.

Thus one of the three Frenchmen summoned by the Sovereigns to assist them in conquering Napoleon, had to be watched by an army of 100,000 men! The *second* was carried off by a cannon-ball before Dresden; and the *third* proved himself, that same day, a sublime *teacher* indeed, but at the same time so unpractical on the field of battle, that his advice was not asked again. Time and events, moreover, had so strengthened the confidence of the Sovereigns in themselves and their generals, that the expediency of summoning foreigners to their assistance was no longer discussed.

At this period, in as far as it emanated from them, the superior conduct of the war was to a great extent well organized; but there was a want of activity, indispensable when the opponent was a Napoleon; too much time was lost before resolutions were matured, and despatches were needlessly trammelled by forms.

In General Blücher's head-quarters, the conduct of business had considerably improved since he had acceded to my entreaties that my propositions for operations, &c., should be made only in the presence of General von Gneisenau, by which means secrecy was better preserved.

The Emperor Alexander had expressly selected the Russian Colonel Theyl for a post near General Blücher, with the wish to do something agreeable to the Commander-in-Chief. This colonel, who had formerly been in the Dutch service, lived, after the French conquest of Holland in 1794, as an emigrant at Münster, where for many years he was the house and table-companion of the General-in-Chief. Blücher received him again at his head-quarters, on the old footing. Theyl was a brave man, but cautious in the extreme.

The order for the flank-march to the right was issued September 24th, and gave the first intimation of this march to head-quarters. No one knew that it was sanctioned by the Sovereigns. The Prussian general, Von Rauch, happened just then to be at the head-quarters of the Silesian army, for the purpose of executing some particular directions relating to the Silesian fortresses, in case the army should be driven back. He best knew the bad state of these fortresses, and he considered the march of the Silesian army to the right as extremely dangerous to them.

Colonel Theyl went still further : he considered that the results of the whole campaign would be inconsiderately perilled by this movement. He availed himself of his *grandes entrées* to the General-in-Chief, to make the most urgent remonstrance

against allowing himself to be carried away by
Gneisenau and me into such hazardous enterprises.
Blücher answered: " Be quiet, old friend; everything
has been maturely weighed;" but Theyl formally
protested against the march. Blücher started, looked
at him in astonishment, and answered : " Colonel,
the Emperor, your master, has sent you here to
report to him, for which purpose I furnish you with
all the necessary materials with the greatest readiness. When you protest against my published orders, you depart altogether from your instructions;
you are not appointed my adviser! I therefore
decline listening to you, and take my leave." Saying this, he left him.

General von Rauch had attempted to force his
opinions upon General Gneisenau; and failing in
this, he tried the same course with the General-in-
Chief, but here he fared still worse than Colonel
Theyl.

General von Blücher made no mystery of these
conversations, and the result was that these two
officers sought and obtained other appointments; but
at the same time the opponents became cautious.*

Until the time of our junction with the Army
of the North, the correspondence with the Crown
Prince of Sweden, which had been entrusted to me,
required very peculiar attention, being more diplo-

* It has been mentioned by many authors who have written
about this immortal hero, that he adhered inflexibly to the conclusions he had embraced, and that when he had once bestowed his
confidence, nothing would make him give it up. Here is the
strongest confirmation of this truth. Blücher broke with a friend
of many years' standing, because he attempted to make him sus-
pect the judgment of the persons who were placed near him to
prepare his operations, and who possessed his confidence.

matic than military. Every word had to be weighed
and considered, with a view to see what consequences might be drawn therefrom. We had found
by experience that the written communications of the
Crown Prince did not at all agree with his verbal
expressions, which we learnt through the Prussian
officers at his head-quarters.

General von Gneisenau, who hated the Crown
Prince with the full energy of his character, was of
opinion that more could be done with him by verbal
intercourse than by written negotiations, and the
General-in-Chief arranged an interview in Puch for
the 7th of October. General Blücher required an in-
terpreter for this,—a part which Gneisenau positively
refused to undertake, but to my great horror made
over to me ; and, furnishing me with impracticable
instructions as to what I should effect, he remained
behind under some suitable pretext.

On his arrival in Puch, the Crown Prince fell on
the neck of his *" cher frère d'armes "* with the *bon-
hommie* of an old soldier, and entered fully into the
propositions which I was directed to make to him,
for the march upon Leipzic, nodding all the time
kindly to the Commander-in-Chief. He then began,
and spoke at first with the finest phrases in the sense
we desired ; but he gradually deviated in essential
parts so materially, that our proposition was no
longer at all the same. He concluded with the
words : " Ainsi nous sommes d'accord." I was
obliged to contradict and refute, but he contrived to
glide over all my arguments with the ease natural to
a Frenchman, and always repeated, turning to the
General-in-Chief, " Mais nous sommes d'accord."
But the being *d'accord* consisted in this, that we

wished for a battle to facilitate the development of
the Grand Army, as well as its advance, and indeed at a time when Napoleon was as yet unable to
attack us with all his forces united,—the Crown
Prince, on the contrary, wished for no battle, either
sooner or later, but he wanted to assume the appearance of having desired, nay, even sought it, and
having been prevented by circumstances. He began
by saying, that it would be rendering the most important service to the Grand Army, to entice the
French army to advance from Leipzic towards the
Mulde, and thereby remove it from the Grand Army.
Granting this, I replied : " If we hide ourselves
behind the Mulde with 150,000 men, this object
can never be attained. Napoleon will in this case
give battle to the Grand Army in the district of
Penig and Altenburg, with superior forces, and we
shall be at too great a distance to take any part in
it."

The Crown Prince assured me this was precisely his opinion, assented to all that was proposed
on our side, and departed with the greatest show of
regard to his " cher frère d'armes." When we got
into the carriage, I said to my General : " Early
to-morrow you will receive his excuses. He will
not venture to decline all participation in the march
forward, but he will find reasons enough for keeping
in the second line, and retreating across the Elbe
on the first cannon-shot, with the fairest professions
that ' All is done only in the interest of the Grand
Army.' " Blücher thought he had expressed too
much good-will, and could not credit such masked
intentions. The result justified my apprehensions.

In a second conference, the Crown Prince was

much more excited, and no longer so circumspect.
The time for important decisions was approaching;
we had already given up the hope of obtaining anything by arguments. The fear of being compro-
mised, and of giving occasion for complaints to the
Allied Sovereigns, who had intrusted their troops to
his guidance, was the only means of forcing him out
of his passiveness.

The English general, Lord Stewart, brother to
the minister Lord Castlereagh, was at the Crown
Prince's head-quarters, for the purpose of watching
the fulfilment of the Treaty of Subsidy, concluded
between England and Sweden, and of apportioning
the money. General Gneisenau was well acquainted
with him, and they both agreed that Sweden was
playing an equivocal part in politics.

The Crown Prince treated the English Commissioner with particular attention, and sought to win
his approval of his views and conduct, in which
attempt however he was not always successful.
Lord Stewart did not hesitate to avow, on some
new instance of intractability in the Crown Prince,
that, according to his instructions, there might be
occasions in which he would be obliged to refuse the
order for the payment of the subsidy.

On the refusal of the Crown Prince, which was
repeated daily, to advance to the battle of Leipsic,
Lord Stewart at last took occasion to fulfil his
threat, undeterred by the Prince's irritability, or his
flattering offers of reconciliation. To this circumstance the plains of Breitenfelde are indebted for
the honour of being trodden by a successor of the
great King of Sweden. The General-in-Chief of
the Silesian army would never have succeeded

in moving him to take part in the battle of Leipsic.

When, on the 19th of October, the generals in command met the Sovereigns in the market-place of Leipsic, just as the Elster bridge had been blown up, the Silesian army was already marching in pursuit of the enemy to Lützen, having the command of all the bridges over the Elster from Leipsic downwards.

I pointed out this measure to the Staff of the Quartermaster Generals of the Grand Army and that of the North, with this observation, that as the Silesian army had hitherto held the centre in the order of battle, and must regulate their movements, the high road to Frankfort seemed their natural line of pursuit, while the line of the Army of the North might lead by Cassel and Düsseldorf, and that of the Grand Army by Würzburg and Mannheim across the Rhine. However, I could obtain no answer either about the pursuit at hand, or the systems and lines in general ; every one was too much engaged for this.*

* Here in the market-place I conversed with General Knesebeck without witnesses, on the subject of our further operations. We were both of the same opinion, that we ought not only to stick close to Napoleon, to drive him over the Rhine, but cross it at the same time with him, and follow him to Paris, to conclude the peace there. Knesebeck, indeed, did not doubt of the acquiescence both of the Emperor of Russia and our King in this plan, but foresaw some opposition on the part of Austria, which might be occasioned by her war in Italy; but he saw the principal difficulty in the entreaties of the generals in command, that some rest at last should be for once granted to their different corps, to prepare for so long an expedition, to provide them clothes and ammunition and repair their arms. The rapid pursuit as far as the Rhine was quite indispensable in order to break up the Confede-

The complimenting the King of Saxony and the Crown Prince of Sweden, the latter of whom was especially interested in showing off his well-preserved Swedes to the Sovereigns *en parade* this day, instead of putting them in movement towards Halle, and lastly, the necessary digesting of the pleasures of victory—all lost so much time that Napoleon gained a start upon us, which we could never recover.

If it had not been for this start, and if the Silesian army had continued its pursuit of him, the combat at Hanau would probably have led to another result; for from Eisenach onward, Field Marshal Blücher found himself every afternoon in the room which Napoleon had left in the morning.

Meanwhile the Grand Army followed from the Werra valley, in the direction of Fulda, and thence undertook the pursuit, whereby the Silesian army was pressed more into the direction of Coblentz, as the Army of the North had not advanced towards the Rhine, because the Crown Prince with his Swedes had found it necessary to despatch some

ration of the Rhine, and to free the troops of the Confederation from the French divisions in which they were still enrolled. Knesebeck hoped that if Blücher undertook to follow Napoleon they would succeed in directing the Grand Army by Würzburg, and the Army of the North, by Cassel and Prussian Minden, to the Rhine.

On this hasty consultation I grounded my communication as an incitement to an activity that excluded all dawdling deliberations. Knesebeck undertook to carry through all the rest in the council of the Sovereigns. Gneisenau, with whom I immediately conversed, (still on the market-place, while our General-in-Chief was being cajoled by the Emperors), was quite of the same mind, and expressed himself (as was afterwards mentioned), publicly to this effect.

business with Denmark, which required a march to Holstein.

Arrived at Frankfort, the Sovereigns thought they might be satisfied with what had been obtained with so much blood, and were of opinion that the continuation of the war was neither necessary nor advisable, as they did not reckon upon a conquest of Holland by General von Bülow, and an attack upon Paris seemed a hazardous operation. Had Napoleon been contented with the Rhine as a boundary, and evacuated the fortresses he still occupied in Prussia and Germany, we should have had peace, but the ever-restless Napoleon would have invaded us again when the Russians returned home.

The Field Marshal, General Gneisenau, and I, in vain exerted all our eloquence to picture the situation of Europe as opposed to this ambitious man; and to show that we had a million of disposable soldiers, against whom he could only oppose the *skeletons* of his beaten armies and discontented conscripts. We were supported in our views by England, but it was to Napoleon himself that we owed the resolution to continue the war, by which his empire fell to pieces, and he himself was banished to Elba. His haughtiness did not allow his reconciling himself to what was inevitable, and the demands which he made for the conclusion of a peace were so arrogant, that the Sovereigns could not consent to them without incurring the reproach of weakness and of neglecting the interests of their new allies.

There was no course left, therefore, but to put in execution what Gneisenau and I had already said. In the market-place of Leipzic, on the 18th of October, when we were asked : " What is to be done now ?"—" Continue," we replied, " what we have begun ; crush the power of the tyrant, and conclude the peace only in Paris ! "

The deliberations on the subsequent military measures were carried on very quietly at Prince Schwarzenberg's, in Frankfort. I had so thoroughly prepared myself for a march of the Allies to Paris, that I had the details of operations, with all the particulars of time and distance, clearly in my head. Gneisenau and the Minister von Stein were therefore glad to see me drawn into the conferences, although it was not properly my place. General Count Bubna, whose opinion as a soldier as well as a diplomatist had with reason a certain weight with the Austrians, did not wish to cross the Rhine; yet he could only support his opinion by the weak argument, that our passage would be a signal to all France for a national war, to which we were unequal. He therefore submitted to us the guiding principle, that one must carefully avoid driving a nation to desperate resolutions, by offences against its honour.

We opposed to this opinion the expectation that all France would be *with* us when she saw that, not as enemies of the French people, but of the restless Napoleon, we came to Paris with a million of soldiers, humbly to seek peace there.

Count Bubna met with no support ; and perhaps, indeed, he was never really much in earnest in his *military* opposition.

The universal readiness of the Germans to contribute to the completion of the great work, conjointly with the three armies of the Allied Sovereigns and with England, facilitated the resolution to cross the

Rhine on New-year's day, 1814, and to advance in a concentrated force upon Paris. The Silesian army especially urged this hastening the passage of the Rhine, in order to allow the French army no time for reorganization and recruiting their ranks.

The King had gone to Berlin, to regulate the most important affairs of the kingdom, and did not return to Frankfort on the Maine until the end of December, when the Sovereigns with the grand army had already begun the march towards Switzerland for the purpose of crossing the Rhine. His State Chancellor, Prince Hardenberg, had been left with full power to act as his proxy for the votes of Prussia in the great political questions, and we had the advantage of his acquiescence in the necessity of a speedy passage of the Rhine.

The King had hoped that peace might be brought about, and he first learnt in Frankfort that, so far from this, the passage of the Rhine was fixed for the 1st of January. Thrown into the worst possible humour by this news, he sent for Gneisenau and myself, to express to us his dissatisfaction at this crossing of the Rhine, and to reproach us for not having advised against so hazardous an enterprize. We instantly confessed that we had recommended this measure most urgently, as Napoleon had rejected the negotiations for peace, by demanding the most ridiculous conditions. We explained to the King at full length what has been stated above; adding that, of the three Great Powers, Prussia herself had the greatest interest in seeing this warloving Napoleon, who was so inimical towards her, annihilated, if possible, by dethroning him; or, if this could not be effected, by driving Young France back within her old boundaries. Moreover, we could not admit that any danger was incurred by the passage of the Rhine, in a military point of, view. Of two alternatives, one only could occur : either the French people, sated with twenty years' victorious campaigns, were weary and longed for peace, or they would take up arms to defend the principle of the war. In the first case, we should have peace in a few months; in the second, we should maintain a million of soldiers at French cost, which would be the best damper to the love of war.

We confessed that the passage between Basle and Düsseldorf was defectively planned, and that the Grand Army should have crossed at Mannheim. There was, however, no necessity for laying such great stress on the observance of all the rules, since Napoleon could not offer us a decisive battle until we should be united with the Grand Army in the advance upon Paris.

The King listened to us attentively; nevertheless he was not convinced by our reasoning, and persisted in his apprehension that the expedition to Paris would end badly.

Later, on the 26th of January, when the Silesian army entered Brienne, we had the satisfaction of finding the most complete union effected between the armies prepared for action; and of seeing the Silesian army standing at their head, which in principle was its proper place, at that castle of Brienne where Napoleon had made his first studies.

SECTION II.

THE CAMPAIGN OF 1814 TO THE FIRST PEACE OF PARIS.

THE movements of the Silesian army, from the truce to the passage of the Rhine, gave no occasion for criticism, either during this campaign or afterwards. Such, however, is not the case with regard to the movements of this army during the campaign of 1814; and as my object is to furnish explanations which may be useful as contributions to history, as well as at the same time to place the reader in a position for passing an independent, unprejudiced judgment on the justice or injustice of this public criticism, I am obliged here to premise many things which I should have preferred omitting, because they relate to personal circumstances.

Since the re-opening of hostilities (in the middle of August), I had filled the office of Quartermaster-General to the Silesian army; that is to say, I had to prepare everything relating to the great operations, quarters, encampments, marches, partial and general actions.

I was not only fully aware of the importance of my position, but knew also, that in the very rapid movements, advancing and retreating, the duties imposed on me, joined with the study of the ever-varying ground, would demand all my time and powers. I therefore renounced all that could hinder me in fulfilling my duties to their full extent. I gave up all social intercourse; I secluded myself, and observed strict silence on all state concerns; but I have since had cause to lament that I became much estranged from the army, in consequence of my position. On the other hand, I escaped thereby all foreign influence on my own judgment; for the man who entertains the delusion that a discussion upon important subjects, whether with friends or opponents, has no effect on his own opinion, is deficient in experience of human nature.

The course of business was so ordered, that all reports arriving by day or night, of the enemy's movements, and all depositions of deserters, prisoners, or spies, were immediately communicated to me. The propositions for movements, and the dispositions for combats and battles, emanated from me. I laid them before General Gneisenau, with all the motives, and always with closed doors; and when he approved of my plans we went to the Field Marshal, to whom I had again to state the measures proposed, map in hand. No one was present then but Gneisenau, who used to support my plans by new and very acute arguments. The Field Marshal sanctioned them, and I managed the despatches, correspondence, &c.

The Field Marshal *never* made difficulties when the talk was of advancing and attacking. In retrograde movements, even when he had acknowledged their necessity, his vexation at this sometimes overpowered him; however, he soon recovered himself.

After the close of the campaign of 1813, Gneisenau and I approached nearer in our views of the higher mode of carrying on war; he got accustomed to me, and acquired confidence in me; and on all points relating to great affairs, we either quite agreed, or easily understood each other. But this

was not the case when it came to the details of a
march before the enemy, or to the plan of an
attack.

An enterprising mode of warfare had its charms
for me, but I never could feel any enthusiasm for
the *hazárdous*, especially where there was no necessity. From conviction, and a feeling of duty, therefore, I resisted Gneisenau when he wanted to go too
far. In general he demanded too much, often what
was impossible, from the troops. However, he
always heard my reasons, and if I had time to
explain them fully, he often yielded against his own
inclination.

Nevertheless, there was one point on which we
could never come to a thorough understanding. If,
on the one hand, he imposed too great tasks on the
leaders (as he was often forced to admit after my
explanations), on the other hand, he permitted the
subordinate commanders of an advanced guard, division, or corps, to undertake, during the battle, without losing time in asking questions, *everything* that
seemed to them conducive to their object of harass-
ing the enemy.

My objections to this were, that such instructions may be very proper from a monarch to his
Field Marshal, but that it is dangerous to authorize
a subordinate General, who is only one link of a
chain, to act according to what *he* thinks right, but
perhaps what the whole army may think wrong. If
a commander is authorized to destroy the enemy
opposed to him, without enquiring farther, and without knowing whether his measures accord with the
plans of the superior General, then his honour
demands of him to make use of such authority : but

by these means battles may be lost, and the greatest disasters may befall armies. For instance, when three corps of four divisions each stand side by side in a defensive position, and the enemy attacks them with equal strength, leaving a division before one of the flank corps, while he advances to crush the other two with superior forces, there is no doubt that this corps would be able to manage the division opposed to itself; but then the natural consequence is, if one corps leaves the place assigned to it, in the hope of gaining an easy victory with four-fold strength, it is 8 to 11 that the other two corps must succumb.

It ought therefore to be an established principle, that the General should not loose his hold, so to say, of any of the troops under his orders, that he may know for certain where they are when he wishes to dispose of them, and that he may not be necessarily drawn into the follies which they might commit.

The whole thing is so clear, that one can hardly conceive how such false doctrine as I have alluded to can be defended; but Gneisenau persisted in it, and demonstrated: Firstly, that it is ruinous to an army for the principle to be established that no one must attack without an order; for then follows the principle that whoever attacks without an order is responsible for it, and the idle and cowards will take refuge under this maxim. Secondly, that the year 1806 might have sufficiently disabused us of this false theory, that one must wait for orders before dealing with the enemy. Thirdly, that from the moment Frederick II. declared he would cashier any cavalry officer who allowed himself to be attacked, and did not go to meet the enemy, his cavalry was always victorious.

As I must return to this subject in adverting to the battle of La Belle Alliance, I reserve till then the final discussion of it. In the Silesian army all the dispositions for marches and battles, from the Peace to the fall of Paris, originated in the manner described above.

Nancy was the first of the large towns of France which we entered. Gneisenau thought it advisable that our entry should be made with a certain degree of pomp, and that the Field-Marshal should use this opportunity to publish his programme to all France, for which the Nancy newspaper would afford a convenient channel. The Field-Marshal agreed to this. On the 16th of January, when Sacken's advanced guard marched in, Colonel Count Nostitz was sent forward, to announce to the Mayor that he must receive the Field-Marshal in state in the old German town, with a speech in German, of which he must first send in a draft.

Count Nostitz came back with it in the night: Gneisenau composed an answer, of which the Field-Marshal approved, but he insisted that he could not learn it by heart on the way. I was appointed prompter, and placed in his carriage, to din the speech into him. The frightened Mayor had already assembled the notables of the place in the town-hall, when the Field-Marshal entered, surrounded by his numerous suite, and listened graciously to the forced phrases of the Mayor. We could not, on the one hand, mistake his fear of Napoleon, who might easily punish a word too much by a *fusillade*;

on the other hand, our respectable Cossacks were very imposing, with their long, well-pointed *pencils* under their arm, indicating their skill in writing history. But how all faces cleared up when the Field-Marshal spoke out with soldier-like roughness against the *rats de cave*, (a nickname of the functionaries who had the control of the cellars,) and declared the *droits réunis* abolished! The speech was printed, and sent off by the mails (which we allowed to pass everywhere) throughout France.

The Mayor had delivered up an old key, as the key of the town : it was sent to the Sovereigns by express, in the expectation that the keys of all the other towns might soon follow. The grateful town was made to understand that it ought to *fêter* the Field-Marshal by a dinner. It complied. The Field-Marshal drank prosperity to the good town, and everything was going off most successfully, the short-hand writers busily engaged, when General von Sacken rose and said : " I beg of you, gentlemen, to empty a glass with me, to the prosperity of France, and to the peace and amity of this fine country with all the nations of Europe, who offer it the hand of friendship and expect it to be frankly accepted [all the Frenchmen lifted up their hands]. We are come to bring you happiness and freedom ; but you will yourselves perceive, that this is only possible on one condition,—Death and destruction to the tyrant who has been so long the scourge of the French nation and the plague of Europe ! "

The hands of all the French were gradually lowered again, pale and lengthened faces appeared : we soldiers emptied our glasses with General von

Sacken, and were too discreet to expect more from our hosts than downcast eyes and some uncompromising sighs.

General Steigentesch joined us at the Castle of Brienne, sent by Prince Schwarzenberg with directions to continue in some measure the confidential conference of Frankfort. Nothing could be more desirable than that the Prince should send a man like Steigentesch, who, clever, dexterous, and well versed in history and diplomacy, united a good military judgment with vigorous opinions.

Prince Schwarzenberg had observed that our views of the necessity of hurling Napoleon from his throne, were more and more favourably received at the Russian head-quarters; but in the delicate relations existing between the two Emperors, Austria did not think it advisable to enter into any clear or definite explanations as to what ought to be the ultimate object of our policy and military operations. The business of Steigentesch was to find out *what* and *how* we thought of the matter, to refute our arguments, and to point out to us something better. We knew that his talents were highly valued by Prince Schwarzenberg, as well as by Prince Metternich, and that he possessed their confidence. Steigentesch laid before us a complete statement of the views of Austria, supported by all the forcible arguments suggested by feeling and skilful dialectics.

We did not engage in any confutation of Austria's policy, but we unfolded our advantages and the superiority of our military force; we pointed out Napoleon's embarrassed condition, as also that his annihilation depended on us; we endeavoured to prove that if Austria could not bring herself to take part in this annihilation, the Allies could accomplish it without her. We urged the necessity of our all holding firmly together, and assured him that, if Prince Schwarzenberg wished to destroy Napoleon's armies, he might reckon entirely on Field-Marshal Blücher, and on finding thorough obedience; but if, on the contrary, he now wished to delay, we could answer for nothing. Steigentesch was as much convinced as ourselves of the necessity of first humbling Napoleon's haughty and arrogant army, and bringing it back to the state of other European troops; nor would he deny that, if peace were now to be concluded, the dove-like, gentle Napoleon (as he was pictured by the Austrian side) might easily be seduced by his soldiers, unless their insolence were curbed, to undertake new wars, which Marie Louise would hardly be able to prevent. At last, after several long and eager conversations, it seemed to us that we *had come to a perfect understanding with one another.*

During his residence in Blücher's head-quarters, Steigentesch conversed with all the officers employed there, as well as with many others serving in the Silesian army, and found unanimity of opinion amongst them all. On taking leave, he said to us: "My friends, an old soldier feels comfortable with you: you possess the consciousness of strength, and the security which arises from it."

Although none of us ever learned in what terms General Steigentesch spoke of Prince Blücher and his head-quarters to the Princes Schwarzenberg and Metternich, yet the sequel showed that, from this period, Schwarzenberg behaved to the Field-Marshal with particular esteem and friendship, of which he gave proofs a few days later.

General von Sacken was stationed at Lesmont, with the double object of keeping the bridge there (as it was one of the principal points for crossing the Aube), and of separating Marshal Mortier, whom we knew to be at Troyes, from the other marshals stationed on the Marne, between Châlons and Vitry.

There was nothing to be seen of the enemy before us along the Aube, on the high road from Lesmont by Arcis to Mery, on the Seine. The great distance from Troyes to Châlons (which were the two points occupied by the marshals who had retreated before us from the Rhine), joined with the intelligence we had received that there was no centre between the two wings, and that the passages across the Aube were not guarded, occasioned the following considerations :—

1. These marshals, with their small forces thus separated from each other, cannot engage in any serious fight with us, who are advancing along the Aube to the Seine, on the road to Paris, with 140,000 men, concentrated in a great depth, unless they receive considerable reinforcements from Paris, where Napoleon is busy with his new formations.

2. Were the marshals to give us battle, it would prove incontestably that Napoleon was not ready with his new formations, and therefore wished to gain time ; for nothing else could oblige him to run the risk of having his marshals crushed by superior forces, before he could venture a battle to save them. But if he still required time before he would be able to offer battle, then his best course would be—

3. To let his marshals retreat slowly before us

in a line between the Seine and Marne, the right
wing by Melun, the left by La Ferté Jouarre; and
join them there with all his reinforcements, in order
to give us battle.

4. If, however, Napoleon were ready with his
new formations, and considered himself strong
enough to venture on giving battle in the plains of
Champagne, he would have three means of attaining
his object:—

a. To lead his reinforcements by Nogent to
Mery, where he could concentrate his right and left
wings by a retrograde movement;

b. To advance on the Marne, and unite with his
left wing—the strongest of the two—while he moved
up the right nearer to himself;

c. To march upon Troyes, and move up his left
wing.

This last case seemed the most unlikely.

These views were laid before General von Steigentesch, who had no objections to make, and propounded
them to Prince Schwarzenberg.

Moreover, we all agreed that the first thing to be
done was to extricate the Grand Army from the
valley of the Aube, which forms a defile from Bar to
Trannes, before we could come to any decision as to
further operations. General Steigentesch stated
that by the 2nd or 3rd of February, the Grand
Army might accomplish this march. By that time
Napoleon's situation must be disclosed, and we
should be united with York, whom we expected at
St. Dizier about the 28th or 29th.

When the intelligence reached us, early on the
29th, that the enemy was advancing on the road
from St. Dizier, by Mortier, to Brienne, and that the

Cossacks had themselves seen strong columns, no one doubted in head-quarters that it was Napoleon himself who was marching against us, and that we ought to adopt the measures we had prepared for this emergency.

General Sacken received instant orders to join the Field-Marshal at Brienne. Immediately after, an officer was brought in prisoner, who had been dispatched from Vitry the day before, with written orders to Marshal Mortier to join Napoleon, from Troyes, by way of Arcis. Thus informed, we stepped out on the castle-court and erected our telescope to observe Napoleon's approach, as from this height we could overlook the whole plain beyond the town of Brienne to Maizière. Count Pahlen, who commanded Wittgenstein's advanced guard, arrived from Joinville, and went, on the Field-Marshal's invitation, through the town, to station himself, with his cavalry and some Jäger battalions, on the other side, in the plain towards Maizière, so that he covered and concealed the march of Sacken's corps. After the enemy's advanced guard had marched out of Maizière, it halted to wait for the main body, and we saw the whole body of cavalry draw off to the right, and form in line against Count Pahlen.

I reasoned on this as follows :—Napoleon will unite with Mortier, who can be at Arcis this evening if he has received the duplicate of his order ; at least Napoleon will wait for him there, and consequently can effect the junction to-morrow evening. What we see of Napoleon's forces here before us cannot be reckoned at more than 30,000 men. We shall therefore be equal to them in strength as soon as Sacken's corps has arrived. As Napoleon expects to be reinforced by Mortier to-morrow, it is not probable that he will attack us to-day. But the question is, shall we attack him before his junction with Mortier gives him a superiority over us. Such an attack on our part would be a mistake, as in a few days we shall be strengthened by York's corps, and the Grand Army will join us. Lastly, it would be quite contrary to the agreement we had made with Prince Schwarzenberg. Therefore it was resolved :—

1. To await Napoleon's attack; and if that did not take place, to keep the town with Olsuview's corps, and to bivouac Sacken's corps between it and Old Brienne, with the cavalry to the right on the road to Joinville :

2. To retreat towards Trannes, if Napoleon attacked us. When Napoleon began a cannonade about three P. M., Olsuview answered with his twenty-four guns, while Sacken marched through the town to his appointed bivouac. The French grenades set fire to some houses in Brienne, which however did not hinder the defiling of Sacken's corps.

The Field-Marshal got tired of watching from the terrace, and went to dinner. He invited the captive orderly officer to join him; the usual cheerfulness reigned during the dinner. Some French balls went through the castle. The Field-Marshal made excuses to his guest, and directed an officer of his guard to take him to a safe place to finish his dinner; but the French officer declared that he found himself in too good company to leave them.

There was, amongst the guests, a man who, as a volunteer defender of his country, was not a soldier by profession, and was so incommoded by the noise of the balls and the cracking of the falling panels in the walls over our head, that he kept changing colour, and moving his chair here and there, as if he wished to avoid the falling-in of the ceiling. As all eyes were directed on this restless person, the Field-Marshal called to him across the table, " Does this castle belong to you ? "—" To me ? No."—"Then you may be quite easy ; the castle is solidly built, the cost of repairs will not be considerable, and at any rate you will not have to pay for them."

On stepping out upon the terrace again, after dinner, we saw that Napoleon was moving the whole of his cavalry to follow Count Pahlen, who, when Sacken's corps had passed through the town, retreated slowly on the same road, so that the French cavalry penetrated wedgewise between the town and the thickets along the road to Lesmont, where it had steep vineyards in front; while the French infantry stood immovable, with its left wing in a plain, without any covering.

Our cavalry, consisting of 6000 men, under Generals Wasiltschikoff and Count Pahlen, reached the prolongation of the line of French infantry, at the distance of about 1500 paces from it, all which we could see plainly from the terrace.

The Field-Marshal instantly perceived that neither time nor space would allow the enemy's cavalry, who had crept into a *cul-de-sac* on the extreme point of their position on the right, to come to the assistance of the infantry, which was exposed on the left. He could not reconcile himself to leave such a fault unpunished. I undertook to convey the necessary orders to the cavalry. Arrived at the point, we rushed forward; unfortunately the day was already closing. We rode into the Young Guard, and our right wing got as far as the reserve, which stood a good way back, on the road bordered with trees from Brienne to Maizière. We captured two batteries, and the enemy fell into the greatest disorder; but, as often happens in a cavalry fight when all are scattered, all command ceased; the French fugitives ran to their centre, and when, without any order being given, the darkness put an end to the combat, we found that we had brought back only five of the captured guns and some prisoners. While this was going on on the enemy's left flank, a battalion from the right wing got to the vineyards, and some of its skirmishers up to the castle of Brienne, where was the Field-Marshal, protected by one company of his staff-guard.

These skirmishers perceived, by the light of the burning town, some led-horses in the castle-court, and fired at them. Thereupon the Field-Marshal left the castle, with his suite and staff-guard, and rode off to Sacken's corps across the fields, not to block up the way through the burning town. This was the occurrence designated as a surprise at the royal head-quarters.

Returning from the cavalry fight on the right wing, I found the Field-Marshal with Sacken's corps, and reported to him the result of the sudden cavalry attack. This changed his intention of withdrawing Olsuview's corps from the burning town. He exclaimed: "Now the fellow must not sleep in Brienne!" and ordered an attack on the castle by Sacken's corps. This attack had not the expected result; but its object—to make Napoleon sleep in the bivouac, and thus prevent his saying in his bulletin that he had conquered Brienne by arms,— was fully attained.

In the position of the two armies,—the grand one cooped up in a narrow space in the valley of the Aube, and Napoleon standing opposite it to cover Paris,—a battle was not only *necessary* for the Allies, but enjoined by all the rules of warfare. It was resolved upon, and the command of the centre was conferred on Field-Marshal Blücher, and likewise that of the two corps of the Crown Prince of Würtemberg and Giulay ,was made over to him by Prince Schwarzenberg.

On the 31st, it seemed as if Napoleon had intentions of attacking the Field-Marshal in his position of Trannes. Nothing could have been more desirable for us. This position, on advantageous heights, with the left wing well protected by the Aube, and the right by impassable woods, was moreover strengthened by the circumstance that the heights, with their moist clay soil, were difficult to ascend. We therefore deferred our intended attack until the 1st of February, in the hope that Napoleon might attack us, and be thereby already somewhat fatigued before he assumed the offensive. As, however, at twelve o'clock, he still kept quiet in his bivouac, we put ourselves in motion.

I had sketched out the disposition for the battle, and handed it over, by the Field-Marshal's order, to the Sovereigns on their arrival with Prince Schwarzenberg, about noon, just as the battle began. The Emperor Alexander, for whom it was translated into French, and who was well informed about the locality, asked me various questions, and seemed satisfied by my answers.

The heights of Trannes afforded a complete prospect of the field of battle, with the exception of our right flank. During the battle I was sent several times to these heights, where the Sovereigns remained with the reserves, and delivered verbal reports to the King our master, who gave me directions to make the same reports to the Emperor Alexander. General Toll, the Emperor's Adjutant-General, repaired to the Crown Prince of Würtemberg during the battle, and found him just as he had lost La Gibrie, which he had attacked with two battalions, and had announced this to the Field-Marshal, with a request for reinforcements. The Field-Marshal sent his first aide-de-camp, Colonel Count Nostitz, to tell the Crown Prince, "that the battle must be decided on the plain of La Rothière, where Napoleon stood with his principal forces and reserves. Reinforcements he could not send him (the Crown Prince was already above 3000 paces in advance of the centre), but he might attack La Gibrie with twelve battalions instead of two, as soon as we were on the same line."

Before this commission was executed, General Toll arrived, and called out from a distance to the Field-Marshal in German, "The Crown Prince must have reinforcements." The Field-Marshal, behind whom stood General Gneisenau, looked at the General with surprise, and did not answer a word. General Toll repeated his words in a still louder tone. General Gneisenau at last replied : "Everything has been considered, and the Field-Marshal has provided for all that is necessary."

General von Toll then screamed out with sten-
torian voice, "Whoever has the heights, has the
valleys likewise!" and on receiving no answer, he
repeated his words incessantly.   I knew that he
was not personally acquainted with the Field-Marshal, nor with any of us, and was so irritated by his
behaviour, that I called out to him in a loud voice,
"He who holds the valleys has the heights; and
he who attempts to decide a battle on a false point
only deserves to be beaten."   On hearing this,
General von Toll in a fury turned his horse, and
galloped off to the Emperor, who sent an aide-de-
camp later, to say that "he had placed a division
of the grenadier corps under the Field-Marshal's
orders, desiring that he would dispatch one brigade of it to reinforce the Crown Prince of Würtemberg."   Upon this I was sent off again, to
prevent the Emperor from seeking to decide the
battle on a wrong point, misled by an erroneous
statement of the circumstances.   I soon convinced
the Emperor that the battle must be decided on the
plain near the great *chaussée*, and not on the thick
wood on the heights; but His Majesty wished some
troops to be sent to the Crown Prince ; he also
ordered that the reserve cavalry under the Grand
Duke Constantine should be placed at the Field-
Marshal's disposal, and commissioned me to tell
him that the entire reserve, including the Guards,
should be ready to support him.*

---

* I convinced myself that the Emperor desired this reinforcement of the Crown Prince from personal interest in him; and this,
indeed, was afterwards explained by the marriage concluded
between him and a sister of the Emperor, which was then still a
secret.

The Field-Marshal did not receive this intelligence in vain; since Prince Schwarzenberg, who, through Steigentesch, knew exactly his way of thinking, had entrusted him with a great command, he must wish for Napoleon's destruction. The fact, too, of the Emperor Alexander having placed the reserves at his disposal, was considered by him as an exhortation not to spare Napoleon, and to employ even the Russian guards, if his own troops did not suffice.

The day was unhappily too short, or Blücher's intention would have produced an extraordinary result. If, however, we could have continued our exertions during the night, the result must have been greater by the morning. This was the Field-Marshal's wish, and I was sent to propose it to the Sovereigns.

On the heights of Trannes, just as night was coming on, I represented to them that the battle was as good as won; we only now required the capture of La Rothière, to which we were advancing, the place being merely defended by the Young Guard without artillery, since we had taken five and a half out of six of their batteries.

The next question was,—Should we, after taking La Rothière, continue our march, take Brienne, allow the enemy no rest, and early the next day avail ourselves of the disorders arising during the night to destroy him? or should we, after taking that place, conclude our day's work, allow the men to rest, cook, and feed the horses, and begin again on the morrow by break of day?

The two Sovereigns were of the same opinion, that it would be better to allow the troops to rest during the night, as a portion of them had been marching ever since daybreak, and to begin fresh in the morning; and this decision was well founded. As the enemy had shown no inclination to fly, he would certainly hold the town of Brienne, which he could easily defend. Then, confusion might easily arise amongst ourselves, advancing in such a dark night, a danger which was increased by the circumstance that the troops collected on the field, from different armies and nations, did not know each other, and on account of diversity of language could not understand one another.

The Sovereigns arrived the following morning at the castle of Brienne, which I had just entered with the advanced guard, and from whence I was watching Napoleon's march upon Lesmont.

The Emperor Alexander made me report to him what I had seen, and afterwards took me into a room alone. Here he desired to know what were my views as to further operations. I replied,—That under all circumstances our guiding principle must be to pursue the defeated Napoleon most vigorously, and to make the best use of our enormous superiority over him :

" That Napoleon's interest was now to concentrate his forces in his rear, not too near Paris, in order to give his great battle, whereas ours was to hinder this concentration :

" That he had, by crossing the Aube, separated himself from Macdonald and his main force of cavalry (which General von York was driving before him), probably with the intention of joining Mortier; or perhaps he had, on the other hand, directed Marmont to make a junction with Macdonald :

" That the Grand Army, with its six corps, was at Brienne, on the shortest line to Paris, by Langres and Chaumont, and might with some exertion march in six days to Paris :

" That Sacken's corps, united to the Grand Army (together with a detachment from Langeron's), had its reinforcements on the road from Nancy to Châlons, and formed a principal component of the Silesian army :

" That the Silesian army, *en échelons*, between the Marne and Mainz, would *certainly* have Macdonald in front, and perhaps Marmont too, on the Marne :

" That York had orders to advance boldly, and to attack with his 20,000 men ; that he was marching upon Châlons, and depended on the support promised to him. This would make it necessary for Sacken (the seventh of the corps assembled here) to march off immediately to the right to effect a junction with York, to secure thereby the reinforcements following, and to advance toward Paris along the Marne, parallel to the Grand Army, which must keep to the Seine ; so that the Silesian army would connect the Grand Army with that of the North, which was taking the direction of Rheims ; and the Allies, extending in wedge-like form from Rheims to Troyes, would advance together upon Paris." *

* Amongst other reasons that made it necessary for Sacken's corps and a weak portion of Langeron's (now representing the Silesian army, as the Field Marshal was with them), to approach on the right, near to the rest of the Silesian army advancing *en échelons*, there was this special one, that the Crown Prince of Würtemberg, General von Wrede, and Count Wittgenstein had fallen into the advanced line (in which Sacken was) from Brienne

I

The Emperor approved my views : he believed, like myself, that Napoleon was marching back from Lesmont, by Arcis and Mery; but he did not approve of all the six corps of the Grand Army following immediately in this direction, not only because Napoleon would infallibly break up the bridge at Lesmont, but because it would be better for the Guards, who were still at Trannes, to go back to Bar-sur-Aube, in order to regain from thence the great chaussée to Troyes.

I replied, that by this step two days' march would be lost, which must produce a stoppage in all the movements, and, likewise, that we did not at all want the bridge at Lesmont, as the stone bridge at Dienville was at our command for the Guards, by which we could easily regain, on the left bank, the chaussée from Lesmont to Mery.

The Emperor had, however, already given definite orders for all the reserves to retreat to Bar-sur-Aube. He refuted my arguments by declaring that there was no chaussée from Dienville on the left bank of the Aube ; and without one, it would be impossible to proceed on such bad roads. Moreover, Count Colloredo was marching in that direction. I thought I discovered some political reasons which disinclined the Emperor to any great haste in the pursuit ; it seemed to me as if he wished to gain time by delay, not to cut Napoleon off from the means of making

to Châlons, and that it was the more necessary to restore the *ordre de bataille*, as the lines of communication of these three corps with Switzerland passed by Langres, while the Silesian army had its line of communication with the Middle Rhine right and left of Mainz by Nancy, and both lines of the reserves must run parallel to, but not cross, each other.

his peace by the congress at Chatillon.* It also seemed to me, that he did not at all like my declaration that, if Napoleon offered battle, and the Grand Army were inclined to accept it, the Silesian army, with its strength of 50,000 or 60,000 men, might, by marching along the Marne, take possession of Paris.

Before he dismissed me, I drew his attention to the great distance between the road from Châlons, and that from Nogent to Paris; and earnestly entreated that Wittgenstein's corps might advance in the space between the Marne and the Aube, if the Crown Prince of Würtemberg, Wrede, and Giulay, crossed the Aube at Lesmont, to follow at Napoleon's heels.

The Emperor promised that Count Wittgenstein should march on the right bank of the Aube, and his advanced guard under Count Pahlen between the Aube and Sezanne. He also promised, that besides this corps, General Seslawin, with twelve regiments of Cossacks, should be placed between Blücher and Count Pahlen. I specified the direction by Sezanne and La Ferté-Gaucher, as the proper one for this general. The plan hereupon concerted with the Commander in Chief, Prince Schwarzenberg, was quite in accordance with the proposition I had made to the Emperor.

On the 4th of February, Blücher was in Sommesous with 24,000 men: he had taken possession of Sezanne in the evening of that day, and thereby rendered it impossible for Macdonald and Sebastiani

* Before I went into the Emperor's cabinet, I had heard that a courier was gone, or immediately going, to Chatillon, with fresh instructions.

to unite with Napoleon, without making a considerable détour in the direction of Paris.

Intelligence reached us here, that Napoleon had retreated to Troyes, and consequently made a flank march. Thereupon I made the following representation to Field-Marshal Blücher : That by this march, Napoleon had got quite out of the reach of the Silesian army. Had he wished to cross the Seine at Mery, and then at Nogent, he would not have taken the détour by Troyes; consequently he could only have taken the line of retreat by Sens, or stationed himself at Troyes, to gain some days' time.

In the first case, Napoleon would move farther and farther away from the Silesian army, who would have a double duty to perform : 1st. To keep the French troops on the Marne separated from Napoleon ; and 2nd, by a march to the left to prepare the junction in case of necessity, upon all points of the line of march, of the Silesian with the Grand Army, in the advance along the Marne.

In the second case, three corps (the Grenadiers, Guards, and Colloredo's) would oppose Napoleon in front ; and three corps, (the Crown Prince of Würtemberg's, Wrede's, and Giulay's,) would be on his left flank, not far from Troyes; with Wittgenstein between us and the Aube.

But there would be no occasion for the Silesian army to act differently in this than in the former case, for it would then be for the Grand Army to come to us to form a junction.

My views met with approbation.

The 5th of February was spent in intercepting the retreat of General Sebastiani from the Seine, on which occasion we captured 30 loaded ammunition waggons, which were of very great value to us, as York's corps had left behind on the Rhine its park columns Nos. 1, 3, and 5, until they could follow, filled with the ammunition which had not yet been given out, and only column No. 13 marched with the corps.

On the 6th, General von York restored the bridge of Châlons; on the 7th, the ammunition was completed, and on the 8th, operations recommenced, in pursuance of the following general considerations.

Macdonald had retreated on the post-road from Châlons to Epernay, and Château Thierry. A high causeway runs along the Marne from Epernay to Château Thierry. The chaussée continues in the valley of the Marne. Cross-roads, practicable for artillery, there are none; consequently it is clear that Macdonald must cross the Marne at Château Thierry.

At La Ferté-sous-Jouarre the post-road runs again along the left bank of the Marne, towards Meaux. At Trilport it again crosses to the right bank. It was probable that Macdonald would march by La Ferté and Trilport, if we did not anticipate him at La Ferté, in which case he must throw himself by circuitous and cross-roads into the road from Soissons to Paris. But then his junction with Napoleon would be rendered as difficult as possible.

If it should afterwards become the natural task for the Silesian army to keep the two marshals separated from Napoleon, the question would then remain how far time and distance would allow of this, without losing its prescribed relation to the Grand Army in the advance. We might assume that

we should occupy Troyes on the 5th and 6th at far-
thest. We did, in fact, occupy Arcis on the 3rd or
4th; and as a line from Rheims to Troyes cuts
through Epernay, Vertus, and Arcis; on the 8th,
when we should have to begin our operations from
Châlons to Vertus, the Grand Army would have
about two days' start of us on the road to Paris.
I therefore made the following proposition :—

That York should follow Macdonald with about
18,000 men to Château Thierry ; Sacken, with about
20,000, should follow Sebastiani's cavalry by Montmirail to La Ferté, and there cut off Macdonald's
passage.

That the Russian general Olsuview should remain
with about 4,000 infantry and 24 guns in Champeaubert and its environs. The corps of Kleist and Capczewitsch, about 15,000 strong, should unite with him on
the 9th or 10th ; Sezanne would then be occupied by
General Carpow with his Cossack regiments, until the
arrival of General Seslawin.

This proposition was adopted.

When we took possession of Vitry, which was not
defensible, although it had walls and ditches, I proposed that it should be speedily palisaded, and armed
with the guns taken at La Rothière. This measure
of precaution was adopted, and it was certainly of
great importance to us, to obtain by this means a
place secured against a *coup de main* ; but unhappily
the town had too little room for establishing hospitals
and magazines.

The troops were billetted and fed by their hosts,
as the season was still too rough to bivouac regularly,
and live by requisition on the villages, which, at the
same time would have made pillaging unavoidable.

On February the 9th, Olsuview cantonned his troops at Champeaubert, Baye, and Etoges; he had Sacken at Montmirail in front, York at Dormant on his right, General Carpow at Sezanne on his left. No disaster, therefore, could happen to him, nor could the enemy fall upon him unexpectedly. General Carpow, who was at Sezanne, belonged to Sacken's corps.

Who could have thought that General Carpow, pressed by the enemy, would leave Sezanne, and retreat upon Montmirail, without giving the least information of it to General Olsuview at Baye, or to General Blücher at Etoges?

In the course of the 9th, a report reached General Blücher from General Carpow at Sezanne, that his Cossacks had been driven back the day before, by the enemy advancing from Villenoxe to Sezanne with superior forces.

Soon after, despatches, dated the 6th, arrived from Bar-sur-Seine; one from the Emperor Alexander saying: "Wittgenstein is too weak, and therefore Kleist must join him without delay; on the other hand, Winzingerode, with his corps coming from the Netherlands, is placed under General Blücher's orders." Another arrived from Prince Schwarzenberg, saying, that he "will not follow Napoleon, who has retreated from Troyes to Nogent, but prefers marching to the left by Sens to Fontainebleau. Kleist must take the direction of Nogent-sur-Seine to join Wittgenstein, who is still somewhere between the Seine and Aube."

This occasioned a complete alteration in the disposition made at Brienne. The Grand Army extended its left wing still further to the left, and by Kleist's movement drew the Silesian army after it. As to the enemy, I concluded from General Carpow's report and other intelligence, that Napoleon had sent a detachment from Nogent by Villenoxe to Sezanne, in order to retain the road from Sezanne to Paris in his power; and perhaps, if it was his intention to remain at Nogent, to cut off, by the possession of Sezanne, the Silesian army from advancing farther along the Marne.

General von Gneisenau considered the enemy's advance from Villenoxe upon Sezanne as merely a reconnoissance of no importance.

Head-quarters were removed from Vertus to Etoges on the evening of the 9th. About eight o'clock, as Field-Marshal Blücher was sitting at table with all his staff and other officers quartered in the castle of Etoges, a Russian officer rushed into the room exclaiming, "The enemy is here!" On this alarm, a Russian battalion, quartered in the place to cover head-quarters, advanced, and all the officers assembled on horseback; however, not a shot was heard, and we did not learn until afterwards that a body of the enemy's cavalry (only some squadrons of Polish lancers had been seen together) had fallen on General Olsuview's quarters at Baye, and that not till several of their attacks had been repulsed had they retreated on the road from Baye to Sezanne, whence they had come.

On this I represented to General von Gneisenau that closed squadrons coming from Sezanne announced not only the occupation of Sezanne, but at the same time their resolute attack indicated an *offensive* power stationed between Sezanne and Baye. The first thing therefore to be done was to recall

General Sacken from Montmirail to Champeaubert.

General Gneisenau was altogether adverse to this proposition, as he could not convince himself that danger threatened us from Sezanne. All my representations, made in the dark night on horseback, in the open field, without the aid of any map, could only induce him to say that "decisive orders should be given to General Sacken to relinquish the march to La Ferté-sous-Jouarre, and remain stationary at Montmirail:" that his reports would announce whether any force of importance was approaching Champeaubert by Sezanne, in which case he would retreat into the position of Champeaubert. General Gneisenau said, in conclusion, "Then it is likewise at Sacken's option to retreat from Montmirail upon Château Thierry, where he can cross the Marne conjointly with York, and unite with Winzingerode beyond Rheims. If he takes up the position of Champeaubert, he will keep open the line of retreat upon Bergères, where he will to-morrow find and form a junction with Olsuview, and the corps of Kleist and Capczewitsch, 15,000 men strong; then there will be 39,000 men *here*, and 18,000 at Château Thierry. If Sacken retreats upon York, then there will be 38,000 men united at Château Thierry, quite independent and perfectly capable of resistance, and we shall have 19,000 here."

If it was impossible to obtain a definite order for General Sacken's retreat to Champeaubert, which the Commander-in-Chief ought certainly to have given, instead of leaving it at the option of a subordinate general either to remain stationary or to come back, and decide thereby the fate of the

army, yet it might be still possible to induce
Sacken to retreat if an officer were sent to him
accurately informed of all the reports and circumstances, who could lay them before him, to assist his
decision.   I chose for this purpose my aide-de-camp,
Lieutenant von Gerlach, who had already executed
several commissions to General Sacken, and in
whose opinion he stood high. I gave him instructions
what he would have to do, and directed him to report
himself, before he rode off, to the Field-Marshal, and
General Gneisenau, who were not far from us, while
I looked after other affairs.

The execution of the order sent from the royal
head-quarters on the 6th, was notified to Prince
Schwarzenberg by a rifleman despatched to him.

Besides the above-mentioned order concerning
Kleist's corps, another order, dated the 7th, arrived
from Bar-sur-Seine, from the Emperor Alexander, to
this effect: " In case the Silesian army should
succeed in reaching Paris, it must not march into the
city, but await the arrival of the Sovereigns."

This order, together with the withdrawal of
Kleist's troops, left no doubt that the Emperor
Alexander entertained apprehensions that the Silesian army would pursue its object—Paris—with
too great eagerness, and thought that this might
be most surely damped by—

1. The withdrawal of troops : for Winzingerode
could not join the Silesian army before two or three
weeks ; and

2. By the order not to enter Paris.

Moreover, these various orders prove that the
situation of the Silesian army was considered to be
perfectly free from danger, even down to the 7th

of February, at the head-quarters of the Sove reigns.

I then made the following proposition :

"That the Commander-in-Chief should order Kleist to take the direction of Nogent. There are two ways to do this—a peaceful march by Arcis and Mery, or an aggressive one by Sezanne and Villenoxe; in the latter case, the forces of this corps might still be reckoned as a part of the army. Kleist's corps ought to be at Châlons on the 9th, 10th, and 11th, and Capczewitsch at Vitry. In the peaceful march the two corps would cross each other. It seemed, therefore, the most judicious plan to concentrate Kleist, Capczewitsch, and Olsuview (19,000 men) on the 10th at Sezanne, in addition to General Seslawin, who was still expected there."

It must be observed, that at the time this resolution was taken, nothing had yet occurred to indicate that the enemy was marching on Sezanne.

My proposition was adopted, according to which the Silesian army would have been posted on the 10th of February on the three great roads to Paris, —18,000 men on the post-road, 20,000 on the lesser road, and 19,000 (along with Seslawin, Count Pahlen, and Wittgenstein) on the road from Sezanne to Paris. In Sezanne the subsequent operations would be arranged, and the better as we could reckon on receiving there news also from Count Pahlen and Wittgenstein.

The attack on Baye, on the evening of the 9th, led to no alteration of the preconcerted dispositions, especially as the march of Kleist's and Capczewitsch's corps was so directed that if, on the 10th, need required, they could both turn aside from any point of their march upon La Fère Champenoise, into the camp at Bergères.

News arrived in the night of the 9-10th, that Napoleon was marching with his Guards through Villenoxe ; further intelligence reached us before noon on the 10th that Napoleon had slept at Sezanne on the 9th, and moreover that neither Wittgenstein, Count Pahlen, nor Seslawin were on the right bank of the Aube.

We therefore now knew that Napoleon had been at Sezanne early on the 10th, with a considerable mass of troops, unpursued by the Grand Army, and not hindered by anything in his projects. He must have chosen one of these courses :

1. To attack Olsuview.

2. To attack Sacken, without meddling with Olsuview.

3. To march in the direction of La Ferté-sous-Jouarre, in order to unite with Macdonald.

The 4th course, namely, to march from Sezanne by La Fère Champenoise, in the direction of the chaussée between Châlons and Etoges, had become quite improbable, since no enemy had appeared between Sezanne and La Fère Champenoise on the 9th, but all had gone off toward the west.

On receiving this news, the Field-Marshal found himself in a most painful state of uncertainty. He could not act himself, because he had left that to Sacken, from whom he had yet received no intelligence.

Towards noon my aide-de-camp returned, and brought me word that General von Sacken had considered the expulsion of his Cossacks from Sezanne a matter of no importance whatever, and had therefore marched off from Montmirail to La Ferté-sous-Jouarre. On my inquiring, "How is this possible? how can he venture to act so in opposition to his orders?" I learned, that when my aide-de-camp reported himself before starting to Field-Marshal Blücher and General Count Gneisenau, the latter inquired what instructions he had received, and made this addition to them :—"Tell General von Sacken, that if he finds that the expulsion of General Carpow from Sezanne means nothing *serious,* he may in God's name continue his march to La Ferté."

My aide-de-camp added, that this was certainly quite contrary to the verbal instructions I had given him, but as he had to transmit orders from Field-Marshal Blücher, and General Gneisenau had ordered this addition in presence of the Field-Marshal, there was nothing left for him but to execute it faithfully.

It seemed to me not at all improbable, that General Gneisenau had made the addition; but it was incomprehensible that he should have concealed from me this complete alteration of all the preconcerted measures.

From all we had learnt during Lieutenant von Gerlach's absence, it was not difficult to perceive, that the course taken by Sacken was a mistaken one, and might precipitate us into great misfortunes. I instantly proceeded to General Gneisenau, made my aide-de-camp repeat in his presence what he had told me, and asked whether it was correct,—whether there had been no misunderstanding. General von Gneisenau replied: "It is quite correct; I did add this order to your instructions." He would not however share my views that this was a great misfortune. It was noon; not a shot had yet been heard: Lieutenant von Gerlach had just ridden through Champeaubert, and found all quiet there; General Gneisenau therefore concluded that Napoleon was marching straight upon Montmirail, or towards La Ferté. In either case Sacken would manage to avoid him.

The march of head-quarters towards Sezanne, to form a junction with the columns of Kleist and Capczewitsch, had commenced. On the way we heard firing at Baye: we comforted ourselves with the thought that the ground was woody and would give Olsuview (who was deficient in cavalry) the opportunity of halting and retiring without loss; but we soon received intelligence that Olsuview, who had been attacked by very superior numbers, had succumbed. We had got tolerably near La Fère Champenoise, in the wild districts. The march to Sezanne could not be continued,—we halted. The troops were weary and required some rest. Under these circumstances Kleist's corps could not be ordered from La Fère Champenoise to Nogent.

In this state of things it was quite necessary to remain with both corps at Bergères the following morning, and to re-assemble Olsuview's corps. This was done. We formed effectively about 14,000 men, counting 500 horse; and as there was an immeasureable plain behind us in the direction of Châlons,* it was very probable that Napoleon would make use of his victory over Olsuview to attack us before noon, as he had a large body of cavalry which

---

* The two corps were reckoned at 17,000 men, but 3000 were still four days' march behind.

he could not employ so advantageously against Montmirail as in the plains of Champagne.

It would have been worse than foolhardy to throw ourselves without any cavalry into these plains ; we therefore resolved, in case we were attacked, to retreat from Bergères upon Epernay, along the slope of the vine-clad heights, where the enemy's cavalry could not touch us.

We were however *not* attacked, and the enemy only showed himself behind Etoges, which place was occupied by him. As Napoleon had bivouacked in Champeaubert on the night of the 10th, we assumed that he had marched to Montmirail, in which direction we did, indeed, hear a cannonade from the afternoon to the evening of the 11th.

Had Sacken remained at Montmirail, instead of marching off to La Ferté, he might have proceeded to Viffort, joined General von York, and with about 38,000 men awaited there Napoleon's farther movements, and eventually crossed the Marne at Château Thierry.

Although the communication between the Field-Marshal and Sacken was interrupted, the connection with York was still maintained through Epernay. From him we learnt in the forenoon of the 13th, that, after a successful combat on the 10th, Sacken had driven Macdonald across the Marne at Trilport, and thus separated him completely from Napoleon ; that on the night of the 10th he had heard of Napoleon's march to Champeaubert, and that of an advanced guard to Montmirail; that on the 11th, he had marched back towards Montmirail; but at Vieux Maisons had been obliged to form against Napoleon, who was already coming from Montmirail to meet him.

Thus far went the accounts, when, on the 13th, about 800 horse from Kleist's corps arrived at the camp at Bergères, so that we could advance, at least not quite destitute of cavalry.

The attack upon Etoges, from whence Marmont was dislodged and pursued to Fromentières, took place the same day. The Field-Marshal remained at Champeaubert, from whence the march upon Montmirail was continued on the following morning.

At Vauchamp there was very hot fighting, and the enemy displayed extraordinary boldness, together with a great deal of cavalry, which pushed with unusual assurance even between our close columns. A Cossack officer, commanding a detachment of Cossacks at the Field-Marshal's head-quarters, took a Captain of the Old Guard prisoner, who told him that Napoleon was in front, after having made a night-march from Château Thierry, where the corps of Sacken and York had been driven across the Marne, after two days' fighting. This was the first intelligence we had received of the issue of the combats of the 11th and 12th, and it was confirmed by the depositions of other prisoners.

We had been forced to deploy and defend ourselves against the attacks of the cavalry, which were very well supported by the artillery. The enemy's infantry was engaged in marching through Vauchamp, and a mass of cavalry appeared in the prolongation of our left wing, surrounding us.

Our position was very disadvantageous,—Kleist on the right wing,—Capczewitsch on the left,—the chaussée in the middle. Our march and attack had lost their object; Sacken's and York's corps were in safety; and as we had the enemy advancing with superior force in front of us, it was time to place ourselves in safety, before the enemy's infantry joined the fight. We commenced our retreat. I watched the movements of the cavalry surrounding our right wing, discovered their head, and the direction in which they were marching, so that I could measure on my map the distance they had to traverse in order to reach the plain between Champeaubert and the wood of Etoges ; for this was the point where we were threatened with most danger, unless we got there with our infantry before the enemy's cavalry, which consisted, in my reckoning, of about 6000 horse.

At the commencement of the retreat, the Field-Marshal, with General von Gneisenau, resolved to remain with General Capczewitsch ; and I, observing from the right wing all around us, was to regulate the pace of the march.

On the right flank we were not at all pressed,—not even pursued in earnest. General von Kleist marched as fast as he could, in order to get before the enemy's cavalry on the plain of Champeaubert, between the wood of Etoges and a great pond—a passage about 1000 paces broad, which the enemy must pass.

I sent my aide-de-camp to the Russian general Udom,* to urge him to occupy the wood at this passage. I despatched several officers successively to the Field-Marshal, to recommend the utmost haste in the retreat, as I saw that General Capczewitsch was loitering quite unnecessarily, and wasting time in cannonades.

The Field-Marshal had just been praising General

* General Udom commanded the remnant of Olsuview's corps of about 1800 men and 15 guns.

Capczewitsch for the calm manner in which he retreated: when my first officer arrived, recommending
the utmost haste, he was unfavourably received.
The second and third were scolded more and more
roughly; and on my repeated remonstrances that the
distance between Kleist and Capczewitsch was continually increasing, the Field-Marshal sent me word:
"If Kleist did not run so immoderately fast, all
would remain compact."

Before I could explain the positive necessity that
Kleist's corps, with its right wing on the wood and
its left on the pond, should close the access to the
plain to the enemy's cavalry—whence in that case
no more danger could reach us—an order arrived to
General Kleist to halt on the spot, and to wait for
Capczewitsch. General Kleist obeyed, although he
had already reached the pond, and was only 1500
paces from the passage he wished to occupy, and
which the enemy's cavalry could not force without
infantry and artillery. Meanwhile my aide-de-camp
also returned, who had not found General Udom
by the wood of Etoges, but near Etoges in retreat,
as ordered by General Capczewitsch. Thus, this
important means of facilitating our retreat also
escaped us.

General Kleist sent forward his cavalry (about
1200 horse), to take up the position between the
pond and wood. He sent to ask the Field-Marshal
whether he might not continue his march to the
passage; but before the answer could arrive, the
enemy's cavalry had formed in several divisions,
one in rear of the other, and driven Kleist's cavalry
back into the wood towards Etoges, and consequently
was already on the plain which we had to traverse

with the infantry when General Capczewitsch arrived with the heads of his columns from Champeaubert.

It was here that the Field-Marshal and General Gneisenau adopted my proposition, to place our numerous artillery upon the chaussée in the centre, with Capczewitsch's corps on the right, and Kleist's on its left; to march on in close order of battalions in a long square, without any stoppage, to the entrance of the wood of Etoges. It would be nearly dark, according to my calculation, when we got there. From the rear of this square (which in the retreat formed the head), I was to direct the march and regulate the pace; the Field-Marshal was to remain in the centre. The chaussée from Champeaubert to the wood of Etoges, ran along an insignificant elevation, which it left to the right, and upon which Capczewitsch's corps proceeded, headed by three battalions, and a Russian half-battery of well-mounted horse-artillery, who did not require the chaussée.

Here, from whence I could see perfectly the whole circuit of the enemy's cavalry, I continued with the troops at a good pace; I prevented the artillery officer, who was a German, from firing with ball at the cavalry deployed against us, but directed him to be prepared to fire with one-ounce canister-shot. Kleist's corps was unceasingly attacked, but contrived not only to repulse bravely the cavalry that dashed forward against it, but to keep up its position' in the march so well, that I was able to continue my pace. The firing at the head (now the tail), shewed that it was hardly pressed from Champeaubert. We had reached the point, I think, where the road to Baye and Sezanne turns off to the right, when

General Gneisenau sought me out, and measuring
the distance we had still to travel to the wood, exclaimed : " Our exertions are useless, we cannot get
to Etoges ; we must throw ourselves to the right on
Sezanne." The unfavourable nature of our situation,
and the tactical relations of the moment, might support this opinion : on the right we had vineyards,
in which cavalry could not molest infantry ; moreover, we should approach the Russian light cavalry
of the Guards, and might reckon on a junction
with them as soon as we had reached Baye ; it
was, besides, more easy to accomplish a retreat to
this place, than across the plain to the wood of
Etoges. But the arguments against this movement
were, that we carried with us a number of guns quite
disproportionate to our infantry, and it was very
doubtful whether we had sufficient strength of horses
to transport them on the cross-road. Moreover, as
the enemy was already on the road to Baye, the
artillery must remain surrounded by the infantry, on
quitting the chaussée,—a circumstance which would
prevent the latter's profiting by the vineyards, if we
did not wish to run the risk of losing the guns.
And, lastly, the deviation to the right would cause
such loss of time, that the enemy might bring up his
batteries (defiling from Champeaubert), to fire on
our long square with case-shot, which we could only
avoid by continuing in quick march on the road to
Etoges.

But if by a deviation to the right toward Sezanne
we could not evade the danger of succumbing to the
united attacks of artillery and cavalry, how much
more unfavourable, even than our tactical, would our
strategical relations be ! Our convoys and reserves

were all proceeding to Châlons : General Udom and our cavalry had retired in this direction, after being driven from the battle-field, and expected us at Etoges, or in the camp at Bergères, where we should find our baggage and provisions. If we marched upon Sezanne, it could only be with a view to regain the connection with General Udom and with Châlons, round by the Marais de St. Gand. We had two miles to go to the camp at Bergères on a well-known chaussée, where we should find straw and provisions. Sezanne was just as far from us, and no one knew the road, which was described as very heavy. It was problematical whether we should find General von Diebitsch in the night, or whether his instructions would allow him to escort us on the following day. But even supposing that we got our wearied troops (without a single horseman) to Sezanne, and remained lying there without provisions, straw, or wood, we should still be four (German) miles from the camp at Bergères, and eight from Châlons. When General Udom (from whom we were quite separated, and with whom we could only communicate through Sezanne) recognised his position the following morning, he would have no other resource but to retire two miles across the Marne at Epernay, or four miles to Châlons. He could not engage in a combat. This was a consideration which ought to prevent our venturing on a march from Sezanne to Bergères, and oblige us to proceed toward Châlons, the most natural point of connection with the corps of York and Sacken ; but this march of eight miles, through a plain, with troops so hungry and weary, and without any cavalry, might expose us to a shameful defeat.

I explained these arguments for and against the

movement to the right as briefly as possible to
General Gneisenau, who weighed them all calmly.
I then earnestly entreated him :—" Leave the disposition as it is; we shall certainly fight our way
through, to the wood of Etoges, if we keep firmly
together; I will bore the hole for you. But we
must not delay our march a moment, for in a quarter
of an hour the horse-artillery of the cavalry corps
which has turned us may come on; and then we
are threatened with the danger of having our compact battalions broken by the cavalry."

"Very well," replied Gneisenau ; "let us stick to
the old disposition. You go briskly forwards with
the head; I will take care that all follow in close
order." And accordingly this was done. A hostile
regiment of cuirassiers formed, to make an attack on
the three Russian battalions at our head. These
happened to be the newly formed battalions just
arrived. Their commanders halted and made ready ;
they allowed the enemy to advance sixty paces
before they gave the word,—Fire ! Instead of the
first and second ranks of the leading column giving
fire, the whole battalion fired at once, and exhibited
the spectacle of three *pots à feu.* Nothing hindered
the cuirassiers from breaking into the close battalions,
for not a horse, not a man of them had fallen, but
they had turned about. I thought this was the
moment to make the inexperienced soldiers believe
they had done something heroic : I hurrahed them
loudly, and *Perrot* and *Perebonschek* had their effect.
They moved on briskly, their drums struck up a
march, and all the drums of both corps followed in
this beat.

I now dashed with the Russian horse-artillery

after the cuirassiers, to prevent their making front again, and embarrassing us on the way. The young officer, whom I directed not to unlimber until he could reach the enemy with case-shot, followed at full speed, and came, without any covering, so near the enemy that his zeal made him foolhardy. The cuirassiers made front when they received the first discharge of one-ounce canister-shot, whereupon they dashed off like lightning to the right, by the chaussée, from whence they came, and left the way to the wood quite open to us, which we reached, without the head of the column being again attacked, just as it began to get dark.

On the other hand, the other sides of the long square, particularly Kleist's corps, which was opposed to the enemy's corps of cavalry, had still to stand several attacks, which the troops repelled with praiseworthy coolness, not allowing themselves to be stopped in their march, which was the matter of most importance here. Arrived at the wood, my advice was to lead on the two corps, now confined on the narrow chaussée, in *one* column, without stopping.

It required some time indeed to compress the long square in the wood, but if the troops in the rear at the edge of the wood, guarding it well right and left, awaited their time to be incorporated in the column, the cavalry could do them no farther harm, and the infantry approaching from Champeaubert would have to attack the wood in the dark, where the enemy had no particular advantages. About this time two battalions belonging to the rear went astray, which must have been caused by some faulty arrangement. It was alleged that these battalions mistook the enemy for friends; the same had happened to our opponents in the dark; for as the Field-Marshal was stopping at the entrance of the wood, to see his column defile, some of the enemy's scattered cavalry got mixed with his suite, but were soon recognized and driven away.

The troops received orders to march back into the camp of Bergères, which they had left the day before. All marched on briskly and in good order upon the chaussée, the divisions separated by small intervals. The division of Prince Augustus was the last, and was not pursued on the chaussée; but on entering Etoges, which the Field-Marshal had just traversed with all the rest of the troops, the enemy, who must have penetrated into it by a lane from Champeaubert, fell upon the Prince from the side streets, and a fight began which cost us many men; for a bridge across a swampy ditch fell in, and all who were left behind to shift for themselves were not able to reach the other side by roundabout ways. About midnight, having rejoined General Udom and our cavalry, we reached the camp of Bergères, from whence, after some hours' rest, we broke up for Châlons, where we arrived about noon, February 15th.[*]

[*] The English writer, Mitchel, has published an account of this 14th of February (so unlucky for the Silesian army), after carefully studying all that he could find in the book-trade relative to the combats of this day. There can be no doubt about his anxiety to investigate the truth. He has, moreover, very accurately comprehended the situation of the Silesian army and its intentions. Nevertheless if errors have crept in (as is unavoidable in narrating so many confused events which occurred in part during the night), this imposes on the still living witnesses the duty of explaining them, in order that no inaccuracy may be allowed to go down to posterity.

At Châlons everything now appeared in a new and cheerful light. Accounts came in from the two generals Von Sacken and Von York, and they themselves both entered Châlons on the two following days.

The Silesian army could have reached Etoges on the 14th of February without any considerable loss, before it grew dark, if the Field-Marshal had not, taking pleasure in the slowness of his retreat, quite forgotten the agreement that it should be left to me, on the right wing, to regulate the pace during the retreat. In order to execute the commission entrusted to me, I rode with some officers from height to height, as near as possible to the enemy surrounding us. I discovered the direction as well as the intention of this march, and was able, with map and chronometer in hand, to measure off with the compass the distances which the heads of his columns had still to traverse, in order to turn them into time, and compare this with the time we required to reach the wood of Etoges. The enemy's horse-artillery, being obliged to go at a foot-pace on account of the heavy roads, could not follow his cavalry, and consequently was still far behind.

These calculations showed that if the Silesian army kept up a good pace, it might be in Etoges before the artillery of the cavalry corps could come up. The cavalry, indeed, if it fell into a trot, could be deployed on the plain before we got there; but what could it do without artillery?

General Kleist saw our situation in the same light as I did, and was the more annoyed at the answers I received to my messages, as the arrival of his corps in the wood of Etoges was of importance to the whole, while his stopping was of no advantage even to Capczewitsch's corps. Meanwhile, even after General Kleist had punctually obeyed the order to halt, and had learnt that Udom was *not* in the wood, he did not consider (any more than Prince Augustus or I), our situation to be such as to preclude all hope of a favourable issue. The Field-Marshal and General Gneisenau had given directions for an obstinate defence of Champeaubert—which indeed they gave up in consequence of my counter-representations, but nevertheless this is the strongest proof that they too considered our situation much less perilous than it has appeared to Mitchel. If he has admitted my exclamation " We must hold fast together," as a proof that it must have been an answer to some such expression as " We must separate—

The Commissary of the army had received instructions on the 7th of February to establish a magazine at Châlons, which should furnish the Silesian army with provisions for a fortnight. We found there the detachments of infantry and cavalry, sent to collect contributions, with important magazines. Of forage (which was particularly scarce) we found enough heaped up in two churches to suffice the army for ten days. A cargo of shoes just arrived supplied the necessities of York's and Sacken's corps. We had thus the means of either awaiting our reinforcements, or of advancing towards Paris, with a fresh supply of provisions.

Prince Schwarzenberg's desire to deliver a battle on the Seine, in concert with the Silesian army, decided the Field-Marshal to march off to the left on the 19th of February, so that York's and Sacken's corps had not even two days to recruit.

The reunion of the Silesian army at Châlons forms a natural resting-place, and offers a good opportunity for thoroughly examining General Clausewitz's criticism on affairs from the battle of La Rothière

---

we must save ourselves as well as we can," or still more, "We must yield," this would be a very wrong assumption. Not only I heard no such cowardly expression, but I must protest against the possibility of its being uttered by an officer of either corps. With the spirit that animated the Silesian army, I even doubt that it could have passed the lips of a common soldier. If a female sutler now had used such an expression, she would have been cudgelled.

My words referred to the ordinary mode of keeping the brigades apart in combats, which in an open plain, and before such a great mass of cavalry, exposed us to this danger, viz., that single bold horsemen dashed into the intervals between the brigades, and misled us in the heat of the fray to fire on each other, or to lose precious time by halting.

to the middle of February. This criticism is to be
found in the "Campaign of 1814," in the seventh
volume of his works, published in 1835 by Dümler,
at Berlin.

Even before the appearance of this work, writers
had been disposed to publish critical remarks on the
events of this campaign ; but these were partly built
upon such inaccurate facts, and partly composed with
so little care and correctness, and with such weak
powers of judgment, that it was not worth while to
refute them. But here, in the person of General
Clausewitz, a man stepped forward who failed in
nothing but in the correct exposition of the events
and motives of action, who firmly believed that
he held in his hands all the fine threads of the
entangled web, and to whose censure we should be
often obliged to assent, if everything had been as he
imagined. Here, therefore, a refutation is called
for.

In the historical narrative of this section, from
page 335, nearly all is misrepresented. Page 339
consists almost entirely of inaccuracies.

General Clausewitz's first and principal censure
relates to the Field-Marshal's separation from Prince
Schwarzenberg after the battle of La Rothière. He
says, page 398 : "Instead of making use of the victory to pursue and scatter the enemy's principal
army, Blücher and Schwarzenberg separate."

Pages 335 and 336, he reckons that the allied
troops at La Rothière, without the Guards, and
without Colloredo and Wittgenstein (who were close
at hand) were 74,000 strong, and Napoleon only
40,000. Now as the Guards, Colloredo, and Wittgenstein, amounted to 60,000, and consequently the

allied army had 134,000 against 40,000, let us ask how should this more than triple force have rolled along behind Napoleon on one and the same road, without provisions?

And if 110,000 remained behind Napoleon, and 25,000 struck off to the right, can this be called anything but a pursuit?

Page 399, he calls this march of Blücher's *precipitate* and *mistaken*.

Page 400, he says that by this deviation of Blücher's, we got out of the right line.

Page 405, that, after the victory of La Rothière, the Allies grew presumptuous.

Page 406, that they parted from irresolution and want of unity.

As, in pages 415 and 416, the critic explains the circumstances of the Silesian army, while advancing, quite correctly, to prove that Blücher's troops *had been used with good economy*, it is the less intelligible how he can censure the march which brought Blücher to Sommesous by daybreak on the 4th, and to Sezanne on the 5th.

By this movement Macdonald was decisively parted from Napoleon, while the Grand Army kept its direction with seven corps, and did not want, and indeed could not even miss, the eighth corps absent from the Silesian army in the battle of La Rothière. The critic would have undoubtedly judged differently had he known all the facts as they have been laid down here from the reports.

But page 417 shows how astonishingly he misrepresented to himself the motives of the battle of La Rothière, where he asserts that Schwarzenberg did not wish to give battle, but only to let Blücher *attempt* one with a portion of his forces. The state of the case was as follows:—

On the 29th of January, about midnight, when the Field-Marshal had the burning town of Brienne, with Napoleon, in front, and did not wish, for good reasons (the enemy had shown at least 30,000 men that day), to accept battle on the following day, he had the power of retreating in two directions:—

1. On the chaussée to Joinville, whence he had come, and where he had found General Lanskoy. Count Pahlen had come in the morning in this direction with Wittgenstein's advanced guard, whose whole corps was probably there already; therefore on the 31st, the Field-Marshal could have united his forces with York's and Wittgenstein's in the direction of Joinville, and formed a fighting force of 65,000 men, which would have been so superior to Napoleon's that the Allies would have had no reason to avoid him. This was the simplest, and, at the same time, the most inviting movement. But the Field-Marshal could also

2. Retreat on the chaussée leading to Bar-sur-Aube. From Bar-sur-Aube to Trannes this chaussée forms a long defile, of which the position at Trannes makes the *tête-de-pont*.

By taking the direction of Joinville, the Field-Marshal would have left Napoleon at liberty to take possession of this defile, and throw the Grand Army into the embarrassment of not being able to develop its forces in pathless districts. He therefore made a *sacrifice* when he took up the position at Trannes, but a sacrifice to duty, and Prince Schwarzenberg has acknowledged this better than the critic. After Blücher had taken up this position, it was quite at the option of the Grand Army to manœuvre or to fight. It could do the first upon Troyes, while Blücher held the position at Trannes; Napoleon would then have been obliged to abandon his position at Brienne.

Prince Schwarzenberg preferred a battle, and was right. He bestowed the command of the centre on the Field-Marshal, who was acquainted with the ground and all the localities of Brienne: this again is worthy of praise.

The battle, in which we took sixty-five cannons, was consequently no *attempt*, but was begun with the resolution to employ even the reserves, if the four corps engaged could not effect their object. That the reserves did not engage in the fight, can be no matter of reproach to Schwarzenberg: they were ready on the field of battle. It may be a matter of censure, that Wittgenstein covered us on the right wing against Macdonald and Sebastiani, and Colloredo against Mortier on the left, and that these two corps were left out of the battle; but then the critic ought to have stated where he would have employed them. We had in front more troops than we could deploy, and Wrede already outflanked Marmont.

The reproach that the Allies grew presumptuous after the victory of La Rothière, is the most uncalled for of all. It does not apply to the Grand Army, which marched humbly enough by Bar-sur-Aube upon Troyes,—nor to Blücher, who from the 3rd to the 8th of February busied himself merely with getting his rear clear to Châlons, and making a place of arms of Vitry. On the morning of the 8th, while Napoleon was still at Nogent, the Field-Marshal was in the line from Epernay to Etoges, consequently in no way inviting for Napoleon, who must have resolved, even the day before, upon the march to Sezanne, since he got there on the 9th. But Sacken did not advance to Montmirail till the 9th, which opened a prospect of success to Napoleon.

But if, perchance, Sacken had remained on the 9th at Etoges, what advantage would Napoleon have reaped from his march, praised as so masterly ? Nothing but lost time. Let us honestly confess it,—luck favoured him in this expedition.

There are again numerous inaccuracies in the narrative of the occurrences of the 8th of February.

It is said in page 422, that Blücher decided that Sacken and York should reunite their forces at Montmirail :—he never thought of it.

Page 423, that Blücher marched off in the direction of Sezanne, where he supposed Napoleon to be, and pursued the enemy to La Fère Champenoise.

We never supposed that Napoleon had made any halt at Sezanne, nor was there any hostile force between Sezanne and the Field-Marshal.

Pages 423, 424, that York reached Montmirail after Sacken :—York was not there at all.

Page 425, that Blücher heard of the defeat of his corps on the 13th of February, in the camp at Bergères :—he first heard of it during the combat of the 14th.

Page 426, that Napoleon came with 40,000 men, to meet Blücher who had 55,000 :—it should be : who had likewise 40,000, but divided in three positions ; for neither time nor distance would allow the 15,000 who were following, to be brought up to Olsuview's combat, or those of Sacken or York.

What can be expected from criticism based on such incorrect statements? But this is not all. Beside many things on which the critic was wrongly informed, there were others of which he was quite ignorant. Amongst these are the circumstances of Kleist's corps being called off to the Grand Army, and Winzingerode being sent, on the other hand, to the Field-Marshal.

Page 428, he calls the march to La Fère Champenoise a movement not fully considered.

Page 429, he again censures this movement, and says: "Blücher would apply a blister where bleeding was necessary."

This proves sufficiently that the critic was quite ignorant of Blücher's motives, and flatly imputed wrong ones to him, which he could easily censure, as he had pronounced them to be such beforehand.

Had he known,—1. That Kleist was called away; and, 2. That Blücher was always the same in good or bad fortune, the most obedient and punctual of Lieutenant-Generals ; that he never made difficulties, and always executed faithfully the commissions he received in order to preserve the confidence bestowed on him, and to be able to act the more freely when he stood alone,—had he known all this, he must have said here, as in page 416, that the troops of the Silesian army were used with good economy.

Page 430, there is again a motive invented for Field-Marshal Blücher. "Blücher advanced on the 13th, because he believed Napoleon to be marching off against the Grand Army." Now, on the same page his advance that day is censured, in consequence indeed of two facts utterly incorrect :—

1. That on the 10th, he sent orders to the two corps to form a junction at Montmirail ; and,

2. That he heard of the discomfiture of his corps before he marched off on the 13th.

When in such important points the materials are false, it is impossible to pass any but a perverted judgment.

Let us now resume the thread of events. How Field-Marshal Blücher, on the summons of Prince Schwarzenberg, joined him on the 20th, in order to give battle—how he again separated from the Grand Army—and rejoined it once more after the battle of Laon, on the day of the *affaire* of La Fère Champenoise, in order to march together to Paris,—is all made out so clearly in the 7th section of the "History of the Campaigns of 1813-14,"* that there is no necessity for corrections or further explanations here, especially as the critic testifies his approval of the resolutions, marches, &c.

General Winzingerode, who arrived at Rheims at the time of the Field-Marshal's separation from the Grand Army (23rd February), was an experienced soldier, who, one might have thought, could have been trusted for using the right means of attaining a clearly prescribed object. On the 26th, General Winzingerode announced to the Field-Marshal, from Rheims, that he was going, in accordance with his orders, to advance from Rheims in the direction of Meaux. The most advantageous line to take in this advance, considering the country and the roads, was from Fismes by Oulchy-le-Château.

* See Part III.

According to the information sent from Rheims
on the 26th, Winzingerode could conveniently reach
Oulchy by the 1st or 2nd of March ; and this was
what the Field-Marshal expected. But instead of
following the instructions of his leader, General von
Winzingerode joined with General von Bülow to take
Soissons, a miserable nest, which had been taken by
Czernitschew with a few battalions, and again abandoned. Some *cadres* and recruits had thrown themselves into the place ; and 47,000 effective troops
invested this nest, instead of 6,000, the utmost that
would have been necessary.

Even when Winzingerode learnt, from the aide-
de-camp despatched by the Field-Marshal from La
Ferté-sous-Jouarre, that the latter was on the right
bank of the Marne, he remained in cantonments in
the valley of the Aisne without stirring.

The Field-Marshal had resolved, that if he found
Generals Winzingerode and Bülow with 40,000 men,
or even the former alone with 30,000, he would begin
to act on the offensive, and give battle with some
80,000 men to Napoleon, who could not oppose
50,000. But he was obliged to relinquish this idea,
as up to the evening of the 2nd of March no troops
from the northern army joined the Silesian at Oulchy-
le-Château. He decided on retreating behind the
Aisne, wishing to get rid of the baggage ; it was sent
forward by Fismes and Berry-au-bac.

The army was to begin to move about noon,
and to follow the baggage to Fismes, where it would
find a strong position behind the Vêle, from whence
it could without difficulty cross the Aisne at Ponta-
vaire and Berry. General von Winzingerode wrote,
on the night of the 2nd or 3rd, on the subject of the

negotiations on foot for the capitulation of Soissons, with as much importance as if they demanded the whole of his strength and that of the 47,000 men investing the place.

The Field-Marshal, who perceived that if Soissons was not in our hands by the 4th, its blockade must be raised, and was quite ignorant how it was to be effected, or what preparations Winzingerode had made at Vailly for crossing, repaired to Busancy. On his way thither he received the news that Soissons had capitulated, and that nothing more hindered their march through that town. As we could certainly cross the Aisne most conveniently there, I proposed to let the baggage proceed in the old direction ; but to order the troops, who were still on the main road from Oulchy to Soissons, not to turn off to the right, but to continue their march by Soissons. This was agreed to, and spared them a circuit.

I was not present at the first interview between the Field-Marshal and his two new generals, therefore I do not know whether any words of censure fell from him. I can only assert this much, that the Field-Marshal had a great partiality for Winzingerode, whom he counted one of the most distinguished swordsmen of Europe, and that he loved Bülow for his fiery chivalrous character. He could not, however, forget that he had been deprived of his battle at Oulchy, as " the swaggerer Napoleon" (the name he gave him since Prince Wenceslas Lichtenstein narrated to him his last conversation with Napoleon) so much deserved a sound thrashing.

When afterwards, in the town of Soissons, the Field-Marshal made his corps march past, Bülow standing at his side, I was present. Our men looked remarkable, with their thin faces blackened by bivouac smoke, and long strangers to the luxury of a razor, but with an expression of energy and bodily strength—with tattered cloaks, badly patched trowsers, unblackened leathers, and unpolished arms, —the cavalry on thin, ill-cleaned, but neighing horses,—all with a true martial bearing.

My eyes were constantly turning involuntarily to Bülow and his suite, on whose faces I fancied I could the more easily read what was passing in their minds, as I had just met a portion of Bülow's corps, in fine brilliant new uniforms, with pink and white cheeks, neatly curled locks and glittering arms. "Some rest will do these men good," said Bülow, with great seriousness, of our tattered soldiers, while perhaps he meant in his heart : " my men too may soon look the same." From his suite more was heard.

General Gneisenau, who had known many of these persons from the time when the *Tugend-bund* was a power, and who had learned to esteem them as vigorous and honourable men, asked me if I had observed the impression our ragged troops had made on our trim ones, and told me, laughing, that one of his old friends had given him a lecture on the means of sparing the troops. This occurrence could not, in my opinion, lead to any alteration in his views, since he never spared himself, and did too much himself to demand little from others. I, too, had been treated to some such phrases, but I soon settled the matter by stating the fact, that the spruce red-cheeked youths of Bülow's corps had still much to do before they could come up to our tattered soldiers of the Silesian army, out of whom the wind had already sifted all the light chaff.

The next day I encountered a conversation of quite a different kind. The fusion of the two corps of York and Kleist was stated to be a troublesome occurrence, at a time when every one could foresee that peace was no longer distant; because then the Allied Powers would claim advantages to be drawn from the war, according to the measure of strength each brought with it to the Peace Congress.

I granted this in theory, but I rated the intellectual powers developed so much higher than the material ones, that it was just by these soldiers of the Silesian army, tattered, accustomed to every privation, proved and respected by all Europe, that I wished the impression which each Prussian demand would make on the Allies, to be calculated. I felt my superiority in this discussion so strongly, that I did not like to continue it, because the cause for which I spoke was *pure*, while that of my opponent, to say the least, was not.

The Field-Marshal's mode of action since the opening of the war, lay clearly exposed : he had no reason to be ashamed of it. Chance led him to take the part of a leader in the way to battle ; and as he had fallen into it without affectation, he could not without affectation give up his part.

Bülow had chivalrously decided the fate of three battles, and the honor of the Prussian army was quite as well maintained as that of the Silesian army. Circumstances had not imposed so many privations on his corps; they had favoured him, he had not been obliged to bivouac. Who would censure him on that account? but there was no merit in this, and to wish to set him high above the Field-Marshal, because the latter had been compelled to fatigue his troops by forced marches or bivouacs, was arrogance. But it was more than this, when Bülow's followers tried to set their unbeaten General above the Field-Marshal, because the latter had just been defeated single-handed by Napoleon, and had retreated before him; while the former had forced a miserable tumble-down place with a weak garrison to capitulate. And here, for the first time, I heard the opinion expressed, that it would have gone badly with the Field-Marshal, if Bülow's corps had not opened Soissons to him, to cross the Aisne. I repelled at once this presumption.

In the negotiations for the capitulation of Soissons, a man was employed who had the reputation of being an overweening boaster; and the notion he entertained of having done something quite extraordinary, was supported by the opinion which had sprung up in Bülow's corps, that he had been the saviour of the Field-Marshal.

Later, when letters arrived from the Grand Army, every one poured out congratulations that the Field-Marshal and the brave Silesian army had been so wonderfully saved from destruction by the surrender of Soissons. General von Gneisenau was so sensitive to this truly ridiculous rumour, that he searched out its origin; and told me, some time after, that General Bülow had used expressions in a report to the King, which could only lead to the assumption that without the capitulation of Soissons the Field-Marshal would have been lost.

These were the means employed to give an importance to the fall of Soissons sufficient to account for the large blockading force engaged, and for its consequent failure in meeting the Silesian army.

However, all this might have passed, as it was without influence on the present and future. But General Gneisenau's old friends claimed the whole of his time, with great success. After every conversation he had with them, I found him absent and gloomy. Nay, some days later, this man, generally so clear-sighted, began to consider our situation as uneasy, critical, and dangerous. When, on seeing this, I took my little tablets from my pocket, and compared the numbers of combatants, taken from the daily reports, of the armies united on the Aisne—above 100,000 men, — with the forces which Napoleon opposed to us; and when, moreover, I mentioned the service we had rendered the Grand Army by moving towards Paris, and showed that everything was now tending to a happy end,—Gneisenau, who was generally so independent, adduced the apprehension, that by reason of the weakness of our army, we should not be able to obtain good conditions of peace at the Congress; and in doing so, he fell into the same train of thought, and almost used the same words I had heard from Bülow's followers.

To hear such opinions repeated by Gneisenau was the last thing I expected; and it struck me forcibly, when I immediately perceived what must be the consequences of this false turn of mind, if I could not manage to bring him back to the right way. I have often found by experience that there is nothing so hard to confute as an erroneous conclusion in politics, when it is firmly rooted, by becoming the basis of any line of conduct. Gneisenau wished to avoid admitting what he must have begun by asserting, namely, that our allies would act trickingly and faithlessly towards us. To admit this of the Emperor Alexander, and to wish to make it current in the world through General Gneisenau, was an idea which could only spring from an intriguing or ill-organized head. I felt that I could not carry on a confutation with the necessary coolness, or without bitterness; I therefore left the political question quite in the background, and merely spoke against the proposition which Gneisenau had deduced as its result; namely, that we ought to pass from this *active* mode of warfare into a passive one, that the Grand Army likewise might do something at last.

These words did not sound pleasantly on the eve of a battle; and I had enough to do to prove that, whether we took an active or a passive course, a battle was unavoidable.

An attempt had been made to impress Gneisenau with the notion that Napoleon would not attack us, and that he would quietly withdraw when he found us in the strong position of Laon; but that if he did attack us, this would be an infallible proof of his great superiority, and then prudence would recommend our not accepting a battle; we ought rather, under the protection of our superior cavalry, to avoid fighting. To such false conclusions I could only reply, that I hoped, "if Napoleon did attack us, that we should, according to our old custom, go at the right time to meet him, as we had done in the battles on the Katzbach, of Leipzic, and La Rothière, in order that the fame the Northern army had justly earned at Grossbeeren, Dennewitz, Leipzic, and in the conquest of the Netherlands, might not be perilled by the Silesian army."

I was obliged to be contented with this: I thought, "With time comes counsel." Meanwhile my opponents gained ground, and to my sorrow I could not help observing that my relation to General von Gneisenau altered daily. Instead of our former open, confidential consultations, my propositions were now rejected shortly and coldly, as unsuitable to the political circumstances of the time; and I felt some bitterness that the influence of strangers should so totally have warped the judgment of the man who, from his position with Field-Marshal Blücher, and the confidence his great military glory had inspired in the Sovereigns and all the Allies, exercised such an important influence on the termination of the two years' struggle. To continue for a short time the exertions which agreed so well with Gneisenau's noble character, was all that was now wanted. If in my heart I felt deeply wounded and depressed, I endeavoured all the more to persevere unchanged in my official duties.

On the 5th of March, the enemy's cavalry came as far as Corbeny, without its being reported to the Field-Marshal.

On the 6th, when Napoleon's approach was announced to him by General Winzingerode, he gave orders to assemble the corps on the plateau between the Aisne and the Lette, and repaired himself with his suite towards the left wing. I rode quickly forward. When I got to Craonne, the rifle-firing of the rear-guard, consisting of two battalions, had begun in that place. Winzingerode's corps had assembled on the plateau an hour after the time; consequently, contrary to express orders, the rear-guard was not posted at the passage at Berry, nor the corps in Craonne, which would have furnished a singularly strong position for a corps having a plain in front,—just what we required with our great superiority in cavalry.

It was quite impossible to retake the lost Craonne, as the rear-guard consisted of only two battalions, and Winzingerode was much too distant with his corps. I sent an officer to inform the Field-Marshal of the loss of Craonne, and of the strong position Napoleon had thereby gained against us, in consequence of General Winzingerode's disobedience.

I rode to meet the Field-Marshal, and made my report as follows:—"General Winzingerode, who ought to have occupied with his corps the impregnable position of Craonne, and posted his numerous cavalry in the plain in front, has, instead of this, given up possession of both to Napoleon, who is now as firmly established as ourselves on the plateau. To attack him in the strong position he has gained would cost us many men, and is the less advisable, as no superiority of force can avail in this attack, when the attacking party cannot bring more men into action than the defending party. As Napoleon will undoubtedly now proceed himself to attack us, since time presses him, but does not press us, we ought to wait for him. But as the greatest part of our cavalry, nearly 20,000 strong, must be withdrawn from the plateau, since we cannot employ it there; and as we can find position behind position, in which not more than 10,000 men can be deployed, and as the occupying two such positions, with a reserve of 20,000 men, would suffice to resist Napoleon's forces without danger, I propose :—

" 1. That immediate orders should be given to the corps who are now on the march, to halt and bivouac on the plateau, wherever they are.

" 2. That a corps of cavalry of 10,000 horse with 40 guns should be formed, and ordered to march off immediately to the left, to cross the Lette, and take the direction of Craonne, from whence it may fall on Napoleon's rear at daybreak.[*]

" 3. That orders should be given to Bülow's corps to march off immediately and take possession of Laon.

" 4. That instructions should be given to York and Kleist, to be in marching order by daybreak; and,

" 5. That the corps of Winzingerode, Sacken, and York, should be drawn up in defence of the plateau.[†] "

The Field-Marshal assented at once to my propositions. Winzingerode contrived, by offering some unmeaning excuses, and declaring himself very willing to destroy Napoleon, to induce the Field-Marshal to give him the command of the 10,000 horse destined to turn the enemy. I was not a little frightened when I heard of this appointment, and did not doubt for a moment that the whole thing would turn out a failure. It had seemed to me the most natural and simple plan that the Field-Marshal himself should cross the Lette with these

---

[*] This proposition was made at five P.M. It became dark about six. The distance to be traversed was four leagues, and the time allowed for this was twelve hours.

[†] These corps together amounted to about 70,000 men.

10,000 horse, and hasten their march to Corbeny; and that he should then draw York and Kleist to some point on the right bank, from whence they could take Napoleon on the right flank, and, if he did not care for that, in the rear.

What would have become of Napoleon, if, involved in a fight with Sacken at Bray, or turned on the side of Ailles or Vauclere by York and Kleist supported by cavalry and artillery, he had been forced to make front on three sides, without having any means of retreat but by the impassable valleys from the plateau to the Aisne? With the bridgeless Aisne and Soissons occupied by us, such a retreat must have ended in a complete defeat.

By General Winzingerode's fault the proposed manœuvre was not put in execution. The Field-Marshal could do nothing but inform General Sacken of this, and order him to retreat on Laon. But this order reached the plateau too late: a most bloody struggle had begun.

Sacken retreated, according to his instructions, from one position to another, as far as Froidemont. Napoleon's eagerness in the pursuit, in which however he could not touch Sacken, showed what results we should have had if Winzingerode had acted up to his instructions.

The Russian corps reached Laon in very bad humour. The loss of Sacken's and Winzingerode's corps in killed and wounded was considerable, but disproportionately great in superior officers. The Russian generals looked upon this fight as altogether useless, and the dead as wantonly sacrificed. They did not acquit the Field-Marshal, though the fault was committed by one of themselves. The Field-

Marshal ought to have known that the easy, dis-
obedient Winzingerode was not fit for such a command.

Although the result of the day might not be
liked by Bülow's followers, yet chance willed that in
their opinion the Prussian troops had suffered no loss
at all. General Gneisenau however thought differently, and declared himself adverse to my views.

A conversation I had with General Bülow, led
me to conclude that the idea of sparing the Prussian
troops did not originate with him, and that he had no
part in the influence exerted on General Gneisenau.

The Russian generals, Von Sacken, Count Woronzow, Wasiltschikof, and others, spoke with their
usual openness, by which I perceived that they were
quite strangers to these notions of *keeping the Prussian troops out of the fight.* I endeavoured to quiet
and soften them; and, while I totally denied that
any alteration had occurred in the principles which
guided the Silesian army, I referred to the impending battle, which we might hope would terminate
the war.

General von Gneisenau was besieged by his old
friends to such a degree that it became very difficult
for me to see him alone, which indeed he probably
wished to avoid, as he knew my dislike of their
political principles.

My health had hitherto withstood the great
exertions unavoidably attached to my employments.
I was accustomed to be disturbed in sleep, for a
night seldom passed without my being awakened
up several times; my natural cheerfulness raised me
above the usual little annoyances. But the vexation
I had endured since our arrival at Soissons told

upon me so much, that I was taken with a violent fever on the evening of the 7th, which continued on the 8th.

General Gneisenau was aware that since our departure from Mery, I had been studying the position of Laon very carefully, and that I had weighed maturely all its advantages and disadvantages. He had paid no attention to this subject, but depended on my studies for taking possession of the position, and resuming the offensive from thence. He therefore required my assistance, and the more urgently as there was no superior officer at Laon prepared to draw the advantages possible from the position.

Napoleon's movements led us to conclude that he would attack us at Laon.

The Cossacks had captured one of Napoleon's secretaries in the neighbourhood of Craonne, and brought him to Laon. He was a Hanoverian, who had, as early as 1806, executed secret commissions for the French to the Prussian general Lecoq, at Hameln. Deliberate in his answers, he seemed to make it his object to exaggerate Napoleon's power and resources, and, with an affectation of German frankness, to make each individual who spoke with him believe that Napoleon had marched with 60,000 to 70,000 men to the battle of Craonne, and had two Marshals behind him, coming from Fismes, with about 20,000.

A true-hearted German appointed private secretary to Napoleon was a contradiction in itself. Accidentally the man was known to me by name, as so contemptible that, in his present position, I could content myself with laughing in his face at such declarations. This scamp was brought to Gneisenau, who instead of treating him with contempt, as he would have done formerly, gave ear to his statements, so that (as I afterwards learnt) *he believed* in this strength of Napoleon.

On the 8th of March I collected all my strength, and after orders had been given to draw up the army behind the heights of Laon, I entered into a long statement of the details of our position, and the measures we ought to take. Gneisenau agreed, and placed great importance on my health permitting me to join in the battle, which we foresaw would take place the following day. My fever had so far abated the following morning, that I was able to perform my duties till evening, when it returned violently.

The battle of Laon, as well as Napoleon's mistakes, and the use we made of them, are related in my "History of the Campaign," &c.* I will only observe here, as it is the proper place, that from the moment the fog cleared off, I stood with my telescope resting on an old wall of the ruined castle, watching the three approaches which were at Napoleon's command for his march to Laon.

I considered it most improbable that he should attack our right wing, as that was the strongest point of our position. It would have been most desirable for us that the offensive combat should take place on the road between Laon and Rheims, because in *this* direction General Count St. Priest, with 16,000 men, must come in a day or two, if he had not already arrived.

The hill and town of Laon were occupied by 17,000 men, and this garrison quite sufficed to defend

* See Part III., Section 7.

them against the strongest adversary, long enough
to allow of his being attacked in flank and rear.
90,000 men stood covered behind the hill to support its defence, till the aggressor should become
wearied, when they might crush him by a vigorous
attack with superior numbers.   This was the general
disposition prescribed by the locality, but particular
circumstances intervened.

The garrison of Soissons had orders to approach
the army at Laon by La Fère, and it was assumed
that these troops could arrive on the chaussée from
La Fère to Laon, about noon on the 9th.   This
necessitated a disposition which should secure the
prescribed direction of their march till noon on the
9th ; and accordingly, on the 8th, Winzingerode's
corps was advanced, and at the same time posted
parallel to the chaussée from La Fère, keeping the
village of Classy occupied in front.

When, about ten o'clock on the morning of the 9th,
(much earlier than was expected), General Rudczewitsch arrived behind Laon with the troops from
Soissons, the reason for leaving Winzingerode in his
advanced position ceased ; and this corps would have
been ordered to move into the covered position behind the hill, had not some fresh circumstance just
then occurred which made it necessary to take a
different course.

When the fog dispersed, we discovered the enemy's
left wing on the Soissons road to be so weak, that we
could with certainty assume it to be impossible
Napoleon could venture to attack the strong
position of Laon with this small number of troops.
Towards noon we indeed knew that a hostile
column was marching on the chaussée from Rheims

to Laon; but we could not reasonably suppose that two wings, separated by so great a distance, *without a centre*, would commence a serious attack. I therefore conjectured that either a centre would still make its appearance in the direction of Bruyères, or that Napoleon intended to unite with Marmont, either by moving to the right himself, or by making him move to the left. In the first case Winzingerode's corps would be at hand (with his left wing on the pivot Laon), to keep Napoleon in check, or to beat him at the passages of the Ardon brook, Chivy, and Leully, and to assist later in the general battle.

I proposed to prolong the right wing by giving the distinguished General Wasiltschikof the commission to go round by Clacy with his cavalry and powerful horse-artillery, to turn the enemy's left wing. By this measure Winzingerode's corps would remain unweakened in its position, and General Wasiltschikof be left independent in his movements. If Napoleon allowed himself to be turned in this manner, we might assume that it was his intention to move to the right to meet Marmont. We could decide on no other offensive movement until we had discovered his intentions.

My proposition was received. Even before Wasiltschikof proceeded as far as Mons-en-Laonnais, some of the enemy's divisions advanced to Ardon and established themselves there. We continued on the defensive, until we discovered, by means of telescopes, that Napoleon had formed a flank against Wasiltschikof, and engaged in a cannonade with him.

This was the moment for the definitive dispo

sition of the battle. General Bülow received orders to attack Ardon vigorously, and to separate the enemy's left wing, under Napoleon, from the right, under Marmont; in doing this he was much assisted by his reserve of cavalry on the plain between Leully and Bruyères. This order was most successfully executed, and the result proved that Napoleon had no intention of going to meet Marmont, since he fell back upon Leully.

The next thing was to fall upon Marmont, with all our disposable forces, to annihilate him. In this movement we had to consider the hill of Laon, with its garrison of 17,000 men, as a fortress to be left to itself: we could then dispose of all the rest of the troops for our attack upon Marmont. But the question was, where should we catch him?

The wind came from the west. Marmont must have heard (on arriving at Fétieux) Napoleon's firing; and therefore it seemed *probable* that he had marched from Fétieux by Parfondry upon Bruyères. Then, as it grew dark, he could have arrived between Bruyères and Leully, and the attack upon him must therefore be made in this intermediate space.

It was settled that the attack should be made by the corps of York and Kleist, supported by Sacken and Langeron, and they received orders to hold themselves in readiness. But it was necessary first to discover where Marmont was to be attacked, and for this purpose the Field-Marshal sent me to the left flank. When I got to Chausous I found two 12-pounder batteries of Kleist's corps brought up, and the cannonade was just opened by some batteries raised by Marmont at Athis. I no longer doubted that the whole of this hostile corps was on the chaussée from Rheims, although it could not be reckoned at more than 20,000 men.

The advance of this corps on the chaussée was the most desirable thing that could happen for our disposition, as it was only necessary to fall with an extended front upon Marmont, who was wholly isolated.

The Field-Marshal and General Gneisenau, from their point of observation on the ruined castle of Laon, had discovered by the cannonade at Athis that Marmont was on the chaussée, and had not left it to turn towards Bruyères. I therefore met General Count Golz, who was already bringing to Generals York and Kleist the order to attack, as well as directions to Generals Sacken and Langeron to advance to support them.

The cannonade on the road from Rheims, had been indeed scarcely heard on the heights of Laon. It was therefore probable that Napoleon, who could not see so far, knew nothing at all about it.

The Field-Marshal quitted his point of observation when night came on: his indisposition compelled him to lie down, but never was a General more sure of victory than he was after he had despatched the order to attack. Marmont had run into the net,—whether by his Emperor's orders or by his own want of caution, has never been clearly made out.

The conduct of this defensive battle on the Field-Marshal's part was very simple, and so was the attack on the other side.

From Napoleon's position, with his right wing at Leully, his left behind Clacy, and both resting on the

Ardon brook, he could not possibly proceed to attack the hill of Laon in earnest, as long as Winzingerode's corps of 25,000 men were posted behind Clacy. We must therefore look upon his attacks as mere attempts to prove the firm attitude of the Field-Marshal and of the Russian leader behind Clacy.

Nevertheless, in perusing the report of the battle, which appeared in 1843, twenty-nine years later, in the History of the Campaign of 1814, we find the description of a battle fought with alternate advantage, and the results of which were quite uncertain until its conclusion. This impression is occasioned principally by the writer's treating the partial fights, both important and unimportant, as all of equal consequence : there are besides some inaccuracies in the narrative. He says, in page 87, that the Field-Marshal retired from the field of action about noon, on account of indisposition : this is incorrect. When I returned from the left wing, just as it began to grow dark, to the point where the Field-Marshal had remained since the morning, I found him still on the same spot ; and it was not until he had given all the orders for the day that we led him to his dwelling. In the same page we read that, "in the attacks this day on the enemy's left wing very different results would have been obtained, had it been possible for the Field-Marshal to head them himself." This is a hard accusation against the leaders, who deserve it the less, as the contrary can be proved, namely, that all the Field-Marshal's important orders on this day were just as well executed as if he had been able to carry them out in person.

The writer of this report makes no mention of the arrival of the Soissons garrison at Laon by La Fère ;* he appears too not to have even known the reasons why Winzingerode's corps was stationed behind Clacy, either in reference to its covering the march from Soissons, or of keeping Napoleon closely shut in by the Ardon brook. We can therefore excuse him, when, in page 88, he is so indignant that the offensive movements of the Allies produced no result, whereas the Field-Marshal considered their preventing Napoleon's leaving his enclosed position a sufficiently satisfactory one.

After midnight a staff officer arrived at Laon from Fétieux, sent by General von York to give a verbal report of the combat which had completely dispersed Marmont's forces; he had lost his artillery, above fifty guns, and had fled towards Berry-au-Bac. York continued the pursuit, not to allow him time to destroy the bridge at Berry.

General von Gneisenau sent this officer to me; he answered all my questions circumstantially by my bed-side, so that I was able to plan the disposition for the 10th. I assumed as its basis that Napoleon would no longer be in a condition, now that his Marshals were so thoroughly beaten, to attack the

---

* He has made the mistake of copying from Wagner's report of the battle, that this garrison arrived at Chevrigny on the evening of the 7th, which was quite impossible in time and space. General Count Langeron says in his report:—" Le Général Rudczewitsch encloua toutes les pièces trouvées à Soissons, et brûla les affûts. Le manque total de chariots le força de laisser les blessés, qui furent pris, et soignés par les ennemis. Il marcha par Coucy, St. Gobin, et Charmes (faubourg de La Fère), et vint me rejoindre près de Laon, le 9 Mars, à dix heures du matin."

Silesian army, almost triple in force, especially in such a strong position as that of Laon. Now that we had garrisoned Bruyères, and carefully separated him from his Marshals, he could only communicate with them by roundabout ways. Even had he heard the firing on the chaussée from Laon to Rheims, till the beginning of the night, he must have remained ignorant of the night combat, in which there was no firing; so that it was possible he did not know of the defeat of his Marshals until after daybreak, and consequently he might not have retreated. Now as we could not touch him in the pursuit on the chaussée to Soissons, we must—

1. Let York and Kleist pursue the defeated Marshals, and in doing so, carry out these two objects, —to hinder the destruction of the bridge at Berry-au-Bac, and effect a junction with General Count St. Priest.

2. We must divide the troops still left at Laon into two portions, one of which under Winzingerode and Bülow must remain in the position of Laon, until it was ascertained that Napoleon had retreated, in which case they must follow, and force him to a battle ; and the second portion must,—

3. March under Sacken and Langeron towards Chevrigny, on the Lette, parallel to Napoleon's line of retreat, in order to be able at any moment to wheel to the right in case he drew off, or to anticipate him on the plateau between Aisne and Lette, if he delayed too long.

According to this disposition, the army would have divided into three portions, whereof one, under York and Kleist, would consist of about 25,000 men, and the two others of about 35,000 each, *i. e.*, just Napoleon's strength after his loss at Craonne.*

As I could not leave my bed without exposing myself to all the consequences of checked perspiration, I sent my aide-de-camp Von Gerlach to General Gneisenau, with the written disposition, and instructions to explain everything to him verbally. He reported, on his return, that General Gneisenau, as well as the Field-Marshal, had understood it all perfectly, and accepted the disposition unaltered, as the Field-Marshal's signature testified. I therefore made out the orders, and by daybreak was informed that all the corps were already marching to their destinations.

With great tranquillity, in the full conviction that the day just dawning would bring us important results, I repaired to the Field-Marshal, whose large ante-room was quite filled with officers. Amongst them I observed many Russian generals, who were come to congratulate him on the result of the previous day, and also some inquisitive people and critics, and those croakers who are to be found at all head-quarters, when great events frighten them.

In pushing my way through the crowd, I observed General Gneisenau standing at a window, conversing with an old friend. I approached, to report myself well again ; the General called out to me, " It is well you are come—the disposition must be altered immediately." I stepped nearer, supposing that he had received some important news of the enemy. He went on: " The disposition you have

---

* I do not include in this the 14,000 to 16,000 men under General Count St. Priest, who might be expected to form a junction with York and Kleist on the 12th of March.

planned is too bold, and might bring us to destruction.
All the four corps who have set out must be recalled
immediately. Napoleon will attack us about ten;
Bülow and Winzingerode cannot withstand him
alone; the entire forces of Sacken and Langeron
will be required for this."

It is hard to describe the impression made upon
me by this weak declaration from the mouth of a
man I esteemed so highly. I tried to represent, in
the gentlest manner, that Napoleon's attack was just
the most desirable thing that could happen to us, if
Sacken and Langeron took him in flank and rear;
but as Gneisenau would not at all give in, I entreated
him to retire from the bustle of the ante-room, into
another apartment where we might be alone, and I.
could explain to him quietly all the circumstances.
He replied that there was no time to be lost; besides,
the Field-Marshal was sick, and he, as his deputy,
could not take upon himself the responsibility of
exposing the army to such danger as that in which
I had placed it.

I asked whether information had already arrived
of Napoleon's being still in his position. As no
one could give any certain answer, I represented
the necessity there was of first discovering whether our opponent was not already in full retreat.
I saw that this public discussion between us would
lead to nothing, and that the attention of the assem-
bly was already drawn to our dispute; so, as my
horses were standing at the door, I offered to ride
to a height before the town, on which there was
a windmill, from whence we could overlook the
villages among which Napoleon had been seen on
the previous day. Gneisenau consented to this.

The foreign influence which revealed itself here in so incomprehensible a manner made me fear that my absence might be taken advantage of, to send out the intended counter-orders by the officers I usually employed to convey my orders; I therefore took all my aides-de-camp with me.

I met with General Count Woronzow at the wind-mill, near which I erected my telescope; his out-posts had reported to him that the enemy was still posted opposite them, as on the previous evening. Woronzow was uncertain whether this might not be a cloak to mask their retreat, which was very easy in Napoleon's covered position. At this time (it might be eight o'clock) there was nothing whatever to be seen, neither bivouac fires nor masses of troops. I sent word of this to General Gneisenau, and delayed my return, hoping soon to announce something more definite.

After quietly considering, and repeatedly investigating every circumstance, I could not find any good foundation for the complaints made of my disposition; the ideas forced upon General Gneisenau could only have originated in the political principle of sparing the Prussian troops, however misplaced it was here, when the question was only of reaping the fruits of a battle already won.*

The manner in which I was again treated by General Gneisenau on this occasion, and slighted for new selfish advisers, after such a long and firmly established friendship, wounded me deeply; but I forced myself to suppress my feelings, clearly seeing

---

* I afterwards heard that my opponents had told General Gneisenau I was sick, and that this bold disposition bore all the traces of an attack of fever.

to what discord in the head-quarters of the Silesian army it must lead if it became public, and what mischief it must do the good cause. I was only quite determined not to let my hand be used for intrigues or counter-orders.

Soon after eight o'clock Colonel von Grolmann, chief of the staff of Kleist's corps, came to the windmill, to look for the Field-Marshal, for whom he had a message from General von York. He asked me —"Why do they make us halt?" It was then I first learned that immediately after I withdrew from that unlucky ante-room, orders had been dispatched to all the corps on march to halt wherever the order reached them. Colonel von Grolmann considered this as much a misfortune as I did. I knew that General Gneisenau had a great value for his opinion, and therefore urged him to explain it to him, and to try to procure the order to continue the march. He rode to Laon, but could not succeed in his attempt.*

Some of the enemy's patrols made their appearance. After nine o'clock, General von Sacken came to the windmill, more enraged than I had ever seen him. "You know, General,"—thus he solemnly addressed me—"what respect I have hitherto felt and shown for all that proceeded from the Field-Marshal; but for four days I have totally missed the spirit that formerly guided everything here. Why have they altered the disposition which would have enabled us to give Napoleon his death-blow?"

* I heard later that Grolmann urged General Gneisenau, if he was determined to recall Sacken and Langeron, at least to allow York and Kleist to continue their march to the plateau between the Lette and Aisne, for the purpose of getting between it and Soissons and Napoleon. All this was refused.

On my answering that the march was only delayed, I learnt that by a second order the four corps had been commanded to *return*. Thus the opportunity was completely lost, if not of utterly destroying Napoleon's cooped-up army, yet at least of capturing all his artillery on his retreat.

Napoleon escaped, and there was general displeasure in the allied armies, which was increased by the defeat, a few days later, of General Count St. Priest, by the same French army which ought not to have escaped unpunished from the defiles of Etouvelles and Chivy.

I had not spoken to any one of what had occurred —not even betrayed by a word what I thought about it; nevertheless, the misunderstanding between General Gneisenau and me was soon remarked, and the occasion of it guessed. General von York had not failed to notice the change that had taken place at head-quarters; and being resolved not to be the sport of intrigues, he left his corps, under the pretence of impaired health. Such a public step could not but produce the most disastrous consequences, and every effort was made to induce General von York to remain the short time that must elapse till the conclusion of peace: he yielded. I took the same resolution to wait quietly, although I foresaw that there was an end to the actions of the Silesian army.

On the 11th, we had to proceed on our march, for there was no more forage. I proposed marching towards Rheims, to form a junction with General Count St. Priest, and then advance upon Paris. In this I met with the greatest opposition from General Gneisenau. He wished to repose and scatter the army, and even to spread it out to the right towards La Fère, which would have removed us entirely from the Grand Army. I represented to him that this separation from the Grand Army would be a doubtful measure; and the more so, as all that was now extended to the right must come back again by Laon to the left. But it was in vain.

At last I discovered, from some expressions that fell from General Gneisenau, that the quarters of Bülow's corps had been, without my knowledge, previously arranged on the other side of the Aisne, in the rich district of Noyon, six miles from Laon. In this Capua selected for Bülow's corps, six days were quite lost. Had we, as I wished, pushed on to Neufchatel and Rethel, we should have arrived there on the 12th or 13th. We could have restored the connexion with the Grand Army, drawn St. Priest near us, given the army three days' rest, and reached Rheims on the 17th, or Châlons on the 18th; whereas (according to this unsuitable and perverse disposition) we could only arrive there on the 23rd and 24th. My remonstrances and disapproval were of no avail.

York and Kleist advanced to Corbeny and Craonne, and were unable, on account of the general movement to the right, to do more than guard the bridge of Berry-au-Bac with advanced posts, though it ought to have been covered by a division. After the defeat of St. Priest on the 13th, we had to bear the disgrace of seeing Marmont destroy the bridge before our eyes, after driving away our advanced posts.

Every day I urged on our departure, and that this state of rest should be brought to a close; but a new and ridiculous reason for delay was brought forward. All kinds of gossip were current in Bülow's corps, from the head-quarters of the Crown Prince of Sweden, who had certainly talked a great deal of ridiculous nonsense after his arrival at Liège, which had led to the conclusion that he disapproved of the march beyond the Rhine, and still imagined that the French would call him (the Crown Prince) to the throne of France in the room of Napoleon.

An attempt was made to instil into Gneisenau the notion that the Crown Prince, offended at losing the command of the corps of Bülow and Winzingerode, might advance with his Swedes, and attack us in the rear; and, therefore, the army could not proceed, or abandon the central point, Laon. However, this was something too extravagant, and Gneisenau let it drop, in consequence of my remonstrances.

As we did not know what had become of Napoleon since the affair of Rheims, and news arrived that he had ordered reinforcements to be sent to Rethel from the fortresses in the Ardennes, it was thought possible that, in order to wipe away the disgrace incurred at Laon, he might bring up all his disposable forces, and attack us from Rethel, taking us in flank wherever he found us scattered, and could roll us up. Although I had very little faith in this movement, it did me good service, in getting the army re-assembled on the 15th.

At this time, and until our entrance into Paris, the Field-Marshal was much indisposed; still he was able to hear reports on all important matters, and to sign the resolutions as usual. A change in the chief command would have been very hazardous;

the Field-Marshal indeed wished to remain with the army, that he might be at hand, ready to resume the command as soon as he felt himself recovered.*

In our further progress, after crossing the Aisne, I again met with the greatest difficulties. The old friend was again at hand, and was able to effect more by speaking than by writing. In drawing out the disposition for the march to Paris, I assumed that Soissons (in which there could be but 2,500 or 3,000 men at most), would not be attacked, but blockaded on the right bank by Cossacks, and on the left by 3,000 men, who could intrench them-

---

* The Russian General, Count Langeron, was next in seniority to the Field-Marshal, and he had a great dread of being obliged to undertake the command. This was further increased when he visited him and found him quite worn out. On coming out of his room he said to me, " Au nom de Dieu, transportons ce cadavre avec nous !"

At page 127 of the before-mentioned report of the battle published in 1843, the sickness of the Field-Marshal is so represented as to lead one to conclude it to have been an absence of mind amounting to incapacity. There is no denying that there existed at that time a party whose interest it was to spread this opinion; they did not venture, however, to express it openly, as the physicians and constant attendants on the Field-Marshal could prove the contrary. When this work appeared in 1843, the greatest part of these witnesses were dead. Lieutenant-General Count Nostitz, who had been first aide-de-camp to Prince Blücher, undeceived the author, who expressed his willingness to be set right, and indeed printed the correction in the 11th Number of the " Weekly Military Gazette" for 16th March, 1844. This correction affirms what was true; "that the Field-Marshal was able from his room to conduct, as usual, the operations of the Silesian army, but not a battle, where he was wont to be always in the hottest of the fight." To this I must add that he did in fact conduct all the operations until the battle of Paris; and he was not to be kept back from joining even in this battle, with a green shade over his eyes.

selves on the road to Paris. To this General Gneisenau objected; he would have it besieged, and
bombarded with red-hot balls. I represented to
him that these exertions were useless, and would
scatter our forces, as in that case it would be necessary to leave 6,000 men before this nest.

Through this resistance on my part, it came to
my knowledge that everything had already been
arranged with Bülow's corps, who were to take the
materials for the siege from La Fère, which *he* had
taken, and that he was to give up the conduct of the
siege to General Von Borstell, who was expected to
arrive from Belgium with 9,000 men.

" But till then what is to be done ?" I asked.

" Till then Bülow's corps must conduct the siege,"
was the answer.

In vain I shook my head, observing, " What will
Bülow say to a commission which is hardly fit for
the commander of a brigade?" The whole corps
went off to this glorious destination. I was, and am
still, convinced that General Bülow was a stranger
to this intrigue, but I cannot at all understand that
he should not have observed that this siege must
appear to all well-informed officers of the allied
armies a pretence to cover other objects. A well-
informed officer, of high rank, said to me when he
read the disposition, " Borstell will never come
now."

From the day Bülow's corps was detached from
the Silesian army, General Gneisenau was again
himself, strong and vigorous in judgment, and
energetic in action; and from this time till the
peace of Paris, not the slightest difference of opinion
again arose between us. I avoided speaking to

him on disputed points, although he not only gave me opportunities, but even seemed to wish that I should. He had private accounts of the siege of Soissons from his friend, which he communicated to me, to give me a high idea of the importance of this operation. I never made any answer, nor once mentioned the name of Soissons or Bülow's corps until we entered Paris.*

SUPPLEMENT TO PART I.

The Baron von dem Knesebeck,† General of Infantry, was one of a number of Prussian officers who were already well grounded in the principles of their profession when the war of 1806 broke out, and had carefully studied the French Revolution, and closely observed Napoleon's military career.

---

* When, on account of the complaint in his eyes, Field-Marshal Blücher gave up in Paris the command of the Silesian army, and when His Majesty conferred the supreme command over the corps of York, Kleist, and Bülow (to which was also attached that over the corps of the Elector of Hesse and Duke of Gotha—at that time before Luxemburg and Mainz) on the Russian general Barclay, General Gneisenau resigned his office of Chief of the Staff of the Silesian Army; and by His Majesty's order I repaired to the head-quarters of General Barclay, as chief of the Staff of the Prussian and German divisions, while General von Diebitsch (subsequently Prince Sabalkansky), was appointed Chief of the Staff of the Russian army.

Though I may have succeeded in performing, till our entrance into Paris, my difficult duty in the Silesian army, as the interest of the King and State required, still it seemed to me that I should be fully justified, both for my own sake and that of the State, in declining to accept again a position such as I held in the Silesian army.

† Who died a Field-Marshal in 1848.

As Aide-de-camp to General von Rüchel in Potsdam, he became better known to the King ; and on the evening of the battle of Auerstadt, being then Quartermaster of the King's staff, he rendered him the important personal service of saving him, by his presence of mind, from what seemed almost inevitable captivity. The royal pair felt towards him, in consequence, gratitude that lasted to the end of their lives.

After the peace of Tilsit he retired to his estate of Carve, not far from Berlin ; the King had accepted his offer of resuming his services the moment his Majesty could make use of them. Here, in complete retirement, he watched public events, and occupied himself almost exclusively with the thought how Europe, so heavily oppressed, could be delivered from the hands of the conqueror of the world. He was no stranger to the parties in his native country ; but, true to his principles, he would engage in no secret combinations whereof he did not know the objects and the leaders ; he entertained the firm belief that he should still witness the downfall of Napoleon.

When war broke out in 1809, he hastened secretly to the Austrian army ; but he failed in his object, and was obliged to return mortified home. This fact however, as well as his whole journey, remained a secret.

In 1811 there could be no longer any doubt that Napoleon had resolved upon the destruction of the Russian Empire ; this was the circumstance which Knesebeck had so long considered as the last and only means of leading to the much-desired overthrow of Napoleon, and for which, in his solitude, he had prepared himself by deep study. He proceeded to Berlin, a stranger to the political views entertained there, though he knew all the persons who had gained any influence. He was valued for his judgment and the services he had rendered; he was known to be a great friend to the Russian army, and a personal admirer of the Emperor Alexander; his arrival was therefore taken as a sign that he acquiesced in the general opinion, that Prussia ought to summon all her strength to reconquer her lost provinces, in conjunction with the Russian armies which were to be set in motion forthwith.

His assistance was expected against the so-called French party, who foresaw the downfall of the Russian Empire, and recommended the alliance with France as the only means of safety for Prussia, whose fortresses were in French hands.

But a report began to spread that Knesebeck was *against* the alliance with Russia, and recommended that with France. People remarked that his old friend Scharnhorst, (who, since the new organization of the army, stood nearest the King), kept aloof from him; and they were still more convinced of the correctness of this report, when Knesebeck set off for St. Petersburg, with the ostensible mission to make a last attempt to induce the Emperor Alexander to maintain peace. Napoleon had given his consent to this mission: Knesebeck departed on sledges, the 9th of February, 1812, furnished with French passports, and with special recommendations, as the French Embassy took care to propagate in Berlin, to Lauriston, the French Ambassador at St. Petersburg.

He came back in the middle of March, and his mission was considered a complete failure. It was said that the Emperor Alexander had declared that he sincerely wished for peace, of which indeed he could give no better proof than by protesting most solemnly that he would not overstep his own boundaries; but that, nevertheless, if he were attacked within them, he should know how to defend himself.

If this answer was calculated to convince Europe that Russia was not the party desirous of war, yet with it sank all the hopes of those Prussians who had urged on the alliance with Russia. There was now no other course left for Prussia but the French alliance, nor for all Prussian officers who would not bear arms *against* Russia, but to get their discharge. Knesebeck returned to his solitude, was silent on the subject of his mission even to his most intimate friends, and became Adjutant General to the King in 1813, when he was dispatched from Breslau to meet the Emperor Alexander, with some diplomatic commissions. This was explained as the result of a previous secret mission to Vienna, which rendered him particularly well qualified to bring about a good understanding, not only between Prussia and Russia, but also between Austria and Russia, as Austria had not yet renounced the alliance with France. When, however, the contingent furnished by Austria was withdrawn from the French army, which was hastening to the Rhine, there no longer existed any motive for the continuance of the war, and consequently there was no obstacle to a good understanding between her and Russia.

By these negotiations, which led to the restoration of the relations between Russia and Austria,

General von dem Knesebeck gained a well-deserved confidence in Vienna; and this was the state of things when the war of 1813 began.

In the year 1792, the Duke of Brunswick's regiment, in which Knesebeck then served, being about twenty-five years of age, and Schenck's fusilier battalion, in which I, a youth of seventeen and a half, was serving, had winter-quarters in common.

Knesebeck observed my desire to improve myself, and became my kind useful friend, as he was already my *beau idéal*. From this connection (after time had apparently more equalised our difference in years), sprang up a cordial friendship, which was never interrupted, and which bore during the years of war good fruits for the service of the state: as holding the position he did, near the Sovereigns, Knesebeck knew through me what was required in the Silesian army, and what we were able to do; while, through him, I learnt what was the particular object the Sovereigns had in view.

The "Tugendbund," that is to say, the heads of it, had since 1812 irreconcilably split with Knesebeck, and they had just as little confidence in me. But when General Gneisenau discovered that I quietly held on my course, a stranger to all parties, and that through my friend Knesebeck I had information of all important occurrences at the royal head-quarters, employing my secret intelligence for the good of the Silesian army, he knew how to turn this circumstance to the best account. He had heard that at Bautzen I commissioned an aide-de-camp (who was going back to the King) to inform General von dem Knesebeck from me "that the abandonment of the Kreckwitz heights, attacked on three sides, was necessary." He had learnt that Knesebeck had, in consequence, defended this measure, that the King even had fully approved it, and that the Emperor had been likewise convinced, by the reasons given, of its necessity; he therefore saw in me a means of putting himself well with the Sovereigns, to which he must cling; the rather as his favourite wish, of having the Russian colonel Von Clausewitz appointed to my office in the Silesian army, had been denied him. He accordingly encouraged me the more willingly to keep up a confidential correspondence with Knesebeck, as he perceived that I never defended the measures of the Grand Army, when I was convinced that something better would or should have been done. This explains how General Gneisenau, who did not enjoy the personal confidence of the Sovereigns, maintained himself in an honourable position as Chief of the General Staff of the Silesian army, which it was the object of my especial care to preserve for him, recognizing the great value to the army of his numerous eminent qualities, which, as long as Blücher commanded as General-in-Chief, were indispensable.

But I considered Knesebeck quite as necessary to secure the happy issue of the war, having witnessed the great confidence which the Sovereigns placed in him, although I did not at that time know how well grounded was the cause of it.

In 1819, I returned from a diplomatic mission to the Netherlands, where I found General von Phull (who had left our service in 1807) as Russian Ambassador. I had never seen this learned, interesting, but uncouth man, since the conference of Erfurt in

1806 ; but I was kindly received by him, and as he
only lived in the past, he willingly read to me his
plan of operations for the campaign of 1812, with all
its details.   The first section went down to the concentration of the Russian armies in the camp at
Drissa, the remaining sections continued the retreat
on the road to Moscow.   I was struck with the care-
fulness with which the subsistence of the retreating
armies was calculated, and at the same time so
managed, that the enemy on his advance should
find neither provisions nor men, cattle nor horses ; as
likewise with the precautions taken for preventing,
as much as possible, the population retreating with
the army from impeding the movements of the
troops.

   According to Phull's designs the magazines were
to have been established on the right and left of
the road from Smolensko to Moscow, but the road
itself left quite free.   The army was to retreat
fighting in divisions selected beforehand.   Whenever it made front, provisions were to be brought
into the camp from both right and left; and when,
to avoid being forced into a decisive battle, it
became necessary to continue the retreat, measures
were taken for all the inhabitants, with their cattle
and provisions, to abandon their villages ; not, however, to fly in the direction taken by the army, but
into the woods on the right and left, in a line at
right angles with the road to Moscow.

   With regard to the correctness of the theory I
could not raise a doubt, though I certainly could as
regards the possibility of its practical execution, as
the Russian, perhaps even more than a native of
highly cultivated nations, clings to his clod.

Phull maintained that the whole plan was based on the strength of character and few wants of the Russian peasant, and on the consequent possibility of his leading a nomadic life in his woods. With no other people could such a project be carried through. Phull concluded by saying that the Emperor had fully approved the whole plan of operations, but that he had given out the first portion only (namely, as far as the concentration in the camp at Drissa) as the disposition : he had recommended to him the strictest secrecy as to the rest, whereby he had been deprived of all means of defending his plan, since his first part must have the appearance of patchwork, contemplated apart from all the other portions. The tumultuous scenes which had obliged the Emperor to remove him from the army had proved, moreover, that the superior Russian officers had not been " à la hauteur " to comprehend his plan correctly, far less to honour and to execute it.

When (I believe after Phull's decease) I communicated all this to Knesebeck, he replied, " Yes, it is all literally true." I had not doubted it, but several officers, who had been present in the camp at Drissa, disputed the fact of Phull's having thought of anything beyond this point; some proof was therefore required for Phull's justification, which I wished to have, as I had perfect confidence in his love of truth. Knesebeck grew serious, and replied,—" I could give the proof, but duty closes my lips." These words sufficed to close mine too on this matter; for I quite agreed that, however confidentially we constantly conversed about persons and circumstances, and state measures which we could not call good, my noble friend could not and ought not to violate a promise given, or disclose another's secret.

In the beginning of May, 1844, the third part of "Portraits from Life" (by Hormeyer), fell into my hands, in which I found a report, delivered by Knesebeck to his King, on his mission to St. Petersburg in the spring of 1812. The first question that forced itself on me was, Is this report genuine? The second,—Why is it written in French? and, if it was not a fabrication by Hormeyer, who had been previously accused of falsifying statements, then how could this report get into Hormeyer's hands? I could imagine nothing but treachery; either that it had been abstracted from the state archives of Prussia, or purloined from the papers of the usually cautious Knesebeck.

Setting aside the general interest which pertained to this report, in relation to the history of Prussia, the conclusion testified, that the fact of the power of an inferior Russian force to place insuperable difficulties in the way of a superior enemy, had been clearly recognised by the authorities in St. Petersburg. Were the report genuine, the incontestable conclusion to be deduced from it would be, that the Cabinet of St. Petersburg had taken the resolution *not* to step out of its boundaries, but to wait and see whether Napoleon would take the important step of bringing a war within the confines of this great empire, whereof the aim was its subjugation, and for which he had only insignificant motives to allege; and we should then be obliged to admit, likewise, that the Cabinet had quite agreed on a defensive plan, which, though it could not ensure success, might at least hold out a prospect of a favourable issue to the war.

I could never give up the notion that Napoleon secretly wished, and *must have wished*, that Prussia might reject the alliance he offered to her, and ally herself with Russia, on condition that Russia should send armies as far as the Elbe for her protection.*

At that time Napoleon had no fears of the defection of Austria, and, in this case, he could choose the field for a decisive battle between the Elbe and the Oder, or the Oder and the Vistula. To this battle he might have brought 500,000 men to oppose 250,000, with a good basis for his line of operations, and subsistence for his forces, in the possession of the fortresses on the Elbe, Oder, and Vistula.

By this means he would have lived at the cost of the Prussian state, which he could thus chastise with a semblance of right, in punishment of its defection ; and it might further be with certainty foreseen that the Emperor Alexander would be obliged to accept peace at a great sacrifice, as he would otherwise run the risk of being forced into it by his own people, who, if the war continued, would consider themselves sacrificed to foreign interests.

On these grounds I considered it for the real welfare of Prussia neither to seek nor accept the

---

* " Portraits from Life," 2nd part, page 86. Report of the Chancellor of State to his King, November 2, 1811, gives all the demands made by Napoleon as conditions of an alliance. These were so hard, that we involuntarily come to the conclusion, that they were intended to drive Prussia into the desperate resolution of throwing herself into the arms of Russia.

Russian alliance, and that it was also the interest of the Cabinet of St. Petersburg to act in the same views.

In 1844, my friend Knesebeck was in the country, whither he had retired on the loss of his wife. Hormeyer's indiscretion, I thought, would be very disagreeable to him; and I considered it a friend's duty to write to him (on the 6th of May, 1844) the account of the printing of his report, together with the three questions above mentioned, in case he might judge it necessary to take some steps against this publication. To this letter I received an answer, which, from its importance to history, I copy here verbatim.

"Rödershoff, near Halberstadt,
"May 20th, 1844.

" Your dear confidential letter of the 6th inst., honoured old friend, has done me good in my solitude and quiet sorrow, and the more so as these are the first lines, at any length, from your hand that I have received for many a day; and because, in the second place, they diverted my thoughts from the mournful subject which engrossed them, and carried me back to an epoch when the greatest event of many centuries was preparing, in which it was my destiny to be deeply involved, although in a secret and unostentatious manner.

" Such was the case with the mission on which I was sent in the beginning of the year 1812, the *ostensible* report of which, delivered by me at the time, Herr Hormeyer has now reprinted in the third part of his 'Portraits from Life.' I say reprinted, for, if I do not mistake, it is already published in the 7th volume of the 'Correspondance inédite,' which, as was said at the time, was published by Jomini soon after the peace, and supposed to have been found in the papers in part taken from Napoleon in his flight, in part left behind by him in Paris. Whether this is true, is a question I leave undecided.

"Now what relation this has to my memoir, I will, in friendly confidence, tell you faithfully.

"The genuineness of the words I cannot deny, as I have compared them with the *brouillon*, which, written by my own hand, is still preserved amongst my papers. But how came it to be published? Heaven knows. With my consent it was not done, nor has it been purloined from me. I therefore conjecture (as I have already said) that it was really found amongst the papers taken from Napoleon, as was told me when I first found it in the 'Correspondance inédite;' and this is possible, for, by the wish of the Chancellor of State, I had to write this report, so that it could be communicated to St. Marsan,* and by him to Napoleon; and I took upon myself, at the same time, to foretell therein the fate which afterwards befell him; though, indeed, it could not be foreseen that Heaven, too, would assist us with the scourge of an early frost, and pass such a doom.

"But, in order to explain the affair, I must now go back a good deal farther.

"You know that in 1806 I made the winter campaign with the Russians, and at head-quarters partly of Benningsen, partly of Tolstoy, I took part in

---

* The Marquis de St. Marsan, a Piedmontese nobleman, at that time ambassador from Napoleon to the court of Berlin.—Ed.

several small actions, and in the battle of Pultusk in particular, which I may say I conducted, and gained thereby the confidence of the leaders of the army. When, in the spring of 1807, the Emperor Alexander joined the army, Tolstoy, who was then Adjutant-General, recommended me to his special notice, and the Emperor summoned me to him at Bartenstein. Here it was that I learnt to know and appreciate his noble heart, whose only desire was the happiness of mankind; and a sort of mutual confidence arose between us, on the strength of which I undertook my mission to St. Petersburg in 1812, to lay before him the plan of the campaign I had made out in my solitude at Carve, which was indeed followed *in toto*. To explain to the Emperor my ideas, how the war must be conducted to effect the delivery of Europe, was my secret errand, which was never perfectly known even to the Chancellor of State; the King alone was fully informed of it.

"But to get to St. Petersburg, and to appear accredited there, required an official and ostensible commission, and this consisted in my once more attempting to mediate peace between the two parties, and using every effort to prevent the outbreak of the war. St. Marsan was informed of this, and through him Napoleon; I set off for St. Petersburg, with the consent of the French, and furnished with French passports and recommendations to Lauriston,—joyful at having any pretext to get access to the Emperor Alexander and lay my ideas before him, and deaf to all the execrations which followed me, when it was reported that I was not disposed to let the Russians advance into our country as far as the Vistula, and fight out the struggle on our native soil, which was then the ruling, indeed universal opinion, in order to unite as soon as possible with the Russians against the French. The King alone, who had granted me an interview without other witnesses, and had listened to me quietly above two hours, agreed with me, but said, 'Here all are of another opinion; and the Emperor will beg to be excused from allowing the French to enter upon his territory.' I replied, that with the noble heart I knew the Emperor to possess this would still be possible, if he were convinced that by this way only he would ensure the victory.

"'Then I will send you off, but you will fare finely; tell him only that we stick to our old friendship, but I cannot now help marching against him; I should otherwise lose the whole country, but I hope all will soon change.'

"These were my instructions for the *secret mission;* and as I guessed from the words which fell from Scharnhorst and Lieven that both were working to get the Russians to advance immediately, in order *to force* Prussia into an alliance with them more quickly, I did not delay a moment, only first making a stringent stipulation with the Chancellor of State, on no account to give up another fortress to Napoleon. In my rapid passage through Königsberg I saw some Russian staff-officers already arrived, and York disclosed to me that he had secret orders to put himself in communication with them; I begged him only to wait till I came back from St. Petersburg: he answered, 'I understand, and will tack.'

" With my carriage put upon a sledge I hurried on, and on the eighth day after my departure from Berlin (for that time extraordinary speed) I reached St. Petersburg. Here I found three opinions prevailing:

one party, to which Bagration belonged, wished to push forward as far as possible ; Barclay de Tolly only as far as the Vistula ; Phull saw nothing but his camp at Drissa ; the Emperor, lastly, agreed to accept the struggle on the Russian frontier, but would in no case overstep it. All considered themselves unconquerable with their 300,000 men under arms, and no one would believe me when I spoke of Napoleon's coming with perhaps double that force : even the Emperor was much irritated when I once remarked that 300,000 seemed to me too few.—'Comment!' he exclaimed; 'vous comptez 300,000 Russes pour rien? vous qui avez fait la campagne avec nos troupes?'

"I answered that I had seen how bravely they fought, but he had also two other allies, on which I reckoned quite as much ; these were *space* and *time*. He had both in his favour, if he took the field, and did not make peace ; and against these Napoleon's genius (for which the Emperor entertained the greatest respect) would and could as little avail as his superiority in numbers. His superiority, on the contrary, would only put more hindrances in his way : that of all the Powers of Europe, Russia alone had such advantages over her opponent, which, if properly used, must ensure Napoleon's downfall ; that consequently he (the Emperor Alexander) appeared to me called by Providence to restore freedom to the world, and to loose it from the chains in which it languished ; that this indeed was properly *his* aim and *his* object. And this was also the view of the King, my master ; who would for this end submit to the heavy sacrifice of fighting *a time* against him, his best friend on earth. That to attain this great object, it mattered not whether 20,000 Prussians more fought against him; but what did matter was, that he should begin the struggle with his opponent in the right way; and in order to lay my thoughts on the subject before his wisdom, I had undertaken this official mission to him, and the King my master had sent me. That I trusted to the noble feelings and sentiments in his breast, and hoped he would be gracious enough to hear me.

"'Eh bien, vous me développerez vos idées: je vous donnerais des audiences privées.'

"He then appointed an hour about midnight, and indicated to me a secret door in the Winter Palace, by which, whenever a Cossack should stand there, I might come to him in the evening, and the Cossack would show me the way. Now while I spent the mornings with Romanzow, in trifling talk, and the afternoons mostly with Lauriston, at that time French ambassador at St. Petersburg, partaking of his good dinners, between eleven and twelve at night I frequently found the Cossack before mentioned, who conducted me to the study of the Emperor, who there made me perfectly acquainted with the strength of his armies, as well as the different plans proposed to him for carrying on the war, and listened with great attention to my observations, objections, and private hints, graciously bestowing on me his unlimited confidence. In this way I was at least a dozen times with him, and made him familiar with the idea of always giving ground while fighting, but at the same time never sacrificing his fighting powers; and of considering the line to Moscow as the basis of operations which Napoleon would certainly choose.

"This last opinion gave rise to much discussion, as Alexander at that time firmly believed that Napoleon would choose St. Petersburg as the aim of his operations. When I took leave of him, he said to me, holding fast my hand in his, 'Dites au Roi, que si je venais à Kazan, je ne ferai pas la paix.'

"I held his hand long clasped in mine: he embraced me cordially, and was much moved when I told him that I, for my part, would *never* fight against him; and that when he heard I had re-entered the service of my King, he might look upon it as a sign that the King believed the moment come for publicly embracing again the Russian party.

"Thus I departed from St. Petersburg, on the 7th of March, I believe. That my representations had made a great impression on the Emperor, I felt quite convinced, and the rest I hoped would follow from Napoleon's own advance. Near Riga or Dorpat, in the night, I met with Czernitschef, who was hurrying from Paris, where, as is well known, he had got possession of many important papers. The postilions wanted to exchange horses. We mutually recognised each other by our voices. When I asked what news he brought, he called out to me: 'La nouvelle que 600,000 hommes marchent contre nous;' and I begged him to ask the Emperor whether I had not been right.

" On arriving at Berlin, it became necessary to make an ostensible report of my official mission, which might be communicated to St. Marsan and Napoleon.

"I had considered the matter on the journey. I had already worked at it at St. Petersburg; and as the official object of my mission was, properly speaking, to dissuade both parties from war, I thought that I might very well introduce into my report all the difficulties which the aggressor would encounter in a war with Russia, in some measure, as a prophecy for my own satisfaction; and this is the origin of what you have read in Hormeyer.

"When the Chancellor communicated the report to St. Marsan, the latter was quite delighted with it: he begged me to come to him, and told me that, if anything could deter Napoleon from this war, it would be the military observations introduced by me at the end of the report. The report itself, he added, was too long for Napoleon, but he would send him immediately the concluding observations by express; and it now occurs to me, that on the same forenoon, by the Chancellor's wish, I gave additional strength to my observations, by briefly adding, that the greatest genius would be unable to overcome the difficulties which distance and time opposed to the aggressor who should attempt to penetrate into Russia; and it is possible that the remark so worded stood in the report which St. Marsan sent off—the one found in Napoleon's papers, and copied in the 'Correspondance inédite.' As I have not got the latter at hand, I can say nothing about it with certainty. In my papers I find it only as it appears in Hormeyer; and my *brouillon*, which I can show you when I have an opportunity, is also written in French, as I frequently employed that language in my political missions, though I am not quite master of it, and write it incorrectly. But the precision of expression which the French tongue possesses, and the satisfaction of giving literally the words of a conversation spoken in French, often induced me to do so; I had more reason for it in this instance, as the ostensible report of the mission to St. Petersburg was intended for the French.

"Now then, my dear old friend, I have told you in perfect confidence, and with the garrulity of old age, all that I can at this moment recall to my memory about this mission. My life is drawing to an end. What I have done in the world, and what I am justified in calling my own work, is buried in silence and known to no one. It is therefore pardonable, if in my 77th year I open my heart to a friend when an opportunity occurs, and you will not abuse my confidence.

"And now that I feel disposed to chat, I must tell you, in addition, the great satisfaction I received from what Napoleon himself said on the subject of the report in question. When, in 1814, I again saw St. Marsan at Paris, he said to me, that he wished to impart a fact which would give me pleasure; and he then told me the following:

"When he quitted Breslau, in the spring of 1813, after we had declared against France, he met Napoleon at Mainz: he saw him there for a few minutes only, and delivered his report. He wished me to guess what was one of the first questions Napoleon put to him. He asked him whether he, St. Marsan, recollected a report by a Prussian officer, which he had sent to him in the preceding year, before the Russian war broke out, and the name of the officer. On St. Marsan's mentioning my name, Napoleon immediately said: 'Cet homme a très bien jugé les affaires et la situation des choses: il ne faut pas le perdre de vue. Est ce qu'il est employé?' St. Marsan replied that he believed so, for he had seen me in Breslau, where I had arrived just two days before St. Marsan's departure, on my return from a secret mission to Vienna, in order to proceed thence immediately to join the Emperor Alexander, whom I met at Plocks; but St. Marsan knew nothing about my Vienna mission. Napoleon then hemmed in a thoughtful manner, and spoke about the Russian campaign.

"Now that Napoleon should have thought of that report, a year after, when everything had occurred just as I had predicted, is certainly remarkable enough, and gave me the greatest satisfaction I could receive on the subject.

"Now, dear and honoured friend, I have faithfully related everything to you with the strictest truth; and you will perceive therefrom that I may feel quite tranquil on the subject of the publication of that report, of which moreover I am wholly innocent; and to this hour I am ignorant how it came to be published, since the printed report is not the private report of my secret commission, which I have now confidentially communicated to you.

"The delicacy of feeling towards me, which the King on this occasion again so graciously evinced, has touched me deeply. A friend could not behave more lovingly towards another! If you have an opportunity, present my warmest thanks in return.

"But enough, this letter is already too long: I have spoken too much of myself, and fear that I have become wearisome. Excuse the old man, and con-

tinue as you have been so many years, *my* friend as
I am *thine*.

V. D. KNESEBECK."

To this letter I have to add the remark, that in
subsequent conversations my friend admitted to me
that there must always remain a gap in the history
of the world, if the *motives* of our King and the
Emperor Alexander for disguising the truth in the
records intended for posterity, were kept secret.
Yet he did not wish to quit this world with an
appearance of personal assumption, and left it to me,
after his death, to give to history what appertained
to it.

It may be asserted that I might have given
more; that I might have displayed, together with
the ripened judgment and clear understanding of
one of the greatest strategists, his richly endowed
mind; to this I must reply, that what I have done
was with a full consciousness. The man who cannot be stirred up by noble natures and great
thoughts, may indeed excite astonishment as an
unerring calculating machine; but to him only
whose heart and understanding are kept in perfect
equilibrium, is reserved the power of inspiring
confidence.

Hormeyer has furnished the materials for judging
of the letter dated May 20th, 1844, by giving the
before-mentioned report of November 2nd, 1810.
This report reveals circumstances as they stood on
that day. The letter of my deceased friend shows
how matters stood in the middle of March, 1812, on
his return from St. Petersburg.

PART II.

FROM THE FIRST PEACE OF PARIS TO THE CON-
GRESS OF AIX-LA-CHAPELLE.—ADDITIONS AND
SUPPLEMENT. — THE CONGRESS OF AIX - LA -
CHAPELLE, AND ITS CONSEQUENCES.

FROM THE FIRST PEACE OF PARIS (1814), TO THE SECOND
PEACE IN 1815.

AFTER the peace of Paris (1814), the Emperor of
Russia and the King of Prussia fulfilled their promise to the Prince Regent, of paying a visit to
England. Blücher accepted the invitation which
had also been sent to him. He knew that he was
the favourite of the English nation, and that his
speeches (in which love of one's country, and its
delivery from a tyrant's oppression, were predom-
inant) always found a favourable hearing with the
multitude. He had, indeed, accustomed himself to
public speaking in great assemblages, and delivered
his speeches with so much expression, that they
never failed to produce effect. As might have been
foreseen, he met with great applause in England.

Count Gneisenau and I were invited as being
attached to the Field - Marshal, but I could not
think of accompanying him, as I had to direct the
army's march back, and was appointed Chief of the
Staff to General Count Kleist von Nollendorff, who
undertook the command of an army which was to
remain on the Lower Rhine.

The old German boundaries on the side of France

were restored to their limits before the revolution ; the district occupied by the army of the Upper Rhine, under Prince Schwarzenberg, extended, according to the agreement, from the southern limits of Germany to the Maine, and as far as the Moselle on the left bank of the Rhine. This line of demarcation was to continue only till the Congress should have arranged the affairs of Germany. The fortress of Mainz, being the point of union of the armies of the Upper and Lower Rhine, was to be garrisoned by Austrians and Prussians conjointly. According to this agreement, a governor and a commandant of Mainz were to be named by both Powers, and instructions given to the garrison defining their respective rights and duties. In default of the local knowledge necessary for such instructions, it was settled that they were not to be planned in Paris, but on the spot, by General Count Kleist and the Austrian general Frimont.

General Kleist had to take up his head-quarters at Aix-la-Chapelle, where the seat of government of the Lower Rhine was already established ; for the King had conferred on him the administration of the province conjointly with President Sack. This last appointment was so disagreeable to General Kleist, that he endeavoured to get rid of it, but in vain, as the State Chancellor replied that it depended on himself to undertake as much of these affairs of the general government, as the time left from the command of the army would allow.

The officers and officials appointed at head-quarters proceeded from Paris to Aix-la-Chapelle, while General von Kleist travelled with me and some aides-de-camp by Luxemburg to Mainz, where he and General Frimont concluded the convention about the occupation of Mainz, which was afterwards accepted, as appropriate, by the German Confederation, and in its essential points has been maintained to this day. Frimont and Kleist both dreaded this business excessively, and foresaw the greatest difficulties. I was their common confidant on this point, and endeavoured to facilitate the affair by a preparatory conference.

General Frimont was a brave soldier, and a man of strong character, who investigated every circumstance in a sensible way, in doing which his conciliatory and pleasant manners assisted him; General Kleist was just like him. Before the hour of the conference approached I already saw that no difference would arise, though both sat down to the green table with anxious feelings.

I had undertaken to deliver and conduct the protocol; after some hours the affair was settled, and my two generals were so rejoiced at the happy result that they embraced, and a friendship sprang up between them which continued through life.

Prince Schwarzenberg had said to me, after some conversation we had together in Paris, about the qualities of the Austrian and Prussian officers who were to command together in Mainz: "Avant tout, pas trop de zèle."

General Kleist, who in addition to his above-mentioned qualities, was a noble-minded and good-natured man, knew very little of me, as we had had no official connexion since 1806, when he was reporting aide-de-camp to the King. He had great knowledge of business, and dexterity in the management of complicated affairs; but he was often deficient in the composure necessary for the inquiries which ought to precede decisions. He rendered justice to

Field-Marshal Blücher as a soldier, but he did not like his company. The man of fine manners was displeased with the Field-Marshal's coarse and often rude outside, and his indecorous way of talking, which constantly embarrassed him, and often made him blush.

General Gneisenau he found too unpolished and dogmatical for intercourse, as a younger general. With these opinions, he kept the Field-Marshal's whole head-quarters at a distance; and I, who mixed with them without expressing any opinions, was one of those he wished to avoid. My appointment therefore, as head of his staff, was not agreeable to him, as his reserve clearly indicated. I went on simply performing my duties. When he saw that I did not smoke, nor play,—that I did not like equivocal speeches,—that I was not dogmatical but obedient, he drew nearer to me, and to the end of his life esteemed me not unworthy of his friendship. The successful negotiation with Frimont constituted the beginning of this new epoch, in which he gave me his full confidence in all affairs relating to the service.

On his arrival at Aix-la-Chapelle, General Kleist felt still less disposed than he had been in Paris to take part in the civil administration. President Sack had the reputation of being an honourable, but coarse and arrogant man. He maintained this reputation at Aix-la-Chapelle; he gave moreover full swing to his nepotism, and shewed little talent for the higher order of administration. Kleist, who had, in addition to the Prussian corps d'armée, the Saxon and Hessian contingents under his orders, was fully occupied with this command. He had received instructions, sanctioned by the

Sovereigns, to dispose of his different corps d'armée, in accordance with which one of the corps might be transferred to Marburg and its environs, on condition of its remaining in marching order. This seemed a hint to send the Hessian troops there, as it would be much easier to provide for their subsistence in their own country. The Elector had given the command of this contingent—a corps of 12,000 or 14,000 men, raised in 1814—to his son, the Electoral Prince, who blockaded, and afterwards garrisoned Luxemburg with them.

General Kleist directed His Highness the Electoral Prince to march to Marburg and take up his quarters there; and in informing him of the conditions annexed, he explained that his reason for assigning this position to this corps in particular, was to facilitate their maintenance, and relieve the inhabitants from the burden of quartering strangers.

The Elector did not receive General Kleist's attention in the right sense; he removed the command from his son, placed the corps on a peace footing, and dispersed it. The expostulations of the Electoral Prince were fruitless, so he gave notice of the proceeding to General Kleist, who took the whole thing much to heart. In his good nature, he was on the point of writing to the Elector, and exposing himself to the greatest rudeness. My remark, that he had nothing to do with the Elector, who must be treated with diplomatically, for which he had no authority, brought everything right at last.

The Saxon corps quartered in Coblentz was ordered to Marburg in place of the Hessian corps; as it was necessary, in obedience to the instructions, that one corps should be placed there; and a Prussian staff-officer was sent to Cassel to arrange

with the Ministry about quarters and subsistence.
The Elector would not believe the intelligence; he
sent for the staff-officer, and tried to produce an
effect upon him by announcing himself a Prussian General, who had already filled that dignity
when General Kleist was hardly a major. He asserted that it belonged to the rights of sovereignty
that troops in their own country should receive
orders from no one but their sovereign. When, however, it turned out that the staff-officer had no
authority to prevent what the Elector had, in his
anger, called an execution,—when he learnt from
him that General Kleist only followed higher orders,
and that the question whether his Highness had
power to withdraw at pleasure from the alliance
and disband his troops could only be decided by
the same Sovereigns who had so lately rendered him
such service in replacing him on the throne,—then
the old gentleman began to perceive that he had
been over-hasty, and that he had entangled himself
in a bad business. His propensity to excessive par-
simony had induced him, against the advice of his
ministers, to take the hasty and impolitic step of
dismissing his troops; a step, moreover, which could
not be justified after the diplomatic communications
he had received from Paris.

Before the Saxon corps (after the Elector had
retrieved his blunder) could march back to Coblentz
from their quarters in Hesse, another event occurred
which subsequently led to important results, and
must therefore be mentioned here.

After the battle of Leipsic, the King of Saxony
had been brought prisoner to Friedrichsfelde, and it
was evident that a political change must take place
in Saxony. The partisans of the King of Saxony,

seeing the clemency of the Sovereigns, believed that they could render this change unimportant, if they laid before the Congress of Vienna petitions from the faithful Saxon subjects, praying for the restoration of their king. One part of the plan was to procure similar petitions also from the troops, and from the corps of officers by regiments.

The time of the cantonment in Hesse was employed in obtaining these addresses, by emissaries who travelled from place to place, and worked upon all the officers individually. This affair, so mysteriously carried on, came to the knowledge of General Thielmann, who commanded the corps as Russian Lieutenant-General; he collected all the addresses, and sent them to General Kleist, for him to decide further about them. These addresses were very peculiar, mystical, and diplomatic, and so composed that they could not, when dispatched to Vienna, be treated of as an innocent matter.

General Kleist sent me to Coblentz to speak to all the officers individually on the subject. I said to them that they had served their King with devotion until the battle of Leipzic: that in this battle, however, the Saxon army had come over to us, and renounced their King's policy and their obedience to him. But their acting thus was the cause of their country being treated as an ally and not as an enemy. Now, instead of waiting quietly for a decision about Saxony, the corps of officers had stepped forward; and, supported by political grounds, desired the restoration of the King, whom ten months before they had abandoned on account of his political tendencies. This, to say the least, seemed inconsistent. The Sovereigns had called upon the Saxon army, as Germans, to assist them in the war against Napoleon:

they had obeyed the call: they had left the King, who would not co-operate; and by so doing imposed on the Sovereigns the duty of caring for their future and that of Saxony;—but now they wished to leave us again, and throw themselves into the arms of their captive King. What did this mean?

I soon discovered (as is always the case in secret unions) that this mysterious affair of the addresses had produced the most confused notions, out of which these persons could not extricate themselves. Those who remained consistent were so overawed that no one ventured to speak out plainly: it was as if a dagger threatened them, if they did not declare themselves for the King's restoration.

Eight months later, when the option was given them, one-half of these officers entered the Prussian service. This remark will suffice to show how the addresses originated.

Amongst the inhabitants of the left bank of the Rhine we found a kind of stolid indifference prevailing towards Germany, her language and customs. All interests had turned to France: commercial relations were almost wholly broken off with Germany: the line of custom-houses on the Rhine, and the difficulties of crossing that river, contributed to this result. Between Mainz and Wesel there were no pontoon bridges. The French Government had carefully separated the province from Germany, in order to transform it more surely and quickly into French departments. The officials, as well as those who aspired to become such, acquired the French language and customs; it was therefore no wonder that everything, from fashion down to domestic habits, was brought from Paris.

In this state of things the German language was

almost forgotten. In 1814 we met with few natives on the left bank of the Rhine who could write or speak German correctly. With German works, however important, which had appeared since the war of the Revolution, no one was acquainted. Such were the fruits of French possession after hardly twenty years' rule. Ten years more, and the German character would have perished *for ever*.

After the removal of the troops had been arranged, and their subsistence secured, and when consequently there remained no regular work for the staff and engineer corps to do with the troops, I directed the engineer officers to sketch a system of fortification against France, from Mainz to Nimeguen; and I commissioned the staff to reconnoitre the districts still unknown to us, on the left bank of the Rhine, whose fate was to be decided in the Congress of Vienna.

On the Rhine we had garrisoned the fortresses of Mainz and Wesel. Coblentz, with Ehrenbreitstein, lay in ruins, and Düsseldorf was razed. Cologne had walls and ditches, but was untenable. Wesel and Düsseldorf, being situated on the right bank, were properly French; and Cologne, Coblentz, and Mainz, being situated on the left bank, German points of defence. Napoleon had formerly spent much money on the fortification of Juliers; when however he acquired Wesel, he allowed Juliers to go to ruins. Making the Rhine the basis against France, Juliers stood on the second line, Luxemburg and Saar Louis on the first.

The distance between the first and second lines was great; if, therefore, we decided on fortifying Cologne, a junction road from thence crossing through the Eifel—and if we settled to fortify Coblentz and

Namur, a connecting road between the two latter fortresses—would be most convenient and desirable.

At the spot where the two new roads through the Eifel would cross each other, I projected building a fortress with great spaces for magazines.

Ehrenbreitstein had been blown up carelessly by the French officers: here, as everywhere, they used half the powder furnished for blowing it up, and sold the other half for their own profit. I ordered the old fortifications to be examined: they were still in a good state of preservation.

I now decided on fortifying Coblentz and restoring Ehrenbreitstein; also on fortifying Cologne with the fortress in the Eifel. Drawings and plans were made, and I sent them all to Vienna.

The Würtemberg general, Vahrenbühler, had designed and sent to Vienna a plan for the defence of South Germany against France, from the confines of Switzerland to Mainz. Thus the members of Congress were in possession of full information about the strength or weakness of the German frontiers towards France, even before the countries on the confines had been apportioned.

The ordinary daily duties of the General Staff had grown somewhat lax during the three last campaigns; this I endeavoured to remedy; with this object I made the young officers take to surveying during the summer; and I established a drawing-class for the winter, and directed reconnoissances. This was very useful to us: when Napoleon re-appeared in France in March, 1815, and we were again obliged to march against him, many of these officers were then fit to be employed on Staff duty.

The Congress of Vienna was protracted to a most

unpleasant length. The negotiations about the partition of Saxony in particular were becoming very disagreeable, and it behoved Prussia to show the utmost composure and moderation in this affair. All who had an opportunity of observing the behaviour of the Prussians in Vienna, testify that they hit the right medium.

I had myself undertaken to report to the General in command, upon every point relative to the Saxon army. When the line of division was determined, lists were made out, indicating which soldiers of the corps remained to the kingdom of Saxony, and which had their home in the portion transferred to Prussia. The apportionment of non-commissioned officers and soldiers was to be made accordingly. With respect to officers, the King of Prussia had declared his readiness to receive into his service every Saxon officer who expressed the wish to enter it; and he made this offer, in order that those officers who might be under the necessity of leaving the army on the return of the King, should find positions in the Prussian army, no matter in which of the two divisions of Saxony they were born.

It was assumed, in publishing this measure, that the Saxon corps would remain together till the King of Saxony should have signed his peace, and released from their oaths that portion of his army which, according to the treaty, was to leave him.

Many of the superior and subaltern officers of the Saxon army announced to me their intention to enter the Prussian service, requesting me at the same time to keep this secret, that they might not come into any unpleasant collision with the *exaltés* of the Saxon party; others, still more anxious and cautious, begged to be excused declaring any intention until the King had released them, and the division had actually taken place. These wishes seemed to me and my Commanding General quite fair, and they were stated to be so in the reports. We then quietly waited for the King of Saxony to perform his part.

When, however, Napoleon re-appeared on the stage, everything took a different form. Unacquainted with what was then going on at Vienna, I limited my attention to what occurred in the Saxon contingent, in which there existed a Saxon and a Prussian party, whereof the first was active and blustering, the latter, on the contrary, quietly expectant.

The former kept up a correspondence with the King's suite, and received their definite instructions from them. My position as reporter made it not difficult for me to discover what opinions were entertained by those around the King, who, removed from his country and the affairs of government, was living in captivity. According to their views, the division of the country was a great misfortune and a crying injustice. They thought they might reckon on Austria's opposition, and on Napoleon's assistance, if fortunately he succeeded in re-establishing himself on his throne. They therefore recommended the keeping up a good Saxon spirit, as the King would contrive to protract everything, and would certainly sign no renunciation so long as there was any hope left of Napoleon's star remaining above the horizon. The Saxon troops had only to remain constant, and to resist a division with energy.

This was the state of affairs when, in 1815, Field-Marshal Blücher, with General Count von Gneisenau, joined the army and undertook the command. The Saxon troops, who had been tampered with, began to be very uneasy.

To avoid the appearance of misgiving, the Field-Marshal concentrated the whole Saxon corps around Liège, and placed four battalions of them in the town, where he had taken up his head-quarters, without having a man of the Prussian troops with him. Had the news arrived here that the king of Saxony had absolved them from their oaths, the division would have proceeded quietly; but when intelligence came from Vienna that this act was being constantly postponed, and could not be obtained from the King, orders were given to proceed with the division forthwith.

It was indeed high time to put an end to this state of uncertainty, for we were very near the outbreak of the war; but the execution of this order involved great difficulties: the non-commissioned officers and privates could easily be separated, as nearly one-half of the whole corps belonged to the Prussian portion; but then came the question, who should command these unorganized troops, since the officers could not yet declare themselves definitively?

The Field-Marshal assembled the Saxon Generals, to advise with them, and to bring about an arrangement as gently as possible; but before this could be accomplished, the fact that the division was to proceed without the consent of the King became known, and this appeared to the leaders of the old Saxon party the right moment for resistance.

The battalion of Guards—already prepared for this step—came *en masse*, without officers, in front of the Field-Marshal's dwelling, shouting a *Viva!* to the King of Saxony. Some Saxon officers, however, persuaded the unarmed soldiery to return to their quarters. The Field-Marshal made the battalion march out instantly, and assigned them quarters in Namur, in the midst of the 2nd Prussian corps d'armée.

Some hours later, however, the three other battalions made their appearance before the Field-Marshal's house, with loud cries, and armed with sabres, so that the house-door had to be instantly locked; the windows of the house, and especially of the room in which the Field-Marshal was, were smashed with stones.

I was aware that the house had a second outlet into another street. By this way I got out, and hastening with some staff officers to the nearest main-guard, I summoned the Saxon officer on guard to follow me to restore order, which he did. The rioters gave way for a moment, but encouraged each other again by wild shouts, and with drawn sabres drove the guard farther and farther back. All exhortations were useless, for the loud roar of voices allowed no one to hear his own words. I attempted, with some Prussian officers, to keep back the foremost, but they attacked us with sabre cuts, one of which would have seriously wounded me, had it not been intercepted by my epaulette. One may imagine from this, what danger threatened the Field-Marshal had the rioters got at him.

I drew the guard back into the house, caused the door to be bolted, and conducted the Field-Marshal out through the back door, where our horses stood ready; his suite rode with him quietly out of the town.

Some days before this occurrence, the Field-Marshal had appointed a rendezvous with the Duke of

Wellington for the following morning, half-way between Liège and Brussels.

When we returned from thence, the Prussian troops, who had been ordered into the town, were already arrived. The three Saxon battalions had renounced obedience to their officers, and driven them from the front; then, under leaders chosen from amongst themselves, they marched off, with loud shouts of, " After the Guard!"

Next day, it came out that these battalions had taken up their quarters in villages in the direction of Hannut. They were surrounded by Prussian troops and disarmed, as well as the battalion of Guards in Namur.

I had learnt from several of the officers who had been driven away by the mutinous soldiery, that the latter had been led on by only a few well-known scamps. I desired the list to be given to me: it was handed in from three different quarters, with seven names, the same on each list. The Field-Marshal, and Generals Count Gneisenau and Grolmann, voted for the decimation of these battalions. This measure seemed to me too harsh, as perhaps in this way not a single seducer, but only the seduced, might be caught. Instead of all this bloodshed, I proposed to burn the standard publicly which had been dishonoured by mutiny, and to call upon the battalions to give up their ringleaders on pain of decimation: the Field-Marshal consented to my proposal. The three battalions gave up seven ringleaders, who were immediately disarmed, and shot in front of the mutineers: six of these were on the lists I had received. We had therefore the comfort of a double assurance that no innocent person had been punished.

The remaining portion of the Saxon army had

kept quite clear of the mutiny, and awaited submissively the settlement of the partition.

The Field-Marshal transferred his head-quarters to Namur; and it was here that, in answer to my petition to the King to place me in the line for this campaign, I was informed that my wish would be gratified later, but that for the present I must proceed to the English head-quarters, to keep up the connexion between the Duke of Wellington and Field-Marshal Blücher.

Little as this appointment accorded with my wishes, and slight as were my expectations of being able to render important services in this post, I readily obeyed, although in my early studies of the English language I had not got beyond the " Vicar of Wakefield" and " Thomson's Seasons."

On my departure General von Gneisenau warned me to be much on my guard with the Duke of Wellington, for that by his relations with India, and his transactions with the deceitful Nabobs, this distinguished general had so accustomed himself to duplicity, that he had at last become such a master in the art as even to outwit the Nabobs themselves.

In Brussels I relieved General von Roeder, who thanked Heaven that he was about to leave these head-quarters, where he felt annoyed by daily causes of offence. But in fact his irritability carried him too far. Now one Englishman entered his room with his hat on; another, not understanding him, would answer him by a prolonged " Eh ?" and then, again, proper regard was not paid to his rank. I made him tell me everything circumstantially; and this was of great use to me, clearly showing how unfair it is for any one in the midst of a foreign nation to frame his expectations on the ideas he brings with him, instead of studying the habits and customs of those around him.

My endeavour to stand well with the Duke of Wellington and the officers of the English army was not unsuccessful. I was favoured by the circumstance of their knowing, that since the opening of the war in 1813, I had served on the general staff of Field-Marshal Blücher. This procured me a friendly reception, as the Field-Marshal was in high repute with the whole English army. It is not of rare occurrence that officers of foreign Powers placed near the Generals in Command are the chief intriguers at head-quarters. Against any such suspicion I was protected by my position. In the part assigned to me, namely, to maintain the union between Wellington and Blücher, it was quite natural that I should endeavour to facilitate everything as much as possible to the Duke, in his arrangements with Blücher, for the harmony and vigorous conduct of the army. The Duke soon perceived that, on every point discussed on such occasions, I told him the simple truth, whether it concerned the Prussian army or the relations between the two, and that he could meet me with perfect confidence.

On the other hand, I perceived that the Duke exercised far greater power in the army he commanded than Prince Blücher in the one committed to his care. The rules of the English service permitted the Duke's suspending any officer and sending him back to England. The Duke had used this power during the war in Spain, when disobedience showed itself amongst the higher officers. Sir Robert Wilson was an instance of this.

Amongst all the generals, from the leaders of corps to the commanders of brigades, not one was to be found in the active army who had been known as refractory.

It was not the custom in this army to criticise or control the Commander-in-Chief. Discipline was strictly enforced; every one knew his rights and his duties. The Duke, in matters of service, was very short and decided. He allowed questions, but dismissed all such as were unnecessary. His detractors have accused him of being inclined to encroach on the functions of others,—a charge which is at variance with my experience.

His Military Secretary and Quarter-master-General were tried men; his aides-de-camp and *galopins* were young men of the best families in England, who thought it an honour to devote to their country and its greatest commander, all the energies of their will and intellect. Mounting the best horses of England's famous breed, they made a point of honour, whenever the Duke added " Quick !" to a message, of riding three German miles in the hour, or one mile * in eighteen minutes.

From the questions the Duke put to me, I gathered that he wanted to know how far he might with certainty reckon on the co-operation of Prince Blücher.

The Duke had sent off Colonel Hardinge† to Blücher's head-quarters: he was a man who recommended himself as an officer and a diplomatist by estimable qualities and most agreeable manners. I was of course wholly ignorant in what light this colonel viewed his position at the Prussian head-quarters, and what instructions he had received on the subject from the Duke; but in all our conferences I met him

* Four English.—Ed.

† Governor-General of the East Indies from 1845 to 1848.

with perfect frankness, and soon observed that he had
received very good information from his predecessor
in the campaign of 1814 (Sir Hudson Lowe) about
the characters of the individuals at head-quarters.
He was acquainted with the peculiarities of Generals
Gneisenau and Grolmann, with whom he had chiefly
to deal. He had no apprehension on the score of
differences with respect to the principles of the art of
war, as Wellington quite agreed with them on that
head, but he feared the frequent outbreaks of their
warmth of temper. Everything went to prove that
he wished nothing more earnestly than to maintain
the utmost harmony between Blücher and his own
chief Wellington, whom he so highly valued. It was
of course at the Duke's option to transmit his questions, answers, and propositions to the Prince through
me, or through Hardinge; meanwhile, I was furnished
with far better means for the purpose than Hardinge
was. I had four aides-de-camp, with bureau and
orderlies; I had as many field Jägers and letter-car-
riers* and as many mounted officers as I required at
my disposal; and in my place of Quartermaster-general of the Prussian army, at Blücher's head-quarters,
General Grolmann was my deputy. It was therefore
to be expected that the Duke would choose me as
a mediator; still this did very little towards pro-
moting unity of operations in a combined army of
more than 200,000 men. The Duke was accustomed
to direct *alone* all the strategical operations of his
army; and in defensive battles to indicate from his
central point of observation the moment for assuming
the offensive. In this manner affairs had been conducted in Spain, when the Duke was generalissimo of

* Post-offices were always established in time of war at each
corps of the army.—Ed.

the English, Spanish, and Portuguese armies; and yet he had learnt from experience that the Spaniards obeyed him only just as far as they thought fit, never caring whether the English and Portuguese, who did obey orders, were exposed by such conduct to the danger of complete discomfiture.

The Duke, more than any one in Europe, had reason to know the value of a command which, proceeding from one master-mind, directs great operations and battles. He was necessarily sensible that the manner of conducting business to which he had become accustomed could not now be continued. In talking over his Spanish campaigns and the years 1813 and 1814, I found opportunities for convincing the Duke that I considered any continued success *impossible* for an allied army without unity in the measures concerted. In our numerous official conferences upon our equipments, subsistence by requisition, encampments without tents, &c., for the purpose of fixing the limits of the circle from whence both armies must draw their means of subsistence, I purposely introduced remarks on the strong points of our army, without concealing the weak ones, or passing over the valuable qualities of the English army.

" Our infantry does not possess," I told him, " the same bodily strength or powers of endurance as yours. The greater mass of our troops are too young and inexperienced: we cannot reckon on their obstinately continuing a fight from morning to evening. We must seek our strength not in defensive operations only, but in a simultaneous, bloody, but not long-continued offensive one; attacking late in the evening, so that the fight is hottest at the close of day. To economize their strength is a thing quite unknown to our men. Led by our officers, they expend in *one* hour what might have taken four to consume. By so doing they compel their opponents to make unusual exertions, and just at a time when night prevents heroic deeds and well-performed duties from being properly admired. If they succeed in the evening in penetrating at some point, so that the enemy is forced to concentrate, retreating, then the powers of our army come out in their most brilliant light—their opponent is lost.

" You may depend upon this : when the Prince has agreed to any operation in common, he will keep his word, should even the whole Prussian army be annihilated in the act; but do not expect from us *more* than we are able to perform; we will always assist you as far as we *can;* the Prince will be perfectly satisfied if you do the same."

I was not surprised that the Duke held his peace on these delicate matters. In his place I should have done the same, and quietly awaited the proposition already announced, to concert what should be done in case the enemy did not attack us in the Netherlands, but turned his force against the Grand Army ; and where we should give him battle, if he passed the confines of the Netherlands.

I had as usual prepared these different cases officially, and in German for Field-Marshal Blücher, and obtained his assent and promise to act according to my proposals, if the Duke expressed himself to the same effect. The Duke, with map in hand, followed my verbal statement in French ; he found my propositions quite consonant to his own principles, and assented to everything.

I was perfectly satisfied with this mode of proceeding in all cases, where there was sufficient time to procure the assent of both parties ; when, however, there was danger in delay, this mode would not suffice: unity in the conduct of the army could only be attained, by my being certain that I was the only mediator between the Prussian army and the English General-in-Chief, and by my having full power to make and receive, whenever necessary, propositions in the name of Prince Blücher. General Gneisenau, to whom I expressed these views, knew that I would derogate nothing from the dignity of the Prussian leader, and that I would as little give occasion to the reproach that more might have been done on our part; he acquiesced in my views, and the Prince granted me the necessary authority. This answered to the position conferred on me by the King; and there was therefore nothing else required but to send the necessary instructions to the superior Prussian Generals to obey my summons. The Prince was obliged to leave all the rest to my tact and responsibility, which I had not the remotest intention of throwing off.

In taking this step all was done that could be done to ensure unity in the impending operations and battles; and as about this time I already became better acquainted with the internal relations of the English army, I felt a strong conviction that, if fortune so far favoured us in a battle, that the English army could act on the defensive while the Prussians acted simultaneously on the offensive, we should obtain a brilliant victory over Napoleon.

The Duke of Wellington communicated to me verbally all I wanted to know; and as this included all his secret intelligence from Paris, I considered these communications confidential, and observed strict silence on the subject of them with all the military envoys at head-quarters; amongst these the Russian general Pozzo di Borgo held the most important place, as the Duke seemed to value his diplomatic views, which he tried to turn to good account.

After this statement of the course of affairs as they gradually got into form, we will now pursue the chain of events.

Field-Marshal Blücher inherited from his predecessor in command, General von Kleist, troublesome difficulties in his relations with the authorities of the Netherlands.

When the news of Napoleon's return reached the Hague, the King of the Netherlands, pressed by circumstances, called upon General von Kleist to advance with the Prussian army as far as the Meuse. General von Kleist replied, that, with the best will, he could not obey this summons, as the subsistence of the Prussian troops was not ensured beyond the limits of the Government of the Lower Rhine, and he had no money at his disposal, to live on the Meuse by purchases, neither could he draw supplies from magazines.

The King, who was anxious that all difficulties should be removed as speedily as possible, undertook to provide subsistence, and to settle accounts ultimately with the Prussian Government. Thereupon General von Kleist, yielding to the wishes of the King of the Netherlands, advanced to the Meuse ; when, however, the English troops landed in considerable numbers, and arrived to cover Brussels,— which made it doubtful whether Napoleon would turn against the Netherlands or against the Grand Army collecting on the Upper Rhine,—the Dutch Cabinet grew desirous of shaking off the expenses of providing this subsistence ; and Field-Marshal Blücher received notice to withdraw the troops

again into the Prussian provinces on the Lower
Rhine, or to pay for all he wanted with ready
money, as the English did.   The latter was not
possible, and the first step was no longer the affair
of the Prussian army, but had become the general
concern of the Allies.

The Duke of Wellington had previously expressed
the wish that, if Napoleon advanced against the
Netherlands, the two armies, Prussian and English,
might be opposed to him in such a manner that
Brussels should not fall into his hands unless he
first gained a battle.   This was consonant to the
interest of all parties, and the Field-Marshal had
accordingly advanced to the Sambre, and as far as
Namur.

I calculated, according both to time and distance,
that in case the Field-Marshal was obliged to retire
as far as Aix-la-Chapelle, this junction of the two
armies between the French confines and Brussels
must be given up, and that it could only take place
in the line from Brussels to Liège.   But then the
line of retreat of the English army on Antwerp, as
well as that of the Prussian army towards the
Rhine, would form very acute angles with the basis,
if indeed they were still practicable.

The Duke of Wellington found my calculations,
with their results, correct, and became the mediator
with the King of the Netherlands, who reconciled
himself to the necessity of continuing to furnish in
advance supplies for the Prussian army.

The Duke learned through me that the espionage
of Prince Blücher was badly organized, while he
believed himself to be very secure on this point, and
expected to hear immediately from Paris everything
indicating a march against the Netherlands.   Rely-

ing on this assurance, the movements of the combined Anglo-Dutch-Hanoverian army were arranged,
and the hours calculated, from the moment the cavalry
orderlies were dispatched from Brussels, to the time
which the army would take to assemble at one or
other of the three places of rendezvous.

The calculations themselves were not known to
me ; but, as was ultimately seen, they were made on
the assumption that the orders for assembling the
troops could be transmitted at the rate at which they
could be delivered by day, but not by night. This
mistake occurs too often in calculations. In dark
nights orderlies cannot ride fast on cross roads ; in
the various cantonments they find every one sunk
in deep slumber; and delay in arriving at the rendezvous is the inevitable consequence of a calculation
grounded on the time it will take to execute an order
by day, and not by night.

As it was probable that Napoleon had in view an
attack on the Netherlands, I had taken such measures
that I must hear of any attack on the Prussian army
in the shortest possible time.

As early as the 14th of June, I heard, through
General von Zieten at Charleroi, that the whole
French army was concentrating in front of his advanced posts, and that their attack would probably
be directed against him.

The Duke of Wellington, who usually received
daily accounts from Paris (from whence till now the
diligences went unimpeded to Brussels), had heard
nothing from Paris when I communicated to him the
news from General von Zieten; for the diligences had
not been allowed to cross the frontier, and his spies
had not yet found means of getting to him by cross
roads. It seemed improbable to him that the entire

French army should advance by Charleroi; he expected, in particular, that one column would show itself on the great chaussée to Brussels by Mons, where his advanced posts stood.

It was natural to assume that Napoleon knew where the cantonments of the two armies came in contact; and the nature of circumstances certainly led to the belief that Napoleon would send forward a strong advanced guard in two columns, one of which would come in contact with the right wing of Field-Marshal Blücher, and the other with the Duke of Wellington's left, and thus break the weak line of connection between the two; while he reserved to himself the option of falling on one or other of the two armies.

———

The military measures adopted by General Kleist, in consequence of Napoleon's landing in France, have been hitherto passed over, in order to record them here in uninterrupted connection, as forming the introduction to the campaign of 1815.

When the news of Napoleon's landing reached head-quarters at Aix-la-Chapelle, the General commanding the Army of the Rhine had to ask himself: Will the French nation remain faithful to Louis XVIII., or go over to Napoleon? The latter course was to be expected from the French army.

The skeletons of an army of 100,000 men collected on the Rhine were the main forces available against France within the confines of Germany. The English in Belgium, and the South Germans, together with the Austrians, were very weak. General Kleist was without instructions for such a case. As, however, it was quite evident that decided measures must be taken as speedily as possible, he was ready to execute them at once, on his own responsibility.

In order to solve the question above stated, of such importance to Kleist, I dispatched Von Gerlach, my aide-de-camp, who was best fitted for the purpose, to Paris, with instructions to bring back a positive answer. Gerlach waited for Napoleon's entrance into Paris, and brought back intelligence that every one received him with open arms, and desired the recovery of the left bank of the Rhine. On receipt of this news, Kleist caused Juliers and Wesel to be prepared for defence, Cologne and Coblentz to be made storm-proof, a bridge of hired vessels to be constructed between Cologne and Deutz, magazines established, a police introduced to watch foreigners, &c., &c.

The King of the Netherlands dispatched an aide-de-camp to Kleist, to summons him to his assistance, in case Napoleon made an aggression on the Netherlands; and to give battle, in concert with his son the Prince of Orange, who commanded the Anglo-Dutch army in Belgium. It was in itself a doubtful proceeding to bring the Army of the Rhine (which was still but the framework of an army whose basis was the Rhenish provinces) to the other side of the Meuse, and to make it dependent as an auxiliary force, without further stipulations; and to this must be added, that Belgium, for so many years French in language, customs, and habits, was Dutch only by constraint; moreover, that the troops given up to her at the peace of 1814, clung as old comrades to the Emperor Napoleon, and still wore his uniform with the Dutch cockade. Nevertheless Kleist could not refuse; he was even obliged to make a show of good-will to the Allied Sovereign.

In the conferences held for this object between myself and Sir Hudson Lowe, Chief of the Staff to the Prince of Orange, I laid before my brave friend and colleague a map of Belgium, on which was drawn a broad red line from Marchienne on the Sambre, along the Dyle by Wavre, to Louvain. " Here you have"—so I deduced with German pedantry from the subject and object given—" the strategical line of demarcation prescribed by nature —a westerly, or English—an easterly, or Prussian department." My object was gained. We did not get a step farther ; and on Wellington's arrival, all was recorded in the minutes.

The troops of the Army of the Rhine turned out in good state from their winter-quarters—the recruits well drilled, all well fed, healthy, well clothed, in the best state of discipline, and eager for war. The troops recently placed on Prussian footing were all in the same condition, i, e., the free corps transformed into battalions of the line, the Russo-German Legion the regiments of the Grand Duchy of Berg, and the still unapportioned Saxons.

The Landwehr ordered to join, rapidly arrived. The higher places, from commanders of brigades up-- wards, were filled up at Vienna.

When the Congress of Vienna concluded on the unavoidable necessity of re-invading France, which had revolted to Napoleon, with the armies of Europe —an operation in which England also could this time take an important part—it was considered advisable on the part of Prussia to get an army of 100,000 men in readiness, whereof three corps d'armée, or 75,000 men, could march upon Paris, and 25,000 remain, as a fourth corps in reserve, in the newly- acquired Rhenish provinces. The commands in the new army to be formed had to be distributed; and in doing this advantage ought to be taken of the experience of the years 1813 and 1814. But here great difficulties occurred. It was no secret to Europe that old Prince Blücher, who had passed his 70th year, understood nothing whatever of the conduct of a war; so little, indeed, that when a plan was submitted to him for approval, even relating to some unimportant operation, he could not form any clear idea of it, or judge whether it were good or bad. This circumstance made it necessary that some one should be placed at his side, in whom he had confidence, and who possessed inclination and skill to employ it for the general weal. Gneisenau had proved himself to be such a man during two campaigns; and since it was by these very campaigns that Blücher had gained his European renown, there was no reason for not entrusting him with the command of the Prussian army precisely as in the two past years.

But the more it became known that Gneisenau really commanded the army, and that Blücher merely acted as an example as the bravest in battle and the most indefatigable in exertion, understanding only to stimulate others by fiery speeches, the louder became the discontent of four generals who had commanded armies in 1814, and were senior in commission to Gneisenau.

Count Tauentzien had taken Wittenberg by storm, York had gained a victory at Wartenburg, Bülow at Dennewitz, Kleist at Culm: they had a European fame, they were known as brave and irreproachable officers; such men as these must not be offended. We shall not investigate here how far they had reason to feel hurt; suffice it to say that they

Q

did so, and they had the voice of the whole army with them,—in considering "it a point of honour not to allow themselves to be put under the command of a junior in commission." The same notion prevails in all armies where promotion by seniority is the rule.

It is necessary also to mention here, that since the years 1811 and 1812, a mutual dislike had existed between these generals and Gneisenau, in which Generals von dem Knesebeck, and Borstell, with most of the superior officers, participated. Gneisenau, Boyen, Grolmann, were noted as the most active members of the Tugendbund, who were accused of very anti-royal tendencies.

Gneisenau, who thoroughly knew his antagonists, had adopted the system of opposing them openly and with great energy. If the service brought them in contact, he was cold and reserved; and he manifested a determination to be repulsive, which was indeed richly returned to him.

All this was known in Vienna. The Minister of War, who had to submit the propositions to the King, was Gneisenau's intimate friend, but he had adopted another system for securing influence. He met his opponents with the utmost candour, and succeeded in making many believe that they enjoyed his confidence.

The King, who disliked abrupt manners, entertained the opinion, that Boyen was devoted to his person and to his views upon the affairs of the state and army; by which means he and his friends, Gneisenau and Grolmann, gained great influence, although in consequence of the position they had assumed, his Majesty had an aversion to these friends, which he let them feel.

He knew Blücher well, and considered him, in 1815, indispensable in his position of Field-Marshal to the Prussian army. Under these circumstances, and after all the services Gneisenau had rendered, it was equally impossible to exclude him from the position of Chief of the General Staff, which he had already filled during two campaigns. The four senior generals mentioned above could not refuse to serve under Blücher; and there was an end of the difficulty, when the King decided that :—

In case circumstances rendered it necessary to name a substitute to the Field-Marshal, the senior of the leaders of corps should be appointed. In Blücher's case, at his advanced age, this might easily and frequently occur; and with the system which Gneisenau had so consistently developed, it was easy to foresee in such a case incredible confusion in the supreme command.

It was therefore resolved, to place the three first corps under the orders of Zieten, Borstell and Thielmann (all three junior to Gneisenau), and the fourth (intended as a reserve corps in the Rhenish provinces, and not expected to be brought into action) under Bülow. Tauentzien, York, and Kleist, obtained other honourable appointments, which if they did not quite satisfy them, could give no occasion for complaint.

Generals Count Tauentzien and York remained as commandants in the interior of the country (in the old provinces); General Kleist von Nollendorf received the supreme command over the 2nd German corps d'armée assembling at Trèves.

But before the war broke out, the revolt of the Saxons at Liège gave rise to refractory conduct on the part of Von Borstell, the General in Command of

the second corps, who had his head-quarters at Namur.
He received there the order to disarm the Saxon
battalion of Guards, who had mutinied at Liège, and
to burn their standard publicly.

General von Borstell, taking quite a one-sided
view of his charge, made long speeches, in which he
reprimanded the mutineers, but ended by forgiving
them all; he reported this to the Field-Marshal at
Liège, who had already proclaimed the measure he
had ordered, as full satisfaction for all the Saxons
who had remained faithful.

The Prince restrained his anger at this disobedience; and, in answer to his report, sent General von
Borstell the strictest orders to assemble the battalion,
disarm it, and burn the standard. General von
Borstell wrote back in reply, that it was against his
conscience and responsibility to the King to execute
this order. The Prince thereupon suspended him
from his command, and conferred it in the interim
on the senior general of the corps, General von Pirch
II., to whom he likewise gave the charge of burning
the standard; the Prince then informed the King of
the occurrence. General von Borstell was condemned
by court-martial to imprisonment in a fortress, and
General von Pirch retained the command of the
second corps.

Outbreak of hostilities, on the 15th of June.

When General von Zieten was attacked before
Charleroi on the 15th of June, an event which
opened the war, he dispatched an officer to me, who
arrived at Brussels at three o'clock.

The Duke of Wellington, to whom I immediately
communicated the news, had received no intelligence
from the advanced posts at Mons. I put the question

to him, *Whether* and *where* he would concentrate his army, as in consequence of this news, Field-Marshal Blücher would concentrate his forces at Ligny, if he had not already taken up this position.

The Duke replied: " If all is as General von Zieten supposes, I will concentrate on my left wing, *i.e.*, the corps of the Prince of Orange ; I shall then be *à portée* to fight in conjunction with the Prussian army. Should, however, a portion of the enemy's forces come by Mons, I must concentrate more towards my centre. For this reason I must positively wait for news from Mons before I fix the rendezvous. Since, however, the departure of the troops is *certain*, and only the place of rendezvous remains *uncertain*, I will order all to be readiness, including the Brunswick corps in reserve, and will direct a brigade of light cavalry to march at once to Quatre Bras." Orders were accordingly dispatched about six or seven o'clock. Later in the same day intelligence of the commencement of hostilities, forwarded from Charleroi to Namur, reached me a second time from thence. The Field-Marshal informed me of his concentrating at Sombref, and charged mè to give him speedy intelligence of the concentration of Wellington's army. I immediately communicated this to the Duke, who quite acquiesced in Blücher's dispositions. However, he could not resolve on fixing his point of concentration before receiving the expected news from Mons, but he promised to give me immediate notice when this arrived. He retained his aides-de-camp and secretaries in his business-room.

I went home after ten o'clock, made out my report, having only to add in conclusion the places of rendezvous, and kept a courier in readiness at my door.

Towards midnight the Duke entered my room and said : "I have got news from Mons, from General Dörnberg, who reports that Napoleon has turned towards Charleroi with all his forces, and that there is no longer any enemy in front of him; therefore orders for the concentration of my army at Nivelles and Quatre Bras are already dispatched. The numerous friends of Napoleon who are here (as towards evening the cannonade could be distinctly heard before the gates of Brussels), will raise their heads : the well-disposed must be tranquillized ; let us therefore go, all the same, to the ball of the Duchess of Richmond ; after which, about five o'clock, we can ride off to the troops assembled at Quatre Bras."

All took place accordingly ; the Duke appeared very cheerful at the ball, where all the great people of Brussels were collected ; he remained there till three o'clock, and about five we were on horseback. We overtook the troops, and reached Quatre Bras about eleven A.M., where the enemy had placed his advanced posts opposite the troops of Perponcher's division. As the enemy remained quiet, and intelligence had meanwhile reached me that the Prussian army was assembling at Ligny, the Duke thought it best to ride over to the Field-Marshal, and concert with him by word of mouth, what measures must be taken for a decisive battle with our combined forces. This was immediately put in execution. On the way the Duke said to me : "If, as seems likely, the division of the enemy's forces posted at Frasnes, opposite Quatre Bras, is inconsiderable, and only intended to mask the English army, I can employ my whole strength in support of the Field-Marshal, and will gladly execute all his wishes in regard to joint operations."

I had a firm conviction that what the Duke expressed was his real and fixed intention; but I knew General Gneisenau's distrust of him, and was apprehensive that this might have some influence on the impending arrangements.

It was the main part of my duty, as mediator between the two Field-Marshals, to concert all the operations to be undertaken in common. These were naturally divided into offensive (a march upon Paris), and defensive (the defence of the Netherlands), in case Napoleon were able to collect sufficient forces to attack them before the Allies could advance from the Upper and Middle Rhine. In the first case it was laid down in writing that the English army should advance on the line from Antwerp, by Brussels to Mons; the Prussian army from Liège, Huy, and Namur, to Marchiennes on the Sambre; and from thence the two armies were to march by routes running parallel to each other.

The sieges of two fortresses (one by each army), were prepared in Antwerp and Wesel; the month of July was set down as the time for assuming the offensive.

If Napoleon could not attempt an attack before the middle of June, it might be assumed that the two Allied Armies would be considerably his superior in strength, or that the army he was leading against them would partially consist of rabble hastily brought together.

The Allies had no apprehension of being assailed in the valley of the Meuse; the barren wooded districts, the impracticable nature of the country, and the waste of time which an invasion from this side would entail, left Napoleon no choice. He must take the fertile plains of Belgium for his theatre of war, and the issue hung on his succeeding in beating the two Allied Armies singly.

Measures for avoiding this were recommended by all the rules of war, and the junction of the English and Prussian armies for a defensive battle, from whence they might assume the offensive, was so distinctly prescribed by circumstances and by the locality, that no doubt whatever could be raised on the point.

If the English army were posted at Gosselies with the line of connection and retreat by Brussels to Antwerp in their rear,—the Prussian army at Ligny having the Roman road to the Meuse, their line of connection and retreat, in their rear,—they would be quite unassailable in front by the Sambre. But if Napoleon were obliged to attack one of the two wings, still he would not be able to hinder the other wing, possessed of a secure line of retreat, from wheeling in front of him and cutting him off from the Sambre.

To the north of the chaussée from Sombref to Quatre Bras, consequently in the rear of this joint encampment, the Dyle runs nearly at right angles to the Sambre to Louvain, in a low, swampy country: as its first half, of five leagues, was quite impracticable for large divisions of troops with artillery, this impediment served to strengthen the strategical position of both armies.

The point of concentration for the Prussian army was accordingly marked out between Sombref and Charleroi, and for the English, *en dernier lieu*, between Gosselies and Marchiennes.

The main road of traffic between the one capital, Paris, and the other capital, Brussels, runs by Mons. It was necessary therefore to dispose the cantonments of the English army, so that they might assemble between Brussels and Mons, and at the same time be free on their left wing to unite with the Prussian army. With this view, the Duke placed the light cavalry on the frontier near Mons, the corps de bataille half way to Brussels, and the reserve in Brussels itself and its environs. Head-quarters were naturally in the capital of Belgium, the seat of the Government. The Duke has been reproached with having committed an error in the disposition of his cantonments. There is no foundation for this censure; but it is true that his army reached the rendezvous later than he intended and expected. The chief mass of his forces were posted round about Nivelles, and had he removed his head-quarters thither on the 14th of June, he would have had accounts from Mons early on the 15th; at 9 o'clock he would have heard General von Zieten's cannonade. Had the reserves moved up as far as Genappe as early as the 14th, all the different corps of the English army could have bivouacked within the triangle Frasnes, Quatre Bras, and Nivelles, on the evening of the 15th; and the entire English army would have been ready to assume the offensive at Gosselies on the morning of the 16th.

Thus Napoleon's fate depended on the trifling circumstance of the Duke's leaving Brussels on the 14th; in that case Napoleon would have fallen into the *fourches caudines* on the 16th of June.

The Duke met the Field-Marshal at the windmill of Bry. His corps d'armée had just been placed in their positions, while some officers observed Napoleon's advance from the *tombe de Ligny.* The Duke looked over the measures taken, and seemed satisfied with them. When the heads of Napoleon's attacking columns shewed themselves moving upon St. Amand, the Duke asked the Field-Marshal and General von Gneisenau : " Que voulez vous que je fasse ?" In few words I had already told the latter, that the Duke had the best intentions to support the Field-Marshal, and that he would do all they wished, provided they did not expect him to divide his army, which was contrary to his principles. As few troops had yet arrived at Quatre Bras, and the English reserve (which was directed thither) could not reach it before four in the afternoon, it seemed to me important that Wellington's troops should concentrate in front, somewhere beyond Frasnes, from thence advance in a straight line towards the Prussian right (Wagnilé), and there forming a right angle with the Prussian position, immediately encircle Napoleon's left wing. General von Gneisenau shook his head at this proposition, but I did not know what objections he had to make to it. Now, to the Duke's question, he replied, that the most desirable plan for the Prussian army would be, for the Duke, as soon as his army assembled at Quatre Bras, to march off to the left on the chaussée to Namur, and place himself at Bry in rear of the Prussian army as a reserve. This proposal was grounded on the pre-suppositions :—

1. That Wellington's army could be assembled at Quatre Bras in a few hours.

2. That the enemy would send no detachments against them, so that they could proceed in secu-

rity upon the chaussée in face of the enemy; and, lastly,

3. That the English army could arrive as a reserve to the Prussians before the battle was decided by Napoleon at Ligny.

All these suppositions however were incorrect, for,—

ad 1. How could the right wing of the English army, and its reserve cavalry (considering at what time they received the order to concentrate at Nivelles), reach Quatre Bras from Grammont before nightfall?—Wellington's march from thence to Ligny (one German mile and a quarter farther), with his *whole* army, was consequently *quite impossible* on the 16th.

ad 2. I had seen with my own eyes a division of French troops at Frasnes, but it was impossible to calculate its strength. Generally speaking, I considered the position at Quatre Bras beyond measure bad. There were two not inconsiderable woods in front, to the right and left, for whichever party could get possession of them; the horizon is bounded by the heights of Frasnes, and the tactical position in *front* of the chaussée from Quatre Bras, and *behind* or *upon* it, is equally imperfect.

ad 3. Supposing Field-Marshal Blücher could reckon on the certainty of Wellington's army being in rear of his lines at Bry, at six o'clock, as a reserve ready to advance, he imposed on himself the task of holding out for five hours against the attacks of Napoleon.

But in this case the English army must march off from Quatre Bras at four; and Gneisenau knew, *through me*, that at this hour *the reserve* could hardly have arrived there after a march of five or six

(German) miles. This proposition, therefore, was by no means favourable to the Prussian army, since it was based upon impossibilities, nor could it be accepted by the English leader, who had the Dutch troops under his orders; because, in taking a flank march to the left from Quatre Bras, he must give up the two roads leading from the enemy to Brussels, and expose the capital of Belgium, which was quite contrary to his instructions.

The Duke looked at his map, and did not answer one word. I saw how much he disliked the proposition, and therefore made the following observations :—

According to this proposition the English army must wait till the whole is assembled, in complete inactivity, at Quatre Bras, at a distance of 12,000 paces from the Prussians, without being able to render them the least assistance. If, however, the English army advances to the point where the Roman road intersects the chaussée from Quatre Bras to Charleroi (one German mile and a half), they would not then be more than 6000 paces from the Prussian right wing, and by deploying to the left, they would touch upon Field-Marshal Blücher, and have favourable ground for fighting and manœuvring. The corps of the Prince of Orange will have little farther to march to the point of intersection specified, from Nivelles than from Quatre Bras; and the right wing from Ath is even nearer the former.

In this manner I avoided publicly mentioning the Duke's erroneous calculations as to the time in which his army would be assembled, as well as Gneisenau's incorrect calculations as to the arrival of the English army at Bry; and the Duke eagerly caught at my proposal, saying, " Je culbuterai ce qu'il y a devant moi à Frasnes, me dirigéant sur Gosselies."

General Gneisenau refuted all that was said in favour of this movement by these few words : " It is too long and insecure ; the march from Quatre Bras to Bry is, on the contrary, safe and decisive." The Duke replied : " Well ! I will come, provided *I am not attacked myself.*"

On our return to Quatre Bras we found Marshal Ney fully engaged in the attack, which had begun on the farm of Germioncourt, occupied by us. The enemy, with their two corps d'armée, displayed such great superiority over Perponcher's division, that it was evidently impossible, unless some extraordinary circumstances intervened, to hold Quatre Bras ; yet from the moment the buildings at this junction of roads fell into the enemy's hands, not only would all connection with the Prussians be completely interrupted, but in like manner that with the main body, the corps de bataille of the English army, which was on its march from Braine-le-Comte to Quatre Bras, while the reserve was maching thither from Genappe. In that case no other retreat would remain to Perponcher's division but to fall back on the reserve. The Duke endeavoured to impose on his antagonist by a firm attitude, and gained so much time that Picton was able to arrive at Quatre Bras, and deploy on the road.

But even now, with his two divisions, Wellington was hardly half as strong as Marshal Ney ; and he had no expectation of being reinforced shortly, except by the Brunswick corps of about 8000 men.

In this very critical moment the Duke took a resolution worthy of a great commander : he directed his left wing to attack the village of Pernimont, already lost, and proceeded to meet Marshal Ney with all the strength he possessed.

The Marshal, who had his right wing resting on Pernimont, his centre at the farm, and his left on the wood pressed forward, *tambour battant*, in columns three deep with small intervals.

The weakness of the English Army, advancing to meet the French, was concealed from them by the tall corn ; two 9-pounder batteries effectively enfiladed the right wing column. On its falling into disorder, a pause ensued : reinforcements arrived to the Duke on two sides ; he gained the most complete victory.

The first intelligence I sent the Prince, after our return from the windmill, could leave no doubt of the Duke's inability to come to his assistance ; nevertheless, by a brave resistance, he had rendered him the great service of keeping back and occupying 30,000 of the enemy,—precisely Napoleon's superiority over the Prussian army. I subsequently sent notice of the Duke's grand resolve. I gave information of its successful progress ; from and after five o'clock I caused this to be repeated to the Field-Marshal verbally by aides-de-camp, and by reports in writing.

When it was already dark. I received notice in presence of the Duke, that a Prussian officer had come by the chaussée from Sombref, just as a detachment of French infantry had outflanked the left wing of the position at Quatre Bras. On the chaussée, the officer had been shot off his horse ; on being afterwards found, by the Nassau troops, he stated that he was charged with a message for me. The whole affair was somewhat confused, and it was never cleared up ; I mention it here only, because it was ultimately discovered that this officer had been dispatched to me with intelligence of the Field-Marshal's retreat, of which I remained ignorant.

Before the final close of the day, the enemy facing the English army were driven back on all points, towards Frasnes, but they still held the Farm of Germioncourt, in front of the Duke's centre. The Duke said to me, that at all events the two Allied Armies would assume the offensive next morning, and consequently it was a question whether it were not best to capture the Farm at once, before the day closed, or defer it till the next morning. I declared in favour of the immediate capture, as the enemy showed themselves dispirited, but we were *en bon train;* its capture the next morning would cost many men. The Duke shared my views : he ordered the assault, and we gained the Farm without loss.

During the night no intelligence reached me, which I attributed to the circumstance of the enemy's having rendered our communication on the chaussée insecure. At daybreak I sent out my aides-de-camp to seek by cross-roads communication with the Prussian army. It was essential to know whether the Field-Marshal were in a condition to assume the offensive, which the Duke was now able to do, his whole army, including the corps of Prince Frederick of the Netherlands, being now assembled.

The Quartermaster-General of the English army had ridden out with the same object with which I had charged my aides-de-camp ; he came back with the news that Field-Marshal Blücher had quitted the battle-field of Ligny. Of this there could be no no doubt, for the Quartermaster-General, Colonel

Delancy, had spoken with General von Zieten, who formed the rear-guard. The Duke and I were both much surprised at this news. The Duke looked at me, as if he wished to ask whether I had known the thing and concealed it from him on good grounds. But on my saying quite naturally, "This is probably the account which the officer, who was shot down, was bringing me," and adding, "but now you cannot remain here, my Lord," he immediately entered with me as usual on the measures to be taken.

As we knew nothing farther of the Prussian army but the direction of their retreat upon Wavre,—moreover that Bülow with his corps had taken no part in the battle,—and that Napoleon had not pursued,—I argued thus: "Things cannot be so bad; the Duke must retreat to a point on a line with Wavre. We shall then have intelligence of the state of Blücher's army; and until we have, nothing can be decided." This was quite the Duke's opinion: he had selected the position of Mont St. Jean; meanwhile came the question whether he should make his troops, weary with their preceding day's march, break up at once, or first let them rest and cook. He preferred the latter, but was apprehensive that his rear-guard might in consequence be involved in severe fighting. I could not share this apprehension. The enemy had only bivouacked on the 16th (the previous day), in the dusk of the evening; and in such cases it was always Napoleon's custom in his wars in Germany, to allow his troops first to cook, and to break up at ten the next morning.

The English cavalry, part of which had only arrived that morning at Quatre Bras, must at any rate feed first; and could then together with the whole of the horse-artillery, form the rear-guard, for which the ground was well adapted.

The Duke allowed his people to cook, at the risk of sharp fighting on the part of his rear-guard. At nine o'clock an officer arrived from Wavre, with verbal messages to me, just as I was sitting with the Duke on the ground. I knew that this officer spoke French and English, and therefore indicated to him by a motion of my hand that he might say to the Duke what he had to report to me. He did so. The Duke put some questions, received sensible and satisfactory replies, and by these was induced to declare to me that "he would accept a battle in the position of Mont St. Jean, if the Field-Marshal were inclined to come to his assistance even with one corps only."

The consequences of this—how we got from the battle-field of Quatre Bras into the position of Mont St. Jean, and how Field-Marshal Blücher answered, that he would come to his assistance with all the strength he had—I take for granted is all well known. It is to be found in the history of the campaign which I published at Cotta's in Stuttgard, in 1817.

Very early on the 18th of June, the Duke of Wellington examined all the details of his position. I visited with him, on horseback, the environs, the farm of Hougoumont, and the front of the line, and then hastened to the left wing, by Papelotte and Frischermont upon the plateau. I examined its accessibility, until I was driven back by a French patrol coming from Planchenois. From what I had seen, I was convinced that a bold advance on the part of Field-Marshal Blücher upon the plateau by St. Lambert, must lead to the greatest results, as

R

the enemy appeared to pay no heed whatever to this right flank, probably because Napoleon assumed that he had annihilated Blücher's army at Ligny. I wrote down on a sheet of parchment my views upon the march of the Prussian army, in form of a disposition for the conduct of the two Allied Armies, according to three different cases, and read it to the Duke of Wellington. "I quite agree," he called out to me; and adding the mention of this concurrence, I dispatched an aide-de-camp to the Field-Marshal, with the verbal addition, that if two corps of the Prussian army were to take possession of the plateau, the battle, in my opinion, would be strategically decided.

Just as I was despatching my aide-de-camp, I received intelligence that General von Bülow, with the 4th corps, was marching in the direction of the English army; I therefore charged my aide-de-camp, in case he met him, to let him read the sheet intended for the Field-Marshal, in order that he might immediately understand what was intended, if I sent him notice later which case had occurred.

The Field-Marshal entirely approved of the disposition I had planned. General Bülow (whom my aide-de-camp met) had already directed his march as I proposed, when he received the official order for it from the Field-Marshal, and almost simultaneously from me the intelligence that the case had occurred in which he was to advance by St. Lambert and Frasnes upon the plateau.

The battle began so hotly, that I was apprehensive Napoleon might succeed in running down the English army on some one point, and driving them from their position before the Prussians could arrive on the plateau to support them. For this reason

I was anxious to hasten the march of the Prussians, and spoke with the Duke (after the battle had begun) about the strength and weakness of his line of battle.

Not fearing for his centre and left wing, I considered his right wing the weakest point; and Hougoumont, in particular, I deemed untenable in a serious assault by the enemy. This the Duke disputed, as he had put the old castle in a state of defence, and caused the long garden wall towards the field of battle to be crenellated; and he added, "I have thrown Macdonell into it,"—an officer on whom he placed especial reliance.*—"But how will it be," replied I, "if the enemy advances on the Nivelles road, towards which the garden of Hougoumont has no wall, but only a very light, indefensible hedge, and consequently all but the house must be given up. But the house, without the garden, will not hinder in the least the attack on the English right wing." I repaired thither with the Duke; he drew in his right wing (which was extended to Braine-la-Leud), raised a battery which swept the Nivelles road, and stationed some infantry in its rear, to cover by offensive movements the access to the garden from this side.

Should Napoleon now wish to turn the right wing of the English army by Braine-la-Leud, Wellington could make the whole of this right wing wheel back on its left, and as soon as the Prussians arrived, simultaneously assume the offensive from the left wing.†

* Now Lieut.-General Sir James Macdonell, K.C.B.—ED.

† The Duke of Wellington had retired from Quatre Bras in three columns on three roads; and on the evening of the 17th, Prince Frederick of the Netherlands stood at Hall, Lord Hill at Braine-la-Leud, and the Prince of Orange with the reserve

After these measures had been taken on the right wing, a serious attack commenced on the left. This was the most dangerous point, on account of the connection with the Prussian army; and as I could be of most use there in directing, on their arrival, the Prussian troops, who were totally unacquainted with the field of battle, the Duke wished me to proceed thither, and at the same time to take care that his left wing acted in full concert with the Prussian army. With this view he referred his generals of the left wing to me.

I arrived on the left wing at the same moment that General Picton (who fell on this occasion) was repulsed in his attack on the enemy's 1st corps.

The enemy's infantry in advance, close to the

at Mont St. Jean. This disposition was necessary, as these three roads were at Napoleon's command for his advance upon Brussels. On the 17th, Napoleon had followed, and pushed forward from Quatre Bras to Rosomme by Genappe; on neither of the other roads had a man of the enemy been seen.

Early on the 18th, about nine o'clock, the offensive battle was warmly begun by Napoleon, though his left wing did not step beyond the Nivelles road. These circumstances permitted Prince Frederick to move up to the army, which he would infallibly have done, had not fresh circumstances occurred. The Duke had pledged himself twenty-four hours before to accept a battle at Mont St. Jean, if Blücher could reinforce him in this position with one corps—25,000 men. This being promised, the Duke arranged his means of defence, when he unexpectedly heard that, besides the promised corps, Blücher was already on his march with all his forces to break in by Planchenois on Napoleon's right wing and rear. If three corps of the Prussian army pushed forward by the unguarded plateau to Rosomme, *as was not improbable*, then Napoleon would be driven off from his line of retreat by Genappe, and it was very possible that he might also lose his line of retreat by the Nivelles road. In this case Prince Frederick of the Nether-lands, with his 18,000 men (who might be considered superfluous in the position of Mont St. Jean) would be able to render the most important services.

chaussée, were attacked by a brigade of English cavalry before they reached the flat ground extending from La Haye Sainte to Papelotte. The remaining force of the enemy's infantry were thereby forced to retreat, and got so divided on the further side of the flat ground, that they were less able to offer resistance to an attack of cavalry, unsupported as they were by cavalry or artillery.

Two brigades of English cavalry, of three regiments each, stood on our left wing; I urged the commanders of both to cut in upon the scattered infantry, observing that they could not fail to bring back at least 3000 prisoners. Both agreed with me fully, but, shrugging their shoulders, answered: "Alas, we dare not! The Duke of Wellington is very strict in enforcing obedience to prescribed regulations on this point."*

* I had afterwards an opportunity of asking the Duke about these regulations, which I could do the more freely, as the two officers in question were amongst the most distinguished of the army, and had rendered the most signal services with their brigades in the action that day. The Duke answered me: "The two generals were perfectly correct in their answer, for had they made such an onslaught without my permission, even though the greatest success had crowned their attempt, I must have brought them to a court-martial; for with us it is a fixed rule, that a general placed in a pre-arranged position, has unlimited power to act within it, according to his judgment: for instance, if the enemy assails him, he may defend himself on the spot, or meet the enemy from a covered position; and in both cases he may pursue them, but never further than the obstacle behind which the position assigned him lay; in one word, such obstacle, until fresh orders, is the limit of his action."

I was obliged to admit that these precepts, hitherto unknown to me, were, as rules, most judicious. I had propounded and defended such myself in my discussions with Gneisenau; still it seemed to me a point worthy of attention, that though the precept must be acknowledged unconditionally correct for infantry and

From the left wing I despatched officers in continual succession to Field-Marshal Blücher, to keep him accurately informed of the events of the battle. After 3 o'clock the Duke's situation became critical, unless the succour of the Prussian army arrived soon.

artillery, yet, for cavalry, an exceptional rule ought to be allowed, namely, that a plain on the other side of the obstacle should be reckoned within the extent of their movements.

The Duke replied, that the case I had in view could neither alter or modify the fixed principle. It was of paramount importance that a general who finds himself in a defensive position should, at no moment of the action, lose the free disposal of all the troops under his orders. In the battles of Vimiera, Talavera, Busaco, and Salamanca, he had allowed himself to be attacked, with the view of assailing the enemy with superior forces as soon as he laid himself open, and of causing thereby confusion in his disposition, or a partial discomfiture, which might lead subsequently to a general defeat. For this object it was necessary:

1. That the commander-in-chief standing on an elevated point of his position, telescope in hand, should investigate by his own observation, and the reports he receives, the disposition of his antagonist, and discover means of hindering the co-operation of his forces; and,

2dly. That the leaders of troops should set themselves in motion the very moment they receive their fresh orders. But this could not be done, if they were engaged in their own enterprises unknown to the General in Command.

Now supposing in the case I mentioned, the six regiments of cavalry had made their 6,000 prisoners, it remained very doubtful whether they could have returned to their position in half an hour. When cavalry is once scattered, no one can foretell to what that may lead. The charms of pursuit are so great, that no trumpet-signal can arrest it. Moreover, when cavalry regiments are scattered, and each rider drives some captives before him, whose well-filled pockets and knapsacks he has a right to consider his own, a long time elapses before such a regiment is again drawn up ready for action.

But if in the most fortunate results one has not always command of time, how much less is this the case when incalculable difficulties unexpectedly intervene in the pursuit; as, for instance,

On the receipt of my reports, it was resolved not to await the arrival of the whole of Bülow's corps on the plateau, but to advance out of the wood as soon as the two twelve-pounder batteries arrived.

At four o'clock the Field-Marshal began his cannonade, as well as his advance against Planchenois, and about six Napoleon's final desperate attack ensued.

From my station at Papelotte, I could overlook the advance of the enemy's reserve from La Belle Alliance against the Duke's centre; and as the advanced guard of the 1st corps (General von Zieten) had already appeared in the position on the nearest height, I begged Generals Vandeleur and Vivian to hasten immediately with their six regiments of English cavalry to the assistance of the distressed centre. On account of the arrival of the Prussian corps they were no longer wanted on the left wing. These regiments marched off, and reached the centre in good time to make some brilliant charges.*

if the enemy should succeed in restoring order, and defending himself on a body of close cavalry hastening to his support, who can then calculate that the pursuit will be ended at a given time? who can foretell that a hard fight of long duration will not ensue, during which the main army would remain paralysed? Who would expose himself to such accidents, and for what purpose? To make a couple of thousand prisoners, which may perhaps have no effect whatever on the decision of the battle! And supposing those prisoners were made, still the troops would have lost their first freshness, and no longer render the services in the hard battle, they would have done without this interlude.

I was obliged to acknowledge the Duke's reasons to be striking, and soon convinced myself that in the continual discussions I had held on this subject, without being able to carry my point, I had already become soft myself, and that I had contracted laxer ideas than the strict but correct school permits.

* This march of the brigades of Vandeleur and Vivian from the left wing to the centre of the English line of battle, is very

Almost simultaneously with the movement of these regiments, the enemy advanced with infantry against the left wing at Papelotte.

General Zieten's advanced guard, which I was expecting with the utmost impatience, suddenly turned round, and disappeared from the height just as the enemy took possession of Papelotte with his Guards. I hastened after this advanced guard on the other side of the height, from whence I saw them in full retreat. General von Zieten, whom fortunately I soon overtook, had received instructions from the Field-Marshal, to close up to him, and wished very properly to effect this by going by Papelotte; but he changed his intention, when one of his officers, whom he had sent forward to ascertain how the battle was going, returned with intelligence that the right wing of the English was in full retreat. This inexperienced young man had mistaken the great number of wounded (by musketry) going or being

correctly described, as far as regards time, occasion, and execution, in the report of the battle by the English Captain Siborne. But the author has been misinformed as to *who* gave directions for this movement. I should certainly make no mention of this circumstance (for it is a matter of perfect indifference to history, whether A or B issued the order), were not my report of the battle, which was written years before the appearance of Siborne's work, thereby exposed to being censured as inaccurate.

Captain Siborne appears not to have been the least aware that in the position I held with the Duke of Wellington, I was stationed on his left wing, nor to have heard what charge I had. I never heard anything of an independent movement on the part of General Vivian, nor did I ever hear that the Duke had verbal negociations, through his aides-de-camp, with other Prussian generals besides me. This would have been contrary to the agreements, with which Captain Siborne was unacquainted. However, this is a mere matter of indifference, as his statements with regard to the co-operation of the allied forces are perfectly correct. [Added in the year 1846.]

taken to the rear to be dressed, for fugitives, and accordingly made a false report. On my assuring General von Zieten of the contrary, and undertaking to bring the corps to the appointed place, and since in any movement *downwards* from Papelotte he would not only find difficulties, but also lose the time for co-operation, he instantly turned about and followed me, and continued to advance until it grew dark, driving the enemy before him.

By this retrograde movement of General von Zieten, occasioned by this false report, the battle might have been lost, as it would have altogether prevented the corps from reaching the field of battle; whereas, by marching on Papelotte, its advanced guard was in full action a quarter of an hour later.

When the enemy had been driven out of Papelotte; when I had brought two batteries from Zieten's corps, to important points previously selected ; and when the enemy enfiladed on his line, and on the flank formed against Blücher, gave way, I hastened, with a battery of Prussian artillery, to the centre of the English line, which still kept up a musketry-fire, though the guns were silenced. I met the Duke in the neighbourhood of La Haye Sainte, holding a telescope raised in his right hand : he called out to me from a distance : "Well! you see Macdonell has held Hougoumont!" This was an expression of pleasure that his brave comrade had answered his expectations. The enemy's right wing, as far as the chaussée, was already in full retreat, pursued by Zieten's corps.

The enemy's centre, however, from the chaussée almost to Hougoumont still remained immoveable. But when the mounted battery on the height of La Haye Sainte opened its fire, the retreat began also on the other side of the chaussée, as the balls from the batteries of Bülow's corps already swept the French line far beyond the farm of La Belle Alliance. The Duke said to me, that he would cause his whole line to advance ; and accordingly he repaired himself to its centre, between La Haye Sainte and Hougoumont. When the line of infantry moved forward, small masses of only some hundred men, at great intervals, were seen everywhere advancing. The position in which the infantry had fought was marked, as far as the eye could reach, by a red line, caused by the red uniform of the numerous killed and wounded who lay there.

This advance of such weak battalions, with the great gaps between, appeared hazardous, and General Lord Uxbridge (afterwards Marquis of Anglesey), who commanded the cavalry, drew the Duke's attention to the danger; the Duke, however, would not order them to stop, as the English cavalry formed a second line, ready to support the infantry, should the French still be in a condition to attack it. There was, probably, also a political motive for this advance. The Duke, with his practised eye, perceived that the French army was no longer dangerous : he was equally aware, indeed, that with his infantry so diminished he could achieve nothing more of importance ; but if he *stood still*, and resigned the pursuit to the Prussian army *alone*, it might appear, in the eyes of Europe, as if the English army had defended themselves bravely indeed, but that the Prussians alone decided and won the battle.

When the two leaders afterwards met, it could be arranged with good grace that the Prussian army should undertake the pursuit.

About midnight, at Waterloo, returning from the

pursuit, which I had continued with the Prussian army to Genappe, I said to the Duke,—"The Field-Marshal will call the battle 'Belle-Alliance.'" He made no answer, and I perceived at once that he had no intention of giving it this name. Now, whether he was afraid of thereby prejudicing himself or his army, I know not. Meanwhile, he had probably already called it the battle of Waterloo in his previous report to England, for he was in the habit of naming the battles he won in India and Spain after his head-quarters.

After this battle I enjoyed a greater share of the Duke's confidence, which was uninterrupted. He had seen that I had the welfare of all at heart, and that I entertained towards him the reverence due to those talents as a commander, which did not more distinguish him than the openness and rectitude of his character.

On the march to Paris, the Prussian army made longer marches than the English; and when in the morning I made my daily communications to the Duke, I took the liberty of respectfully calling his attention to this, and suggesting that it would be better if he kept the same pace as his ally. He was silent at first, but on my urging him again to move more rapidly, he said to me: "Do not press me on this point, for I tell you, it won't do. If you were better acquainted with the English army, its composition and habits, you would say the same. I cannot separate from my tents and my supplies. My troops must be well kept and well supplied in camp, if order and discipline are to be maintained. It is better that I should arrive two days later in Paris, than that discipline should be relaxed."

Of the two military events which occurred on the

march to Paris, the storming of Cambray and of Peronne, I need only say, that the remarkable order in the preparations for them struck me as forcibly as the excellent manner in which they were executed by persons who had gained their experience in Spain.

In few words the Duke designated which division of troops should make fascines in a thicket, and which should bind the ladders of eighteen steps (collected in store from the nearest villages), together in threes. He designated the point of attack, and all the rest went on of itself. The battalions in two contiguous columns, behind a swarm of tirailleurs, carried the fascines, covered with arms perpendicularly before them, as a protecting wall, and the ladders on their shoulders, all just as if they had been on the practising-ground.

During the march on Paris, Field-Marshal Blücher had at one time a prospect of getting Napoleon into his power; the delivering up of Napoleon was the invariable condition stipulated by him in every conference with the French Commissioners sent to treat for peace or an armistice. I received from him instructions to inform the Duke of Wellington, that as the Congress of Vienna had declared Napoleon outlawed, it was his intention to have him shot whenever he caught him. But he desired, at the same time, to know what were the Duke's views on this subject, for should he entertain the same as himself, he wished to act in concert with him.

The Duke stared at me in astonishment, and in the first place disputed the correctness of this interpretation of the Viennese declaration of outlawry, which was never meant to incite to the assassination of Napoleon. He therefore did not think that they could acquire from this act any right to order Napoleon to be shot, should they succeed in making him a prisoner of war. But be this as it may, as far as his own position and that of the Field-Marshal with respect to Napoleon were concerned, it appeared to him that, since the battle they had won, they were become much too conspicuous personages to justify such a transaction in the eyes of Europe.

I had already felt the force of the Duke's arguments before I most reluctantly undertook my mission, and was therefore little disposed to dispute them. "I therefore," continued the Duke, "wish my friend and colleague to see this matter in the light I do; such an act would hand down our names to history stained by a crime, and posterity would say of us, that we did not deserve to be the conquerors of Napoleon; the more so as such a deed is now quite useless, and can have no object."

I made use of these expressions only as far as was necessary to dissuade the Field-Marshal from his idea. It is not unimportant to preserve to history the motives which actuated the Field-Marshal in giving me this commission. With this view I have introduced, in the Appendix, three notes from General von Gneisenau relating to this subject.

The Duke of Wellington must have received instructions from his government to re-introduce King Louis XVIII. everywhere as the dispossessed Sovereign, for he induced the King to follow him from Ghent, and, when he had his head-quarters at Château Cambresis, to make a solemn entrance into this town under his protection.

The Emperor Alexander had not expressly declared whether they would re-impose King Louis on the French nation, in case Napoleon were expelled.

Prince Blücher had probably received instructions on the subject unknown to me, for he avoided all contact with the King, and instructed me to do the same.

It had not escaped the Duke's notice that I held back. He invited me one morning at Château Cambresis to come to him, in order to communicate to me various important despatches; and when I had read them, he said, " We must have some further talk about this; but now we must ride out to meet King Louis XVIII., and we will talk of it on the way."

I made an excuse that I had no horse; but he replied, that one of his stood ready saddled for me. And so I was drawn into this ride against my will; at the conclusion of it I could not avoid the King's saying to me many obliging things about the services which the Prussian army had rendered to his cause in the battle.

Wellington had obtained his object, when it was reported in the newspapers that the Duke had gone to meet the King, riding between a Russian and a Prussian General. I consoled myself by thinking that my Russian colleague, Pozzo di Borgo, was, like me, obliged to appear an actor against his will. Before we got to Paris, a courier reached me from the royal head-quarters, with the charge to deliver to the Duke a letter of congratulation from my King, with the order of the Black Eagle.

I was present at the conclusion of the Convention of St. Cloud, and have given the details in my history of the campaign. The Duke of Wellington showed on this occasion a remarkable degree of patience with the long-winded discourse of Monsieur Bignon, in whose opinion it was contrary to the honour of the French army to retire on the other side of the Loire. As there was no end to the chattering and declaiming, I at last said: " My Lord, let the gentlemen chatter, and let us attack, that we may end the matter." This had an effect.

I was now charged by Prince Blücher to represent to the Duke that it was necessary to appoint a Governor and Commandant of Paris. Each of the armies had to name an officer for the post. Prince Blücher was desirous that General von Zieten (who had so distinguished himself in this campaign) should be appointed Governor. General Gneisenau urged that Prussia ought by preference to fill up the post of Governor, because the Prussian army was the strongest. The Duke answered me, that he must consult with the Field-Marshal on the subject.

I immediately communicated this to the Field-Marshal, along with an inquiry from the Duke, whether it was the Prince's intention to make a solemn entrance into Paris.

The Prince had his head-quarters at St. Cloud. From thence I received a letter from General Gneisenau (No. 5 in the Appendix), appointing me Governor of Paris. At the first moment, in truth, I felt quite confounded by this nomination. I had been charged to negotiate this appointment for a General who, by his rank and personal character, was particularly well fitted for it; and now he, with whom I had to negotiate, desired this place for me. This had all the appearance of an intrigue ; for who could know that the Duke took this step without my having the remotest suspicion of his intention? However, Blücher and Count Gneisenau knew me well enough to be sure that I could not do anything so unworthy ; moreover, this appointment was but provisional, until the arrival of the Sovereigns. The Duke of Wellington gave me thereby a proof of his confidence, which I valued more highly than the Commander's Cross of the Bath, which he presented to me by order of the Prince Regent. When I had obtained accurate information of the views of both Field-Marshals on the occupation of Paris, I was able to organize the affairs of my government on a sound basis. The Duke of Wellington would not quarter any troops in the city, but established a camp of 20,000 men in the Bois de Boulogne, with a detachment (to lighten the service) encamped in the Champs Elysées. These troops were to obey my directions, should I require their assistance, within the city of Paris. Field-Marshal Blücher would have the infantry of the 1st Corps d'Armée quartered in Paris, and, according to the Prussian rules of fortress duty, these troops were placed under my orders. I divided the city into two halves, right and left of the Seine.

On the right bank, an English colonel with six *Mairies,* on the left a Prussian colonel with the same, were placed as two commandants under my orders. In each Mairie (under these commandants) a staff officer or captain was appointed, to enforce order in quartering the troops, &c., and to redress complaints in the first instance.

Marshal Massena was at the head of the National Guards. I invited him to come to me, in order to concert with him the internal service, according to Article 9 of the Convention ; he excused himself, pleading sickness, and sent General Hulin instead, as next in command to himself. To him, as well as to the two Prefects of the Seine and of Police, and the Postmaster-General, I made known what was necessary for our mutual relations.

With the first-named Prefect, as the chief authority of the city of Paris, ·I had to regulate the quartering, subsistence, &c., and with the two latter, my relations to the police, gens-d'armerie, and secret police. I did not conceal from myself that I stood in the most difficult position with regard to the latter. Were it hostilely disposed towards us, concealing from me what was going on, I should have to endure it patiently; I had no means of compelling it to act with straightforwardness toward me.

The Prefect of the time being, M. Decazes, had behaved in the Hundred Days in a manner calculated to inspire confidence; and, true to his oath given to the King, he would not accept of any appointment or employment from Napoleon. I had in the first place to get information from him on all points; and I adhered to the principle laid down, of troubling myself only with such subjects of police as affected our military security. I had to keep an eye on the French army, and to know what officers and privates were still in the city, or came back from the Loire, and remained openly or secretly in Paris.

It is in fact hardly credible, that no proprietor or tenant of a house in Paris, should have been under the obligation of giving notice to the police if he received strangers in his house during the night. I took this for some new irregularity, and wished to put a stop to it at once; but M. Decazes explained to me, that this was a very ancient prerogative of the city of Paris; and that neither during the Revolution nor in Napoleon's time, could any alteration in this foolish privilege be effected. He explained to me how, in consequence, the police possessed no other means but a well-ordered espionage, for obtaining information which could certainly be acquired much more cheaply, quickly, and surely, through notices from the owners of houses themselves, and on their responsibility. He concluded by saying, that the measure I had in view could only be carried through by force, and would cause the greatest excitement, during which excesses of all kinds would be unavoidable. That, without wishing to presume, he must warn me against it; and the rather as he could answer for it, that no greater danger to us could arise from strangers creeping in, than what under existing circumstances threatened us every day.

The suburbs of Paris, for instance, on the news of the loss of the battle of La Belle Alliance, had been furnished with arms and ammunition to defend Paris. With the capitulation this object had indeed ceased, but this dangerous class of workmen were still armed, and the suburbs were connected with the Fort of Vincennes, commanded by an officer devoted to Napoleon, who had a great store of arms and ammunition at his disposal.

We had quite forgotten Vincennes in the capitulation. But what was then easy to obtain, was now more difficult. On referring to the Duke of Wellington, he was of opinion that King Louis XVIII. could easily remedy the evil, by appointing a commandant of Vincennes devoted to himself, in room of the Bonapartist. In short, the general opinion was, that it would be better not to talk of the thing, but to *secure* ourselves until a remedy could be found.

M. Decazes considered the disarming the suburbs an indispensable measure; but he was apprehensive that if this were done by the Allies, and by force, (necessary in this case), a portion of these fool-hardy people would resist, and a general resistance might arise from that of individuals, which might needlessly cost much blood. He proposed that I should leave it to him to disarm them gradually, which could best be done on Sundays chiefly (when the work-people of the suburbs assemble to talk over their business for the coming week), and he considered himself the most proper person to do this, as against him, their Prefect, they entertained no distrust.

After mature consideration, I agreed the more willingly to this proposal, as I perceived that there was no fear of a dangerous *émeute*, as long as the French army was engaged on its march and sub-sequent establishment on the Loire; consequently not for the next fortnight. The most complete success justified this conclusion.

With regard to the custom of the townsmen re-ceiving strangers into their houses, without giving any notice to the police, I considered that what Napoleon had not achieved was not to be effected by me, in my temporary position as Governor, with-out setting many other more dangerous things in the balance. Moreover, the funds at the disposal of the police were so considerable that much could be effected by this means. The income from the rent of gambling-houses was assigned to the police for their objects, and this rent amounted at that time to seven or eight million francs.

I deferred therefore all measures until I should find means for radical remedies, and met the Prefect of Police with entire confidence, only stipulating that I must be accurately informed of everything, official

as well as secret, in any way relating to my office.
I neve rhad cause to repent this.

The Prefect of the Seine, Count Chabrol, inspired
me, on a short acquaintance, with full confidence,
by his honourable, open behaviour. I had planned a
disposition, by which I could remain master of the
city in case of a reduction of the garrison of Paris.
This plan included barricades, and a species of block-
houses, which, erected on the squares where the
main streets terminated, would give the means of
effectually sweeping the principal streets by guns and
musketry. The city of Paris was to bear the cost
of these fortifications, which would not be trifling.
The Prefect did not in any way refuse, but he represented to me the exhausted state of the city funds,
with a petition to spare them, " as he was obliged
to expend so much in maintaining harmony between
the citizens and the soldiers quartered on them, and
avoiding all complaints."

It was evident this measure would be quite superfluous if there were expectations of peace being soon
concluded. On this ground, and having convinced
myself that my barricades could be built in three days,
I put off this measure.

On the 7th of July, when I had taken possession
of Paris, in answer to all inquiries how this or
that thing was to be managed, I replied: " Just as
in the previous year, 1814, when a governor of Paris
had likewise been appointed by the Allies." I
thereby removed from the French authorities all
apprehension that we intended to behave this time
differently, and everything went on without my
being obliged to direct each trifle. I could always
alter afterwards whatever I thought injudious.

Quarters were assigned to me in the palace of

the Prince of Neufchatel and Wagram, who had recently lost his life in Bamberg, from falling out of a window. On the following day stores of wine, cooks, plate, &c., arrived at my dwelling, and it was explained to my aides-de-camp that as I wished everything to go on as in the previous year, forty covers would also be served daily to me by the city of Paris. I instantly sent all back again, with the remark, that as a Prussian general I had my own cook and field-kitchen : I therefore thanked the city of Paris for its attention, but I declined to put it to any expense. Furthermore, a sum of 2,000 francs daily income from the rent of the gambling-houses was assigned to me, with the remark, that a similar income had been raised by the Governor appointed by the Allies in 1814 ; moreover, that by ancient custom it was likewise due to every French governor ; and General Maison, who acted in that capacity during the Restoration, had continued to receive it. Under these circumstances I saw no reason for declining this allowance, which had been paid even in time of peace. Accordingly, I directed the revenue derived from the gambling-houses to be paid, in decades of 20,000 francs, into the Prussian general state-fund, into which this income, in fact, continued to flow for four months and a half—the period during which I occupied the post of Governor.

This rejection of all personal advantages placed me in a situation quite independent of all French authorities, and of the city of Paris, and contributed not a little to my power of maintaining my position, till its close, in a manner conformable to the dignity of the armies and governments I had to represent. I could the more strictly insist on the troops quartered in Paris being well supplied, and that, with strict maintenance of discipline, they should be treated with the respect to which, as victors, they had a double claim.

Among the French marshals, Macdonald, during his command over the Prussian corps in 1812, had conducted himself as a man of honour; neither he nor Oudinot had been any annoyance to Prussian subjects when quartered upon them. I therefore paid my visit to both immediately on entering upon my office, and received their visits in return. I declined the visits of all other persons and authorities, on principle.

During the whole time of my government I lived exclusively for my duty, and quite secluded from social life, as much because I had no time for its enjoyments, as because I deemed it expedient from prudential reasons. On principle, I never took the slightest notice of all the threatening letters and anonymous reports of plots on my life.

Among the difficult tasks to be performed was the restoring of the treasures of art collected in Paris by Napoleon, the fruits of his conquests. On receiving this commission, by the decision of the ministers of the Allied Powers in Paris (to whom I was referred in political affairs), I first resolved on the removal of the chariot in the court of the Tuileries. The size and weight of the horses had rendered it necessary to attach them with considerable fastenings of iron into the masonry. I borrowed from the Duke of Wellington a company of Sappers and Miners, known for their dexterity and strength. I asked their commander how much time he required, with his company, to detach the four horses from their fastenings, and to lower them down from the triumphal arch upon transport waggons. He undertook to effect this in six or eight hours, by day or night.

Marshal Massena and General Hulin, who were disliked by King Louis XVIII., had been removed, on his arrival at Paris, from the command of the National Guard, which had been conferred on General Dessoles, the old chief of General Moreau's staff. In our intercourse I had found him an honourable man, desiring nothing more ardently than to see the King's power firmly established on a durable footing; whilst, in designing means for this end, he was moderate and sensible. I acquainted him with my plan of getting the chariot quietly removed by night, and thereby sparing the King two annoyances; first, this being done before his windows in open day; and secondly, his giving a forced official consent, which could not be agreeable to him in the face of his people. General Dessoles entered fully into my views, and recognised in them a peculiar delicacy toward the King's person. The King, whom I never saw (to avoid all false judgments with respect to himself), had been informed, through Dessoles, of many things I wished him to know; I therefore commissioned this general to disclose to him my intention, but to him alone.

He did as I wished, but shortly after returned from the Tuileries, describing to me the excitement into which the King had fallen on this occasion, and transmitting to me at the same time his demand, that I should pause in the execution until he had averted this removal by diplomatic negotiations. The King bitterly complained on this occasion of the little regard evinced toward him by the Sovereigns, and their endeavours to degrade him in the eyes of his people.

I had received accurate information from the Ministers of the Allied Powers how this affair stood. Even before the Peace of Paris in 1814, the Allies had re-demanded their treasures of art, and proposed to the King to restore these to them of his own free will, as property unjustly taken. On the King's showing hesitation, they intimated that, if he disliked the proposal, they would *take* these purloined treasures. Thereupon the King represented to them that the people clung to these conquered treasures, which it was his intention to restore, but they must allow him time. This was conceded; but as often as he was reminded afterwards that this time had expired, unmeaning excuses were alleged, and it was evident he had no intention to give up the works of art.

These causes had produced, in 1815, the resolution to take back the works without any diplomatic negotiations, and to disregard any protestations; my instructions therefore implied that I was not to allow anything to stop my removing them. I accordingly requested General Dessoles to disclose to the King that I had definite orders, and must proceed to execute them on the following night. The work was begun at nightfall; but about midnight I received information that it had been interrupted by a division of the Guards, who came from the palace, and that the progress was impeded. The Garde du Corps, commanded by old emigrant friends of the King, exercised at that time great influence over him. It was not improbable that these friends, admitted into the secret, had made an attempt to intimidate us, and in this manner to carry the King's purpose of preventing the removal; and, indeed, it was thus explained subsequently.

Next morning I charged General Dessoles to express to the King my regret at the occurrence, with an urgent request to him, to give the necessary orders that the like obstruction on the part of his Guards might not recur on the following night, or I should be obliged to take serious measures against his Garde du Corps. I concerted with Dessoles for the following night, that he should secretly keep two battalions of the National Guard under arms in the Louvre, at my disposal. The next night the same scene was repeated, with the difference that the interruption of the work this time proceeded not from within the palace, but from the populace outside. The National Guard might very well be employed against the King's insolent, and generally hated, Body Guard, but not against the people; I therefore ordered the work to be immediately relinquished, and caused the National Guard to withdraw.

But now the season for forbearance had expired, and any continuance of moderation would be weakness. The following morning I ordered four battalions of Austrian troops and a division of cavalry, under Major General Prince Bentheim, to form a square round the triumphal arch, and removed the four Venetian Horses in open day. A large mob collected around the palace, and a portion became very vociferous; I had the guns well loaded in their presence; no one ventured to interrupt the work, and by evening the Horses were in the Austrian barracks.

General Dessoles had represented to the King,

with great frankness, that he must submit to what was inevitable, and not take the voice of the *canaille* for that of the nation. If he followed the will of the mob, he would get into difficulties with the Allies, of whom he stood in too great need.

Towards noon the King sent me word that he had found himself compelled to withdraw the command of the National Guard from General Dessoles, and to confer it on Marshal Oudinot. The causes alleged for this step were never made known to me officially; meanwhile, if the King may be censured for depriving a man of honour of the command, he must at least be commended for giving it to another honourable man in his stead.

After the Horses had been taken down, I had the Venetian Lion also removed; and gradually cleared the Museum of all the foreign property, without the recurrence of any hindrance.

The French Government had to put up with what they could not prevent; they only refused to return to the Pope his statues and pictures. The reason for this refusal was taken from the diplomatic declaration of the Allied Sovereigns, according to which all treasures of art *forcibly* carried off by Napoleon were to be returned to their respective owners. The Pope's treasures had been taken from him, as from all the other Sovereigns, but a most exorbitant war-contribution had been at the same time imposed upon him. A petition for its reduction had been rejected; but under the impossibility of raising the sums required, Napoleon had at last allowed some millions to be charged on the purloined treasures. This was entered in the Treaty of the Peace of Tolentino, signed by the Pope. The Most Christian King therefore maintained that the

Pope's treasures of art had not been in any wise seized, but *fairly earned* by treaty.

However ridiculous these arguments might appear in sound reason, it was necessary to respect diplomatic forms. My proposition therefore ran thus : to deal with these treasures just as Napoleon had chalked out, viz., first to carry them off by military force, as the rights of conquest, and then to enter upon diplomatic negotiations so far as circumstances should make it necessary.

The conference of the Ministers of the Allied Sovereigns referred the settlement of this affair to the three Field-Marshals present in Paris : they did not hesitate to empower me to take back the treasures by military force. The written instruction sent to me (No. 6, Appendix), is, as far as I know, the only dispatch with the signatures of the three Field-Marshals, as I was the only military authority placed under their joint orders.

The presence of the three Sovereigns in Paris materially increased my difficulties in carrying on business, as no Frenchman was ever satisfied with my decision, but always appealed to one of the three Sovereigns. The delivery of reports required in consequence demanded an expenditure of time and powers, to which in the long run I was unequal, with the number of officers allotted to me for the labours of government. Meanwhile I had the satisfaction of finding that the measures I took were not only uniformly approved, but that they had likewise the expected results, although I had often to make respectful expostulations against the inclination of the Sovereigns to rule paternally in the conquered capital. The great mass of the French people are very intelligent, but there are many vain, egotistical, and quarrelsome individuals amongst them, who must be summarily dealt with. One who yields appears to them weak; he who changes his measures, inconsistent and trifling.

The Emperor Francis imparted to me, through Prince Schwarzenberg, the supplications and complaints sent to him; he was soon convinced by the information he obtained on these occasions, that I did not act passionately, or without regard to circumstances : this gained me his confidence in process of time.

The Duchess de St. Leu had great means at her disposal. The Prefect of Police continually complained that she employed them in Napoleon's interest, which called for the utmost attention on the part of the police, to watch her intrigues, as well as to obviate the evil influence of her distributions of money. However disagreeable it was to me to proceed against women, and especially members of the former Imperial family, yet I saw the necessity of removing from Paris this lady, who was forming a successful opposition, and endangering the public tranquillity. I therefore directed an aide-de-camp to inform her, that I had heard she was purposing to travel to Switzerland; and as I made it my especial duty to provide for her safety, as her journey took her through the quarters of the Allied Armies, she would receive from me the necessary passports and directions for her safety.

Some hours later, her Chamberlain made his appearance, to notify to me that, by order of the Duchess, he had immediately requested an audience of His Majesty the Emperor Francis, who had decided that the Duchess might remain quietly at Paris. I replied, that I awaited the Emperor's orders, but that the Duchess had done very wrong to betray her secret and mine; and I asked, whether he had also notified to the Emperor, that at ten o'clock the following evening the post-horses, with an escort of four Prussian hussars, and four French gens-d'armes, would be at her hotel, accompanied by an aide-de-camp, who would hand over to her the necessary passports, and arrange for her departure.

Thereupon the Chamberlain was dispatched a second time by the incensed Duchess, to inform the Emperor that she was to be removed from Paris by force. The Emperor inquired, " By whose orders ?"—" By order of the Military Governor."— "Then I can do nothing," was the answer returned by the Emperor to the Chamberlain.

The Duchess must have comprehended that I had knowledge of her secret connections, and that much worse might befall her if the Emperor Francis did not protect her;—she departed punctually.

The Emperor Alexander took most notice of the complaints brought to him, and protected with partiality all the French who turned to him. The secret police had intimation, that in the hotel of the Swedish Ambassador, where the Crown Princess of Sweden was dwelling, a carefully served-up dinner was daily brought to a closed room at the back of the house. The police soon ascertained that Napoleon's eldest brother, Joseph, who was married to a sister of the Crown Princess, was concealed there.

I was empowered by my commission to arrest all the male members of Napoleon's family; however, I could not invade the hotel of an ambassador of an

Allied Monarch, to arrest any one there. On the other hand, it was very strange that the ambassador of an Allied Power should secretly harbour a person who, according to the diplomatic measures of all the Allied Powers, ought to be arrested. I stated the case verbally to the Emperor Alexander, inquiring of him whether I should occupy the environs of the hotel with a military force, and demand of the Swedish Ambassador to deliver up the ex-King. The Emperor maintained that there must be some error at the bottom of this : he promised to take cognizance of the matter, and give me information. Until then I was not to take further steps. I recommended his Majesty to keep the secret, that the ex-King might not privately escape.

A few days after this, the Emperor sent an aide-de-camp to me early in the morning, with a message that I was right ; the ex-King Joseph was concealed in the hotel of the Swedish Ambassador. Immediately after I learnt that he had escaped during the previous night by a back door of the hotel, and had set off for the Loire, furnished with false but valid passports, which he had obtained through Russian mediation. I did not spare the Emperor Alexander the embarrassment of a circumstantial verbal report of this flight.

Under these circumstances, and after filling for nearly five months the difficult post of Governor of Paris, I was much rejoiced to be able to lay it down, and the more so, as during the whole time no excess had occurred worthy of mention.

I had provided in the best manner for the welfare of the city of Paris ; and in a fraudulent affair, in which it had been contrived to involve the Allies, I had decided, as impartiality required, to the advantage of the city funds, which thereby gained some millions.

On my retirement, the city of Paris wished to testify its gratitude to me; and Count Chabrol, who knew that hitherto the city funds had not had to bear any charge for me, and who was also aware of my disliking to receive anything that could be rated at its money value, with great delicacy arranged that the city of Paris should present me with the great Egyptian work (not then purchasable), after King Louis XVIII. had first bestowed on his good city the copy intended for me.

After laying down my office, the King, at my request, granted me a private audience, in which he spoke with as much candour and confidence as if I had been one of his adherents. I thought that I ought to make use of this opportunity to warn him against some persons, and to recommend to him others whom I had found by experience able and trustworthy men : amongst these was the Prefect of Police, M. Decazes, respecting whose qualifications the King made particular inquiries. In conclusion I represented to him, what the extent of my experience had taught me during five months, the difficulties of his situation, if he yielded to the emotions of his heart, with the expectation of awakening thereby an echo in the hearts of his people. I described to him the influence which the unfeeling rule of Napoleon had had on the impressionable French, and how all his endeavours to attach them to himself by moral and religious means would turn out unsuccessful, unless he combined these with a cold measured strictness, to which Napoleon had accustomed them, and without which his power would break against the wild unruly state of the people.

At first, the King listened to my representations with intense attention, but he afterwards became greatly agitated and burst into a flood of tears; I paused, and stood several minutes silent in his presence: he could not recover himself, and I respectfully retired to the ante-room. I had not wounded him, and therefore I supposed it was the truth and independence with which I described his difficult position that had so painfully affected him. The King sent for those persons I had pointed out as deserving his attention, and examined their capabilities for high offices. M. Decazes was soon after appointed Minister of Police, and the other persons named by me were likewise promoted.

APPENDIX.

No. 1. "To the Royal Major-General Von Müffling, Grand Cross, &c., &c.

"The French general De Tromelin is at Noyons, with the intention of proceeding to the head-quarters of the Duke of Wellington to treat for the delivering up of Bonaparte.

"Bonaparte has been declared under outlawry by the Allied Powers. The Duke of Wellington may possibly (from parliamentary considerations) hesitate to fulfil the declaration of the Powers. Your Excellency will therefore direct the negotiations to the effect, that Bonaparte may be delivered over to *us*, with a view to his execution.

" This is what eternal justice demands, and what the declaration of March the 13th decides ; and thus the blood of our soldiers killed and mutilated on the 16th and 18th will be avenged.

" Compiègne. June 27th, 1815.

(Signed)   " Von Gneisenau."

---

2. " To the Royal Major-General Baron Von Müffling, Grand Cross, &c., &c.

" Your Excellency will give notice to the Duke of Wellington that we have sent an officer to the five Deputies from Paris, in order to accompany them to the head-quarters of the Sovereigns.

" A halt and armistice is denied them, but it has been declared that after the Conquest of Paris, we Prussians would agree to a truce under the following conditions :—

" 1. The delivering up of Bonaparte alive or dead.

" 2. The cession of the fortresses of the Sambre, Meuse, Moselle, and Saar, including Longwy.

" 3. The occupation of the provinces of the Marne, including Château Thierry and Epernay.

" 4. The cession of the Castle of Vincennes.

" 5. The restoration of the treasures of art to the nations from which they were taken.

" 6. Indemnification for the costs of the war.

" Your Excellency will inform the Duke on these points, in order that no scruple may arise respecting them on his part, which however I do not expect.

" Perfect liberty is left to the Duke to stipulate

T

for *himself* to act as he pleases, according to the views of his Cabinet.

"Guiory, June 27th, 1815.

　　　(Signed)　　" COUNT N. VON GNEISENAU."

"P.S.—The Deputies have had no written answer.

"The Prince von Schönburg is charged with their escort, the Count von Nostitz with the negotiations, and Count Flemming with the redaction.

"The capture of Peronne is very important."

---

3. "To the Royal Major-General Baron Von Müffling, &c., &c.

"I am directed by the Field-Marshal to request your Excellency to communicate to the Duke of Wellington, that it had been his intention to execute Bonaparte on the spot where the Duc D'Enghien was shot; that out of deference, however, to the Duke's wishes, he will abstain from this measure, but that the Duke must take on himself the responsibility of its non-enforcement.

"It appears to me that the English will feel embarrassed by the delivery of Bonaparte to them; your Excellency will therefore only direct the negociations, so that he may be delivered up to us.

"Senlis, June 29th, 1815.

　　　(Signed)　　"N. VON GNEISENAU."

4. " To the Royal Major-General, Baron von
Müffling, &c., &c.

" When the Duke of Wellington declares himself against the execution of Bonaparte, he thinks
and acts in the matter as a Briton. Great Britain
is under weightier obligation to no mortal man than
to this very villain ; for by the occurrences whereof
he is the author, her greatness, prosperity, and
wealth, have attained their present elevation. The
English are the masters of the seas, and have no
longer to fear any rivalry, either in this dominion or
the commerce of the world.

" It is quite otherwise with us Prussians. We
have been impoverished by him. Our nobility will
never be able to right itself again.

" Ought we not, then, to consider ourselves the
tools of that Providence which has given us such a
victory for the ends of eternal justice? Does not
the death of the Duc d'Enghien call for such a
vengeance? Shall we not draw upon ourselves the
reproaches of the people of Prussia, Russia, Spain,
and Portugal, if we leave unperformed the duty that
devolves upon us?

" But be it so !—If others will assume a theatrical
magnanimity, I shall not set myself against it. We
act thus from esteem for the Duke and—weakness.

" Senlis, June 29th, 1815.

(Signed) " COUNT VON GNEISENAU."

---

5. " To the Royal Major-General, Baron von
Müffling, &c., &c.

" In answer to the inquiries made by the Duke
of Wellington of your Excellency, on the subject of

T 2

the entry into Paris, I have just received the Field-Marshal's orders, and he has charged me to explain that :—

" He is quite indifferent about the entry into Paris; that he intends to keep his head-quarters here, and merely have a lodging in Paris, to go with few attendants, and only for a short time. He has no wish to give the Parisians the spectacle of a formal entry.

" With regard to the appointment of a Governor, I have the honour to inform your Excellency that the Duke has written with his own hand to the Field-Marshal, stating that he had given your Excellency no answer yet on the subject of the nomination of a *Commandant of Paris* (so the letter is expressed), but that he wishes to propose to the Field-Marshal that your Excellency should be appointed to the post. The Duke on this occasion, says of your Excellency : 'There is no person who, in his situation, has done more to forward the objects of our operations ; and it appears to me, that having had so much to do with us both and with our operations, he is the person who ought to be selected.

" The Prince has answered him, that he had, indeed, chosen Lieutenant-General von Zieten for this post, and even conversed with him on the subject ; but since it is the Duke's wish, he gladly nominates your Excellency.'

" St. Cloud, July 15th, 1815.

(Signed) "Count N. von Gneisenau."

6. " A Son Excellence M. le Général Baron de Müffling.

" Monsieur le Baron,

" Monsieur Antoine Canova, qui est arrivé dans cette ville il y a quelques jours, ayant été député de la part de Sa Sainteté le Pape pour réclamer du Gouvernement Français les objets d'art et de science injustement dérobés à l'église de St. Pierre et à l'état Romain, par les armées de la République Française depuis la Révolution, ayant annoncé aux Ministres des Souverains alliés que les instances qu'il a fait au Gouvernement de Sa Majesté très Chrétienne, conformement à ses instructions, n'ont pas eu de succès, et qu'on refuse de les livrer sinon à la force armée ; et vu qu'il parait juste et nécessaire aux Souverains alliés, que les dits objets d'art et de science soient rendus sans délai au Pape et à l'état Romain :

" Nous avons l'honneur d'adresser la présente à votre Excellence, afin qu'elle puisse prendre telles mesures qu'elle jugera convenables pour mettre M. Canova à même d'effectuer sans opposition l'objet de sa mission ; et pour cet effet nous prions votre Excellence de mettre à sa disposition, les mêmes moyens et protections militaires qu'elle a déjà fourni aux agens de Sa Majesté Impériale et du Roi des Pays-Bas, qui ont surveillé la restitution des objets d'art appartenant à leurs dites Majestés et au Grand Duc de Toscane.

" Agréez, Monsieur le Baron, l'assurance de notre considération très-distinguée.

(Signé) " SCHWARZENBERG.
WELLINGTON.
BLUCHER."

" Paris, le 20 Septembre, 1815."

SUPPLEMENT.

THE CONGRESS OF AIX-LA-CHAPELLE, AND ITS RESULTS.

IN obedience to my instructions, I remained in France with the army of occupation, at the head-quarters of the Duke of Wellington, who by invitation of Louis XVIII. spent the winter of 1815-16 in Paris, where there was still much to regulate concerning this army.

During this time I wrote the History of the Campaign of 1815, and employed my leisure hours on higher works of mensuration.

Napoleon had commissioned Colonel Tranchon to survey the four " Départements réunies." He established a network of principal triangles along the base of Ensisheim, carried these triangles along the Rhine and Meuse, and there connected them with the great Crayenhof triangles, which stood in connection with the French measurement for ascertaining the value of a degree terminating at Dunkirk, and these again with the two bases measured in England.

Tranchon had been interrupted in his surveys by the war. Already, at the first Peace of Paris, we had stipulated that this map should be delivered to us ; however, this was not done till the second peace in 1815. I had retained it in Paris, and sketched out a plan for completing it, which was approved by the King and fully accomplished by 1818. I was empowered to employ a number of hopeful young officers in surveying during the summer, and in drawing in classes during the winter, and to combine these with military instruction in staff knowledge.

The principal triangles constituting the basis of

this map were carefully measured with the best instruments : I considered them adapted to the measurement of degrees. I founded upon this the proposition for carrying on similar triangles from the Rhine to the basis of Seeberg, and then, as circumstances permitted, to Berlin; and for measuring, by means of beacons, the terminating points in distance as well as time, in order to obtain the measure of a degree of longitude, which, to the regret of many astronomers, had never yet been accomplished. The King likewise approved of this proposition.

The measurement of time by means of beacons had already been practically executed by Herr von Zach, in the Seeberg observatory at Gotha, in the Thuringian measurement of degrees, and I had been his chief assistant. I recommended this method in a lecture which I gave in the Bureau des Longitudes at Paris, and proposed to the French savans to make, conjointly, a measurement of degrees between Dunkirk and Seeberg.

I have given the history of the measurement of a degree of longitude between Dunkirk and Seeberg, in the seventh volume of the German journal Herta, (June, 1826) edited by Professor Berghaus, after having already made known the results, namely, the discovery of the flattening of $\frac{1}{315.2}$ in the Astronomical Reports of Professor Schumacher, 1823 (No. 72.) To avoid repetitions, I refer the reader to these publications.

I spent the summers of 1816-17-18 in Coblentz, from whence I directed the surveys : with my assistants I selected the angles of the principal triangles between the Rhine and the Seeberg Observatory, and observed them with a Reichenbach circle.

The winters of 1816-17 I spent with the Duke

at Paris, where preparations were already making for the Congress to be held at Aix-la-Chapelle in the spring of 1818. We were accurately informed of the wishes of King Louis XVIII., who considered his Government so far strengthened as to be able to dispense with the occupation of the European Powers. His minister, the Duc de Richelieu, coincided in this view, to which he had already gained over the Emperor Alexander, as well as the Russian Ambassador, Pozzo di Borgo.

The cost of maintaining, as well as the burden of quartering, the army of occupation were certainly heavy for the departments occupied. The uncertain state of the French kingdom was a consequence of Napoleon's government, and of the various views of parties who were indeed checked by the army of occupation in giving public vent to their hatred, but could not be reconciled thereby.

When Louis XVIII. had again obtained an apparently quiet possession of the throne of his ancestors, the emigrants, the companions of his misfortunes, stepped forward with the modest wish, that now when the principles of monarchy and legitimacy had come out victorious from the struggle, something too might be done for them, whose estates had been confiscated, and who had thereby become homeless, without receiving any indemnification for all their losses. No objections could be advanced against this proposition. At the time when they quitted their country, it was deemed a moral duty—an honourable sentiment—to remain true to their king, and to follow his call into foreign parts. They had lost their property in consequence of taking this step, and had been condemned to lead a life full of cares for more than twenty years in foreign lands ;

they had grown old in the interim, but had remained constant. Now, then, they wished also to reap the fruits of their heavy privations. It was a moral and religious obligation on the King to provide for men who had not, indeed, reconquered his kingdom for him, but re-entered it victoriously with him. The King felt this duty : he was ready to fulfil it, and it was only necessary to watch attentively what could, and what ought to be done.

The confiscated estates of the emigrants had been sold : they had passed into private hands at the invitation of the government. The sums produced by the sales had been paid into the state funds; the nation had enriched itself by the confiscations. A new confiscation to the prejudice of the purchasers, in order to make restitution to the emigrants, could not take place without violating all the principles of justice, and producing a fresh revolution. The acquisitions had been made under the safeguard of the existing laws of the State. It was proposed to restore their estates to the emigrants, and to indemnify the present possessors by giving them from the national fund the same sums as they had paid for them ; but a period of twenty years had altered the state of property to such a degree, that, even were it possible to find out the former condition, it was quite impossible to join together again properties many times divided, and employed for very different objects, or to be just to those who had costs of improvements to produce. The project of re-procuring for the emigrants the natural possession of their estates had therefore to be abandoned.

The purchasers had, without exception, acquired them cheap, and in some instances for a nominal price. Such property confiscated in consequence of the owner's fidelity to his master was not for every one's market ; and the apprehension that the posses-sion of such estates could not be considered quite firmly established, was decidedly expressed after the Restoration.   Property acquired in such a manner, without contracts or the signatures of the former owners, could never be sold for its real value, even before the Restoration.   When two properties of equal value lay side by side, the one an old family estate, the other the confiscated estate of an emi-grant, the former generally fetched double the price of the latter ; and this manifested the popular belief of the insecurity attached to such a purchase.

In vain Napoleon exerted all means to create confidence in the inviolability of such purchases.   He had gone so far as to introduce into the conditions of the Légion d'honneur, that this *légion sacrée* should uphold the sanctity of national sales ; never-theless, in the printed announcements of sales of private estates, at all the corners of streets, he could not prevent the insertion in the preamble, in letters the length of a finger, that the estate in question was not such debased national property.

This need not surprise any one, for the history of the last century shows the same results amongst all nations.   Even in the present day, estates confiscated at the time of the bloody revolution in England, and publicly sold under the guarantee of the State, have not the same value as those transmitted from undisturbed family possession ;* and we must rejoice that it is so, for it bears witness of a voice concealed within the human breast, which sets *moral* right against *declared* right.

* What the author had in his mind when he wrote this passage it is hard to guess.—ED.

Louis XVIII. had it in his power to adjust this evil state of affairs, and to close the still open book of the revolution. Some purchasers of emigrants' property gave him a hint to this effect. They sought the former owners of their property on their return, stated to them how cheaply *they* or their fathers had purchased, and volunteered the payment of arrears to them, on condition of their legal consent to the purchase. Some sensible emigrants agreed to this proposal. The value of the estates had greatly increased from the time of confiscation to the present, and the arrears were considerable. From the day of the signature of the contracts, such estates acquired equal value with all others ; the advantage to both parties was clear, and nothing could be more tranquillizing or conciliatory on the part of the government, than Louis XVIII. giving the widest extension to this system.

The King ought to have favoured it, and to have granted exemption from stamp fees, he ought even to have set premiums on such agreements. But, alas ! passions on all sides stood in the way. The republicans had no wish to see the revolution closed, the partizans of the ex-Emperor made every effort to prevent any obstacle arising in the way of his return, which they still hoped for. They wished him to continue to be the necessary and indispensable hope of the oppressed people ; lastly, the emigrants were dissatisfied with this prospect, hoping to obtain still more in their favour from the distressed King; an indemnification for emigrants was resolved upon by universal consent, and the King thought he might congratulate himself on a successful work. From this day forward the voluntary agreements ceased ; an impenetrable wall was raised between the emigrants and the purchasers of their properties; the guarantees for the future quiet possession of these failed; the estates of the emigrants retained their depreciated value; and mistrust, revived and increased, passed soon from sighs and complaints, to a loudly expressed wish that Napoleon might appear again.

Such was the state of affairs when it fell to the lot of the Duc de Richelieu to play the difficult part at the Congress of Aix-la-Chapelle, in 1818, of describing the prosperity, tranquillity, and harmony of the French Empire, in order that it might be relieved from the heavy burden of the army of occupation.

The Emperor Alexander had wonderfully facilitated the commission of his former Governor of Odessa. Alive to all that was comprehended in the words "to do good—to do right," he had declared himself on the first day of his arrival at Aix-la-Chapelle, and after the first conference with the Duc de Richelieu, in favour of the withdrawal of the army of occupation. The following day he sent for me, wishing to hear my opinion on the internal state of France. The views I propounded to the Emperor accorded very little with what the Duc de Richelieu had alleged, and the security he had given, that after the departure of the Allies, no disturbance of the tranquillity of France need be apprehended. The Emperor was well aware, indeed, that the parties opposed to the King were still powerful, and widely spread; but he took these for old soldiers still panting for war, who would find their counterpoise in the pacified landed proprietors; he was quite confounded when I represented to him, that on account of the great spoliation of national property, it was natural that the class of purchasers of this property should desire earnestly Napoleon's return; and that it was vain to hope for a continuance of the tranquillity of the country, so long as the King gave no guarantee that fortunes acquired by and during the revolution were inviolable property. It was not sufficient that the King had convinced his marshals and high state functionaries of this; the great mass of the people were in the same condition, and required this security still more than the highest state officers who had retained their places. To this, I added my views on the error committed in giving indemnification to the emigrants. The Emperor caught at my notion with warmth, and asked: "Have you spoken with the Duke of Wellington on this affair?" and on my answering in the affirmative, "What reply did he give you?" "Vous mettez la main à la plaie." The Emperor looked down, and after a pause asked: "Are you then also against the withdrawal of the army of occupation?" I replied, that if the Sovereigns withdrew their army in the fair hope that all germs of future disorders in France were stifled, and all the King's stumbling-blocks removed, I could not share in this simple belief; but if the question was, whether the continuance of the occupation in its present form gave any expectation of another and a better result, I must declare my opinion, that it could lead to nothing. The King of France was striving to gain the love of his people, and thought that to show sympathy was the surest means to succeed. Our occupation was a hateful measure to the whole French nation; and the King showed on every opportunity that it was, to say the least, an oppressive burden to him, which he wished to shake off. The Sovereigns had hitherto refrained from exercising any influence on internal affairs, and contented themselves with giving good advice which had not been listened to.   If now the Sovereigns resolved on *prescribing* to the King definite steps for tranquillizing his country, and on not quitting France until these steps were taken, then only I should consider the continuance of the occupation advantageous.

The Emperor here interposed, "that such constraint imposed on the King would only increase the evil, and did not come within the lawful rights of the Sovereigns." He declared himself in favour of the withdrawal of the army of occupation, and added a hint, that it would be too late now to conclude otherwise.

When I communicated this conversation to the Prince State Chancellor, I added that the army of occupation had a double object ; to maintain tranquillity in France, and to secure punctual payment of the sums of money stipulated in the Peace of Paris.   "The first we give up ; with regard to the second point, guarantees must be agreed upon, for we must not deceive ourselves,—as soon as the army is withdrawn, attempts will be made on the part of the French to release themselves from the money-payments under some pretext or other."

The Prince State Chancellor did not see every thing so *couleur de rose* as his colleagues did.   He coincided in my view, that the departure of the army of occupation ought to be made contingent on the payment of the arrears ; but he thought there was no prospect of obtaining this, as England and Russia had no more demands to make upon France ; it was therefore most important now to make such agreements that Prussia and Holland, who on an outbreak in France would be first called upon to act, should not stand *alone*.

The Duke of Wellington had undertaken the construction of fortifications in Belgium for the King of Holland, with French money; but as everything was calculated for five years, he had (like ourselves in the fortifications on the Rhine) scarcely got through half.

The State Chancellor, in his propositions for securing the boundaries of the Confederation, as well as for erecting fortresses, reckoned on vigorous support from the Duke of Wellington and the King of Holland, and ready compliance on the part of Austria. He was right as to the latter. As, on the one hand, the army of the Netherlands, with the prudent economy of the King, was sufficient for him, but was, on the other hand, quite insufficient, with fifty fortresses and forts, to defend the country successfully against a hostile invasion from France, Prince Metternich wished that Prussia should have a considerable force in her western provinces, which might, on the first signal, hasten to the assistance of Holland, and afford her protection until England could arrive with an army, and all Europe united could come forward.

No difficulties were made on our side. Austria and Prussia undertook conjointly to carry on negotiations with the King of the Netherlands, and to make arrangements in common with the Duke of Wellington, in Brussels, where the King of the Netherlands had resolved to take up his residence in the winter of 1818-19.

As the command of such auxiliary corps was to be given to me, I was chosen to go to Brussels as plenipotentiary from Austria and Prussia conjointly. After a conference, to which I was admitted,

between Princes Metternich and Hardenberg, at
which the motives of my mission were discussed, I
received directions to sketch out my instruction myself, which was considered quite appropriate, and
signed accordingly.

I arrived at Brussels at the same time as Prince
Metternich and the Duke of Wellington. The
Emperor of Russia and the Empress-mother had
arrived there on a visit to the Princess of Orange.
My business was introduced during the festivities
ordered for these high guests, but I had soon occasion to perceive that his Majesty, the King of the
Netherlands, was little inclined to enter into serious
negotiations with me. The King had considered it
a duty, in his difficult political position, to treat the
Dutch and Belgians alike as faithful and devoted
subjects; he declared publicly that, in spite of the
difference of language, religion, and customs, the two
peoples had become perfect friends after a union of
three years' duration, and he eulogised his army as
animated by the best spirit and deserving of full
confidence. Under these circumstances an envoy
could not be welcome to him, whose commission tes
tified to apprehensions on the part of Europe, which
in accordance with his self-imposed duty he was
bound to contradict *in toto*. I hoped however to
overcome these difficulties with ease, by representing
as the motive of my mission, the restlessness of the
French, combined with the wish of the Allies to be
enabled to support his Majesty at the right moment,
in case of an unexpected attack on the still unfinished
fortifications. Were these facts once admitted, agreements between the English and Prussian army would
be indispensable.

But, alas! I was soon compelled to acknowledge

that reasons still more cogent determined the King
of the Netherlands, while keeping up due forms,
to enter into no conference, still less into any proposition. The King had not forgotten that in 1815
Field-Marshal Blücher had brought no well-filled
military chest, like the English army, to pay ready
money for the subsistence of his army; and a fresh
circumstance had occurred in addition, to call forth
his Majesty's dissatisfaction against Prussia.

According to a resolution of the Confederation,
Luxemburg had a Prussian garrison conjointly with
the troops of this Grand Duchy, and likewise a Prussian Governor and Commandant. This was not
agreeable to the King of the Netherlands. His
Majesty stipulated, as a condition of the execution of
this resolution, a claim that the right flank should be
consigned to the troops of the Netherlands, and
directed this demand not to the Confederation but to
Prussia. The thing in itself was of little importance,
but the Prussian Government could not take independent resolutions in the affairs of the Confederation. Being charged, on the occasion of my mission, with the settlement of this affair, I proposed
that the Belgian battalion destined for the occupation should enter Luxemburg. On the part of
Prussia no rank was claimed. The town was the
undisputed property of the King of the Netherlands;
but, on the other hand, the circle of works around
it, as well as the barracks and other military esta-
blishments were the property of the Confederation,
and the disposition for their defence was the affair of
the Confederation, in which the King my master
could in no way interfere.

My representations were fruitless. The King
persisted in not placing his battalion in the garrison

U

until his claim was allowed.   After the departure of
Prince Metternich and the Duke of Wellington from
Brussels my principal business was protracted : for
months I was amused with an interchange of notes ;
and as France in the interim appeared quiet, and the
Netherlands drew continually closer to England in
their commercial relations, the proffered assistance was
considered daily more and more superfluous. Under
these circumstances, after the loss of five months,
I asked for my passports, and arrived in Berlin in
the month of March, 1819.

The circumstances recorded in this Supplement
appertain to the Congress of Aix-la-Chapelle and its
results ; consequently to the history of the affairs of
Europe.

PART III.

CAMPAIGNS OF THE SILESIAN ARMY UNDER FIELD-MARSHAL BLUCHER IN 1813 AND 1814.

FROM THE ARMISTICE TO THE CAPTURE OF PARIS.

Published at Berlin in 1824, from notes taken at the time.

"La critique est aisée, mais l'art est difficile."

SECTION I.

Composition of the Silesian army before the close of the Truce.—Secret instructions for operations.—Verbal additions to them.—Condition and internal relations of the army.—It advances into the neutral territory.—Commencement of hostilities.—Action at Sieben Eichen.—Bonaparte arrives with his reinforcements at Löwenberg to give battle.—The Silesian army retires.—Interrupted action at Löwenberg.—Blücher resolves to attack the enemy.—Battle on the Katzbach.—Pursuit of the enemy.

DURING the armistice (of the 4th of June, 1813,) the Sovereigns held a conference with the Crown Prince of Sweden at Trachenberg;* the Emperors of Prussia and Austria had had a previous interview in Bohemia. The plan of operations was discussed and concerted, but kept secret until the day came for distributing the parts to the various actors. A degree of foresight was displayed everywhere which inspired universal confidence.

* As related in Part I.—ED.

According to the new *ordre de bataille*, the cavalry general Von Blücher was at the head of the Silesian Army, which was composed of two Russian and one Prussian corps. Blücher received his secret instructions from the hands of General Barclay de Tolly, on the 11th of August, at Reichenbach. They were clear and appropriate, but contained some exceedingly difficult tasks. The Silesian Army was directed :—

1. To move towards the enemy.

2. Never to lose sight of them, and to approach them immediately if they attacked the Grand Army; but,

3. To avoid all decisive actions.

General von Blücher shook his head doubtfully, General Barclay de Tolly went on to explain that, according to the proposed plan of operations, the Grand Army *only* was to act on the offensive and advance through Bohemia by way of Töplitz; that the Silesian Army must therefore fall back in case the enemy advanced against it, and by so doing draw them into the interior of Silesia. But if the advance of the Grand Army were assisted by this movement, it would then be most important that the Silesian Army should instantly follow the enemy, in case they turned round. Consequently, the main object to be kept in view was to avoid being beaten, and to arrive at the right moment to take part in the grand general battle on the Elbe.

General von Blücher declared to General Barclay that this task exceeded his powers; he had never been familiar with the arts of a Fabius. Another might succeed better; he only knew how to attack. However grateful he felt for the confidence of the Sovereigns, he must decline this difficult command, in which he was to be so strictly limited to defensive operations.

General Barclay and his Quartermaster-General, Von Diebitsch, who was present at this conference, endeavoured to quiet General Blücher, by representing to him that he was taking his instructions too literally. An officer in command of an army of 100,000 men can never be tied down absolutely to the defensive; therefore, if a good opportunity occurred, he might attack and beat his enemy.

Blücher, who was quite satisfied with this interpretation, wished to have it in writing, as a supplement to General Barclay's signed instructions; and as the latter did not think proper to comply with this wish, because the Sovereigns had confirmed the instructions as they were, Blücher concluded by saying, that he undertook the command on condition of his being at liberty to attack the enemy when and where he thought necessary. He urged General Barclay to lay this explanation before the Sovereigns. Should it not accord with their views, it would be for them, in their wisdom, to give him another appointment. Thus the two Generals parted, mutually satisfied.

It is probable that General Barclay did inform the Sovereigns of this conversation, but nothing more ever transpired on this subject, either verbally or in writing.

As General Blücher received no other appointment from the Sovereigns, he took it as a sign of their approval of his views, and considered himself authorized to act quite independently, according to circumstances. This result gives great importance to this conference at Reichenbach, which therefore becomes a matter of history.

The Silesian Army was composed of three corps-d'armée, two Russian and one Prussian, commanded by Generals Count Langeron, Baron von Sacken, and Von York. Langeron's corps ought to have consisted of 46,000 men. He had about 40,000 under arms, in excellent condition, a numerous cavalry, and 170 guns, amongst which were 72 twelve-pounders.*

General Count Langeron, descended from a very old French family, had commanded against the Turks, and had acquired in the army the reputation of a good officer. Six Lieutenant-Generals and twenty-nine Major-Generals served under him.

Sacken's corps ought to have consisted of 19,000 men, but had only about 16,000 under arms. This corps was the remnant of an army which had been employed against the Turks, and had not been recruited for a long time. It was composed of old and well-tried soldiers, and was, in proportion, stronger in cavalry than Langeron's; it had 60 pieces of artillery, 24 of which were twelve-pounders.

General Baron von Sacken, a native of Courland, was reputed in the army to be an active soldier and an able man. He had formerly been condemned by court-martial, in consequence of a quarrel with a superior; but the Emperor, who knew his good qualities, and required men of his energy, did not confirm the sentence. Public opinion reported that he had been soured by this occurrence, and rendered so irritable that his superiors found it difficult to deal with him.

York's corps consisted of about 40,000 men.

* The Russian army carried three kinds of 12-pounders,—18, 16, and 14 calibre. The Silesian army had learnt by experience to look upon the latter kind as a very imperfect sort of ordnance.

The spirit and good-will of the Prussian troops were beyond all description. On the other hand, they were at this time far behind the Russians in arms and equipments. The Silesian Landwehr were particularly ill-supplied with clothes; they were wanting even in shoes at the re-opening of the campaign. Cloth had been got wherever it could be found. There had been no time for taking the usual precautions in making it up, and after the first rain the coats shrunk so much that they barely covered body and arms. Many battalions were altogether without half-boots; they left their shoes sticking when they came to muddy places. The coverings for their head protected them neither from cuts nor rain.

The sick-lists of the first four weeks of the campaign prove how much the health of the men was affected by this insufficient clothing. Later, when the army advanced into Saxony, means of procuring all that was requisite were found there. The cavalry was tolerably well mounted; the 100 guns which the corps possessed were well horsed.

General von York had entered the Prussian service from the Dutch;* he had served at the Cape; he distinguished himself as commandant of the Jäger

---

* Von York's family was of English origin. His ancestor left this country after the battle of Worcester, and went to Sweden. Von York received his first commission in the Prussian service; but on a reduction of the Prussian forces in which he was included, he went to Holland, in whose army he obtained a commission, through the interest of the then English Ambassador at the Hague, Joseph Yorke, Lord Dover. He subsequently re-entered the Prussian service. In 1814 he visited England, and after his return to Prussia, he sent a notice of his family and of his personal history to the late Earl of Hardwicke. This note is given from memory of the contents of this document.—ED.

regiment in 1806, and acquired a military reputation by the orders he executed in Courland in 1812, as well as by the Convention of Tauroggen. Serious, strict, of a firm unbending character, esteemed in the army, persevering in battle, and particularly skilful in maintaining and prolonging an action, he was a welcome associate to General von Blücher, on whom he placed the fullest reliance.

There existed great differences in the Russian and Prussian armies, both in the mode of conducting the war and in the customs and habits of the troops, as well as in the relations of the soldiers to their superiors, and in their maintenance and pay. The utmost attention was requisite to prevent all these causes from giving birth to lasting discord.

Meanwhile General von Blücher did not confine his views to the mere avoidance of all cause of offence; he was desirous also of establishing brotherly harmony, and of so disposing the Russian troops, that they might carry on the war, if not with pleasure, at least without reluctance. He disputed the opinion entertained by many, that we had a right to require the Russian army to adopt German customs while they were in Germany; he wished, on the contrary, that we should conform to theirs; he laid it down as a fixed principle, that the Prussian army ought to earn and preserve the esteem of their allies by great actions. To put forward the Prussian army, wherever it was possible, seemed to him the fundamental condition of his command. Without the assistance of Russia, we were unable to crush the colossus which had threatened us with degradation and eternal slavery: but to desire more than *assistance*, where our own strength did not suffice, would be unfair.

Russia had freed herself in 1812; our turn was now come, and General von Blücher had too exalted a notion of national honour, to balance it against the policy which might teach us cunningly to shift on others the heavy labours whereof we hoped to reap the advantages.

In perfect understanding with the superior Prussian officers, Blücher could reckon on their co-operation; yet he was hindered in the execution of his intentions by a peculiar coincidence of circumstances.

Opinions were much divided in the Russian army as to the expediency of a continuance of this bloody war on the part of Russia. Marshal Kutusof perhaps started the doubt: he gave his voice for peace. But every general employed in carrying on the war, whether in accordance to or against his own convictions, wished to fight under the eye of his Emperor; *i. e.*, in the Grand Army. Appointments therefore in the Silesian Army appeared anything but favours. Moreover the circumstance that neither of the three armies was commanded by a Russian general seemed to many an offence against the rights of honour, or those actual rights springing from the alliance; and the fact of General Count Langeron, who had already commanded armies, being placed under the orders of a foreign general, increased this feeling. There was therefore no lack of discontent, and the cause of it was of such a nature that Blücher was unable to remove it.

To all this must be added the singularly unlucky circumstance, that General Count Langeron had got hold of the secret instructions given to General Blücher, while he remained in total ignorance of the conversation mentioned above, which completely altered the state of things. In accordance with these

instructions—undoubtedly with the best intentions—
Count Langeron chalked out the line of conduct
which he supposed Blücher would pursue, and which
he also made the guide of his own actions.   When,
in consequence of this, things went contrary to
Blücher's orders, Count Langeron believed himself
to be on the right course while Blücher was pursuing
the wrong one.   His generals shared this opinion,
and misunderstandings accumulated, which could not
be prevented, because the origin of them lay in
obscurity.   General von Blücher never dreamt that
his secret instructions had fallen into other hands.

Thus we see, in the first ten days after the commencement of hostilities, that the military objects
General von Blücher had in view were but imper-
fectly attained; his intentions were disturbed, and in
part frustrated, and the internal relations of the
army were troubled by anger and discontent; so
that there was considerable danger that the greatest
disasters might befall us in consequence.

But, as we often see, after a combination of unlucky circumstances in the history of states, in the
fate of armies, as well as in the private relations of
men, fortunate moments reappear, which when seized
with a vigorous hand, extricate all concerned from
the most embarrassing situation : thus there arose for
the Silesian Army, in the battle on the Katzbach, a
star of hope, which shed its light upon them and
guided them faithfully to the gates of Paris.

The corps of General Baron von Sacken was
posted on the right bank of the Oder, at Breslau.

A portion of the corps of Count Langeron (about
12,000 men), under the orders of Count Pahlen,
were cantoned at Landshuth : the rest assembled on

the 12th of August on the Zobtenberg, where York's corps was already concentrated.

The country (from Upper Silesia to the Elbe) in which the armies on both sides had remained, during the armistice, was exhausted; only the intermediate neutral district, including the town of Breslau, could serve to maintain the army until the new harvest. It might be foreseen that the enemy's army would, on their part, forage as much as they could in this district; and as the neutral territory had an extent of two days' march, such a loss could not be prevented on the part of the Silesian Army (on their advancing through this district at the close of the armistice) for forty-eight hours. But what if the French army attempted this foraging during the armistice? By complaining of the violation of national privileges we should not recover what we had lost. For this reason it was the earnest wish of the General-in-Chief von Blücher to find an occasion for occupying the neutral territory, without however commencing hostilities before the termination of the armistice. A second reason was of still greater importance. It was known, by means of a well-organized system of espionage, that the French army stood *en échelon* from Goldberg to Bautzen. It was probable that, as soon as Bonaparte received intelligence of the march of the Grand Army through Bohemia, he would concentrate all his forces at Dresden, to give them battle with superior numbers before the other Allied Armies could come up.

The armistice and the neutral territory attached to it were singularly favourable to such a mode of proceeding; for should Austria make her declaration of war on the 10th of August, Bonaparte, by immediately setting all his *corps-d'armée* in motion, could bring those that were now posted on the confines of Silesia, and those now opposed to the Crown Prince of Sweden, into the neighbourhood of Dresden by the 16th of August. The Silesian Army would be obliged in that case to allow all these preparations to proceed quietly, and could not venture even to enter the neutral territory before the 17th.

But were it possible to find some pretext for sooner occupying the neutral ground we could by this movement,—

1. Deceive the enemy as to our strength and plan of operations, as they would suppose that we were advancing to assume the *offensive,* and

2. We should gain two days' march (the width of the neutral territory) in case he drew off his forces for the purpose of concentrating them on the Elbe.

In fact intelligence reached us on the 13th that hostile patrols in the mountains (towards Schönau) had entered the neutral ground and ventured to make requisitions. Thereupon the army received immediate orders to advance into the neutral territory, and attack the enemy wherever they found them within the confines of this territory; they were however not to pass these limits, but to remain on this side the Katzbach until the close of the armistice, which was to follow shortly. This order was executed on the 14th, 15th, and 16th of August. The enemy kept very quiet in their old encampment at Goldberg and Liegnitz, behind the Katzbach, but occupied the villages and other important points on the right bank, which gave rise to some skirmishing.

This entrance upon the neutral territory gave occasion to a multitude of remarks in the Russian corps, which spread and were loudly repeated in the army. It was said that this was against the intentions and instructions; that General Barclay, who properly commanded the army, would not think it right; that he ought to repair to the Silesian Army and lead it himself; that the Russian corps could not be placed under the orders of General von Blücher, &c. These expressions came round to Blücher's ears, but, however unpleasant they must have been to him, he took no notice of them, and continued the same demeanour toward the Russian troops.*

The reports brought in, on the morning of the 17th of August, stated that the enemy was still quietly remaining in his camp behind the Katzbach. The General-in-Chief ordered a reconnoissance toward Goldberg. The Quartermaster-General von Gneisenau conducted it. A tirailleur-fire commenced. General Gneisenau attacked the enemy in the village

* This entrance upon the neutral territory gave rise to a correspondence between Neumark and the head-quarters of General von Blücher. There were still commissioners at Neumark from the belligerent Powers, who had met there to watch over the execution of the conditions of the armistice. The French Commissioner complained in a note of the violation of the Convention and of national rights. The Russian and Prussian Commissioners, ignorant of the circumstances which had led to this violation, communicated these complaints to General von Blücher, and called upon him to remove all causes of grievance.

Blücher laid before our Commissioner the proofs that the French army had first allowed themselves to act against the Convention; and as this had brought upon him the duty of protecting the neutral subjects of his king against the aggressors, he would not allow himself to be disturbed in the performance of his duty; but, on the other hand, he would strictly respect the truce till the hour of its close. This was not considered sufficient. Demands were sent from Neumark for the army to turn back. The General-in-Chief wrote to the Prussian General von Krusemark, "that an end must be put to diplomatic fooleries and note-writing. He would beat time without notes."

of Rochlitz, situated on the right bank of the Katzbach ; they defended it in earnest. The firing was
kept up by the Prussian advanced-guard till dark,
when it drew back, in accordance with the disposition, as far as Seichau. That same night the
enemy withdrew from the camps at Goldberg and
Liegnitz.

On the receipt of intelligence on the 18th, the
army marched off in three columns : The 1st column
(Count Langeron's corps), through the mountains, by
Schönau and Steinberg. The 2nd column (York's
corps), to Goldberg. The 3rd column (Sacken's
corps), from Liegnitz upon Haynau.

Some prisoners were made, and the enemy was
pursued by Pilgramsdorf to Lauterseiffen, where a
rear-guard was posted. There seemed to be no doubt
that the enemy would concentrate their forces on the
Elbe, and measures were taken accordingly to follow
them without loss of time, so that the advanced-
guard should never lose sight of them.

On the 19th the march in three columns was to
be continued to the Bober, and across it. The right
wing (Sacken's corps), was to cross at Bunzlau : the
centre (York's corps), at Löwenberg. The left wing
was to pass the Bober at Zobten, and join the centre
in the camp beyond Löwenberg.

The left wing first reached the Bober at Zobten,
found the enemy on the left bank, and took them for
the retreating rear-guard.

The advanced-guard of Langeron's corps, under
General Rudczeweitsch, attacked them warmly. It
was most probable that the enemy had intended this
day to concentrate the three corps which had stood
facing the Silesian Army, and did not expect to be
attacked at Zobten. Meanwhile the advanced-guard

of Count Langeron's corps, pressed forward by Sieben Eichen, as far as the road from Lähn to Löwenberg, and separated thereby the 11th corps of the French, which was marching from Lähn to Löwenberg, from the 5th, which was stationed in the latter place.

This the enemy would not permit; they therefore collected their forces to recover their communication, and succeeded in doing so. As, however, Langeron's advanced-guard had fallen in with the baggage of the 11th corps, and would not give up this advantage so easily, an obstinate fight commenced, which only ended at nightfall, by the advanced-guard retreating across the Bober, and remaining at Zobten reunited with the corps.

While this was going on in that quarter, York's corps marched in two columns from Goldberg to Löwenberg, the General-in-Chief being with the one advancing along the chaussée. When this column arrived in the district of Lauterseiffen, reports were sent in by General von York, (who was with the second column,) that his right flank patrol had discovered a hostile corps on its march, which, on becoming aware of the movement of the Silesian Army, had halted on the Gräditzberg, and taken up a position there. This had compelled him to advance with three brigades, to keep back the enemy, and prevent their taking the army in the rear. The accuracy of the information could not be doubted, but how this hostile corps had got into the midst of the Silesian Army remained incomprehensible. The Bober could only be crossed at two places, at Löwenberg and at Bunzlau.

By accounts received that morning, General von Sacken must have already reached Thomaswalde, and consequently the retreat to Bunzlau was cut off from the hostile corps on the Gräditzberg. As Lauterseiffen was in our hands, and we had a corps of some 30,000 men at Zobten, it would be easy to cut off the enemy's retreat from Lauterseiffen likewise, if General von York succeeded in detaining them on the Gräditzberg long enough for the troops to come up from Zobten. The enemy would in that case be forced to lay down their arms. An aide-de-camp of the General-in-Chief, with some swift horses, was dispatched from the district of Lauterseiffen to recon-noitre the enemy on the Gräditzberg. He found them there, and learnt from a prisoner that they were the 3rd corps, consisting of about 20,000 men, under Marshal Ney. On his report, the General-in-Chief founded the following disposition :—

General von York was to observe the enemy, and if they drew off, he was to endeavour to detain them, or at all events to follow them.

General von Sacken was directed to place himself in front of the enemy, in case they drew off towards Bunzlau, as the whole army could then follow them.

General Count Langeron received instructions to send a part of his corps immediately by Lauterseiffen to Deutmannsdorff, to leave his advanced-guard at Zobten, and to follow later with the rest of his corps towards Deutmannsdorff, in order to cut off Marshal Ney from Löwenberg. Count Langeron replied that his troops were too much fatigued to perform this march, and refused to do so, even when a Russian general, who happened to be at head-quarters, and perceived the importance of this movement, pro-ceeded himself to Zobten, to see that the disposition prescribed was put in execution. It grew dark, in the meantime, and Marshal Ney escaped by a night march beyond Bunzlau.

The General-in-Chief was in a most difficult and unpleasant predicament. What was the reason of Count Langeron's refusal? Was it a false view of the strength of his corps? Was it a false view of the political interest of Russia? Was it opposition, in consequence of his dissatisfaction at being placed under the orders of a Prussian general? What was to be done? Should he or could he apply the strict forms of the service? Would this be advisable in such an isolated situation, and in a crisis like the one impending?

The discontent existing in the army might easily come to an outbreak were the General-in-Chief inclined to punish; and the entire machine, on whose co-operation the Grand Army relied, must come to a standstill.

The Prussian general had also to think of his country.

In this critical situation the General-in-Chief resolved to regard the disobedience of Count Langeron as a misunderstanding, and to pass it over lightly. He had nothing left for the future but to remain with this corps, and to wait and see whether any fresh instance of disobedience to orders given by himself in person should occur, when there could be no excuse of misunderstanding.

On the 20th, the corps of Count Langeron remained at Zobten; York's corps proceeded along the chaussée, the advanced guard attacked the enemy, who occupied the heights of Weinberg and Plagwitz, as a *tête de pont* in front of Löwenberg, and drove them away after a combat of some hours' duration.

General von Sacken, on his side, attacked Bunz-lau, and dislodged the enemy, who toward evening blew up a powder-magazine, whereby the town was very much damaged.

The whole of the right bank of the Bober was now in our hands. The enemy had destroyed the bridges, and this, as well as the blowing up of the powder-magazine, seemed to indicate that it was their intention to continue their retreat. It was naturally supposed that the hostile troops would withdraw in the night from the camps at Löwenberg and Bunzlau, on the left bank of the Bober, and preparations were accordingly made for restoring the bridges next morning, in order to pursue the enemy.

But the next morning the camp at Löwenberg remained unaltered. Troops were seen marching up the Bober towards Löwenberg; and, judging from the clouds of dust, considerable numbers were likewise on their march from Lauban to Löwenberg.

At Sirkwitz a small bridge over a mill-stream had been repaired by York's corps; a weak division crossed it, to reconnoitre the march of the troops pro-ceeding up the Bober. They found them to be the Würtemberg contingent, with whom they engaged in a fight, which ended in the retreat of the troops of York's corps across the Bober.

The enemy's movement was altogether inexpli-cable, until towards noon, when he at last began to restore the bridge at Löwenberg.

Following the chaussée from Löwenberg to Lau-terseiffen, about a quarter of a mile from the Bober bridge, you reach a village of the name of Plagwitz; it is long and very much scattered, lying between two mountain ridges, which run parallel to the Bober, and terminate in a tolerably steep slope towards Plagwitz. The ridge to the left, on which lie some houses of the village of Weinberg, is about half a (German) mile long, but only from 300 to 400 paces broad at its summit. The way thither from Plagwitz is hardly practicable for artillery, on account of its steepness; another road, however, running in the opposite direction from Ludwigsdorf, is quite practicable for artillery. This ridge and the village of Plagwitz were occupied by York's corps.

The other ridge, to the right of the chaussée, is far longer, and in that part where the village of Höfel is situated, it is moreover considerably broader; until after some indentations, it ends at Zobten. Upon this ridge, between Höfel and Plagwitz stood only some Russian advanced posts.

When the enemy began to restore the bridge, a 12-pounder battery fired upon them from the heights of Weinberg, and the General-in-Chief ordered Count Langeron to occupy the heights between Höfel and Plagwitz, with proportionate forces. But the passage of the Bober by the enemy took place so soon after, that they had gained these heights, brought up their artillery, and got possession of the village of Plagwitz before the Russian brigade arrived; which, on finding that the enemy had anticipated them on the heights they had been appointed to defend, formed in line between Höfel and Zobten.

York's corps was disposed with its right wing on the heights of Weinberg, and its left in a wood on the chaussée, with the village of Lauterseiffen about three-quarters of a mile in its rear. The centre stood on undulating hills, which could only be reached by the enemy's heavy artillery from the ridge between Plagwitz and Höfel. In the valley a warm tirailleur-fire had commenced.

Hitherto the General-in-Chief had been unable to find out the intentions of the enemy; but when we saw from the Weinberg heights the whole hostile army defiling in close columns and with great haste through Löwenberg, and great clouds of dust rising continually upon the chaussée from Lauban to Löwenberg; and when, at last, a messenger found means of crossing the Bober, and brought the news that Bonaparte himself was arrived, we could no longer doubt that it was his intention to give battle. Our position was bad, chiefly from this reason, that Count Langeron's corps at Zobten was at too great a distance from the left wing of York's corps; however the ground was very favourable for breaking off the action that had commenced.

The General-in-Chief ordered the retreat. General von York drew off from the right wing, and brought his main force behind Lauterseiffen. The execution of this movement was in great part unnoticed by the enemy, while one brigade held the wood between Lauterseiffen and Plagwitz with swarms of tirailleurs. Night fell just as we abandoned the village of Lauterseiffen.

According to the disposition, Count Langeron's corps marched from Zobten by Neudorf and Armruh, into a position behind Pilgramsdorf, his advanced guard in a second column by Petersdorf to Neu Wiesen, where it halted. York's corps took up a position behind Ulbersdorf, with his advanced guard at Neudorf. Sacken's corps, according to report, had likewise been attacked at Bunzlau; he had received orders not to engage in any action, and to retreat into a position between Adelsdorf and Leisersdorf, with his advanced guard at Algenau.

In this position the army had the rapid Deichsel* in front, and this little river, covered on both banks from Pilgramsdorf to Adolfsdorf with dwellings, gardens, and hedges, did not allow of troops crossing in a body. The General-in-Chief was therefore able to wait quietly until the enemy disclosed his mea- sures, without being forced into a battle. We had the advantage of an open prospect on the left bank of the Deichsel.

In the course of this day, the Prussian Landwehr was engaged for the first time. It had been a mere skirmishing fight, and they had shown themselves brave but inexperienced, as was to be expected of young troops : the loss in consequence, in killed and wounded, had been considerable, and exceeded 2000 men. It may be assumed that, from the greater skill of their tirailleurs, the enemy's loss was not so considerable.

The action at Lauterseiffen had ended. The question now was, what would the enemy do next? Should he with such considerable forces penetrate still further into Silesia, he would give time to the Grand Army to gain Dresden and the line of the Elbe ; and as this was the main object of our ope- rations, we could wish for nothing better. But it was also possible that Bonaparte might turn back from the Bober towards Dresden : it was therefore necessary to force him to develop his strength in our view before we retreated a step further.

The position of the army on the Deichsel was well adapted to this object, and there was none

* A mountain stream.

other to be found on the line of retreat but the position behind Goldberg, which would have allowed of our awaiting the enemy, and calculating his forces without incurring any danger.

The General-in-Chief disclosed his intentions to the commanders of the three corps: to engage in no battle, but not to quit the Deichsel until it was evident that the enemy was advancing to give battle, with superior numbers, and until he had deployed his forces before our eyes on the left bank of that stream.

In case of a retreat it was determined that the army should proceed in three columns:—Count Langeron's corps, on the chaussée, to a position behind Goldberg:—York's corps, by Neudorf to the Rennweg, his centre by the Katzbach, his rear-guard at Rosendau:—Sacken's corps by Seiffersdorf and Giersdorf, on the right bank of the Katzbach.

The General-in-Chief reserved to himself to determine when the retreat became necessary. In a conference which he held with Count Langeron on the morning of the 22nd, the latter expressed a wish for the immediate retreat of the army; he considered it the most judicious, indeed necessary, measure, and urged the General-in-Chief to put it in execution. Blücher stuck to his disposition, and as not a shot had yet been fired, towards ten o'clock he repaired to York's corps from Pilgramsdorf.

Shortly after Langeron's advanced corps at Neu Wiesen was attacked, and driven back towards Pilgramsdorf. The enemy showed about 10,000 men, and the head of a second column between Neu Wiesen and Armruh, all which the General-in-Chief accurately observed from a height behind Ulbersdorf. Nothing was yet to be seen in front of the corps of York and Sacken, therefore the General-in-Chief took the enemy's movement for a reconnaissance.

A message soon after arrived from General Count Langeron, to say that he had been attacked by such considerable forces that he had found himself obliged to commence the retreat, according to the disposition. In vain the General-in-Chief dispatched an aide-de-camp to stop this retreat—in vain he rode thither himself; for, on reaching Pilgramsdorf, he found the enemy already in the place, engaged in a skirmish with the rear-guard. There was nothing left but to give the order to retreat to the rest of the troops.

The General-in-Chief continued to observe the enemy as long as possible, but could not discover more than about 20,000 men, who did not advance with the eagerness they usually displayed when Bonaparte was at their head. He was convinced that Bonaparte had turned back, and sorely regretted that his intentions had been frustrated by the precipitate retreat of Count Langeron. He proceeded to Goldberg, in order to have a conference with this general, but he found the town quite deserted, and no troops behind Goldberg. An aide-de-camp was instantly dispatched to the Prussian rear-guard, with orders to throw six battalions into the town, and these luckily arrived before the enemy. Some aides-de-camp, sent after Count Langeron, found him at Seichau, on the chaussée to Jauer, in full retreat. The General-in-Chief sent him orders "to turn back instantly and resume the position at Goldberg." The fate of the army hung on this movement: General Count Langeron executed it.

General von York had lost his rear-guard by the

occupation of Goldberg; early on the 23rd therefore he directed a brigade to advance from Rochlitz until it reached a position parallel to Goldberg. Count Langeron's corps reached the position behind Goldberg, but the Wolfsberg, which should have secured the left flank, and gave to the position its peculiar strength, was already in the hands of the enemy, who were forming behind this hill for the attack on Langeron's corps. The capture of Goldberg seemed to them probably too difficult, as one attempt had completely failed. The town had old walls, which had been prepared for defence during the night, as far as time allowed, and judicious use had been made of them.

Almost at the same time the brigade belonging to York's corps, on the left bank of the Katzbach, had to encounter an attack of the enemy's cavalry. The country there is flat, but to the south and southeast of Goldberg it is wooded and hilly. It was impossible to compute the enemy's strength; a captain, whom we took prisoner, told us that he had seen Napoleon that morning. A number of troops appeared in the neighbourhood of Neudorff.

The army was divided by defiles, and Count Langeron's corps alone had a tactically strong position, which was however much weakened by the loss of the Wolfsberg. Should the enemy advance towards Kroitsch, Goldberg and the position behind it must be immediately abandoned; this would entail the necessity of giving up the whole position on the Katzbach.

The General-in-Chief, therefore, about one P.M., gave the order for breaking off the action, and beginning the counter-march to Jauer, where he intended to concentrate the whole army. The loss of

Prussian troops again exceeded a thousand men. Count Langeron's corps had lost hardly half that number; meanwhile they had repulsed the enemy several times, maintained their position, and silenced the firing; and now, after marching and counter-marching the whole night, they had again to make a stout march. This excited great discontent. General Count Langeron wished to remain quiet; this was not allowed, and he consequently believed that this new counter-march enabled him to prove clearly that it had been perfectly unnecessary to make him return to Goldberg on the previous night.

The actions were broken off in a very skilful manner, and the retreat commenced in the best order; meanwhile night fell, and gaps arose in York's corps, which was marching on cross-roads. One column in consequence got scattered, and could not be brought into order again until the morning of the 24th of August. Four battalions of Landwehr, which went astray, and knew not where they were, fell in with the Russian baggage, marched with it, and so at last reached Schweidnitz. This circumstance greatly irritated General von York; he thought that the Prussian army would be quite ruined by fatiguing marches and incessant exertions before it came to a battle.

Peculiar circumstances—especially the difficult task imposed on the army of never losing sight of the enemy, yet never engaging in any decisive action with them—had demanded great exertions. This moreover gave occasion to very contradictory orders in the course of a few hours, according to the various accounts received. An accurate survey of the circumstances was necessary, in order properly to estimate the proceedings of the General-in-Chief; without this he must appear irresolute, and at variance with himself as to what he really wanted. Discontent among the foreign troops, inexperience in his own, and amongst their leaders dissatisfaction, and demands which could not be fulfilled,—truly such a state of things required speedy help, and this was only to be sought for in some great and successful event in the war.

But the General-in-Chief had taken his resolution to receive battle on the open hilly ground to the back of Jauer, in case the enemy advanced further. If they remained stationary, he would go himself to meet and attack them. Should the battle be lost, things could not be worse than they were; and if he gained the victory, everything would probably be put straight.

On the 24th, the enemy quietly remained in their positions at Goldberg, and behind the Katzbach, and the same on the 25th. This made us believe that Bonaparte had marched off with a portion of his army, although we could arrive at no certainty on the subject, and spies reported that a considerable army was still standing in front of us. On the 25th intelligence reached us, through some partisans, roaming about in the neighbourhood of Haynau, that the enemy's third corps had passed Haynau on its march back to Bunzlau. The General-in-Chief resolved, in consequence, to attack the enemy on the 26th. All was prepared in the army, and the two days' rest had given time to put the arms again into good condition, and to complete the ammunition and provisions.

Baron von Sacken had displayed in some previous affairs all the qualities of a good general. The General-in-Chief was not yet personally acquainted with him; he repaired to his head-quarters on the 25th, to testify his approval of him, and to learn his views on the situation of the Silesian Army. He left him very well satisfied, for he found that, if the leaders of the other two corps entertained opinions which did not accord with his own, General Baron von Sacken entered fully into his views.

Orders were therefore given, on the evening of the 25th, for the army to break up. The intentions were to advance as far as the Katzbach, to await the enemy on the edge of its left valley, then to engage their attention in front, and fall upon them, on the right flank and rear, with Count Langeron's corps and a portion of York's corps, which was to cross the Katzbach in the neighbourhood of Goldberg. But, in order to facilitate the march to the Katzbach, and to keep the enemy in uncertainty as to the disposition, the march was ordered in three columns:—

1st column. Count Langeron's corps was directed to advance on the chaussée from Jauer to Goldberg, by Hennersdorf, Seichau, Lasnig, and Rochlitz. As this chaussée skirts the foot of the wooded mountain chain which runs down from Hirschberg and the Bohemian confines, one brigade of the corps was to proceed upon the wooded heights, to cover the march to Goldberg.

2nd column. York's corps was directed to march by Alt Jauer, Brechtelshof, and Nieder-Crayn, to the Katzbach.

3rd column. Sacken's corps was to march by Dohnau to the Katzbach.

By this disposition, the corps of Langeron and York were divided in their march from Alt Jauer to Nieder-Crayn by the Neisse, a turbulent brook running in a valley about 150 feet deep, of which the ridge to the right is the highest. From this ridge a plateau extends towards Liegnitz, which may be considered a plain, as it is only slightly hilly, and the springs (near which the villages are situated) pour great quantities of water into the Katzbach.

The corps of York and Sacken were, therefore, closely united on this march as far as Nieder-Crayn, after which Sacken's corps remained alone on the above-mentioned plateau, and the corps of Count Langeron and York united. If Count Langeron was left to his own resources during the greatest part of this march, still he possessed the advantage of finding, during its course, two positions well adapted to a corps of 15,000 to 20,000 men, which, with the flanks secured, are almost impregnable. The principal position is behind Hennersdorf, where the right wing rests on Schlaup, the left on the mountains, having the village of Hermsdorf in its rear. The second position is a German mile further on, with Seichau in front. It requires fewer troops, but does not command the opposite hills, which the first position at Hennersdorf does in a very advantageous manner. As in both positions the right wing rests on the Neisse, and the left on the mountain-chain, the necessary measures for covering the wings are the same in both. Hence the necessity for one brigade to march along the mountains, to cover the left wing. The right was secured by the march of York's corps.

The advanced posts of Langeron's corps were stationed in Prausnitz and Rochlitz on the 25th. Those of York's corps along the Katzbach, and those of Sacken's corps (touching York's), towards Liegnitz.

THE BATTLE ON THE KATZBACH.*

On the morning of the 26th, the advanced posts stationed in the district from Prausnitz to Kroitsch (where the Neisse flows into the Katzbach), reported that the enemy was advancing, and already driving back the outposts.

The General-in-Chief, who was with the central column (York's corps), made the army continue to march, until the reports became so decisive about eleven A.M. that he could no longer doubt the enemy was advancing, perhaps to seek him out, and offer battle. He therefore gave orders for all the corps to halt, and to draw up concealed, until the enemy's intentions were more developed. Should the enemy make no farther advance by one o'clock,—that is, in two hours, thus showing that his movement was only a reconnoissance, the army would continue its march according to the former disposition.

A violent storm of rain had set in, which prevented anything being seem. The General-in-Chief halted at Brechtelshof, where York's corps took up a position, while the chief of the staff repaired to the advanced guard in order to observe the enemy's movements. At Christianshöhe he met with the Prussian rear-geard, which was retiring before the enemy in such a manner, that no flankers even were left behind, to keep the enemy in sight. These troops could give no other account, but that the enemy had crossed the Katzbach in considerable masses, and were following by Nieder-Crayn upon the plateau.

* Colonel Cathcart, in his "Commentaries on the War in Russia and Germany in 1812-13," mentions this battle as one of the most brilliant and decisive victories recorded on behalf of the Allies. Marshal Macdonald commanded the French army.—Tr.

The enemy had sent out no flankers either, it was therefore possible to get near enough to observe what follows.*

A numerous body of cavalry, which might be computed at 3,000 horse, with many batteries, was discovered coming from Nieder-Crayn, with the left wing towards Jänowitz. Infantry followed on the same road, but few battalions were as yet arrived on the plateau. The front, and the attention of the army seemed directed towards Eichholz. This led to the following conclusions :—

If York's corps, resting on the ridge of the Neisse valley, advances rapidly, in an hour it can reach the point where the defile from Nieder-Crayn leads on to the plateau. In this interval of time, from 10,000 to 12,000 of the enemy's troops may have arrived on the plateau, consequently York's corps will encounter at most 20,000 men.

Should the enemy march in two columns (admitting that in the reconnaissance a column coming from Dohnau on the plateau could not be seen), in this case from 30,000 to 40,000 men might be found on the plateau. These would not be quite equal to the strength of the corps of York and Sacken, who would then fight united. There was therefore not a moment to lose for assuming the offensive. Two points were of paramount importance to us, and for the success of our attack: these were—

1. The heights between Eichholz and Christians-höhe, and

2. The little village of Balawic on the edge of the valley of the Neisse.

An officer was now dispatched to General von

* See previous memoirs, Part I., p. 59.—ED.

Sacken, to communicate to him the disposition, and invite him to direct himself with his corps upon Eichholz.

Directions were given to bring up a 12-pounder battery from York's corps, between Christianshöhe and Eichholz, which was intended by its fire to draw the attention of the enemy to this point.

Two brigades and a half were to continue to advance, but without deploying, along the ridge, between Christianshöhe and the edge of the valley. A half brigade was to form the connection between York's corps and that of Count Langeron. One brigade was to remain as a reserve.

Before the troops of this corps had got into motion, a 12-pounder battery opened an unexpected fire from the above-mentioned height at Eichholz upon the enemy who had begun to advance, but was then obliged to halt to engage in a cannonade. It was discovered to be the artillery of General von Sacken, who had, even before receiving instructions, approached Eichholz, and, perceiving the importance of this height, speedily occupied it with a 12-pounder battery, although it lay out of the direction of his line of march. This circumstance, which proved the military correctness of General Sacken's eye, not only mainly contributed to the speedy decision of the battle, but produced a lasting esteem and attachment for him in the whole Prussian corps.*

* The day after the battle the General-in-Chief, speaking of it to some officers and soldiers, said, "We owe a great deal to General von Sacken; his 12-pounders on the Eichholz heights facilitated our work, his cavalry in Sebastiani's rear completed the victory. Let us hold the man in honour." These words were hardly spoken when they were already known throughout the Prussian army. General Sacken accidentally rode down the column of York's corps. The officers saluted him respectfully

The ground was undulating, and the rain so violent, that both causes combined prevented the French army from discovering the approach of our infantry until it had left the little village of Belawic far in the rear. The French infantry rushed to the attack, but in the violent rain few muskets went off, so that between some battalions it came to a hand-to-hand fight, in which the enemy's infantry got the worst. Our infantry continued to advance in conformity to the disposition; it was supported by the artillery, which had formed into one great battery on the right wing; and the enemy's infantry, threatened on its line of retreat, began to abandon the field.

Thereupon the enemy's cavalry made an onslaught, rather to gain time for the retreat, than to decide the combat. Our infantry could not fire; nothing therefore was left for us but to bid defiance, in close masses, to the hostile cavalry, until our cavalry could come to our support.

When our cavalry came up, the horse got too much scattered in the fight, so that they were unable to decide it or rout the enemy, until the Russian cavalry of Sacken's corps took them on the left flank, between Eichholz and Jänowitz, and the two last regiments of the Prussian reserve cavalry came on in close columns.

The retreat of the enemy now became general. Their artillery attempted to save it, but the guns got stuck and overthrown in the steep road on the ridge to Nieder-Crayn, so that five batteries of six

and in silence, as became them. But the soldiers on recognizing him broke out into a prolonged joyful hurrah, as became *them*. General von Sacken acknowledged the value of the one as well as the other of these unaffected expressions of approbation and esteem.

pieces, with their carriages, fell into our hands. Some hostile battalions, forming the rear-guard, re- treated in good order, in squares, beyond Nieder- Crayn, when night set in, and the darkness was intense. The field of battle was so saturated by the incessant rain, that a great portion of our infantry, the Landwehr in particular (who had no half-boots), left their shoes sticking in the mud, and followed the enemy barefoot.

While all this was passing on the right bank of the raging Neisse, the cannonade on the left bank retired farther and farther towards Jauer, and General Count Langeron sent word how he had gra- dually lost the village of Seichau, occupied by his advanced guard, then the position behind it, then the village of Hennersdorf, and gave notice that probably he should be unable to hold his position on the last height. This seemed quite incomprehensible to the General-in-Chief, as Count Langeron must have had about 130 pieces of artillery in that position ; and on this rainy day, when neither cavalry nor infantry could advance rapidly, the guns could operate very decisively.

The General-in-Chief, however, caused the reserve brigade of York's corps immediately to advance on Schlauphof, in order to fall on the left flank of the corps attacking General Count Langeron. When the enemy was totally routed near Nieder-Crayn, with the loss of his guns, the General-in-Chief dispatched an officer of his suite* to Count Lan- geron to acquaint him with the state of affairs, and to concert measures for combining their exertions to make use of the victory. It then came out that Count Langeron had taken his own peculiar view of

* The Author, v. Part I., p. 67—Ed.

the course he ought to pursue, and arranged his measures accordingly. He had entertained the firm belief that the General-in-Chief would accept no battle, but give way as heretofore. In this view he had sent back his whole artillery (with the exception of about thirty pieces of 6-pounders) with an escort beyond Jauer, and had not allowed his troops to offer any great resistance anywhere. The result of this was that the enemy, continuing to push forward his right wing along the mountains, had already reached Hermsdorf by six o'clock in the evening, and would have unquestionably driven Count Langeron from his strong position, had not the occurrences in the neighbourhood of Nieder-Crayn, and the advance of the brigade of York's corps to Schlauphof, forced them to make another disposition.

It was, as may well be conceived, extremely disagreeable to Count Langeron to have formed such erroneous conclusions. He wished to retrieve his mistake, but it was too late. The enemy gained Hennersdorf on their retreat, and when it grew dark retained the position behind this place. The brigade in the mountains had also been attacked, but had gone to meet the enemy, having placed its artillery so advantageously that it had been able to repulse the enemy totally. Count Langeron instantly recalled the artillery he had sent back, and measures were taken, if the enemy (as was likely) retreated in the night, for immediately discovering it and pursuing him at once.

Towards evening the Cossacks on the right wing reported to General Baron von Sacken, that the enemy was advancing in one column across the Katzbach, for the purpose of turning the right flank of the Silesian Army. General Sacken dispatched his reserve against this column, which fell in with it just before it grew dark, routed it, and made a number of prisoners, amongst whom was a general ; whereupon the enemy retreated across the Katzbach. Thus ended the day, which had seen four actions.

We afterwards learnt that Marshal Macdonald had been charged by Napoleon to drive back the Silesian Army into the interior of Silesia. His army was nearly equal in strength to the Silesian Army, and he proceeded according to the following disposition :—

One division (Püthod's forming the right wing of the army) was detached, with orders to advance through the mountains towards Jauer.

The 5th corps advanced on the road from Goldberg to Jauer.

The 11th and 3rd corps, were to cross the Katzbach between Liegnitz and Kroitsch, and traverse the plateau to Jauer.

The 2nd cavalry corps, under General Sebastiani, marched at the head of the 11th and 3rd corps over the plateau towards Jauer.

The 35th division of the 11th corps engaged in action with York's corps, and was driven back by Nieder-Crayn ; and the 36th division retreated without fighting by the little Dohnau bridge, by which it came, and consequently lost nothing but its ammunition-waggons.*

The enemy's 3rd corps could not pass the bridges by which it ought to have gone, and was obliged to seek another passage further down, and thus lost

---

* The 31st division of the 11th corps under General Ledru, about 7000 men with 14 guns, marched on the 26th of August by Spiller towards Hirschberg, and was not engaged in any action on that day.

Y 2

four hours. Its attack came too late, and was repulsed. General Sebastiani was beaten.

Marshal Macdonald was with the 5th corps on the chaussée, but as neither the attack of the right wing (Püthod's division), nor that of the 11th corps, nor General Sebastiani's, succeeded, he was obliged to give up his enterprise.

The result of the 26th of August for the Silesian army was the acquisition of thirty guns with their proper ammunition waggons and some thousand prisoners : their loss was inconsiderable. York's corps had not above 300 killed and wounded.

The next thing was to make the best use of the victory, and to allow the enemy no time to recover and collect his forces. But the rain, like a torrent, continued unceasingly, so that it was hardly possible to kindle or keep up a fire in the open air for cooking.

The General-in-Chief proceeded to Brechtelshof during the night, to send his report to the royal head-quarters, and to give out fresh orders. From hence York's corps received instructions to break up about two o'clock in the morning of the 27th, and to follow the enemy across the Katzbach, in order to make use of the victory. The execution of this order, which only reached General von York about five A.M., met with great difficulties. The Neisse was already much swollen; the infantry waded through up to the waist in water, so that the head of the column only reached Kroitsch about eight A.M., which they found still occupied by the enemy. He was dislodged, and the Katzbach was still passable, but the water rose every moment. In wading through the Neisse at Nieder-Crayn, the column had got very much scattered.

As the enemy's troops showed themselves on the heights behind Kroitsch, York's corps waited there for the troops that were following; and when these arrived about noon, the Katzbach was no longer passable. On the other side there was nothing but hostile cavalry, with little artillery and no infantry.

On the 27th,* the whole day was spent by York's corps in vain attempts to cross. Sacken's corps marched upon Liegnitz, where they passed the Katzbach without difficulty, and pursued the enemy to Haynau. At daybreak Langeron's corps first became aware of the enemy's retreat, and pursued him to Goldberg; they overtook him even before reaching Goldberg, where he had posted a rear-guard to cover his march through the town. About 1400 men, with six pieces of artillery, formed a square which defied Langeron's cavalry. When they were at last enfiladed by the artillery, and gaps arose, Langeron's cavalry broke in and took prisoners all that were not cut down. Thereupon began a flight through Goldberg, which was thronged to excess, and many more pieces of artillery there fell into the hands of the pursuers.

The rapid Deichsel, in general an insignificant stream, was likewise so much swollen that the French were only able to cross it at Pilgramsdorf, with great trouble and loss of time. On the appearance of the cavalry, of the corps of Langeron and York, in the vicinity of this brook, the enemy aban-

* On the 27th of August the battle of Dresden was fought. Napoleon forced the Grand Army to retreat, which, on the 29th, engaged at Kulm with Vandamme, who was totally defeated and taken prisoner.—ED.

doned all their guns and carriages which had not yet crossed over. The number of prisoners and carriages taken here was very considerable.

All the troops which had taken the direction of Bunzlau on the 27th, and succeeded in crossing the Deichsel, escaped beyond Bunzlau on the 28th. Meanwhile, the division that had been engaged with Count Langeron on the 26th made its retreat by Goldberg and Pilgramsdorf upon Löwenberg, where the 5th and 11th corps (as many as arrived in any order) succeeded in crossing the Bober. Afterwards it became quite impossible to cross the Bober at Löwenberg, from its overflowing, and all who only then arrived there were forced to proceed to Bunzlau on the ·29th, and attempt the passage there.

On the 29th of August, Langeron's corps entered Lauterseiffen soon after the Bober had become impassable at Löwenberg, and just as a number of fugitives from the district of Plagwitz were marching off to Bunzlau. The corps would have pursued them, had not a hostile column been just then seen approaching Löwenberg from Zobten. This was Püthod's division, which, after making various attempts to cross the Bober from Hirschberg to Lähn without succeeding anywhere, now wanted to cross at Löwenberg.

General Count Langeron caused his advanced guard to occupy the heights of Weinberg, by which movement Püthod's division was quite cut off from Bunzlau. He then ordered the attack. This ended in the entire division, with guns, carriages, eagles, &c., being either captured or cut down, after refusing to lay down their arms when they were surrounded. The officers and soldiers who attempted to throw themselves into the water, in order to reach Löwen-berg, were drowned; a few only swam to the other bank.

The 3rd corps, after an inconsiderable affair at Bunzlau, reached the left bank of the Bober.

Some battalions of Prussian troops, which followed the enemy into the town of Bunzlau, took the bridges and penetrated into Tillendorf. The enemy however turned about, and forced them to retreat, which they did under the protection of Russian troops; and this ended the pursuit of the enemy.

Such were the results of the battle on the Katz-bach, which, though not bloody in itself, was as important in its consequences as the most bloody battles. Till the 3rd and 4th of September prisoners continued to be brought in on all sides; the country militia (*Landsturm*) in the mountains on our left flank took an active part in this. From 18,000 to 20,000 prisoners, above 200 pieces of artillery, and more than 300 ammunition and hospital waggons, baggage, &c., remained in our hands. But what was of greater consequence than all the rest, was the spirit that now pervaded the army, which must be considered the result of this battle.

The General-in-Chief had shown that he well knew how to seize the proper moment for passing from a prudent defence to a bold attack, which must produce great results. After the battle he had done everything to instigate them all to exert their utmost strength in the pursuit; and his words—"with some bodily exertion now you may spare a new battle," —had turned out true.

The army was itself amazed at the great results, as each individual had only been able to notice a small part of the pursuit. All united in praise of the leader, and the approbation of rescued Silesia was in itself an agreeable reward for the Russian soldiers.

General Langeron felt his error; he had retrieved it in a brilliant manner. It was now become evident that the contumacy he had shown was occasioned chiefly by his apprehensions, and that he was neither wanting in zeal nor good will. The General-in-Chief overlooked the past, and thought only of the means of preserving harmony in future.

General Baron von Sacken had done so much in this battle, that it would have been ungrateful of the Commander-in-Chief not to acknowledge it. However, General von Sacken perceived from the distinctions conferred on him by the Sovereigns, what honourable mention must have been made of him.

Thus by *one day's* work all discord, all ill-humour in the heart of the Silesian Army was removed, and in the subsequent seven months, until its dispersion after the peace, no complaint, no discontent again occurred. Every one served willingly under General von Blücher, and the deeds performed by this army, in the years 1813 and 1814, will sufficiently prove to posterity that it must have been animated by a rare spirit of confidence and concord.

August 30th.—The army approached the Bober; on the 31st it advanced to the Queiss. The enemy retreated from its left bank, after some inconsiderable actions.

September 1st.—The General-in-Chief caused the army to rest, fire a *feu de joie*, and sing a Te Deum. He had issued the following proclamation :—

"Silesia is freed from the enemy. To your courage, brave soldiers of the Russian and Prussian armies under my orders, to your exertions and perseverance, to your patience and endurance of hardships and privations, I owe the good fortune of having snatched a fine province from the hands of a greedy enemy.

" In the battle on the Katzbach, the enemy came to meet you with defiance. Courageously, and with the rapidity of lightning, you issued from behind your heights. You scorned to attack them with musketry-fire : you advanced without a halt ; your bayonets drove them down the steep ridge of the valley of the raging Neisse and Katzbach.

" Afterwards you waded through rivers and brooks, swollen with rain. You passed nights in mud. You suffered from want of provisions as the impassable roads and want of conveyance hindered the baggage from following. You have struggled with cold, wet, privations, and want of clothing ; nevertheless you did not murmur, and with great exertions you pursued your routed foe. Receive my thanks for such laudable conduct. The man alone who unites such qualities is a true soldier.

" A hundred and three cannons, two hundred and fifty ammunition waggons, the enemy's field-hospitals, their field-forges, their flour-waggons, one general of division, two generals of brigade, a great number of colonels, staff, and other officers, eighteen thousand prisoners, two eagles, and other trophies, are in your hands. The terror of your arms has so seized upon the rest of your opponents, that they will no longer bear the sight of your bayonets. You have seen the roads and fields between the Katzbach and Bober : they bear the signs of the terror and confusion of your enemy.

" Let us sing a song of praise to the Lord of

Armies, by whose help you overthrew the foe, and in public worship thank Him for the glorious victory vouchsafed to us. Let a thrice-repeated volley conclude the hour which you consecrate to devotion. Then go seek your foe anew.

(Signed)   "Von Blucher."

SECTION II.

Bonaparte advances with reinforcements by Bautzen.—Takes up
the army defeated on the Katzbach, and goes to meet the Sile-
sian army to offer battle.—Combat at Hochkirch and Glossen.—
Interrupted action at Reichenbach and Görlitz.—The Silesian
Army marches by Ostritz on the right flank of the King of
Naples.—Combat at Löbau.—The Silesian Army advances to
Bautzen.—The situation of both armies considered.—Neces-
sity for concerting a new plan of operations.

SEPTEMBER 2nd.—The army proceeded with the
advanced guards as far as the Neisse. On the 3rd,
it crossed the Neisse by two bridges—a pontoon and
a trestle-bridge—and encamped on the Landskrone.
This day our partisans turned the left wing of the
French army; at Würschen, in their rear, they
took a battalion which was escorting an ammunition
waggon, and blew up the ammunition which they
could not bring with them.

On the 4th, the army, in three columns (of
which the centre one consisted of the Prussian
corps d'armée), proceeded by Bischofswerda to concentrate at Bautzen.

When the advanced guard came out by Hochkirch, it engaged with the enemy's rear-guard, which
retired slowly. Great clouds of dust were observed
in the plains of Bautzen, moving toward us. Soon
after, the enemy's rear-guard also faced about, and
drove back our advanced guard through Hochkirch.

An Italian horseman was captured, who deposed
to having done duty in the course of the day as
orderly to Napoleon, who, at the head of his guards,
had joined the army not far from Bautzen. A
young man from Bautzen was brought in, who

deposed that he had seen Napoleon ride into Bautzen about noon. At last a messenger arrived with the certain intelligence that Napoleon, who was come with great reinforcements from Dresden, was marching against us.

The Commander-in-Chief determined to avoid a battle. He kept back the army behind the Löbau Water, and left the advanced guard only to defend the Stromberg until it grew dark, by which means the army gained time for a safe retreat. At night they re-entered the position on the Landskrone, leaving only the advanced guard posted by the Löbau Water, at Glossen.

September 5th.—Bonaparte advanced with his columns. Our advanced guard retreated to Reichenbach, and there engaged in a cavalry fight, which detained the enemy, indeed, but probably cost both sides equally dear. The Commander-in-Chief observed the enemy's advance from the Landskrone. He did not wish to give orders for the farther retreat, before it was clearly seen that the enemy was moving out with strong columns by Reichenbach. When this took place, towards evening, the left bank of the Neisse and Görlitz were abandoned to the enemy.

Hitherto no mention has been made of the Russian corps under General Count Pahlen (of which General Count St. Priest afterwards took the command), which was posted at Ladnshut. This little corps followed all the movements of the Silesian Army in its marches and countermarches, without exerting any influence on the operations, or engaging in any important action. It was now ordered to advance in a line to the Neisse, and henceforth it made a part of Langeron's corps.

September 6th.—The partizans reported that on the evening of the 5th Bonaparte had already marched back with his troops towards Bautzen. An employé of the imperial head-quarters, who was taken prisoner, confirmed this report. The same news was brought in by the scouts, who also reported that the King of Naples commanded the corps left at Görlitz. Thereupon the Commander-in-Chief promptly resolved by manœuvring to force back the King of Naples to Bautzen, or, should he engage in the defence of the Neisse, to attack him so that his loss must be considerable.

The country between Görlitz and the Queiss consists of flat heights overgrown with wood, so that the party in possession of the ground between the Neisse and Queiss cannot be discovered or observed by any force stationed on the Neisse.

The army marched off to the left. An advanced guard remained in front of Görlitz to mask its march. According to the preconcerted disposition, the various corps were to station themselves at Ostritz, on the 8th of September, in such a manner that their bivouac fires might not be seen from the Landskrone. After crossing the Neisse (at Ostritz) the army was to march upon Löbau and Reichenbach, in order to attack in the rear the army under the orders of the King of Naples stationed on the Landskrone. This movement might have produced great results, but the march of the Silesian Army was discovered by the enemy. The King of Naples retreated, and it was impossible to overtake him.

The enemy's 8th corps, under Prince Poniatowsky, stood at Herrnhut. On receiving intelligence of the approach of the Silesian Army he retreated upon Löbau, where he occupied all the issues by which

an advance could be made. These could not be left
in his possession.

General Count Langeron had the charge of dis-
lodging Prince Poniatowsky with a part of his corps.
He selected General Count St. Priest for this duty.
On the 9th of September the latter advanced against
the enemy from the mountain ravines running between the roads from Görlitz and from Herrnhut to
Löbau.   After a warm resistance Prince Poniatowsky
retired behind Löbau, where he took up a position,
from whence however he retreated in the night
towards Bautzen.

The Commander-in-Chief now formed a junction
(September 10th) with the Austrian general Count
Bubna, who had advanced with 8,000 to 10,000 men
from Zittau, and taken up a position at Schluckenau.

The enemy still occupied Bautzen. The Commander-in-Chief removed his head-quarters to Herrnhut: his main forces were posted in this district.
The army found here means of subsistence for a short
time: the district of Bautzen was quite exhausted.

As the route by Schluckenau, Neustadt and Stolpe
to Dresden was shorter than the one from Bautzen
by Bischofswerda, the enemy could at any moment be
forced by manœuvring to abandon Bautzen.

On the 11th of September intelligence was received, by which it seemed probable that the enemy
had intentions of abandoning the left bank of the
Elbe and keeping Bautzen and its environs only long
enough to exhaust them totally, and so render our
pursuit more difficult. Thereupon the General-in-
Chief resolved on forcing the enemy to give up
Bautzen and its district to us on the 12th.

Count Langeron's corps was pushed forward in
the mountains from Schirgswald towards Neusalz ; by

this movement it threatened the enemy's line of communication between Bautzen and Dresden.

York's corps marched to Rumburg. The advanced guard and Sacken's corps observed the enemy in the neighbourhood of Bautzen, and took possession of the town on their quitting it and retreating to Bischofswerda.

The enemy took up a position, with the right wing on the Elbe, opposite Königstein, in a curved line by Neustadt, Bischofswerda, Camenz, Königsbrück, and Grossenhain. To the north of this line, they had been driven back across the Elbe, by the army of the Crown Prince of Sweden, and only continued to occupy the fortresses of Wittenberg and Torgau, as *têtes de pont.*

Bonaparte stood with his principal forces in and near Dresden. Although he had sent a portion to oppose the Grand Army, and another against the Silesian Army, yet he could still in one night reunite his whole strength, and attack with superior numbers whichever of the two armies laid itself open to him. This reason alone would have prevented General Blücher from approaching Dresden nearer than Bautzen, and thereby exposing himself to the chances of an unequal combat; but there were other reasons besides.

Admitting that the General-in-Chief should succeed in driving the army across the Elbe, the result of this movement must be that the Silesian Army would be posted on the Elbe on *some one* point, or on several, between Schandau and Grossenhain. They would be, in that case, in a barren district, amidst forests, in which it was impossible to live; but this was not the greatest disadvantage; there was still another, namely, that the army would be imme-

diately obliged to fall back on the defensive, for it
was impossible to cross at Dresden ; they would
have to seek another passage. Even if they found
one, still they could not leave the right bank of the
Elbe without the enemy's immediately discovering
it, and making their counter arrangements to impede
a new movement.

All these reasons combined made General von
Blücher decide on proceeding no farther, and on
taking up such a position as to be able to give way
as heretofore, should Bonaparte advance against
him. It was however now time to concert a fresh
plan of operations. If on the re-opening of the campaign, after the armistice, each leader was to act
for himself, only keeping in view some important
general principles, it became necessary now, when
the army was approaching the Elbe, to make special
and timely agreements for future operations, in order
that the Allies might take full advantage of their
superiority in men, and that no army might be
exposed to the danger of being beaten singly.

SECTION III.

New plan of operations.—The Polish Army reinforces the Grand
Army. The flank march of the Silesian Army to the right is
secretly prepared.—Bonaparte advances to Bischofswerda.—
He returns to Dresden. The Silesian Army marches towards
Grossenhain. — Combat at Grossenhain. — Combat before
Meissen.—The Silesian Army crosses the' Elbe at Elster.—
Combat of Wartenburg. — March to Düben. — Bonaparte
advances.—Agreement with the Crown Prince of Sweden.—
The Silesian Army evades the battle, and goes with the Army
of the North to the Saale.—Opening of communications with
the Grand Army.—Bonaparte marches by Wittenberg.—The
Silesian Army advances against Leipzic.—Battle at Möckern.
Combat at Leipzic.—Battle of Leipzic.

BY all accounts, we may assume, that at the
opening of the campaign the French armies were
weaker than those of the Allies. The former had
suffered so much greater losses in battle, that the
Allied forces (including Bennigsen's corps, then on
its march from Poland through Silesia) must have
exceeded them by 100,000. They had, namely,
400,000 men ; Bonaparte 300,000, or 4 to 3.

The surest means, therefore, of terminating the
war successfully, was to engage in daily combats,
even if they decided nothing. If in this way, after
some time, an equal number of men on each side
(say 100,000) were put *hors de combat*, the Allies
would still be 3 to 2 ; and then would be the time to
crush Bonaparte at once in a grand battle.

This was the general opinion at the head-quarters
of General von Blücher. Officers were dispatched
by him to the head-quarters of the Grand Army
and of the Crown Prince of Sweden, to learn what

opinions prevailed there. The accounts from head-quarters of the Grand Army were very gratifying; the Sovereigns displayed everywhere the greatest constancy, and an unshaken determination to complete the great work they had begun. But the accounts that came from the Army of the North were not so satisfactory.

The Crown Prince of Sweden was born in France, and in consequence of his situation and relations could not lay claim to unconditional confidence. In the battle of Gross-Beeren,* General von Bülow had acted with a sense of chivalry; the Crown Prince had on the contrary displayed a degree of caution, which naturally excited some apprehensions in the Prussian army. In the battle of Dennewitz,† General von Bülow had thrown himself *alone* against a far superior enemy, and had been left to defeat him *alone*, the Crown Prince only arriving on the field after the battle was won. It was thought that he had had it in his power, with 50,000 fresh men, to make use of the enemy's defeat to destroy him; but not only was this *not* done, but the report spread that he had even hindered General von Bülow in a pursuit which would have produced the greatest results. These opinions and rumours had spread the notion in the Russian and Prussian armies, that the Crown Prince must have particular relations in which the obligation to spare the French was involved.‡

---

* In which Marshal Oudinot was repulsed on the 23rd of August.—TR.

† In which Marshal Ney was defeated on the 26th of August. —TR.

‡ Two causes mainly contributed to give rise to this notion. The *first* was the decided assurance given by the French officers in

General von Blücher, who was accurately informed of all that took place in this army, thought it necessary and conducive to the good cause, in future operations, to remain with the Silesian Army in the vicinity of that of the North. The Grand Army was too much weakened to be able to act independently against Bonaparte without reinforcements. The Sovereigns were therefore desirous that the Silesian Army should make a flank march to the left, and cross the Elbe, in order to form a junction with the Grand Army, while General Bennigsen might advance with the Polish army, and take up the place of the Silesian.

As General Bennigsen was not yet near enough to allow of the flank march of the Silesian Army, General Blücher had still sufficient time to make a remonstrance, whether it would not be more expedient for General Bennigsen to join the Grand Army, since he could do so undiscovered by the enemy; whereas the flank march of the Silesian Army to the left could not be kept one day concealed from the enemy.

A confidential officer was dispatched with this message, in order to represent (should this reason

Saxony, that the Crown Prince who had grown up in their camps, and had learnt with them the trade of war, was fighting only in appearance against the Great Nation. The *second* cause lay in the Prince's general position. who, though a less powerful ally, commanded his own army. The general has but *one* course to pursue; the prince and general has a double course; his actions as soldier are always subordinate to politics. It is therefore so much in the nature of circumstances that his steps should be observed with prejudice and mistrust, that it would have been superfluous to mention it here, if this mistrust had not had such important influence on the war that it necessarily appertains to history. The sequel will show this.

appear insufficient), that on account of the policy of
the Crown Prince of Sweden, no activity could be
expected from him as long as he remained alone, and
was stationed on a separate theatre of war; and
therefore General von Blücher was disposed (leaving
some troops to mask his departure, and cover the
main road to Silesia) to turn to the right towards
the Crown Prince, and induce him to cross the Elbe
in concert with himself.

The first reason was considered quite weighty
enough at the Royal head-quarters, and General
Bennigsen received orders to draw off in rear of the
Silesian Army, in order to join the Grand Army by
Zittau and Leitmeriz. The latter was, on the arrival
of Bennigsen's corps, to begin its march, to force
Bonaparte to abandon the Elbe, and to accept a
battle in the plains of Saxony.

These movements might begin at the end of
September, and the duty General von Blücher had
to undertake was to make such movements with
the Silesian Army as should facilitate the Grand
Army's operations in debouching from the Erzgebirge; and then, if it were still possible, take part
in the battle which must follow. The General
kept his plans secret, and quietly prepared for their
execution.

The Prussian corps, under General Count Tauentzien, formed no part of the Army of the North; it was
destined to blockade fortresses. But in addition to
this duty, General Count Tauentzien had taken measures for appearing in the field with a corps of about
20,000 men; and as it would be necessary in this
case to have some regard for the requisitions and
wishes of the Crown Prince, it was not possible for
him to evade them. His corps was therefore posted

on the left wing of the Army of the North, in some sort as if belonging to it.

As the King of Naples was stationed with a French corps at Grossenhain and its environs, the General in command invited General Count Tauentzien to draw near to him, and drive away the King of Naples, for which purpose he would consign to him any additional troops he required from the Silesian Army.

General Count Tauentzien began his march, and fought a successful cavalry action at Mühlberg. This attracted the enemy's attention, and he altered his position so that the attack upon Grossenhain could not follow. Meanwhile the General-in-Chief had obtained his object, of pretending that he considered the district of Dresden so important, that he wished to draw additional reinforcements in this direction from the Army of the North.

During this time, more troops were gradually pushed forward from the mountains to the right of Camenz and towards Königsbrück. The pontoons (two Russian companies with 100 canvas pontoons) were left at Görlitz, in order to be able to direct them singly, and without exciting attention, toward the point of passage. The enemy had drawn in his semicircle in front of Dresden, and abandoned to us Neustadt, Bischofswerda, and the right bank of the Rade.

Blücher had already removed his head-quarters to Bautzen, on the 15th of September, and drawn in his corps from the mountains to a camp near this town. A few insignificant actions took place. A partizan, Major von Falkenhausen, crept through the Dresden Heath, and surprised a bulwark of waggons on the glacis of Dresden. A cavalry fight subsequently took place in the district of Königsbrück, in which a Saxon colonel was taken prisoner.

Bennigsen's corps marched away in rear of the Silesian Army, and the time drew near for the flank march of the latter to the right. On the 17th of September the first troops of Bennigsen's corps reached the district of Zittau, and the last were to arrive there about the 25th or 26th.

This flank-march to the right of the Silesian Army was much facilitated by the enemy, and apparently from a singular cause. General Blücher's son, commander of a Prussian hussar regiment in the Grand Army, had been severely wounded in an action, and left lying on the field, and had fallen into the hands of the enemy. His father wrote to him, and sent the letter openly by a trumpeter, to the French out-posts. In order to keep them in ignorance of his head-quarters, he dated his letter from Bischofswerda. This place was occupied by four battalions of Prussian troops belonging to the advanced guard. Towards evening, on the day following, the enemy advanced against Bischofswerda with a considerable army, and drove out the four battalions. It was immediately known that Bonaparte in person was with these troops.

He passed the night at Harta; he sent for the Burgomaster of Bischofswerda, and made inquiries about General Blücher, whom he supposed to be at Bischofswerda. Thus it seems that he had trusted to the date given by the General-in-Chief, and sought him at Bischofswerda to beat him there, where there was no advantageous position for an army.*

* Perhaps the officers who were about Bonaparte at that time

September 22nd.—The enemy advanced from Bischofswerda towards the position of Förstgen (a German mile and half from Bautzen, on the road to Bischofswerda,) into which our advanced guard retreated.

On the retreat an opportunity offered for cutting into the enemy's infantry, of which the Prussian and Russian cavalry in concert made skilful use, and brought in some 100 prisoners of the Westphalian guard.

The advance of the French army proceeded so slowly this day, that, putting this together with the accounts from the Grand Army, the Commander-in-Chief naturally assumed that the enemy would retreat again on the following day. He therefore determined on striking a blow that must be felt, and which would facilitate the secret plan of the flank-march to the right; this was the more inviting as it could be done without danger, or any great loss on our side. In advancing from Bischofswerda to Förstgen the enemy had not attended to his left wing, probably supposing that we had drawn up all our forces at Bautzen. General von Sacken was accordingly moved up from Camenz to Marienstern, in order to pass the Schwarzwasser, in case the enemy should attack us in the morning of the 23rd, and take him in the rear. In case, however, the enemy did not attack us by noon, General von Sacken was ordered to march straight to Bischofswerda, turning the sources of the Schwarzwasser by a high causeway, and there await the retreat of the enemy, who would be attacked in front by the two other corps d'armée.

could tell whether this was the case, as   rcumstances led us to conclude.

The enemy not having attacked us by noon on the 23rd, the Commander-in-Chief proceeded to the heights of Förstgen, to lead the attack as soon as General von Sacken should have gained sufficient ground. But Sacken's corps failed in executing the plan; they missed the right roads, and set out so late that they were entangled in defiles when night set in. Meanwhile the enemy gained time to retreat, and when our columns reached Bischofswerda, the following morning, it was already abandoned. Consequently there was no other use to be derived from this expedition of the enemy but that the Silesian Army moved off to the right undiscovered, to advance by forced marches to the passage of the Elbe, in the vicinity of the Army of the North.

September 25th.—The general movements began, but they were of such a nature as to prevent their intention becoming clear to the enemy until the 27th, when General von Sacken advanced to the attack upon Grossenhain, drove the enemy on this and the following day to Meissen, engaged in a sharp cannonade on the 29th, and also attacked with his infantry the villages occupied by the enemy on the right bank. The army, covered by this movement, marched off in the rear of General von Sacken.

General Prince Scherbatow remained behind in the neighbourhood of Bautzen, with about 8000 men, to cover Silesia, and to conceal our departure from the enemy as long as possible.

The Silesian Army entered Herzberg and its environs on the 1st of October, and Jessen on the 2nd. In the night of the 2nd and 3rd, a bridge was constructed across the Elbe at Elster, with the canvas pontoons, seventy-two of which were required.

October 3rd.—The army began to defile in the morning.

Before leaving Bautzen, Blücher had dispatched a confidential officer to the Crown Prince of Sweden, to inform him that, since the Army of the North was too weak to operate alone on the left bank of the Elbe, he would come with the Silesian Army and cross at Elster on the 3rd ; he therefore invited the Crown Prince to cross the Elbe at the same time, and to advance towards Leipzic. What was then only conjectured was afterwards proved, namely, that the Crown Prince did not believe that the general of the Silesian Army really intended the expedition he announced ; for though he had declared himself ready for such a passage, yet the General-in-Chief learnt on his arrival on the Elbe, that no preparations whatever had been made in the Army of the North for crossing on the 3rd. This not only rendered the passage of the Silesian Army more dangerous, but also enabled the enemy on the 2nd to move a corps from the neighbourhood of Wörlitz (opposite the Crown Prince), which reached Wartenburg, opposite Elster, in the evening.

General von Blücher would not be diverted from his purpose by anything, and as soon as the troops began to defile across the Elbe he dispatched an aide-de-camp with this intelligence to the Crown Prince, and to enquire where the Army of the North had crossed.

York's corps was at the head. Count Langeron's formed the reserve. Sacken's corps could only arrive towards evening by forced marches from Meissen.

The village of Wartenburg had been formerly fortified by the enemy, as they had found it an advantageous point for crossing to the village of

Elster. The arms of the old Elbe, the barricades that had been constructed, and the dams used as breast-works, converted the village into a kind of fortress. It was considered unassailable in front, having only two entrances by long dykes, which traversed the old Elbe.

The Prince of Mecklenburg received orders to attack with his brigade the village of Bleddin, and after capturing it to turn Wartenburg. While the Prince was taking Bleddin, firing was kept up with the enemy entrenched in Wartenburg.* As this however cost men, and as it took longer to turn Wartenburg than was at first expected, General von Horn grew impatient; he led the troops of his brigade on one of the dykes leading to the entrance, overthrew the hostile troops stationed there, and penetrated with them into the village. The enemy lost here a number of guns, and retreated towards Wittenberg. The cavalry had been left on the right bank of the Elbe, as it would only have been under the enemy's fire on the left, yet could not have been deployed against Wartenburg. Had it been at hand, the enemy would have suffered considerable loss. Two cavalry regiments, which were sent after the Prince of Mecklenburg, came just in time to cut in. We captured eleven pieces of artillery, with a multitude of ammunition waggons, and made some hundred prisoners, who were considerably increased when our cavalry joined in the pursuit later in the evening.

An officer belonging to the corps of the Crown Prince, who had been present in the action, was dispatched to him, to acquaint him with the results of the day.

---

* Bertrand's corps; who had moved from Dessau on receiving intelligence of Blücher's march.—TR.

It might be expected that the Crown Prince would now cross the Elbe; but whether he would engage in a decisive battle was quite another question. The General-in-Chief therefore determined to secure the means of retreat by an intrenched camp at Wartenburg, in case Napoleon should fall upon him with his whole strength. Accordingly, on the 4th of October, 4000 workmen were ordered out from the army to intrench an encampment of this kind from Wartenburg to Bleddin. In pursuance of the proposed plan it was to be put in a defensible state by the 10th of October.

York's corps buried their dead, and got again into fighting condition.

Towards noon Sacken's corps moved forward by Wartenburg, and the army made half a march more as far as Kemberg.

Circumstances had caused York's corps to take the right wing, and Sacken's the left. One hundred prisoners (taken near Gräfen-haynchen) belonging to the 7th corps d'armée were brought in by York's corps, and decided intelligence also arrived that Marshal Ney had left Dessau and joined the 4th corps d'armée at Delitsch.

The army reached the Mulde on the 5th and 6th. The enemy had destroyed all the bridges, and were still stationed on the 5th opposite Düben, to which they set fire. On the 6th they retreated to Eulenburg.*

General von Sacken pushed forward his light

---

* An intelligent Russian officer was dispatched from hence with a few Cossacks to creep through the hostile army, and to take accounts from the Silesian to the Grand Army. Leaving Leipzic to the left, he lay in woods by day, marched by night, and reached the Grand Army in safety.

cavalry between the Mulde and Elbe, and sent his advanced guard to their support as far as Mockrehna, (between Eulenburg and Torgau), while his Cossacks extended their excursions beyond Wurzen.

On the 8th Sacken's corps marched to Mockrehna, and the skirmishing was so much assisted by this movement, that the number of prisoners taken on this side in four days amounted to about 1000.

Alone and without the co-operation of the neighbouring army, the General-in-Chief could now proceed no farther. His army consisted of about 60,000 men, and his intrenchments at Wartenburg could not be completed before the 12th of October. The enemy appeared to be concentrating his forces at Leipzic and at Wurzen on the Mulde.

On the 7th of October the General-in-Chief had an interview with the Crown Prince of Sweden, in which it was arranged that both armies should march upon Leipzic, where they might expect to find only a small hostile force. The Crown Prince's army was about 90,000 strong, Count Tauentzien's corps included.

The movements of the Silesian Army for reaching Leipzic on the 9th were prepared, indeed, but had not yet commenced, when news arrived that Napoleon had quitted Dresden with his army on the 7th, and was advancing against us on the chaussée from Meissen to Leipzic. This intelligence rendered an alteration in our plans necessary, which required a consultation with the Crown Prince. The confidential officer, sent by the General-in-Chief for this purpose, came back early on the 9th, bringing intelligence that the Crown Prince wished to retreat behind the Elbe, and only consented to remain on the left bank on condition that General Blücher would resolve to cross the Saale in concert with him, in order to take up a position behind that river. This was a movement of a very peculiar kind, which however facilitated the connection with the Grand Army on the most exposed point on the enemy's rear.

Although by this movement the Silesian Army lost its line of communication, still it was of the utmost importance to remove every reason that might induce the Crown Prince to retreat across the Elbe. The General-in-Chief therefore directed the Silesian Army to march off to the right in the afternoon, and to cross the Mulde at Jessnitz the same day and following morning. A disaster might have befallen the army here, had the enemy been more attentive and General von Sacken less resolute. An orderly officer was the occasion of this.

On the morning of the 9th the army stood thus: —York's corps between Düben and Jessnitz; Count Langeron's at Düben; Sacken's at Mockrehna; his advanced guard before Eulenburg. Now, on this day York's corps was to move to Jessnitz, Count Langeron was to replace York, and Von Sacken Count Langeron at Düben. It was arranged that an officer should be sent from each corps to the head-quarters of the General-in-Chief, in order that he might know the way between the latter and the head-quarters of his corps, and transmit safely all urgent orders either by day or night.

On the morning of the 9th, when this orderly officer from Sacken's corps ought to have taken the disposition to General von Sacken, he was not to be found, having already gone back to his corps. It was necessary to send another officer, and General von Sacken received the order three hours later than had been calculated.

Bonaparte had meanwhile attacked Sacken's advanced guard at Eulenburg, and pushed forwards to Mockrehna; so that, when General von Sacken received the order to march to Düben, the enemy was marching with his main army between him and that place.

Count Langeron's corps and the head-quarters of the General-in-Chief waited at Düben for Sacken's corps till three P.M., and began to move, when it was reported that he was seen approaching on the road from Eulenburg, on the right bank of the Mulde. But this was the enemy, who captured some officers and baggage at Düben. Langeron's artillery in reserve marched in its usual order in rear of the columns, and the enemy might have carried it off had they known how to make proper use of the misunderstanding ; they were however so slow that there was time to send some guns and infantry against them, which kept them in check. They were thus in the middle between us and the corps of Langeron and Sacken, and the latter might have easily incurred great losses ; but he had timely information of the occurrence, and perceiving how important it was not to get separated from the army, he marched the whole night through, going round Düben in a semicircle ; so that on the 10th the whole Silesian Army stood united with the Army of the North on the left bank of the Mulde, the bridges over which had been destroyed.

In conformity with the preconcerted *ordre de bataille*, the Army of the North ought now to have moved to the right towards Halle, where a detachment from it, under General Count Woronzoff, was already stationed. But the Crown Prince gave General Blücher to understand that he could not move from the Elbe, on account of his communication with Sweden, as well as his detachments, blockades, &c.; he therefore requested the General-in-Chief to take the right flank with his army.

This new demand was most annoying; if the Crown Prince found it inconvenient to quit the Elbe, how much more so must it be to General Blücher, who had his basis in Silesia, and had detached General Prince Scherbatow to Dresden. It was considered at head-quarters a proof that the Crown Prince wished by this means to reserve to himself the option of joining or not in a general battle. This could not be practicable if the Army of the North, proceeding step by step between the Silesian and Grand Armies, was obliged to follow the movements of both. What was to be done? If General von Blücher yielded, the object of the passage of the Elbe would be *partially* lost; if he did not yield, it might come to a formal breach between the Crown Prince and himself, and then the object would be *totally* lost. He therefore consented to this demand likewise, and directed Count Langeron and York to set out as early as noon on the 10th, and to move towards Zörbig. Sacken's corps required more rest after its long night march, and therefore remained at Jessnitz and Raguhn on the Mulde.

In the afternoon of this day, on the way to his new head-quarters, the General-in-Chief had an interview with the Crown Prince. Some persons present observed that there was less confidence shewn on Blücher's part in this conference than in the first interview.

The Crown Prince communicated the news that Augereau's corps was on its march from Erfurt to Leipzic, which showed that the enemy was concentrating his forces for battle, and he conjectured that Bonaparte would try to beat the Northern and Silesian Armies with superior numbers, and then march against the Grand Army. As we must not expose ourselves to this danger, we ought to retire immediately behind the Saale, in order to take up a strong position in the district of Bernburg.

The General-in-Chief von Blücher was rather of opinion that, by drawing near the Grand Army we should oblige Napoleon to leave the plains of Leipzic, to take up a position in the neighbourhood of Erfurt; but, if the movement on the Saale were intended to produce any great effect, we must take up a position at Halle, all united ; with the right wing resting on the ponds of Dieskau and Bruckdorf (where these obstacles and the Elster would prevent our being attacked) with the whole of the cavalry on the left wing, and with five bridges across the Saale between Halle and Scope, at our command in case a retreat became necessary. In this position we could accept or avoid a battle ; we should protect the approach of the Grand Army, and have the advantage of anticipating Napoleon on the Middle Saale, if he retreated in that direction.

The Crown Prince had many objections to make to this position; he asserted that he had become well acquainted with it in his affair at Halle in 1806, and persisted in his opinion that we could march up the left bank of the Saale with much greater security than from Zörbig to Halle.

Blücher yielded, on condition that the Crown Prince would pass the Saale at Wettin and take up a position there. The latter promised to construct a bridge there immediately, and to extend his left wing only as far as Alsleben.

The General-in-Chief ordered up his pontoons to Wettin to make a second bridge there himself. He intended to push on behind the Saale to Halle, and hoped to get the Crown Prince to follow him. But these circumstances made it necessary for him to put himself in closer connection with the leaders of the Army of the North, Von Winzingerode and Bülow, as also with the military envoys who were at that time at the head-quarters of that army.

General von Bülow acquiesced fully in the views of the General-in-Chief, that it was only by battles that Napoleon could be driven out of Germany, and that they ought therefore to make use of every opportunity to give battle, while with equal loss of men on both sides our superiority would constantly increase.

With regard to the Swedish corps, as it was evidently the Crown Prince's wish to spare it and to avoid considerable losses, the rest of Europe would have seen perhaps greater activity on his part, if these 20,000 Swedes had not formed part of his army.

Early on the 11th of October, the two corps took their departure from Zörbig for Wettin; Sacken's corps was also directed thither by way of Radegast and Löbegün. The advanced guards remained stationary.

It was reported on the march, that the pontoons could not reach Wettin before the afternoon. This was unpleasant; still we expected to have the use of the bridge which the Crown Prince had promised to construct, so that it should be ready by day-break.

An officer was sent forward to ascertain whether it was serviceable.

Just as the columns were crossing the chaussée leading from Magdeburg to Halle, this officer came back to report, that not only no bridge was constructed, but that not a man in Wettin or its environs even knew that such a thing was intended. In this perplexity, the General-in-Chief instantly resolved on following the chaussée from Magdeburg as far as Halle, with the corps of York and Count Langeron, though this was a forced march, which lasted in fact to the following morning. Sacken's corps remained on the left bank of the Saale before Wettin, till the bridge of boats was ready, when they crossed over and marched to Langenbogen.

Blücher seems now to have taken the resolution no longer to yield in consultations with the Crown Prince, but to rely solely on his own forces ; he determined to decide in future without reference to the latter, and to communicate to him only his *decision*.

On learning that the Silesian Army was posted at Halle, the Crown Prince made General Count von Woragow move on the 12th from Halle to Eisleben.

The General-in-Chief directed General Count St. Priest to occupy Merseburg on the 12th, and distributed the army in the nearest villages on the left bank of the Saale, to give it a day's rest. This day news arrived by Lützen and Merseburg from Altenburg, from the Grand Army, that the King of Naples was stationed in front of it with considerable forces. From the Army of the North news came that the *entire* French army was marching upon Wittenberg, and had altogether abandoned Leipsic and its environs. These accounts were contradictory : however it was possible that the King of Naples had orders to follow, by forced marches, to Wittenberg.

This could only be observed in the neighbourhood of Leipsic, through which the King of Naples must in that case pass. But as long as he did not follow the troops marching to Wittenberg, we could not assume that Napoleon had any real intention of going on the right bank of the Elbe, for it was not at all like his mode of warfare ; it would indeed have been egregious folly on his part, to expose the King of Naples to destruction in the middle of Saxony, in order to begin offensive operations which must shortly lead to succumbing himself, like the King of Naples, under the superiority of the Allies.

Blücher therefore resolved on allowing his army rest, to prepare for battle, until one of two cases should occur, namely :—

1. The King of Naples following Bonaparte to Wittenberg ; or,

2. The Grand Army approaching near enough to give battle in concert with himself.

A third plan, viz., of joining with the Crown Prince to strike a blow on the portion of the French army which had already crossed the Mulde, was given up, because the General-in-Chief felt, from experience, convinced of the impossibility of moving the Crown Prince to such an enterprise, at least in his present position.

A fourth plan, namely, of throwing himself, with the Silesian Army, between Napoleon and the King of Naples, would have been a mistake, as the army was too weak for this ; and the junction, now nearly completed, of all the Allied Powers, in a position where the enemy could hardly escape a great battle, made it a duty to forego hazardous undertakings. In case the King of Naples should march by Wittenberg, Blücher would make a rapid movement in front of Magdeburg, on the left bank of the Elbe.

For the purpose of procuring intelligence, on the 13th the cavalry of the advanced guard was ordered to reconnoitre Leipsic, and the infantry was moved into the position of Bruckdorf. The same day the Crown Prince sent word that the enemy had passed through Wittenberg with four corps d'armée, and driven back the blockading corps towards Rossla; that General Count Tauentzien had crossed the Elbe there, and joined that corps; and that the enemy had then penetrated into Dessau, and placed a strong garrison there. The Crown Prince, firmly convinced that it was now evident the entire French army had thrown itself on the right bank of the Elbe, and apprehensive for his line of retreat, communications, &c., had given orders for his army to cross without delay to the right bank of the Elbe, by a bridge constructed at Acken. After communicating this in writing to the General-in-Chief, the Crown Prince added, that His Imperial Majesty the Emperor Alexander had informed him that, in certain cases, he (the General-in-Chief Blücher) was to put himself under his (the Crown Prince's) orders. As an important case of this kind had now occurred, he had to request him to follow his movements on the right bank of the Elbe, with the Silesian Army, with the least possible delay.

A confidential officer, who came on this occasion from the head-quarters of the Army of the North, had found great apprehensions and the most discordant opinions existing there. One party thought that Napoleon would march upon Magdeburg, another that he would join Davoust in Mecklenburg, a third supposed Berlin to be his object, a fourth, Stralsund, to revenge himself upon Sweden. But others went further still; they foresaw reinforcements to the fortresses on the Oder, and Napoleon effecting a revolution in the heart of Poland, and requiring no communication with France.

Accounts had already reached us that Marshal Marmont was in and about Delitsch, and that he had only taken the direction upon Eulenburg on the morning of the 13th.

We found out later, by reconnoitring, that the enemy occupied the village of Möckern, in front of Leipsic, with infantry backed by artillery; and the country people reported that troops were quartered in all the houses in Leipsic.

According to intelligence received from headquarters of the Grand Army, the King of Naples was still stationed in front of them.

Putting all this together, the General-in-Chief became convinced that Napoleon had no intention whatever of removing the theatre of war to the right bank of the Elbe, but that he wanted to mislead the Army of the North, and the Silesian Army, to cross that river, in order then to make a rapid movement to meet the Grand Army with all his forces. He sent his written answer to the Crown Prince by an officer well informed on every point, who was to conjure him verbally to give up the intended movement across the Elbe, and recall the troops which had already gone over.

This relieved Blücher from the necessity of making any reply on the subject of the supreme command claimed by the Crown Prince; he had never heard of it before, and he did not believe that the Emperor of Russia had mentioned as a decided agreement what had been perhaps expressed under quite different circumstances.

Before the answer from the General - in - Chief reached the head-quarters of the Crown Prince, an event had occurred which was more effective than any representations in producing an alteration in the Crown Prince's resolution. Some French troops on the right bank of the Elbe got as far as the bridge at Acken, and fired at it, which induced the officer in command there to render the bridge impassable.* The army was consequently obliged to remain on the left bank.

* The French troops who made their appearance at this bridge did Napoleon bad service, for, had it not been for this, the Army of the North would have crossed the Elbe on the 13th, and either followed the same route as General Count Tauentzien (who was hastening by forced marches, on cross roads, to Berlin, in order to reach it before the enemy), or would have been at all events absent from the battle of Leipsic. Had Blücher shown less resolution at that time, and had he followed the Army of the North on the 14th, it is a question how the campaign would have ended.

It is necessary here to draw attention to the fact that Napoleon's intention was *wholly* or *partly* foiled by trifling circumstances, as he has been severely censured for the movement to Wittenberg. Without wishing to assert that he could not possibly have done anything better, let us put ourselves in his situation: the country was not favourable to him, or at least was no longer so. From patriotic feeling, no Saxon would give him intelligence. Paid spies could not pass through the country; for, in spite of all arrangements, the Cossacks did not even let our own pass without ill-treating them. For this reason, the French army was at this time so ill supplied with intelligence, that Napoleon only heard of the march of the Silesian Army from Bautzen to Elster *after* the affair at Wartenburg.

The Grand Army in or behind the Erzgebirge could not be forced to accept battle; but as the Allies formed at this moment two armies which were far apart, the rules of war required that Napoleon should attack and beat one of the two; consequently,

Reports reached us on the 14th which quite confirmed Blücher's conjectures, that the French army was marching back from Düben to Leipsic. These reports spread rapidly at head-quarters of the

that he should seek the united Northern and Silesian Armies. This decided him. He left the King of Naples behind, to observe the Grand Army, quitted Dresden on the 7th, and was at Düben on the 9th, with his army concentrated. Hitherto no objections can be made to his plan, or fault found with his activity.

Napoleon saw that we avoided a battle. He was quite unable to discover at Düben, on the 9th, which direction we had taken. He naturally concluded that if we wished to avoid him, we could only do so by retreating across the Elbe. And was it not so? Did not the Crown Prince wish to retreat across the Elbe? There was no other means of preventing this but Blücher's retreat behind the Saale, as above related. But this movement was, in fact, so little in the usual order of things, that Napoleon must, in justice, be pardoned for not conjecturing it on the 9th and 10th.

But supposing he had known at Düben, on the 10th, that the combined Northern and Silesian Armies had retreated behind the Saale, as he must have known that the Grand Army was advancing against Leipsic, what should he have done? Make a flank march to the left, to force the Saale, and compel the combined armies to give battle? It was a question whether they *would be compelled*, and then it might be foreseen that this would demand more time than the Grand Army required to take Leipsic from the King of Naples.

Ought he to have turned round, to go to meet the Grand Army? The argument against this was, that the Grand Army was not yet advanced far enough out of the defiles to give a decisive battle, and, consequently, the combined Northern and Silesian Armies had time enough to hang on to Napoleon, and to place him between two fires if he moved against the Grand Army.

Napoleon probably said to himself: I have not succeeded in forcing the combined Northern and Silesian armies to accept battle. I have but four days left before I must meet the Grand Army; in these four days I will attempt, by feints, to draw the two armies across the Elbe, and then strike a rapid blow on the Grand Army. If I do not succeed in drawing them across the Elbe, I shall at least keep them close to it; and then, by making a forced march to Leipsic, I shall get there so much sooner, that I

Grand Army; the Army of the North must have
been as well aware of this as the Silesian, for on the
12th and 13th they took some prisoners at Delitsch,
belonging to troops which had come from Düben.

The General-in-Chief had already offered to advance straight upon Leipsic with the Silesian Army,
in case the Grand Army made an attack upon it.

At last, on the morning of the 15th, news arrived
that the Grand Army intended, on the morning of the
16th, to attack Lindenau with one corps, on one side,
and Wachau with the whole army on the other side;
and the General-in-Chief was invited to advance as
he had proposed. The Silesian Army proceeded
that day to Skeuditz; Sacken's corps as a reserve to
Gross-Kugel.

General Count St. Priest marched from Merseburg to Güntersdorf, and had the charge of spreading
the news that the Silesian Army was advancing to
Lindenau.

Information of the intended attack by the Grand
Army on the 16th, together with news of the advance of the Silesian Army, must have reached the
Crown Prince's head-quarters before noon on the
15th. Had he, like the Silesian Army, advanced
some miles that day on the road by Delitsch to

shall have at least one day left to beat the Grand Army before
they can arrive.

That it was a mistake to leave a corps behind at Dresden, and
that Napoleon ought to have given up Leipsic, and removed the
theatre of war to Thuringia, is acknowledged, and cannot be
disputed; but when he was once arrived at Düben, what ought he
then to have done? It is to be wished that his censurers had told
us this. Had General von Blücher allowed himself to be drawn
across the Elbe, and had Napoleon then defeated the Grand Army
at Leipsic, nobody would have censured him, and future ages
would have admired the march to Wittenberg.

Leipsic, he could have taken part in the battle of Leipsic on the 16th. But he marched towards Petersberg, and removed his head-quarters to Halle on that day.

Blücher did not know with certainty where he should find the enemy. He believed that he had already returned with all his forces from Düben to Leipsic, and ordered the whole of his cavalry and horse artillery to set out at daybreak. The infantry and foot artillery were to cook and be ready to march by ten o'clock.

It was reported tolerably early that the enemy was in occupation of Freyenrode and Radefeld. When the General-in-Chief arrived on the heights of Litschena, he saw a hostile alignment, which he could not overlook, and of which he was unable to compute the strength, as he naturally supposed that the left wing rested on Lindenthal, and must be partly covered by the wood of that name. Towards Leipsic the villages were occupied just as on the previous days, but no troops were discovered on the heights.

After reconnoitring and putting all the accounts together, it appeared probable that the enemy had taken up his position in the district of Hohen-Ossig and Podelwitz, and would accept a battle there, where he had the advantages of well-protected flanks and free motion at the same time.

The next question was, what was to be done in this uncertainty; whether it were best to proceed with the whole army to Leipsic, leaving the enemy on the left flank, or, without considering consequences, attack him in his position, and follow him?

Blücher had still some hope that the disposition

and summons sent from head-quarters of the Grand
Army would persuade the Crown Prince to advance
on the road from Delitsch to Leipsic; and in this
case the Silesian Army might venture at once to
advance straight upon Leipsic, the rather as firing
could be heard on the side of the Grand Army and
at Lindenau, and consequently they would not have to
encounter the *whole* French army; but the English
envoy, Lord Stewart, who just then arrived at head-
quarters from the Crown Prince's, communicated to
the General-in-Chief the fact that the Prince had
marched to Halle.

Blücher had now no option left but to order his
attack on the enemy, in the supposition that he
would retreat on the causeway from Radefeld to
Hohen-Ossig.

Count Langeron, who had recalled General Count
St. Priest after his march on the left bank of the
Elster from Merseburg to Skeuditz, received the
charge to drive the enemy out of the villages of
Freyenrode and Radefeld; General Sacken to follow
Count Langeron with his infantry and reserve;
General von York to leave his advanced guard on
the chaussée to Leipsic, in the valley of the Elster,
and to take with his corps the road on the heights
beyond Litschena, and then proceed to the attack
of Lindenthal.

The General-in-Chief wished to discover by this
preliminary movement the position and intentions of
the enemy.*

* Lord Stewart rode back at once to Halle, to inform the
Crown Prince that the Grand Army was engaged in battle, and
that General Blücher was going to attack, and conjured him still
to make every exertion not to be the *only* one-left out of the
battle.

BATTLE OF MÖCKERN.

Count Langeron found Freyenrode and Radefeld already abandoned by the enemy, and met with no resistance. When he had traversed the village with the infantry, he was fired at by a French battery situated between Radefeld and Hayn. The position of this battery was in the direction in which Blücher expected the enemy to retreat. When, however, Count Langeron brought up a superior force of artillery against it, the enemy unexpectedly turned upon Lindenthal, and York's corps was soon engaged in a warm cannonade; while the enemy showed a line with the right wing towards Lindenthal, and the left towards Möckern, and abandoned the wood, together with the village of Lindenthal.

This required an entire change of disposition. Without waiting for further directions General von York changed front, so that he rested his right wing on his advanced guard, and turned his rear towards Lindenthal.

The General-in-Chief ordered Langeron's corps to move by and through Lindenthal, in one column, through the wood, with the cavalry and horse artillery at the head, in order to see whether more hostile troops were marching on the two roads from Düben and Delitsch to Leipsic, and in that case to stop them, and if possible crush them by a sudden onslaught.

General Baron von Sacken was ordered to remain with his infantry as a reserve at Radefeld. General Emanuel had been previously charged to examine with his Cossacks whether there was a hostile army on the heights of Hohen-Ossig, and Blücher would not leave Radefeld until he knew for certain that he had nothing to fear for his left flank.

General von York in his advance approached his advanced guard, which took the village of Möckern after a hot fight.

Count Langeron's corps met a hostile corps marching on the road from Delitsch to Leipsic, and engaged in a fight in the villages of Gross and Klein Wetteritz, into which the enemy had thrown some infantry. This occasioned a great interval between the corps of York and Langeron, and Marshal Marmont's corps now appeared fully developed in a position on easy heights, his right wing resting on Eutritsch, his left on the Elster, behind Möckern. Blücher ordered the whole of the cavalry of Sacken's corps, under Lieutenant-General Wasiltschikoff, to deploy with intervals in this space; but as it did not quite fill up the gap, and it also appeared that the hostile force in front of Count Langeron was not as considerable as Marmont's corps, he ordered Count St. Priest to move to the right by the brook flowing from Lindenthal to Eutritsch, and charged him to attack Marshal Marmont's right wing with a battery of thirty-six 12-pounders, and in his advance to keep close with his left wing to the above-named brook.

While this movement was preparing, General York lost and regained Möckern; the village took fire, but the enemy captured it once more, and threw a considerable force of infantry into it. General York thought it now time to advance straight against the left flank of the enemy's position; he executed this movement with two brigades, while he left Möckern on the right. The enemy had brought up the greatest part of his artillery here, and occasioned thereby a very considerable loss to the two advancing brigades. At last he even moved the infantry of his left wing to meet them, and the fight became a standing one. General von York had but one brigade still at his disposal, for the third was employed, together with his much reduced advanced guard, on a fresh attack on Möckern.

It was about this time that General Emanuel reported that no hostile force was stationed on the heights of Hohen-Ossig, and now General Sacken received orders to advance to General York's support. But he could not move up to him under an hour, and by that time night fell. York brought his last brigade to the support of the two brigades engaged between Möckern and the enemy's position. The enemy's left wing advanced against him in close columns of infantry, with batteries intervening. General von York's artillery opened a hot fire on them, and some powder-waggons blew up in the midst of the infantry. This scattered the masses ; some disorder arose, and the moment was favourable for attacking the enemy's infantry with cavalry. York perceived it ; he put himself at the head of the first regiment of cavalry, directed the attack, and caused the other cavalry regiments to follow. His infantry moved after them in masses, and this decided the battle in a few minutes. The enemy's left wing, surrounded by our cavalry, could not retreat upon Gohlis, but threw itself upon its right wing and centre towards Eutritsch.

Had General Count St. Priest been near enough at this moment to attack the masses of infantry squeezed together in front of him, and to increase the disorder so as to afford opportunity to Sacken's cavalry (under Lieutenant-General Wasiltschikoff) to break in upon them, the greatest part of Marmont's corps might have been destroyed; but St. Priest was still engaged on his march when night began, and Marmont's corps drew off through Eutritsch, and retreated with another column on the great chaussée from Lindenthal to Leipsic, across the brook which runs from Eutritsch to Gohlis. Sacken's corps did not arrive till after it was quite dark. York's corps passed the night on the field of battle. He had captured forty guns, an eagle, and some thousand prisoners; his loss was very considerable: nearly every officer of rank was wounded, and on the evening of the battle the corps did not amount to more than 13,000 men.

Count Langeron's corps executed its commission completely; it had prevented the 3rd and 7th corps from joining Marshal Marmont, driven the enemy to the Parthe, and captured his guns and a number of powder-waggons. Fifty-four pieces of artillery, captured by both corps, were collected together on the 17th of October.* An officer was dispatched from

* As this narrative of the battle of Möckern is entirely founded on the views entertained in the Allied Army, and as it is necessary, for the perfect survey of a battle, to know also the relations and views existing on the other side, it will not be uninteresting to describe here, from the best sources, what took place in the French army.

The 6th corps (under Marshal Marmont, Duc de Ragusa) marched from Düben to Delitsch on the 12th; he had not been there eight hours when he received orders to march to Leipsic. When he arrived there, the King of Naples (who wished to give battle to the Grand Army) made him advance to the heights of Stötteritz, and on changing his idea, march back again to Leipsic on the 13th.

On the $\frac{13}{14}$th October the Emperor Napoleon arrived at Leipsic. He ordered Marshal Marmont to place himself, with the 6th corps, about a mile and a half from Leipsic, in such a position that he might make head against the Silesian Army. The Marshal selected a position with his right wing on Lindenthal, covered the field of battle by way of Skeuditz, to bring news of the victory to the Grand Army.

The road from Skeuditz, through the low plain, is very difficult to travel by night, from the number of

by the wood, and his left resting on the Elster and Pleisse, keeping Möckern in front. He informed the Emperor that this position was suitable for the purpose; but, in order to detain the Silesian Army, two more things were necessary:

1. More men, as the position was calculated for 30,000 men; and he had but 15,000 infantry and 1,500 cavalry, with 84 guns.

2. Some intrenchments on the most important points.

The Emperor replied that he placed the 3rd corps in addition under the Marshal's orders, and that he was to begin the intrenchments. This was done. Nothing came of this assignment of the 3rd corps, as it was still on its march to Leipsic.

On the 14th, an officer and two sappers, who had been taken prisoners at Delitsch early on the 13th, and had ransomed themselves, returned, and brought intelligence that the Grand Army was advancing. The Marshal reported it to the Emperor.

On the 15th, the adjutant of a corps of French patrols came back, and reported that he had himself seen columns advancing from Halle, on the road to Leipsic. The Marshal reported this to the Emperor.

On the night of the 15-16th the bivouac fires of the Silesian Army could be seen from the tower of Lindenthal, in the direction of Skeuditz. The Marshal himself ascended the tower. The picquets had also seen the infantry of the advanced guard of the Silesian Army approaching on the road from Halle to Leipsic. The Marshal sent word to the Emperor that he would be attacked on the 16th.

On the morning of the 16th a message came from the Emperor to say that the Marshal was quite mistaken; the Silesian Army was on the left bank of the Elster, and he had nothing but cavalry opposed to him. He was to break up immediately, and move through Leipsic, on the heights of Stötteritz, against the Grand Army. The 4th corps (which was much weaker) was to take up the position of Lindenthal.

Marshal Marmont was obliged to obey, and set his troops in motion, all but the advanced guard, which he left behind in the position, with out-posts towards Radefeld, to cover the march.

About ten o'clock the columns of the Silesian Army made their bridges and deep places in the meadow land; consequently the news sent by this officer did not arrive as soon as Colonel Count von Golz, first aide-de-

appearance. The Marshal found his situation difficult, because he foresaw that, on the one hand, his rear-guard must encounter a disadvantageous fight at the passage of the Parthe, and that, on the other hand, without the 3rd corps, he would not be equal to the Silesian Army. To end this perplexity, he sent an officer of his staff to Marshal Ney (who was in the town of Leipsic), to know definitively whether he could reckon on being reinforced by the 3rd corps. He received for answer: "Yes; the 3rd corps is arrived." This answer decided the Marshal to let the 6th corps halt and deploy between Eutritsch and Möckern, to accept battle.

Delmas' division (of the 3rd corps) had arrived in the neighbourhood of Breitenfelde, on the right wing of the 6th corps, and the position of the latter was much strengthened by it, for it could not be attacked without the aggressors exposing their left wing to that division.

The Marshal formed only *one* line with his three divisions of the 6th corps. He had not troops enough for a reserve. As he saw that the principal attack was directed against his left wing, he ordered a movement to the left in semi-divisions, by which means his forces were disposed in six échelons.

At one moment, when the fight was at the hottest, an opportunity presented itself for attacking the Prussian infantry with cavalry. The Marshal calculated on prolonging the action for some time by this movement, and of obtaining moreover from 600 to 800 prisoners. His cavalry was on the left wing; he gave the order to attack, but it was not executed. On the order being repeated, the cavalry did attack, but the favourable moment was gone by; the thing was a failure, and the cavalry, in retrograding, rode completely over a battalion of infantry.

When, by its violence, the action was drawing nearer and nearer to a decision, the Marshal placed himself at the head of one of his old infantry regiments, and advanced against the Prussian infantry. A 12-pounder battery at its head fired with case-shot on the Prussian masses, and caused great devastation amongst them. At this moment a grenade fell into a powder-waggon, and three powder-waggons, belonging to a 12-pounder battery, in the midst of the French masses, blew up. Many men were thrown down, and the Marshal himself was injured; the camp to the General-in-Chief, who set out the following morning to transmit the captured eagle.

The General-in-Chief sent without delay accounts of the issue of the battle to the Crown Prince, but making no mention of the movements of the Army of the North. The English envoy had however effected this much, that the cavalry General von Winzingerode was directed, on the 16th, to support the Silesian Army with 5000 horse, belonging to the Crown Prince's corps.* General von Winginzerode was at Lindenthal early on the 17th. The General-in-Chief pointed out to him that he would render him most service by turning the enemy's right wing, and taking up a position at Taucha, with the double view of maintaining the passage over the Parthe, and establishing a line of communication on this side with the Grand Army, which would answer better, and be much shorter than the one by Skeuditz. General von Winzingerode agreeing, marched off there directly.

On the morning of the 17th, Sacken's corps took

battery left off firing, and the infantry dispersed. The Prussian cavalry took advantage of this moment to make an attack, which left the French infantry no time to recover, while the Prussian infantry advanced in close columns.

These combined attacks decided the retreat, which the Marshal covered with his right wing, which had not yet been engaged, and, in doing so, he was again wounded by a musket-ball. He traversed Leipsic in the night, and crossed the Parthe.

Delmas' division, which was pressed by Count Langeron's corps, was obliged to remain on the right bank of the Parthe, by orders of Marshal Ney. It was this division that was attacked on the 17th by the cavalry under General Wasiltschikow.

* Lord Stewart brought the news himself at the moment the battle was hottest; he staid to the end, and then rode back to the Crown Prince's head-quarters at Halle.

the place of York's on the field of battle, and the latter moved to the rear in the neighbourhood of Möckern, in order to put itself again into fighting condition, to provide itself with ammunition from the captured powder-waggons, to transport the prisoners and guns to Halle, &c. &c.

The rest of the troops were ordered to cook early in the day, to be ready for anything that might be undertaken in the course of it. When the General-in-Chief rode out early to visit the outposts, he found the enemy still at Eutritsch and alongside the brook of Gohlis. Some tirailleur firing had commenced. He gave orders to go round Eutritsch upon the chaussée from Wetteritz: it was deserted by the enemy, who had retreated the whole length of the Parthe on the left bank. A rear-guard, however, was still posted between Eutritsch and Leipsic, composed of all kinds of forces, who made a show of maintaining this position. In this case it formed a *tête de pont*, and under its protection the enemy could always advance with superior numbers from Leipsic against the Silesian Army. This the General-in-Chief wished to prevent, in order that he might keep his army disposable: he therefore directed General von Sacken to attack the village of Gohlis, in the expectation that the rear-guard thus threatened or surrounded on its left wing would retreat to Leipsic; but the enemy had placed a strong garrison in Gohlis, and General von Sacken could advance but very slowly.

The General-in-Chief had no other troops between Eutritsch and the Parthe (where he himself was) than the cavalry of General Sacken's corps. Meanwhile, as the advance to Gohlis took so long, he resolved on making an attempt with this cavalry to drive away the enemy's rear-guard. The peculiar disposition of the enemy gave rise to this resolution.

The line of communication of this rear-guard with its main corps extended as far as could be seen, through the Halle Gate at Leipsic, thus far beyond its left wing. Its right wing rested on the Parthe, consisting of cavalry, which stood on the same line with the infantry.*

Four hussar regiments under Lieutenant-General Wasiltschikow advanced in columns against the hostile rear-guard, under a hot fire from the enemy's artillery; at the proper distance the two first regiments set off at a galop, and fell upon the cavalry of the enemy's right wing. This did not wait for the attack, but retreated behind the infantry towards the Halle Gate.

Wasiltschikow's two regiments of cavalry followed in the rear of the enemy's infantry and artillery, as far as the Parthe bridge; on the way they captured a battery and powder-waggon, made some prisoners and cut down some infantry. The enemy's line of infantry, deserted by its cavalry, remained in the middle of the field formed into squares, and assumed so good an attitude that the cavalry could make no impression on it. Had there been some battalions of infantry, or some artillery at hand to attack it, it would have paid still more dearly for its faulty disposition. But the cavalry was obliged to abandon again the houses in front of the Halle

* A worse disposition was hardly possible; indeed, it has been observed that infantry generals, who know nothing but the tactics of their own arms, when they get cavalry under their orders, generally place it in a line with the infantry.

Gate, and the enemy's infantry retreated to Leipsic before Count Langeron's corps reached the neigh- bourhood of Eutritsch.

During this time Gohlis was likewise taken; the enemy had not only defended it obstinately, but retaken it once, so that General von York was obliged to bring up part of his infantry to the fresh attack.

The General-in-Chief had attained his object, the enemy had been driven away from the right bank of the Parthe, with the exception of some houses and intrenchments near the Halle Gate. Should the enemy wish to advance under their protection, with an army out of Leipsic, there was still time enough to take all the measures suitable to the circumstances. But for continuing offensive operations it was necessary to cross the Parthe. This in the vicinity of Leipsic was difficult for two reasons: first, on account of the swampy bank; and, secondly, because the enemy's entire force could hinder the passage there. Farther up towards Tau- cha the enemy was not so strong, and the little river presented fewer difficulties.

The General-in-Chief therefore turned his views in that direction; he ordered a portion of Lan- geron's corps to cross the Parthe, in company with General von Winzingerode, and move down the river, his right wing resting on it, until, arriving on a line with the remaining portion of Langeron's corps, they should have driven the enemy from the left bank. This other portion was then to cross and assume the offensive, while the corps of York and Sacken remained on the defensive between the Parthe and the Pleisse.

These two last corps together amounted to about 20,000 men, and their surest means of maintaining this angle was to attempt to drive the enemy from his houses and intrenchments in front of the Halle Gate, and raise some twelve-pounder batteries, so as to command this gate and the bridge over the Parthe.

If this movement succeeded, the right wing's point of support would be quite secure; but it was always a very hazardous undertaking, with a corps of 25,000, or at most 30,000 men, (the probable strength of Langeron's force,) to attack on the left bank of the Parthe, Leipsic, the enemy's central point. However the General-in-Chief had no option: he could not leave the Grand Army to itself; he could not remain on the defensive, and allow the enemy to turn all his strength against the Grand Army. He must undertake the attack, comforting himself with the thought that, if he were beaten, his movement would at least facilitate the victory of the Grand Army. Just as he was about to begin this operation, he received intelligence that the Grand Army would not attack on the 17th, but on the 18th, after Generals Bennigsen and Colloredo should have closed up on the 17th.

The actions of the 16th had produced no satisfactory results in the Grand Army. Count Giulay had not taken Lindenthal. Shortly after, news came from the Army of the North that it had begun its march, and could form a junction with the Silesian Army in the evening. Both accounts could not but be most acceptable to the General-in-Chief. Under these circumstances, brilliant results might be expected from the battle on the 18th.

The General-in-Chief broke off the fight, and made Count Langeron's corps move into bivouac;

its right wing on Eutritsch, its left in the direction
of Taucha, and advanced posts on the Parthe.

All was preparing for the battle on the 18th.
The Crown Prince of Sweden appeared determined
to take part in it : he treated the battle of Möckern
as a fight of small importance, and Blücher was
willing to let this pass, provided the Army of the
North would but move into line on the 18th. But
it had not yet arrived, when the Crown Prince made
new and unexpected demands. He wished to see
the old *ordre de bataille* immediately restored ; that
is to say, that he should move on the right wing of
the Silesian Army.

The foregoing considerations, on the situation of
the Silesian Army on the 17th, distinctly show that
it was cooped up between the Parthe and Pleisse in
a defensive position from which only the bold spirit
of its leader, or the sacrifice of himself for the
general advantage of the whole, could extricate it.
To say nothing of the time that would be lost in
relieving the Silesian Army, it would have been
perfectly useless to move with a strong army into a
defensive position which 30,000 men could defend.
The General-in-Chief therefore refused this demand.
The Crown Prince, on arriving at his head-quarters
at Breitenfelde, sent an aide-de-camp to desire a
conference : Blücher declined it.

At the commencement of the campaign, in all
his relations with the Crown Prince, Blücher kept
the military point of view only before his eyes. In
the present instance, he saw in the Crown Prince
only the future King of Sweden, and viewed his
relation to him as simply a political one. He therefore dispatched a confidential officer to General von
Bülow, to communicate his plan to him, and invited

him to act as he had done at Gross Beeren and
Dennewitz; and in case the Crown Prince gave no
orders, to move across the Parthe without them.
He left it to General von Bülow to discuss this
matter with General von Winzingerode. Bülow
answered, the same night, that he would not fail,
when the good of his country and of Europe was in
question. General von Winzingerode would not be
backward either. Thus all was now prepared for the
battle on the 18th.

When, in the night of the 17-18th, there came a
second invitation to a conference from the Crown
Prince, in order to consult about the *attack* on the
18th, the General-in-Chief accepted it, and repaired
at daybreak next morning to the Crown Prince's
head-quarters at Breitenfelde.

His Royal Highness Prince William of Prussia,
the King's brother, was then with the Silesian Army.
Blücher requested him to be present at this conference. It must give far greater importance to the
transaction, if what all Europe expected this day
from the Army of the North were discussed in the
presence of a Prince of the Blood. The result of
the conference was, the declaration of the Crown
Prince that he could not attack on the left bank of
the Parthe, unless General Blücher gave up to him
for this day 30,000 men of the Silesian Army.

The General-in-Chief, keeping the interest of the
whole in view, consented without hesitation; but he
determined to remain himself with these 30,000 men,
since they constituted the greater half of his army.
Count Langeron's corps was placed under the Crown
Prince's orders. As the General-in-Chief returned
from the conference on the heights of Eutritsch, firing

had already commenced in the direction of the Grand Army.

An aide-de-camp brought orders from the Crown Prince to Langeron's corps, to march towards Taucha, and there cross the Parthe. This disposition would have obliged this corps to march back for two hours, and then again forwards, to get into the enemy's vicinity, where it was already. It would moreover have caused an unnecessary pressure on the bridge at Taucha, as the entire Army of the North intended to cross there, and the whole day would probably be lost in the useless march. Blücher therefore sent the Crown Prince word that Count Langeron's corps would await his orders on the left bank of the Parthe, in the district of Abt-Naundorf.

General von Bülow sent to inform the General-in-Chief that he would cross the Parthe on the shortest line with General Langeron's corps, and requested him to hasten his passage as much as possible, to support this movement.

The enemy was posted on the Parthe, and had planted some artillery on a ruin near Neutsch. Three Russian 12-pounder batteries, of twelve guns each, were brought to bear upon the enemy's artillery, and soon silenced it. General von Sacken attacked at the same time the intrenchments and houses at the Halle Gate in Leipsic.

Hearing that Bülow was still at a considerable distance from Taucha, and the firing in the direction of the Grand Army increasing in violence, Blücher resolved not to wait for Bülow, but to force the Parthe at Mockau. He was induced to take this resolution principally by seeing very few troops on the other side of the Parthe; but with good telescopes, he perceived a column moving from Leipsic towards the windmill of Stötteritz. He was therefore afraid that the greatest part of the French army might turn against the Grand Army, to bring the battle to a decision before the Northern and Silesian Armies could come up.

The first portion of the infantry encountered no other difficulties in crossing at Mockau, than having to wade through the water up to the waist. A very imperfect flying-bridge was subsequently formed of barn-doors, gates, &c.

The enemy drew back, took up a position with his principal masses at Schönfeld, and opened a tirailleur fire in the neighbourhood of Abt-Naundorf.

Langeron's Cossacks spread themselves from the Parthe to Paunsdorf, where they formed a junction with the Cossacks of the Grand Army under the Hetman Platow. The Saxon Hussar and Uhlan regiments came over to us on the left bank of the Parthe; the General-in-Chief ordered them to cross over, and join York's corps, which this day formed the reserve.

The columns of the Army of the North only reached the neighbourhood of Paunsdorf by Taucha about noon, and filled up the interval there between the Grand Army and the Silesian. The remainder of the Saxon army then crossed, and fell in with General von Bülow. It was two o'clock. Count Langeron now advanced with his masses, and supported the attack of the infantry on the village of Schönfeld by a warm cannonade. General von Bülow also advanced on the side of Paunsdorf. Reinforcements were seen hastening from Leipsic towards Schönfeld; thereupon Blücher sent word to Sacken to increase his fire, and to make a show of capturing Leipsic. This had the effect of stopping the hostile troops destined for Schönfeld.

Blücher supported the attack on Schönfeld by a cannonade from the right bank of the Parthe. The fire of the enemy's artillery, posted behind Schönfeld, was partially drawn by these means to the right bank of the Parthe. The combat in Schönfeld continued with alternating success, but great vigour, until nightfall; Count Langeron, with a large force of infantry, maintained his position in the village, after it had already been some hours in flames. The enemy drew back toward Leipsic, behind the brook and defile of Reudnitz, and occupied the villages of Volkmannsdorf and Reudnitz during the night.

Sacken's corps had suffered considerably from the long-continued musketry fire. In the afternoon it was reported that the enemy had opened his way through the Lindenau pass.

The Silesian Army could overlook the semicircle formed by the Allied troops round Leipsic on the east side; and as the troops were advancing everywhere, the enemy had no way out but by a retreat towards the Saale. The General-in-Chief therefore gave orders to General von York to make a night march to Merseburg, leaving it at his option either to take the direction of Döllnitz, or to cross the Saale at Halle, to march up its left bank. From Merseburg General York was to proceed according to circumstances, to harass as much as possible the retreating enemy. He set off accordingly, but Sacken's corps was now too weak to make head against the enemy's attempts; Count Langeron's corps, therefore, received orders to restore the bridges across the Parthe in the night, and to cross to the right bank, as the Army of the North no longer wanted its assistance. The fatigue of the infantry however, the dark night, &c., prevented the immediate execution of this order. The corps did not reach Eutritsch till eleven next morning.

There is no denying that the General-in-Chief demanded a great deal from his troops, but they had in return the satisfaction of rendering great services, and hearing this universally acknowledged.

It was Blücher's intention, on discovering the enemy's retreat, to proceed with Count Langeron's corps, the shortest way across the Elster, in order to overtake the enemy in the plains; but in reconnoitring the Elster, it appeared that the only practicable point for the corps to pass was at Skeuditz, and consequently it would be necessary to make a great circuit.

It was not till past eight o'clock in the morning of the 18th, after the fog had dispersed, and General von Bülow had commenced his attack upon Reudnitz, that the General-in-Chief acquired any certainty as to the enemy's retreat. But Langeron's corps had not yet crossed the Parthe, and when it arrived Sacken's corps was so involved in the action, that it was necessary to support it with infantry and artillery. Blücher could therefore only order the cavalry of both corps to follow in the enemy's rear by Skeuditz and Lützen. They marched off about noon.

It might have been ten o'clock when Bülow's corps advanced in columns out of the village of Reudnitz towards Leipsic. The enemy sent troops to oppose him; meanwhile Blücher discovered a point on the right bank of the Parthe, from whence a 12-pounder battery could open an advantageous fire upon them, and the whole ground, up to the suburb, was soon cleared of the enemy. Bülow's corps now attacked the suburbs. The troops of Langeron's corps, which first crossed the Parthe, were sent to make an attempt lower down the river to penetrate into the town, and to get round the gate which was barricaded and guarded by three guns.

The first regiments that arrived were regiments of the line, not accustomed to fight singly ; they drove the enemy from the buildings, and advanced in masses, which however suffered considerably without getting possession of the gate.

About this time a French officer, with a trumpeter and a flag of truce, brought a citizen of Leipsic to the first picquets. The citizen delivered a letter from the magistrates to the General-in-Chief, begging that the city might be spared, and an armistice granted, in order that they might deliver up the city to us. The singularity of the proposition consisted principally in the authorities making it (according to the citizen) with the consent of the French governor of the town.

The same proposition was sent to Prince Schwarzenberg and the Crown Prince of Sweden, and it seemed that the object of the French was to gain time. The General-in-Chief sent back the citizen with an officer of rank, to declare to the French governor, as well as to the magistrates, that he was very willing to spare the city, and would cease all hostilities if it was given up instantly. The propositions made by the French officer confirmed the opinion that his object was to gain time ; the firing, therefore, against the Halle Gate was vigorously continued. Blücher, however, prohibited shells from being thrown into the city, not to set it on fire.

The musketry fire of Bülow's corps was heard

advancing farther and farther in the town ; when about one o'clock the tirailleurs of Sacken's corps stormed the Parthe bridge, which the French abandoned, probably because they were afraid of being taken in rear from the side of the town, and cut off.

The access by the bridge was instantly made practicable, and the enemy was pursued to the esplanade. Masses of troops rushed after him ; the General-in-Chief, with his suite, all pressed forward to the esplanade, where such a scene presented itself as is hard to describe. As far as the eye could reach, guns, powder-waggons, bread and baggage-waggons, &c., were so huddled together, that it seemed hardly possible for a foot-passenger to wind his way through. Some horses were still attached to the waggons, others were cut off. Servants and fugitives ran round and round this labyrinth seeking a way out.

During this time the bridge at the gate leading to Lindenau had been destroyed by the enemy, and all who did not swim through the river were taken.

When Blücher saw that there were troops enough of Bülow's corps moving on the esplanade, he gave orders to his troops to remain outside the gates, not to fill the town too much.

The Sovereigns arrived on the market-place of Leipsic, while the fire was still kept up at the Lindenau gate. The enemy had some guns with his rear-guard, and fired on the town, probably to hinder the restoration of the bridges. However, as his fire was not answered, and the bridges were not touched, he soon ceased firing.

A general agreement was entered into, that the

Silesian Army should march off to the right, and the
Grand Army to the left, and that the Army of the
North should go through Leipsic. All the necessary
orders were expedited accordingly. The troops had
made great exertions, but they were rewarded by a
brilliant result, and forgot all past toils.

SECTION IV.

Pursuit of the enemy after the battle of Leipsic.—He is overtaken at Weissenfels.—Combat at Freyburg.—The Silesian
Army goes round Erfurt and Gotha, to cut off the enemy from
Eisenach.—Combat on the Hörselsberg.—Pursuit to Fulda.—
The Silesian Army turns to the right, and goes by the Vogelsberg to Giessen.—March by Limburg and Altkirchen, to cross
the Rhine at Cologne.—The Silesian Army is recalled, to
blockade Mainz on its right bank (Cassel), while the Grand
Army marches to the Upper Rhine.—Resting quarters.

On the 19th the corps of Langeron and Sacken
marched to Skeuditz. On the 20th Sacken's cavalry
brought in about 2,000 prisoners, taken in the district of Rannstädt. The same day the General-in-
Chief transferred his head-quarters to Lützen, where,
during the day, a strong rear-guard, under the King
of Naples, had skirmished with the light cavalry.

Towards noon on the 21st, the army reached
Weissenfels; the enemy deserted the place, and
retreated to the left bank of the Saale. From the
castle at Weissenfels we saw the whole rear-guard
encamped close to the Saale. It was very easy to
reach them with 12-pounders. A battery of 12-
pounders was unlimbered behind the height, and
opened an unexpected fire on them, whereupon they

drew back as well as they could, out of reach of the balls.

The bridge over the Saale was of wood, and *covered*. The enemy loaded it with inflammable materials, set them on fire, and defended the fire; but even without this it would have been quite impossible to put it out.

On the march from Lützen to Weissenfels, an event took place which was highly gratifying to the whole Silesian Army. His Royal Highness Prince William of Prussia, who had staid behind at Leipsic, here overtook the General-in-Chief, bringing him with his own hand his appointment as Field-Marshal by the King, couched in the most flattering terms. The Russian corps attached to the Silesian Army shared in this pleasure as heartily as the Prussians, for they had learnt to value the merits of their leader.*

The pursuit of the enemy was thus interrupted (by the destruction of the bridge) for some time. We learnt at Weissenfels the reason why the enemy had passed the Saale, and taken a direction across the country.

It had been reported to the Emperor, on his arrival at Weissenfels, that the enemy had already thrown a strong force into the defile of Kösen, and broken up the bridge there over the Saale.

Field-Marshal Blücher had now the choice of two ways; either to send to Kösen, to give information

* The old Russian soldiers had nick-named him " The little Suwarrow;" others called him " Marshal Forwards;" and amongst the Cossacks a rumour spread, still more flattering to him, namely, that he was born on the Don, and was, properly speaking, a Cossack; but fate had transplanted him young from his native land to Prussia.

that the enemy had crossed at Weissenfels, and that the bridge at Kösen must be restored (if it was really destroyed) to enable him (Blücher) to cross at once with his army as soon as he arrived ; or to build a bridge at Weissenfels to follow the enemy directly.

No other intelligence had yet been received of York's corps but that it had marched by Halle, and had not entered Merseburg. The Field-Marshal could depend on York's seeking the enemy and *finding* him, for the march to Freyburg would just give him an opportunity of doing so. This town lies in a valley, deeply hollowed out by the Unstrut. The roads on the right bank towards Erfurt, or toward the Upper Unstrut, are all steep and bad. If General von York overtook the French army here unexpectedly, it must suffer considerably. The Field-Marshal consequently decided on crossing the Saale, and summoned the carpenters of the town to construct, with the utmost speed, a bridge of boats or rafts to enable him to cross over before evening. There was no lack of wood—the whole river was covered with rafts and planks.

There was an old master-carpenter in the place who, as apprentice in 1757, had helped to build the bridge by which Frederick the Great had crossed at Weissenfels, before the battle of Rossbach. He proposed to place the bridge on the *same* spot, promising that it should be ready in a few hours. The man kept his word, and the whole army was on the left bank of the Saale in the evening. The Field-Marshal himself repaired in the afternoon to the heights towards Freyburg, and there received intelligence of York's corps. This corps had already overtaken and attacked several of the enemy's columns. On this occasion about 3000 prisoners, taken from the Allies* and transported by one of these columns, were liberated. Some hundred prisoners and some guns were taken from other columns; General von York proceeded on his march towards Freyburg.

The Field-Marshal ordered the cavalry to support General York's undertaking, by pursuing the rear-guard. The enemy thus pressed on two sides was forced to abandon guns and powder-waggons, until the King of Naples at last formed in line on the heights on this side of Freyburg, while as soon as it grew dark General von York drove the enemy, after a warm infantry fight on the road to Mücheln, into the suburb of Freyburg. Although the fight ended at nightfall, the King of Naples was unable to carry away a great part of the baggage and a number of heavy guns and powder-waggons, and they were captured by the Cossacks at the gates of Freyburg at daybreak next morning. The enemy had destroyed the passages over the Unstrut in his rear, and taken the direction of Erfurt. The bridges however were soon restored, and the pursuit continued.

The Field-Marshal had now reunited his whole army, with the exception of Prince Scherbatow, who had arrived in the Wittenberg district, and followed the army.

On the previous evening a cannonade had been heard on the heights of Kösen, and news arrived that a great part of the Grand Army had already reached Naumburg to support General Count

* The greater portion consisted of Austrian prisoners, taken at the battle of Dresden, August 26th, who were dragged along by the enemy, and suffered to *starve*, to make them take service in the French army.

Giulay, who was supposed to be on those heights. The Field-Marshal concluded from this, that these troops had anticipated the Silesian Army in the further pursuit towards Erfurt. The portion of the enemy's rear-guard which had been seen appeared to be in good order, and, according to the assertion of some intelligent people who had seen the French army, it still consisted of 70,000 to 80,000 men, with above 200 pieces of artillery. Napoleon might therefore, without risk, take up a position at Erfurt, and give his army some rest, while the Allies must endeavour to turn the camp and fortress of Erfurt.

The Field-Marshal resolved therefore on making an immediate attempt from Freyburg to turn the enemy's left wing, while he marched up the Unstrut. Could the Silesian Army succeed in anticipating the enemy in the defiles of Eisenach, the result might be the entire destruction of the French army.

On the 25th, the army reached Langensalza. On the 26th, General von Sacken marched upon Eisenach; General von York to the foot of the Hörselsberg, between Eisenach and Gotha. A portion of Count Langeron's corps under General Rudczewitsch was detached against Gotha, and the remainder followed as a reserve.

The two corps of Sacken and York were so thinned that they might be considered as only advanced guards. Just as the advanced guard of York's corps reached the top of the Hörselsberg, the French army was defiling in the valley on the chaussée to Eisenach. The corps was still in the rear, engaged in a difficult march through deep soil (there is no chaussée here, nor had the army marched upon one since Weissenfels), and was not in very close order. Nevertheless it immediately attacked the hostile column on its march. It would perhaps have been better had it remained concealed until more forces came up to join in the attack. The enemy had no option but to lead out some troops from his column to meet the attack, and to pursue his march with the remainder. Hünerbein's brigade had to stand a fight, in which ten officers and several hundred men were put *hors de combat,* and it was not until quite late and dark that it succeeded (on being properly supported) in obtaining possession of the village of Eicherodt, and gaining thereby a strong position on the chaussée between Gotha and Eisenach. The greater part of the French army had already reached Eisenach; but some officers—prisoners—asserted that Bertrand was still behind. An officer who was brought in prisoner in the night deposed that this corps had thrown itself into the mountains on the left to escape by Ruhl.

General Rudczewitsch made about 1,500 prisoners, without suffering any loss himself; General Sacken attained the heights of Eisenach, but was not able, on account of the weakness of his infantry, to engage in any important action, and he had indeed arrived too late for this.

The enemy quitted Eisenach in the night, and we took possession of the town in the morning of the 27th. The Field-Marshal still hoped to cut off Bertrand's corps, before it could escape out of the mountains. General von York had instructions to anticipate it on the chaussée by Wilhelmsthal to Barchfeld.

General Count St. Priest was detached with the 8th Russian corps to Cassel.

General von Sacken was ordered to take with his

corps the direction of Berka and Hersfeld, and
Count Langeron that upon Vach by Marksuhl, following on the enemy's heels.

There are days or seasons in an army, when all
the operations, from the moment they are prepared,
are well understood and executed by the troops.
There are other times and other days when nothing
will go right, when stoppages and difficulties, on
which no one has calculated, arise in the simplest
matters. These difficulties exist rather in imagina-
tion, and are fostered by a certain lukewarmness,
which pervades the execution of orders. Such a
time had now set in with the Silesian Army, but
there was no accounting for the why or wherefore.
Perhaps it was the thought that the enemy must
cross the Rhine, and would march ·so fast that it
would be impossible to overtake him, and then it was
of little consequence to reach the Rhine a day or two
sooner or later. To this must be added, that a report
had spread in the army, that the Bavarian General
Wrede would anticipate Napoleon at Frankfort with
a strong Austro-Bavarian army ; and as there was a
general longing for some days' rest, every one heard
the report with pleasure, and thought there was no
necessity to hurry on.

Moreover nothing could be more disagreeable
and disgusting than to follow in the wake of the
French army. Along the road, the whole way, lay
corpses or dying men ; the prisoners taken had death
stamped on their faces ; in short it was impossible
to think, without horror, of sleeping on the same spot,
perhaps on the same straw, as this fever-stricken
army, which had moreover infected the inhabitants
on their route and consumed all the provisions.

It began to be so cold and disagreeable that the cavalry looked about for stables, and the infantry for more substantial huts than those of a bivouac.

A considerable mountain lies between Eisenach and Marksuhl, which must be traversed; on its north-eastern declivity the chaussée ascends at an angle of inclination of 10 to 12 degrees. On this mountain the French rear-guard was overtaken, and found itself obliged to blow up some of the powder-waggons, that were too badly horsed to be brought up the mountain. Here Count Langeron lost time, and the pursuit was resigned to the Cossacks. The enemy kept the Cossacks in check with the infantry of the rear-guard.* When the Field-Marshal removed his head-quarters to Philippsthal near Vach on the 29th of October, the French rear-guard had already gained a start as far as Hünefeld; and the following day, when the Field-Marshal arrived at Fulda, it was hardly any longer possible to overtake it with infantry, supposing the French could continue on the chaussée to Frankfort. If, however, General Wrede succeeded in anticipating the enemy at the defiles of Gelnhausen, as was possible by all calculations, Napoleon would be compelled either to fight these fresh troops, or, what seemed much more natural and easy, to turn off the road to the right and march to Coblentz. In this case it was important that a corps

---

* The orders drawn up at Eisenach, where the army moved on four roads from thence, caused the Field-Marshal to remain with his head-quarters. The stoppage of the troops, a..d perhaps also the prospect, after so many hardships, of spending one day comfortably in the castle of Eisenach, induced the head-quarters to remain there the 27th. Had they removed that day to Marksuhl, or, still farther, to Vach, more activity would have been shown everywhere, and we should have stuck to the enemy; however, the Field-Marshal could not foresee this.

should march by the Vogelsberg and throw itself into Giessen.

General von Sacken was moving in the direction from Berka to Hersfeld, and was therefore naturally on this line; but when General Bubna entered Fulda on the 1st of November, with an Austrian advanced guard, still fresh and in good condition, and consequently more troops were collected on this road, the Field-Marshal decided to quit it and to take the direction to the right by the Vogelsberg to Giessen.

The army arrived there on the 3rd of November. Sacken's corps occupied Wetzlar. The Cossacks and single detachments were pushed forward as far as the Rhine. The Field-Marshal received information that the enemy had opened a way by Hanau, and crossed the Rhine at Mainz on the 2nd.

It was now necessary to settle what was to be done next. The Field-Marshal allowed his army to take up such extensive quarters for a few days, as in some degree to get refreshed and recruited. All was prepared for continuing the campaign with the utmost vigour. The Field-Marshal was of opinion that the shortest lines ought to be taken, to lose no time.

The Crown Prince was marching upon Hanover; the Field-Marshal therefore thought that it would be the Prince's affair to take Holland, while he himself would penetrate with the Silesian Army into the Netherlands, and cover this conquest of Holland. The Grand Army must in this case cross the Rhine between Mannheim and Mainz, and Paris must be the general aim of all the operations. In order to lose no time for this movement, the army began to stir again on the 7th of November.

On the march Count Langeron's corps formed a

junction with that of General Count St. Priest, who had been detached to Cassel. They marched by Dillenburg and Siegen towards Cologne. The Field-Marshal, with the two other corps, took the route by Limburg and Altenkirchen to Cologne. The plan was to construct bridges at Mühlheim, to cross the Rhine on the 15th, and then to advance by Aix-la-Chapelle and Liège to Brussels.

The chief of the general staff, General von Gneisenau, was gone to Frankfort, to lay this plan before the Sovereigns, to procure their consent to it, and make out the necessary co-operation. But it was contrary to the views and interest of various Powers, and did not therefore receive the sanction of the Sovereigns. Field-Marshal Blücher was recalled with his army to the plains of Frankfort, where the Silesian Army was to blockade Mainz from the right bank of the Rhine, and occupy this river from Ehren-breitstein to opposite Cologne with detachments.

The courier who brought this intelligence met the Field-Marshal at Altenkirchen. The Silesian Army therefore turned round, and arrived on the 15th before Cassel, where the Austrian troops were relieved by York's corps, and marched off the same day to the Upper Rhine.

On the 16th of November, Sacken's corps arrived on the left wing of York's, and (while extending out to the Maine) began the blockade of Cassel in concert with York's corps. Count Langeron's corps was placed, as a reserve, in cantonments between Königstein, Höchst, and Frankfort-on-the-Maine. The Field-Marshal took up his head-quarters at Höchst. The Sovereigns and their ministers were at Frankfort.

SECTION V.

CAMPAIGN OF 1814.

Internal state of Germany.—Organization of the German armies.
—Plan of operations; march of the Grand Army through
Switzerland.—The Silesian Army crosses the Rhine, and drives
Marshal Marmont back to Metz.—It marches to join the
Grand Army at Nancy, takes Toul, and advances by Vau-
couleurs to Brienne.—Combat of Brienne.—Retreat to
Trannes.—The Silesian is reinforced by the Grand Army.—
Battle of La Rothière.

*" Let all sinners be forgiven, and let there be no
more hell !"*

WITH this device the armies had advanced from
Leipsic to the Rhine. In Germany there were in
fact very few persons who still adhered to Napoleon,
and these few were held in general and profound
contempt. They belonged to the class of men who
wish to reap without sowing,—revellers, thieves,
bankrupts, and some perverse professors, who preferred talking to acting, and confounded theory with
practice.

The great mass of the people, with the best and
ablest portion of the nation at their head, had not
allowed themselves to be deceived by Napoleon.
When he assigned sovereignties, honours, splendour,
and extension of power to their Princes, they shook
their heads in doubt, and had forebodings that their
princes would have to pay with blood, money, and
their freedom, for all this glitter.

Where a good-humoured confidence still existed

that the Princes would be able to avert all mischief, the sentences of the mighty man opened the eyes of every one. Palm was executed by foreign power; Becker and many honest men (just because they were such) were dragged about as prisoners, without trial or sentence, in violation of national laws, and in contempt of the reclamations of the Princes.

Napoleon's system, of representing himself as the sole source from whence happiness and justice flowed, had different consequences than those he calculated upon. To destroy him, and with him all that he had introduced, was the wish of the multitude; this was accompanied by the hope, that on his destruction all the nameless misery he had brought upon Germany would cease. Whether it would then be advisable to restore the old German constitution, with all its later abuses, or only its principles with an improved method of carrying them out, was a question which occupied the attention of few people, and these were not allowed by the French police to spread their ideas; but every one was convinced of one fact, that small states like the German States could not have an independent existence, with distinct forms of government, legislation, and policy, without inviting, by their internal disorders, the greater Powers to make use of their strength to maintain or restore tranquillity. Experience had shown how dangerous the exercise of a foreign power, not legally defined, may be for a small state; and therefore the sovereignty bestowed by Napoleon, which totally excluded the notion of German supreme tribunals, was considered the greatest of all evils.

The German Princes hated Napoleon, they wished to get rid of his demands, but to most of them sovereignty was become a necessity: their system of

government, their financial obligations, were based
upon it. If they lost the position of sovereigns,
which had imprinted the stamp of legality on all
their measures for seven years, what confusion, what
difficulties would be created! If it was a troublesome burden to render an account of the principles
and measures of government in future, how much
more must it be to render account of the past!

All Germans who had lost their lands, titles,
property, or dignities, by the Bonapartist revolutionary measures, considered the moment of liberation the fittest time for regaining all they had
lost. A *portion* of these had rendered us important
services, and fought with us; *all* belonged to the
good cause,—we owed them thanks. The spirit of
the age and nation spoke in their favour. There is
no doubt that the Sovereigns would have willingly
wiped off all the injustice of their enemy, even to the
recollection of it; and it seemed at first the most
natural way to restore the old state of things, reserv-
ing to themselves the power of improvement; but
if, on the one hand, this was no longer possible, on
the other hand, had it even been possible, this measure must appear a doubtful one if necessity had not
required some temporary measure.

Napoleon was still opposed to us,—weakened
indeed, but not annihilated. The principal fortresses
from Dantzig to Mainz were in his hands; populous
France gave him the means of repairing his losses in
men; inexhaustible France, that of restoring the
matériel of his army. The distance of the armies of
Austria, Prussia, and Russia from their respective
states, rendered it difficult to draw from thence all
that armies require, and winter now made it impossible. It was just as impossible to procure the things

wanted, for ready money on the spot—none of the Powers had the means of doing so.

The war must be ended. There were two ways of accomplishing this—to cross the Rhine and prescribe peace in the heart of France, or to remain stationary on the Rhine and await Napoleon on the defensive. In the first case we required a multitude of men, being unable to foretell whether we should not have to wage war with the whole French nation; but in this case the war would support itself, and it was the most honourable way of ending it. In the second case, we should exhaust ourselves, and be just as little able to exist without the help of Germany; we should moreover give Napoleon time to collect his scattered forces. It was not difficult to choose between the two. Meanwhile, both in the one and other case, it was necessary to proceed with energy, and without loss of time to place armies in the field.

The governments of the Confederation of the Rhine were accustomed to execute such measures. Napoleon had practised them in it; they were acquainted with the means, and had the necessary authority.

If an attempt was now made to restore the old state of things in Germany, to replace the mediatized sovereignties and abolish the larger ones, everything would be lamed. It would require years to get the imperial armies together, according to the old mode; the time would be taken up by litigation, and the Princes of the Confederation would find their own misfortune in Napoleon's. It seemed the simplest way of proceeding to let all these affairs alone, and to undertake first, what the general interest so loudly demanded, namely, to make *him* harmless who had involved us in all this trouble.

If history judges what took place at Frankfort from this point of view, it will note down to the honour of Germany the fine feeling of patriotism with which young and old flocked to the standards. We had principally reckoned on those countries which had been forced to exchange their hereditary princes for the newly created ones of the Bonaparte family; they were expected to set a fine example, and great exertions were hoped for from them on that account.

All was easily executed where England's and Prussia's restored dominion procured the extraordinary means, but with more difficulty in Hesse and the Duchies of Berg and Oldenburg, where there was a deficiency of arms of all kinds, and from whence all the military magazines, depôts, &c., had been removed beyond the Rhine or destroyed.

For the rest of Germany, the strength of the armies was fixed by a per-centage on the population, and these were divided into six corps.

While treaties of peace and reconciliation were signed at Frankfort, and new German armies formed on paper, and while the investments and sieges of the fortresses in the rear were effected or arranged, the armies remained at Frankfort, and rested and ate, and ate and rested.

There soon began to be a want of forage. The Cossacks roamed for miles from Frankfort, to forage for the horses of the Emperor of Russia; forage was brought for those of the Emperor of Austria out of Franconia by ship to Frankfort. It was evident to every one that some decision must be taken about future operations; but one party wished for peace, another for winter-quarters, and a third wanted to wait for reinforcements. The Field-Marshal stuck to his opinion that we ought to cross the Rhine without halting, leaving the reinforcements to follow as a second division, and the new levies as a reserve. His reasons were these :—that Napoleon had no reserve in the interior, and that none of his fortresses were garrisoned and victualled; that we had reached the Rhine in greater strength than he had; and that, if we marched upon Paris, he must either throw the remains of his army into fortresses, leaving the field open to us; or give up his fortresses, if he kept his army together, and sought his safety in a battle. In neither case would he gain any time. But if we gave him time, he would contrive to arm the fortresses, create new armies, and inspire his people with fresh spirit. The Sovereigns perhaps entertained the same views, but they still wished to make another attempt for peace.

While the Grand Army was extending its movements to the left beyond the Neckar in the last half of November, the Sovereigns dispatched the Baron de St. Aignan from Frankfort to Paris, having communicated to him the conditions on which they were ready to conclude peace.

Napoleon could not bring himself down to his altered circumstances. A French General, with a nominal commission, desired an interview with Prince Schwarzenberg, as *Commandant* of the Allies. The Prince sent generals from all the Allied Powers to Hocheim, for he expected important propositions.

Napoleon offered to vacate the fortress on the

Vistula, if his troops were allowed a free retreat.
This unreasonable proposition, and his reply to the
communications made by the Baron de St. Aignan,
showed that it was impossible to avoid continuing
the war.

In December the armies were considerably
strengthened, particularly the Russian; and three
additional corps were made over to the Field-Marshal for the new campaign; so that his army was to
consist of—

Langeron's corps - - -	35,000 men.
Sacken's - - - -	25,000
York's - - - -	25,000
Kleist's - - - -	15,000
The Elector of Hesse -	24,000
The Duke of Saxe Coburg -	18,000
Total	- 142,000 men.

From these must be deducted 10,000 Hessians,
as it was foreseen that the Elector would only be
able to raise at most 14,000; and the Field-Marshal
could not reckon on the three last before February,
1814.

In the beginning of the year he could operate
with from 80,000 to 85,000 men, who were distributed
in winter-quarters along the Rhine, from the Neckar
to Düsseldorf. On these forces the Field-Marshal
grounded his plan of operations, for supporting the
movements of the Grand Army from Switzerland to
Paris, and those of General von Bülow from Holland
to Paris. The Allied Sovereigns had communicated
to him the general object and the plan of march

proposed for the Grand Army; but the General-in-Chief of the Grand Army requested to be informed by him what movements he had resolved to make with his army. Of all the distinctions hitherto received by the Field-Marshal, this, as a proof of unlimited confidence, seemed the greatest. It deserves to be transmitted to posterity, because the Sovereigns showed by it how well they knew how to honour, and at the same time reward, the Field-Marshal's care, activity, and patriotism.

The general plan of operations must be contemplated from the following point of view.

In 1813 Austria had, in a certain measure, carried on two wars at once; in Germany as an Allied power, and in Italy for herself alone. The war in Italy lay quite beyond the reach of the other Allies; the chief blow must be struck in Germany, where Bonaparte had his principal power. Russia and Prussia were therefore silent about Italy.

Austria furnished her army in Germany, according to stipulation; but as she could not leave her states and her capital quite uncovered, and consequently was obliged always to have a defensive army, she preferred rather to increase her efforts, and to form an army which should be strong enough to act on the offensive, and in case of good fortune, to conquer Italy with a purely Austrian army.

These measures quite fell in with the general interest, and there seemed therefore to be a tacit agreement not to treat them diplomatically; which avoided the necessity of binding the hands of one or other party, or of anticipating the time for settling an endless multitude of cases.

Until the arrival of the Allies at Frankfort, the

war in Italy had exercised no other influence on the proceedings of the Austrian Cabinet, or the relations between the Allies, than perhaps occasioning the attempt of a settlement with Bavaria; but now it was said on the part of Austria, that the operations of the year 1814 must be, in some measure, directed to facilitate the conquest of Italy. Now this again was an affair of general interest, and the Austrian Cabinet consequently met with ready compliance and support, though the affair was not expressed in plain terms on all occasions.

We shall not now enquire whether we should not have harassed Bonaparte far more, if we had attacked him quite in the north, and thus compelled him to separate himself from his Italian army, so that any concerted movements between his Italian and French armies would have led to nothing, instead of directing our principal forces to the south, and approaching the theatre of war in Italy. Particular circumstances have great weight in deciding this question. If we had equal or fewer numbers than Bonaparte, with superior means of intelligence, it was expedient to bring the scene of operations of the German army nearer to that of the army of Italy; if, however, we were superior in numbers, and our enemy in means of intelligence, we ought to remove the theatre of war as far north as possible. But there were strategists who foresaw, in such a case, Napoleon operating on the Danube, and ourselves hastening full of anxiety to cover Vienna. By the situation of Paris, and the necessity under which Bonaparte lay, of resigning his capital as well as the northern and eastern fortresses of his Empire to their fate, if he wished to draw any real advantage from a junction with his Italian army, the operations of the Grand Army from Switzerland acquired a new and important light; and as the Austrian Cabinet wished for this movement, which certainly shortened considerably the line of communication with home, it was universally adopted.

But now came the question, What could, what must, Field-Marshal Blücher do under these circumstances?

Experience had shown that in critical cases the Grand Army was always stronger and more efficient than it knew or believed itself to be. The most natural plan, therefore, was to let Bonaparte fall upon the Grand Army and fight it, while Blücher should rapidly unite with Bülow in Bonaparte's rear, and proceed to Paris. But how would it be if Bonaparte beat the Grand Army, and if the peace party, always lurking at royal head-quarters, like a poisonous plant in the heart of the army, gained the day?

It was, besides, but too well known that this party endeavoured in the most shameless manner to work upon Austria, who on account of consanguinity must be expected to show some forbearance towards Bonaparte. It was, indeed, the general opinion that this Cabinet might be easily made to waver in the resolution of overthrowing the tyrant's throne. As an Austrian Field-Marshal commanded the Grand Army, this circumstance was not unimportant.

Taking all these things into consideration, Blücher decided on keeping with the Grand Army, and the rather, as he was too weak at the commencement of the campaign to act independently.

A strong corps had to be left before Mainz, as the forces blockading this place, on both banks of the Rhine during the winter, when no bridge of boats could be constructed, must be in a condition to withstand the garrison, unless Frankfort-on-the-Maine were to be exposeed to the danger of being pillaged.

The conquest of Holland was almost completed, but that of the Netherlands (the Field-Marshal's favourite notion) must be given up, as General von Bülow was too weak to attempt it, and no one could dare hope that the Crown Prince of Sweden would do anything to assist it. This Prince had expressed himself in very passionate terms against a passage of the Rhine, and General von Bülow had been obliged to disengage himself from him to a certain extent by force, in order to free the old Prussian provinces and Holland.

It might be foreseen that, with proper precautions on our part, the enemy would neither defend the Rhine from Manheim to Coblentz, in earnest, nor accept a decisive battle before he reached the Saar. The Field-Marshal consequently sent word to Prince Schwarzenberg that he would arrive before Metz by the middle of January.

The space between the Moselle and the Meuse, occupied by the six fortresses of Metz, Thionville, Saar Louis, Luxemburg, Longwy, and Verdun, the left flank being also very well covered by the fortresses on the Meuse, Sedan, Montmedy, and Mezières, which block up all the roads at right angles to that river, seemed quite made for receiving Bonaparte's army.

What enormous difficulties should we have found in attacking him in this great intrenched camp! Had he taken up a position behind the Moselle, with Thionville in front of his left wing, and Metz in front of his right, who would have attacked him there in front? And supposing we had advanced between the Moselle and the Meuse on his right flank, he had only to cross the Moselle, and he could have taken up an equally strong position between Thionville, Saar Louis, and Metz, or he might have taken up one between Longwy and Luxemburg. Thus the locality offered him numberless positions where he could never be *forced* to give battle; and with the various rivers, unfordable in spring, he could not fail, in the course of this movement, to find opportunities for falling on one or other portion of the army with superior forces. He had shown at Dresden that he understood how to choose, and was tactically skilful in making use of, such positions. There he had no strong fortresses, or only two;* he had not the two parallel rivers; yet how much trouble he gave us there! In case we left him alone, and wished to march to Paris by Troyes (where an army of reserve was probably forming), if he had allowed us quietly to march on and then followed us, should we have ventured to continue the march to attack Paris?

It might therefore be expected that we should find Bonaparte between the fortresses; and there seemed to be only two causes that could hinder his making a stand on these points :—first, if he believed that all our forces would press forward from the Upper Rhine towards Langres; or second, if we anticipated him by surprise. The Field-Marshal resolved on attempting both, and kept the strictest secrecy as to his intentions, with all the apparent openness respecting his situation which his followers

---

* The mountain Castle of Königstein could only have been important to Bonaparte inasmuch as it secured his passage across the Elbe.

were used to from him. He complained at his head-
quarters of Höchst, of the inactivity to which he
was condemned, spoke of his winter-quarters; and
after having hitherto declined all the friendly invita-
tions from Frankfort to remove his head-quarters
thither, declaring that " he would not rest," now, on
the 25th of December, he took up his quarters in
Frankfort, saying, that as he must now at any rate
spend the winter in inactivity, he would as soon that
it should be at Frankfort.

The General War-Commissary of the Silesian
Army had previously assembled the Deputies from
the Governments on the Rhine, to regulate with
them the winter-quarters, and subsistence of the
army. While these were now disputing in Frankfort
about the distribution of the burdens, and in German
fashion deducing their rights from Charlemagne, the
passage of the army across the Rhine was secretly
prepared. A number of Frenchmen who were
settled in various countries of Germany had been
brought together and detained at Frankfort, that
they might not betray what was passing amongst us.
As there was no trace anywhere of our intentions
being betrayed or guessed at, but as, on the contrary,
the burden of winter-quarters was the general subject of conversation in Frankfort, and it suited our
system to spread this account, the Field-Marshal
had all these Frenchmen conveyed to Mainz on the
26th of December.

The character of this war, the composition of the
Prussian Army, which contained the kernel of the
whole nation, and the enthusiasm with which the
Silesian Army fought for the great European interests, induced the Field-Marshal never to let an

opportunity slip in which he could cheer and strengthen the spirit of his soldiers, and elevate their feelings of honour and love of their country. The celebration of certain days, the conclusion of certain seasons, and the commencement of great undertakings under favourable auspices, were amongst the opportunities of which he thus availed himself. The custom on New-year's night of taking leave of the old year, and welcoming the new one, was turned to account by the Field-Marshal for *concluding* and *beginning*. He determined that as the clock struck twelve at night on the 31st of December, the Silesian Army should cross the Rhine at three points—Manheim, Caub, and Coblentz. A short proclamation to the soldiers, and another to the inhabitants of the left bank, were prepared. In the latter he said, " All who have pleasure in fighting for Bonaparte may go away, to seek death and destruction in his ranks." This phrase was written less for the inhabitants of the left bank than to raise the pride of our soldiers.

The passage was safely effected on all three points. The French troops had placed redoubts opposite the mouth of all the rivers flowing from Germany into the Rhine, from whence manned vessels could enter the Rhine. General von Sacken resolutely attacked the one situated opposite the mouth of the Neckar; his men sprang into the ditches, and mounted the breastworks on each other's shoulders. The garrison of the redoubt and six pieces of artillery were taken. The redoubt situated opposite the Lahn was attacked by General Count St. Priest; the enemy abandoned it, and four iron guns were found in it. At Caub the enemy made little resistance. A bridge of *canvas pontoons* had been constructed; and though these pontoons had been used with great advantage by Field-Marshal Blücher during the whole campaign of 1813, and all the twelve-pounder batteries had gone over them, yet here there was this difficulty, that even a small quantity of floating ice would have destroyed the bridge.* Just as the troops were crossing at Caub, a postilion was caught who was bringing instructions to the General commanding at Coblentz (Durutte) what to do in case we crossed.†

The Field-Marshal discovered by this, that Marshal Marmont would take up a position at Kayserslautern, where Durutte was to join him; in case he could no longer do so by Kirn or Oberstein, he was to take the direction of Birkenfeld.

The Field-Marshal now pushed forward rapidly with York's corps, by Creuznach (where the communication with General von Sacken was opened by Alzey, on the chaussée from Meissenheim, Lautereck, Coussel, and St. Wendel to Saar-brück, while General Sacken marched by Kayserslautern upon Zweybrücken, and Count Langeron (after leaving a detachment at Coblentz) invested Mainz on both sides with his corps. On the 8th of January, the Field-Marshal's head-quarters were at St. Wendel,

---

* A pontoon train of this sort consists of frames of the same form as a copper pontoon, which are to be laid down separately. Round these frames, strong canvas, soaked in pitch, is nailed in such a manner that the whole takes the form of an usual pontoon. The canvas resists the water. A carriage is necessary for each pontoon; but these carriages are so light they can be driven on all kinds of roads. If the canvas is easily damaged, it has the advantage of being easily repaired, which is a long process with copper pontoons.

† This was in consequence of intelligence received by Bonaparte of the march of the Grand Army from Basle to France.

but Marshal Marmont had arrived safely that day at Saar-brück, where he joined his forces with those of General Durutte, and destroyed the stone bridge.

Several actions had taken place, in which we took some prisoners, but they were of no other importance than that they raised the spirits of our army, while they still more depressed the enemy's. General von Sacken blockaded Landau with three battalions; and Colonel Count Henkel was detached with some battalions and squadrons to take speedy possession of Trèves.

Marshal Marmont made a show, on the 9th, of making a stand at Saar-brück. The Field-Marshal accordingly ordered a cavalry movement for the 10th, by which his two wings would have been encircled, and which was to be followed on the 11th by the passage of the infantry across the Saar and an attack. Marmont retreated on the 10th, and marched through Metz on the 12th. The Field-Marshal established his head-quarters this day at St. Avold. The advanced posts were pushed forward to the gates of Metz. Trèves was occupied, and there were flying parties before Thionville and Luxemburg. General von Sacken sent out parties towards Nancy, and endeavoured to connect himself with the Grand Army by Saarburg. It was necessary to take new resolutions without delay; they depended on the enemy's movements and on the news from the Grand Army.

The Silesian Army on the Saar was about 50,000 strong; of the reinforcement to follow, Kleist's corps was to enter Coblentz on the 19th. The Elector of Hesse was to follow him immediately. The latter was destined to remain stationary between Luxemburg and Thionville, in order to observe and keep in check all the contiguous fortresses. The Duke of Saxe-Coburg's destination was to blockade Mainz and relieve Count Langeron, who together with Kleist was to reinforce the army by degrees. General von York had instructions to reconnoitre closely the fortresses of Metz, Thionville, and Luxemburg, and to attempt if possible a forcible attack on one or other of them.

It might be foreseen, that such an undertaking would exceed General York's strength, though the garrisons in all the places were weak ; meanwhile the object of making a show of strength to the garrisons, and of throwing uncertainty on the direction of the march, was attained. During this march of General York the enemy's troops retreating from Alsace, abandoned Nancy, and the light-troops of Sacken's corps took possession of the place. The Field-Marshal entered it with Sacken's corps on the 17th, and there received news of the Grand Army, which had advanced on its line of march nearly as far as the Silesian Army. General Count Wrede had had an *affaire* in the district of Remiremont, and was advancing by Epinal to Neuf-Château. He was nearest the Silesian Army, as Count Wittgenstein had met with hindrances in crossing the Rhine that retarded him.*

---

* The French newspapers stirred up the people to represent us everywhere as robbers and plunderers, who had come across the Rhine for the purpose of dividing France amongst us. Such representations might seem ridiculous to every other nation, but they had the greatest effect on the French, as there is no people more credulous. The Field-Marshal therefore sought an opportunity to explain our views and conduct. He found such at Nancy, where he made a speech to the Magistrate who gave him welcome, in which he announced to the conquered departments the abolition of the " Douanes " and the " Droits réunis," as well

All accounts of the enemy agreed that Marshal Marmont had retreated upon Chalons, which was the general rendezvous of the enemy's army.

According to accounts received from the Lower Rhine, Marshal Macdonald and General Sebastiani were retreating from the Rhenish Provinces to the interior, probably also to Chalons.

The Field-Marshal now resolved to advance rapidly, to make the enemy believe that he was proceeding to Chalons, but to touch on the grand Army by his left, and for this purpose to march on the chaussée by Vaucouleurs and Joinville to Brienne.

Toul still held out with a weak garrison and few means; when General von Sacken invested it, it surrendered.

The Field-Marshal wanted to make it appear, that we were certain of our affair, and considered the war as quite ended. All the deserters who came over to us were therefore dismissed with passports to their homes; the prisoners even, if they wished it, were publicly dismissed; and it is certain that this mode of proceeding withdrew a multitude of combatants from Bonaparte's army. Our army, cantoned everywhere, was well received by the inhabitants, and the utmost order prevailed.

The advance from Toul was made in two columns. The one, with which the Field-Marshal remained, reached Brienne on the 26th, without meeting the enemy. The second, under Prince Scherbatow, about 10,000 strong, destined to mislead the enemy as to the direction of our march, found the hostile rear-

as the diminution of the Salt Tax. These were the most hateful burdens in France, their abolition must therefore produce the greatest effect. The speech was immediately printed, and copies transmitted to all parts of France.

guard not far from Ligny on the evening of the 22nd.

On the 23rd Prince Scherbatow took Ligny, which was occupied by infantry. On the 25th he took St. Diziers, left Lieutenant-General Lanskoy behind, there to wait for York's corps, while he himself joined General von Sacken at Brienne. York's corps had received orders to march by St. Mihiel to St. Diziers, where it was to arrive on the 28th. It was quite impossible for the Field-Marshal to blockade all the fortresses, of which there were six here in a small circle, Metz, Thionville, Saar Louis, Luxemburg, Longwy, and Verdun. On his retreat, Marshal Marmont had taken all the old soldiers from the fortresses, and left recruits behind in their places. It was a good measure, for in the fortresses there was time to drill the young men, and all the more as the weather did not yet allow of any regular attack. There was a deficiency of artillerymen to serve the guns on the walls. The Field-Marshal wished to take advantage of these circumstances. There were two means of doing this—namely, to escalade one or other of these fortresses with old soldiers (as it might be expected that the recruits would defend themselves ineffectively), or to leave a few Cossacks to watch all these fortresses, since their garrisons could not be drilled for some months, and to keep them in such check by the troops who were to follow as reinforcements, that they would not be able to make any sallies against our lines of magazines. In accordance with these views the Field-Marshal made the following disposition : A weak Prussian Landwehr cavalry regiment was to blockade Saar Louis. General Jouseffowitsch was to blockade Metz, but until his arrival the blockade was to be undertaken by General

Boroscdin, who was afterwards to follow the army. General Kleist was to leave 1000 horse to blockade Luxemburg and observe Thionville, and to march (as soon as the troops should reach Trèves) between Luxemburg and Thionville, and between Verdun and Metz, upon St. Mihiel. As soon as the Elector of Hesse should arrive, the 1000 horse were to be relieved and to follow by the same route.

Of the blockading corps before Mainz the following troops were to march off by Nancy :

January 9th, General Olsuview (with one corps).

January 17th, General Capczewitsch (with one division).

February 1st. General von Korff (with five cavalry regiments) : and General Rudczewitsch (with one and a half division).

February 15th, General Count St. Priest (with half a corps).

These troops would be rendered superfluous at Mainz by the successive formation of the German corps under the Duke of Saxe-Coburg; of the Russian troops only two infantry regiments, one battery of twelve guns, and some Cossack regiments, were to remain before Mainz.

Towards the beginning of March the Elector of Hesse's troops (by stipulation 24,000 men) ought to be assembled at Trèves in perfect condition for service. They were destined to be employed in sieges or blockades.

These were the arrangements which the Field-Marshal made to cover his rear and his line of magazines by Saar-gemines and Nancy, before advancing farther.

Field-Marshal Blücher learnt on his arrival at

Brienne, that Marshal Mortier, who was marching with a corps upon Langres, had retreated upon Troyes, after an *affaire* at Bar-sur-Aube with the Crown Prince of Würtemberg. On the other hand Bonaparte had reached Chalons, and removed his head-quarters to Vitry; Macdonald and Sebastiani could not yet have joined him.

The French army was consequently divided, and one portion separated from the other by the Aube and Marne. The Field-Marshal concluded that Bonaparte would be too weak to act on the offensive, without a junction with Mortier or Macdonald, as he on the other hand considered himself too weak to attack Bonaparte till the arrival of General von York.

The roads were now bad, and except on chaussées it was difficult for the Artillery to proceed. The party wishing to attack would be obliged to give up the advantage of chaussées. In order to observe Mortier more closely and to impede his junction with Bonaparte, General von Sacken was instructed to advance to Lesmont, and push his advanced posts to Arcis. The Crown Prince of Würtemberg observed Marshal Mortier from the other side, and covered the Field-Marshal's left flank and rear with his corps, about 15,000 strong.

Meanwhile, Bonaparte had marched on the 27th of January upon St. Diziers, and driven from thence General Lanskoy, who retreated to Joinville, where he found the advanced guard of Wittgenstein's corps.

At St. Diziers, Bonaparte learned that Prince Scherbatow's weak corps had marched by Montier-en-Der to Brienne, and followed this corps.

Early on the 29th, news arrived that Bonaparte was advancing from Montier-en-Der towards Brienne, and this movement of the enemy was indeed soon seen.

Field-Marshal Blücher ordered General von Sacken with his entire corps to Brienne, and was much in‐clined, in case Napoleon attacked him, to go out to meet him; and the more, as it appeared from an intercepted letter to Marshal Mortier at Troyes, dated Vitry 28th, that he (Mortier) was only to set out on receipt of this letter, to join Napoleon; therefore if a dupli‐cate had reached him safely, he was only to depart on the 29th, and could hardly proceed that day as far as Arcis, whither he was ordered. Moreover, General Count Pahlen, with about 2000 horse, form‐ing the advanced guard of Wittgenstein's corps, arrived at Brienne on the morning of the 29th.

But, although it was not impossible to strike a blow at Bonaparte here, it was our duty to follow a safe course, to avoid a decisive action, and to await the reinforcements that must arrive in a few days, namely, the Grand Army consisting of above 110,000 men, who were already at Chaumont, and General von York, who must already be at or near St. Diziers. With this view, the Field-Marshal decided not to seek a battle, but first to take up Sacken's corps, which must march through Brienne, and then wait and see whether Bonaparte would attack him.

The march of Sacken's corps on the chaussée from Lesmont to Brienne, was concealed from the enemy by a wood, which was however of no great breadth. From the wood to the village of Maizières, through which the enemy must pass, a great plain extends; here General Count Pahlen stationed him‐self, to cover the march of Sacken's corps. The town of Brienne with its two outlets, one towards Montier-en-Der, and one towards Bar-sur-Aube, was occupied by the 9th Russian corps under Lieutenant-General Olsuview, which consisted of the 15th and 9th divisions, but did not amount to more than 4000 to 5000 men with 24 cannons.

Bonaparte placed the whole of his cavalry opposite General Count Pahlen, and at 3 P.M. began to cannonade the town, just at the moment when General Sacken reached it with the head of his columns. The first grenades set fire to the place, and a conflagration subsequently rose in several quarters. Bonaparte's batteries and columns advanced to the right and left of the avenue leading from Brienne to Montier-en-Der.

The Field-Marshal himself occupied the Castle of Brienne, which is close to the town ; so that from the castle-court, a street of the town and the avenue leading to Montier-en-Der form one straight line. As soon as Sacken's corps had traversed the town, it took up a position in column behind it, on the road to Old Brienne, with the cavalry under Lieutenant-General Wasiltschikoff on the right wing. General Count Pahlen had already retreated slowly, and followed Sacken's corps through Brienne. As our troops continued to defile through the outlet of the town leading to Lesmont, which was not on the side towards the enemy, Olsuview's corps had left it unguarded. The day was beginning to close, and it was supposed that the fighting would end, as Bonaparte had not hitherto developed any considerable strength. But now, on the contrary, he advanced with batteries and took the right wing in hand.

After our cavalry had moved through Brienne, from the left wing to the right, as the enemy's cavalry had now in front only heights covered with vineyards, the wood and the town, it ought to have moved upon the left wing opposite ours. This Bonaparte neglected, and the Field-Marshal resolved to punish him for it on the spot.

The cavalry under Wasiltschikoff and Pahlen, advanced, turned Bonaparte's left wing, attacked it as it was getting dusk, and threw the entire wing into great disorder. They captured the hostile batteries of the left wing, but could only carry off five pieces of artillery, being forced to leave the rest, as the horses belonging to them had been driven away.

Just before nightfall, the Field-Marshal, wishing once more to survey the enemy's forces, rode up to the castle. While he was there, some of the enemy's tirailleurs, who had found the Lesmont entrance unguarded, forced their way into the town and up to the castle, where they might have surprised the Field-Marshal and Lieutenant-General von Gneisenau, had they not betrayed themselves by some untimely shots.* Almost at the same moment General von Sacken rode into the town with his suite, to acquaint himself with the state of affairs. In the middle of the town he met a troop of hostile cavalry, by which he was very nearly taken prisoner. An officer of his suite, Colonel Count Rochechouart, fell on this occasion.

On hearing that the enemy was in the town, the troops, who still defended themselves at the outlets, withdrew from thence, and a part only of the town

---

* This occurrence afterwards appeared much misrepresented before the public. Accounts reached head-quarters that the Field-Marshal had been surprised in Brienne, and had contrived with difficulty to save himself. The circumstance that General von Sacken stumbled unexpectedly on the enemy in Brienne, and the Commandant of the Field-Marshal's Staff was taken prisoner, gave some probability to this version of the affair.

was still held by us.   The Field-Marshal gave orders
to eject the enemy totally, and caused fresh troops
from Sacken's corps to advance.   It was reported
after midnight that we had retaken the whole town,
but that the enemy defended the castle so obstinately
that we could not gain possession of it; for they fired
from the windows upon all who approached, who
were seen distinctly by the light of the burning town;
while these could see nothing of the enemy inside
the castle.   Under these circumstances, Field-
Marshal Blücher was content to let matters rest,
and the rather as he only continued to hold Brienne
for the honour of his arms, and in order to mask the
retreat which he had already determined on.   The
flames had gained such a mastery in the town that
many streets were no longer passable.

After the troops had rested awhile, and the
baggage had been sent forward, about three P.M.
the Field-Marshal set out with the infantry and
artillery, and marched to Trannes, where Sacken's
corps took up an advantageous position, with its left
wing resting on the Aube, and its right towards
Eclance.   The Field-Marshal established his head-
quarters at Arconval.   Our cavalry followed the
infantry at eleven o'clock the same day, after the
enemy's infantry had taken possession of Brienne.
The enemy's cavalry followed, and some skirmishing
took place.   Bonaparte took up his quarters in the
castle of Brienne, and occupied Dienville, La
Rothière, and Chaumenil, with three different corps;
he stationed the remainder of his troops near
Brienne.   He remained in this position the 30th,
31st, and till noon on the 1st, without doing anything but make a vain show of attacking us.

In these two days however our situation changed

very much for the better. The Crown Prince of Würtemberg took up a position on the heights of Maisons, occupying Levigny, to cover the Field-Marshal's right flank, while the Grand Army gradually reached Bar-sur-Aube by Chaumont. General Wrede with his corps of about 25,000 men had been posted to the right from Chaumont into the valley of the Marne; General Count Wittgenstein marched still more to the right upon Vassy. General von York did not arrive at St. Diziers until the 30th *; he found that place occupied by the enemy, and attacked and took it, in which operation a gun was captured.

The military condition of the Allies was consequently recovered; the *débouché* from Trannes remained in our power, and permitted us to proceed on the offensive. But it was otherwise with our political relations. Bonaparte had contrived to make some people believe that he was really anxious for peace; and the proposal was entertained of a Congress to be assembled at Chatillon-sur-Seine.

Whether it was advisable for us, in a general point of view, to enter at that time into negociations for peace with Napoleon, or whether we ought not rather to have taken advantage of our superiority, to dethrone him speedily, and to declare freely and firmly to the French nation, that this was the only means of obtaining peace, are questions which it would take too long to investigate here, as they must be preceded by an exposition of Bonaparte's relations to his senate and legislative corps, and of the previous attempts at peace on the part of the Allies. Suffice it to say, that the Allies believed they ought not to decline the proposal of a Congress, which did

* The bad roads, and the necessity of marching in close columns, to be prepared for an attack, had delayed him two days.

not put a stop to operations; and that they ought to prove to all nations their real desire for peace; they perhaps also thought that the Congress bound them to nothing; and if it did not assist their views, neither could it do any harm.

That Bonaparte was not in earnest in his wish for peace, was soon shown.   Well-informed people maintained that he had contrived this conference, mainly with the hope of being able to work upon the Austrian Cabinet.   The relationship might have produced milder views.   Austria might think quite differently of Bonaparte, defeated and taught by experience, than of the conqueror of the world of former days, particularly if she were able to treat with him, in an amicable and befitting manner, on the subject of most importance to her—*Italy:* this seemed far preferable to the uncertain issue of war.

The soldiers, and those who considered the anni-hilation of Bonaparte's power a necessary condition, remained firm in their opinion that the war must be continued in earnest, and the Congress only considered as by-play.   But the other party entertained the contrary opinion, that the war must now be carried on only as a feint.

Field-Marshal Blücher had called forth Bonaparte's legions by his stroke against Arcis.   The peace party at the royal head-quarters wished to know what views he entertained, and at what he was aiming.   It appeared hazardous to the diplomatists to undertake the personal commission of sounding his views: they knew the strength of his character. Prince Schwarzenberg, who knew not what answer to give, undertook to put the question : he sent an officer held in high esteem, to Brienne, who spoke openly and simply.   The Field-Marshal replied in

the same style, with his usual force of expressions:
"We must go to Paris. Napoleon has paid his
visits to all the capitals of Europe; should we be
less polite? In short, he must descend from the
throne which, for Europe's sake and that of our
Sovereigns, he ought never to have been allowed to
occupy. Until he is hurled from it, we shall have
no rest."*

These words were repeated beyond Arconval.
The Field-Marshal represented the great advantage
of our attacking Bonaparte near Brienne, before
he could bring up the remainder of his troops;
and offered himself to make the attack, if he could
only be strengthened, in the absence of York's
corps. But the consideration that the army could
not subsist in the barren valley of the Aube, and
must retreat if it did not attack, had more effect
than all besides. Thus military considerations cut
the knot, and the battle was resolved upon.

By a disposition made at Chaumont on the 31st
of January, a centre was formed of the corps of
Count Giulay and the Crown Prince of Würtemberg,
and placed under Field-Marshal Blücher, in order to
push forward on the 1st of February, and drive the
enemy from Brienne. Its strength amounted to
rather more than 50,000 men. General Count Wrede
formed the right wing; General Count Colloredo
the left — each with about 25,000 men. Count
Wittgenstein was posted beyond the right wing with
16,000 men. The whole of the Guards were so

---

* The author cannot say whether this was the first time that
these views were officially mentioned, but it would appear so;
for about this time, Field-Marshal Blücher began to be much
censured at royal head-quarters, and represented as a man of
exaggerated notions.

disposed as to serve as a reserve, to support the right wing or centre, and took up a position accordingly near Bar-sur-Aube. Giulay's corps could only reach Trannes by 10 or 11 A.M. on the 1st of February.

On the 31st, the enemy's Light Cavalry made a movement from La Rothière toward Trannes, just as the Field-Marshal was in the position. He gave orders to avoid any serious engagement. This so emboldened the enemy, that towards evening he took possession of a wood, which lay in front of the position of the Allies, but not so as to prevent our defending it.

It was natural to conclude that Napoleon intended to attack us the next morning. In expectation of this, the Field-Marshal made no other preparations than to invite the Crown Prince of Würtemberg to be with his whole corps at Eclance next morning. As, however, before noon next day, the enemy did not show any preparations for attacking us, and as General Giulay had arrived at Trannes, and the Crown Prince of Würtemberg at Eclance, the Field-Marshal gave orders to attack.

The task he had undertaken presented no great difficulties in itself, but the strategical disposition for the advance of the Allies, as well as the distribution of the forces, was not at all adapted to the position which the nature of the ground prescribed to the enemy.

Bonaparte had his right wing securely supported at Dienville; his centre was advantageously posted at Brienne; but his left wing at Morvilliers was not supported, nor had it any particular tactical advantage. He was, moreover, unfavourably circumstanced in this respect, that his right wing and centre possessed no other line of retreat but through Brienne, from which place his right wing was more distant than his left.

The point of attack for the Allies was therefore unquestionably Bonaparte's left wing : in that case, he would have been immediately driven back on the *one* line of retreat by Lesmont ; whereas, in an attack on his right wing, he had still the second line by Ronay-sur-Voire open to him.

It was an unfavourable circumstance to the Allies that they had to march some distance to the battle. This could not begin till late on a short February day ; and besides, it might be foreseen with certainty, that a portion of the troops would not be able to get up at all. Moreover, the chaussée from Bar-sur-Aube to Brienne, on which the principal forces of the Allies were advancing, led up to the strongest point of the enemy's position, viz. the right wing and centre ; but they were afraid of leaving the chaussée on account of the bad roads. Another disadvantage was, that 16,000 of the 40,000 men of the right-wing column must, according to the disposition, remain inactive for the battle ; as the left wing, consisting of 25,000, had the same charge. Moreover, the reserve was posted at such a distance, that it could not fulfil its twofold destination. Neither time nor distance would allow it to support the right wing on the day of battle ; and it could not even arrive to reinforce the centre until dark.

The Field-Marshal was afraid, if he advanced too early or too quickly with the centre, that Bonaparte would slip away ; he therefore delayed the attack till mid-day, by which time General Count Wrede might arrive. His intention was, to get possession of the villages in front of him, (of these La Rothière and

La Giebrie were the most important) ; then he would
have it quite in his power, either to keep Napoleon
in check, (who had apparently his main force in the
district of Old Brienne,) should he wish to send detachments to the support of his left wing, or to
attack him with all his strength if this seemed
necessary or advantageous. The progress General
Wrede must make, the start which he must gain,
according to the plan, would determine the rest.
The Field-Marshal, therefore, only made out the
disposition for the first part of his charge.

The Crown Prince of Würtemberg was to
march upon La Giebrie through the wood from
Eclance, and to attack the enemy; General von
Sacken was to march from the position with his corps
and General Olsuview's in two columns, to attack
La Rothière; and General Count Giulay was to proceed on the chaussée from Trannes, bending farther
to the left, to attack Dienville. A notion was entertained that the reserve from Bar-sur-Aube would
only act against La Rothière, and its march was
directed thither. The Grenadiers and Cuirassiers at
its head were made over to the Field-Marshal,
who left them in reserve on the heights of Trannes.

There had been a frost in the night ; the soil on
those heights was clay ; the artillery that had been
brought up could not be moved from the spot, unless,
as proposed by the Artillery-General of Sacken's
corps, one half the guns remained behind in the
position, in order to put a double number of horses
to the other half. The Field-Marshal gave his
consent, and General von Sacken marched to the
battle with 60 pieces, instead of 120.

In order to give a correct idea of the battle, it is
necessary here to mention, that, according to all

subsequent accounts, Bonaparte neither knew nor suspected anything of the arrival of the Grand Army; and an Austrian trumpeter, who deserted from Wrede's corps, was the first to give the French officers information that the Grand Army was approaching.

When about one o'clock it was announced to Bonaparte that the Field-Marshal was advancing, he would not believe it, until later, on the trumpeter's statement, he mounted his horse with the idea of avoiding the battle, and gave the Prince de Neufchatel orders to this effect. When, however, he reached (between Old Brienne and La Rothière,) the Young Guard, who had got under arms on hearing the approaching cannonade, he was received with such enthusiasm, that he thought he ought not to let the moment slip without profiting by it. He therefore exclaimed: " L'Artillerie en avant!" and thus about four o'clock the affair at La Rothière commenced in earnest. On the first reverse, however, Bonaparte abandoned the fight, ate his dinner in the Castle of Brienne, and retreated with his army in the night. These particular circumstances show that Bonaparte came to this battle without any previous wish or intention.

Let us now return to details. The column of the Crown Prince of Würtemberg, conformably to the disposition, remained on the wooded heights, which were only intersected by forest roads, along which it was so difficult to pass that the Crown Prince had got but one battery through. He opened the fight, met with resistance, attacked La Giebrie with some battalions, and took it; but his troops were driven out again, and the action was for some time at a standstill there.

General von Sacken, with about 20,000 men, drove the enemy without much trouble as far as La Rothière. But here the latter raised some batteries outside the village, which were however soon compelled to retreat by Sacken's artillery. When after this (about half-past three), the enemy advanced with the artillery of the Guards, Lieutenant-General Wasiltschikoff went to meet him with the light cavalry of Sacken's corps (leaving La Rothière to the left), and engaged in a combat with the hostile cavalry just as snow began to fall in large flakes. General Wasiltschikoff was forced to give way. The enemy pursued him warmly, and in the snow came unexpectedly on Prince Scherbatow's column of infantry, got under its fire, and was simultaneously attacked by the dragoons of Sacken's corps which had remained in reserve. General Wasiltschikoff rallied his forces, made a fresh attack, and drove the enemy's cavalry quite off the field, behind Old Brienne. He took four batteries on this occasion. The enemy's infantry had thrown itself into the village of La Rothière, where General Sacken attacked it with all his forces. The combat was long and obstinate, the Field-Marshal was obliged to lead on the reserves. It was not till eleven o'clock at night that we got the village quite into our power.*

* If, at the moment of Wasiltschikoff's second attack, Sacken's infantry had followed in the same direction; and if the Russian Grenadiers and Cuirassiers, who had already arrived, had advanced after him, and the Guards had marched to support the attack as far as La Rothière, this battle would have produced a very great result, and annihilated the entire right wing of the French army. But, unfortunately, the Field-Marshal could not superintend the fight, on account of the snow-storm, and he received no report of the result of Wasiltschikoff's attack.

During this time the Prussian General, Prince Biron of Courland, who was employed with five squadrons of Prussian cavalry, in keeping up the communication between Von Sacken and the Crown Prince of Würtemberg, captured five or six cannons in an attack; the Crown Prince advanced by La Gibrie, took eleven guns, and then turned to the right towards Chaumenil, to support General Count Wrede, who, after taking Morvillers, now took Chaumenil also, and, according to his report, captured twenty-five guns.

General Count Giulay found the enemy between La Rothière and Dienville, in a position which appeared too strong for him to attack in front. He therefore directed a part of his corps to cross the Aube at Unienville, to recross it at Dienville, and so take the enemy on the right flank. These troops encountered some difficulties at the barricaded bridge at Dienville. This might have been foreseen; however, the Field-Marshal's object was attained, as the enemy sent a considerable body of troops to oppose Count Giulay: the possession of the bridge and village of Dienville was of no importance to him. The enemy retreated about midnight. Count Giulay's troops immediately observed the retreat, pursued and continued to fight with the rear-guard in Dienville. The loss of the Allies amounted to 4000 or 5000 men: General Sacken's corps suffered most. The enemy lost about as many killed and wounded, and 3000 prisoners. Measured by the standard of modern times, the loss of men in this battle was inconsiderable, but the loss of artillery was of consequence to Bonaparte, as well as the moral impression it made.

The corps of York, Count Wittgenstein and Colloredo, the Grenadiers and Guards, had taken no part in the battle, and yet the army from the first moment it advanced was superior in numbers to the French army. What results then might have been expected for the following days, had all these corps taken their places in the line, and had we accomplished the six marches to Paris in a straight direction and without delay!

The next morning we found a feeble rear-guard before Brienne, which, on the appearance of our infantry, immediately abandoned the town and castle, and followed the French army on the chaussée to Lesmont. By all accounts the army had passed through Brienne during the night, not in the best order. Marshal Marmont's corps, which had fought with General Wrede, did not march back through Brienne, but left it a German mile to the left. The corps of Giulay and the Crown Prince of Würtemberg pursued the enemy on the chaussée from Brienne to Lesmont. General Wrede took the direction of the Voire towards Roney, to prevent the reunion of Marshal Marmont with Bonaparte; Sacken's corps was engaged in getting its guns out of the position of Trannes to La Rothière, where the corps had passed the night on the field of battle, and then proceeded on the chaussée to Brienne.

SECTION VI.

Disposition after the Battle.—March of the Silesian Army on the
Marne.—Occupation of Vitry.—Fight on the Chaussée.—
Taking of Chalons.—Fight at Soudron.—Pursuit of Marshal
Macdonald.—Napoleon advances by Sezannes to Champaubert.—General Olsuview's Fight.—General Sacken's Fight
at Montmirail.—Combats of Generals York and Sacken
near Château-Thierry.—Field-Marshal Blücher's Combat at
Vauchamp and Champaubert. — Retreat and Re-union of
the Silesian Army at Chalons.

THE Sovereigns had arrived on the 1st of February
on the heights of Trannes, just as the attack began.
On the 2nd, they reached about noon the Castle of
Brienne, and there the following disposition was
made.

Field-Marshal Blücher was to approach the
Marne, in order to support the operations of York's
corps upon Chalons.

Count Wittgenstein's corps was to approach the
Aube, and proceed on its right bank, in order to keep
up the communication of the Grand Army with the
Field-Marshal. His advanced guard under General
Count Pahlen was directed to advance immediately
for this purpose. General Seslawin, with twelve
Cossack regiments, was to form the link between
Count Pahlen and the Silesian Army.

Count Wrede, the Crown Prince of Würtemberg,
and Giulay, were to follow the French army by
Lesmont.

The Grenadier corps, Colloredo's corps, and the
Guards, were to make a flank march to the left upon
Troyes.

This disposition, which was made with due consideration of the means of subsistence, as we were totally unprovided with magazines, appeared to all experienced officers extremely judicious and well adapted to the state of affairs. Had it been carried out, and above all had we allowed Bonaparte no time, the war must have been ended very shortly. We were obliged to spread ourselves out in various masses, to live; but as we had nearly 30,000 horse, while Bonaparte could not oppose these with more than 12,000 altogether, there was no danger, if the whole machine only worked together. If the Allies were in an advantageous military situation *before* the battle of Brienne, in how much better condition must they have been *after* the battle!

The following portion of this Campaign, from the beginning of February to the 25th (a period of three to four weeks), is one of the most interesting histories of ancient or modern war. We shall see how Bonaparte, left in so hopeless a condition as he was in after the battle of Brienne, by good fortune, by activity, and by political and military deception, managed so, that twenty-one days later, with forces double the strength of his, we avoided a battle by rapid, almost precipitate retreats—nay, even tried for an armistice.

Bonaparte's natural line of retreat on the 2nd of February was upon Arcis and Mery. It was reasonable to suppose that he would endeavour to concentrate all his disposable forces. To prevent this was the natural duty of both wings; to continue an uninterrupted pursuit, and to annihilate the defeated army, was the affair of the centre. Let us examine in succession what each did. Field-Marshal Blücher could not march far on the 2nd of February. An affair at Ronay-sur-Voire lasted till the afternoon. General Wrede wished to cut off Marshal Marmont's retreat ; but as the latter had the start, he escaped.

On the 3rd the Field-Marshal marched to St. Ouen. The hope of learning something of General York was not realised. Vitry was still occupied by the enemy. A Cossack regiment was dispatched to blockade this place, on the left bank of the Marne. The Field-Marshal was anxious to reach as soon as possible the cross road on which Sommesous is situated. Here the high road from Vitry to Fère Champenoise intersects the chaussée from Chalons to Arcis.

If Marshal Macdonald and General Sebastiani had reached Chalons, and received orders from Bonaparte to join him, their movements would have been much impeded, perhaps rendered impossible, by our taking up a position at Sommesous.

On the morning of the 4th, General Wasiltschikoff's cavalry carried off at Sommesous a convoy of flour-waggons, which was intended to follow the hostile army. It then pursued a convoy of ammunition-waggons, which, on hearing of our advance, retreated towards Sezanne, but was overtaken there at 2 A.M. on the 5th, and captured ; and the rearguard of the escort, of about 100 men, were taken prisoners.

On the 4th, the Field-Marshal took up his headquarters at Fère Champenoise, and left Olsuview's corps behind at Sommesous. Here he received information that Bonaparte had retreated after the battle of Brienne by Piney to Troyes. We could not explain his thus quitting the shortest line of retreat to Paris after the loss of a battle, but by supposing that he had no intention of uniting his forces with Macdonald's ; and as the Field-Marshal naturally assumed that, conformably to the disposition, Arcis must at least be occupied by *one* of the three Allied corps, 60,000 strong, which had crossed at Lesmont, and also that Count Wittgenstein must have arrived between him and the Aube, he was the better able to turn his attention towards Macdonald, who, according to the reports of many of the country-people, was at Chalons, where the report of cannon had been heard on the night of the 4th to 5th.   The Cossacks under General Carpow received orders to push forward from Sezanne to La Ferté Gaucher, and by Barbonne to Villenoxe, to keep up the communication with Count Pahlen.   On the morning of the 5th, reports came from the Cossack regiment in front of Vitry, that a hostile column had come out of that town, and was marching in the direction of Cernon.

The Field-Marshal gave orders for immediate departure, which was unfortunately delayed, because the cavalry stood before Fère Champenoise, and we waited for it.   The army marched in two columns. Sacken's corps from Fère Champenoise to Soudron. Olsuview's corps upon the chaussée from Sommesous to Vitry.   At Soudron, Sacken's corps came out straight upon the enemy's column, which had retreated from Vitry, and was in full march upon Chaintrix, on the right bank of the brook that flows through Soudron.   The day was closing.   The artillery fired on the enemy.   On the second discharge, one of his powder-waggons blew up ; the column fell into disorder, and we took two pieces of artillery, and about thirty powder-waggons.   Had we come an hour sooner, the whole infantry probably must have surrendered, along with the ammunition depôt of the army, which Bonaparte had left behind at Vitry. General Excelmans escorted this convoy with his cavalry.

The same night news arrived from General York, that after a cavalry fight between Vitry and Chalons (near the chaussée), in which the enemy's cavalry was totally defeated, and after bombarding Chalons during the night, it capitulated to him on the morning of the 5th. General York had on this occasion negotiated with Marshal Macdonald, with whom he had had no communication since the retreat from Russia, except having mainly contributed to the victory gained over him in the battle of the Katzbach.

Marshal Macdonald on departing destroyed the bridge of Chalons (one of the finest stone bridges in France), and his troops defended the left bank of the Marne until evening, when he retreated towards Epernay.

On the 6th the enemy's rear-guard was seen in good order, on the two roads leading from Chalons to Paris. It was soon discovered that Marshal Macdonald was marching with the main body upon Epernay, and that but few troops* were marching on the so-called little road to Paris by Montmirail.

At Chateau-Thierry the great post-road crosses from the left to the right bank of the Marne by a stone bridge, and at La Ferté-sous-Jouarre it crosses back to the left bank by another stone bridge. The lesser roads runs by La Ferté-sous-Jouarre on the left bank as far as Trillport.

General von York had not yet restored the bridge at Chalons on the 6th. He that day moved up the remainder of his troops. The exhausted ammunition

* Perhaps only the troops which had retreated from Vitry.

was replaced by what had been captured. On the 8th operations recommenced. Marshal Macdonald continued his retreat upon the great road. The most natural movement for General York was to follow him, and for General von Sacken to proceed on the lesser road, in order to cut him off at La Ferté, in case he loitered.

The Field-Marshal received intelligence that Kleist and Capczewitsch might be in the district of Vertus on the 9th ; he therefore determined to wait for these two corps, with Olsuview's, and to form with all three a reserve for the support of Sacken and York. Accordingly, on the 9th of February, the Silesian Army was disposed as follows :—

General von Sacken, at Montmirail, with about 20,000 men.

General Olsuview, at Champaubert, with about 3,500 men.

General Kleist, between Chalons and Vertus, with about 8,000 men.

General Capczewitsch, between Vitry and Vertus, with about 7,000 men.

General York, at Dormans, with about 18,000 men.

Consequently the army amounted to 56,000 men. Of these 38,000 stood *en échelons* on the lesser road, and 18,000 on the great road.

Vitry was found to be in rather a bad condition. The Field-Marshal placed a small garrison in it, and ordered a palisade and new works to secure it from a *coup de main*. The ramparts were furnished with artillery taken in the battle of La Rothière.

General Count Wittgenstein, instead of remaining on the right bank of the Aube, had crossed it at Lesmont, and summoned General Count Pahlen likewise to the left bank ; so that between Field-Marshal Blücher's army and the Aube there were no troops left, as General Seslawin had meanwhile another place assigned him on the extreme left wing.

Bonaparte, after breaking up the bridge of Lesmont in his rear, had marched on the 2nd to Piney, and united his forces with Marshal Mortier's on the 3rd at Troyes.

The Allied Guards and Grenadiers in reserve marched back to Bar-sur-Aube on the 2nd, to make use of the chaussée leading from thence to Troyes, and advanced towards Vendeuvres. The enemy occupied the bridges over the Barse.*

We ought perhaps to have attacked at once, in conjunction with Colloredo's corps. All the corps that had crossed at Lesmont were *à portée* to *support,* but we *manœuvred* instead ; Count Colloredo extended his corps to the left as far as Bar-sur-Seine, in order to outflank Bonaparte, who by this means gained time.

The forces of the corps of Wrede, the Crown Prince of Würtemberg and Giulay, as well as Count Wittgenstein's, were lamed, as they were obliged to move to the left, and consequently could not push forward upon Mery, which would have been the plan best calculated for striking a great blow on Bonaparte, or for preventing his junction with Macdonald.

Bonaparte left Troyes on the 7th, and reached Nogent that day ; a division of the Spanish army under General la Val entered Provins the same day. Even here many French Generals considered the cause decidedly lost, and made arrangements in their

* It is said that the Grand Army lost Bonaparte for two whole days, and sought him too much to the left.

2 F

private affairs, while they sent couriers from Nogent
to Paris.   Many directed their families to withdraw
from Paris into the interior.

Field-Marshal Blücher stuck to the disposition
which had been given to him in the Castle of Brienne : he did not think that Bonaparte could have
retreated on the road from Troyes by Nogent, as,
according to his calculations, Wrede, the Crown Prince
of Würtemberg, Giulay, and Count Wittgenstein,
must have anticipated him on this road, and compelled him to take the road by Fontainbleau.
Although he had not yet received any information
that all the troops of the Grand Army had crossed
the Aube, he nevertheless gave General Sacken the
commission to keep up the communication with
General Seslawin and Count Pahlen by the occupation of Sezanne.

When, after the affairs at Brienne and La Rothière,
the troops began to levy supplies upon the villages,
many disorders occurred, as must inevitably be the
case when troops are not cantonned and regularly
supplied in their bivouacs.   It was of the greatest
consequence to Field-Marshal Blücher to restore
order, and to avoid giving just cause of complaint to
the French people, to whom the strictest discipline
had been promised.   There were no other means for
insuring this, but to put the army in cantonments.
The accounts of the enemy permitted him to do so,
especially as, with our superiority in light cavalry, we
must be informed of all the movements of our adversary.

Sezanne was occupied by General Carpow with
some Cossack regiments.   From thence a *chemin de
traverse* proceeds by Baye and Champaubert to

Etoges, and another to Petit Morain and Etoges. Between these two roads lies the Marais de St. Gond, which is quite impassable for foot-passengers. The Field-Marshal could only be attacked on the left flank by a force arriving from Sezanne. The roads were too bad to convey artillery on any other cross line.

Baye and Petit Morain were occupied, in addition to Sezanne, when on the 9th, a report arrived that the enemy, coming from Villenoxe on the 8th, had driven back the Cossacks. It was believed that a hostile corps had taken up a position at Nogent, and being uneasy about Count Wittgenstein's corps, it had attempted a reconnoissance.

On the 9th General Carpow was driven out of Sezanne. He retreated upon Montmirail in the direction of the rest of his corps, and sent notice of his retreat thither. General von Sacken had no apprehensions for his left flank, as he occupied all the passages over the Petit Morain; and this little river, which is tolerably deep, offers difficulties, to the passage of cavalry. This report from General Carpow never reached the Field-Marshal, whose head-quarters were at Etoges; nor did General Olsuview (of Langeron's corps), who was cantoned in Etoges, Champaubert, and Baye, ever hear that the enemy was in possession of Sezanne.

In the evening, just as it grew dark, some Polish cavalry made its appearance at Baye. The troops cantoned there had hardly time to get under arms, but the enemy made no use of his advantage. This hostile cavalry could only have come from Sezanne.

The Field-Marshal, who was alarmed by this in his head-quarters, at eight in the evening sent off officers directly to Generals Sacken and York. They delivered written instructions to General Sacken to remain quietly on the 10th at Montmirail, and to watch the movement from Sezanne. In case Bonaparte attacked him, he was not to engage in an unequal fight, but to cross the Marne in concert with General York.*

The officer who conveyed this order was told that General Sacken would have already received accurate information about the state of affairs at Sezanne. Should he know for certain that there was nothing to fear from thence, it would be important that he should continue his march to La Ferté-sous-Jouarre on the 10th. The order to General Sacken was communicated as an instruction to General York, who was at Epernay on the 7th, at Dormans on the 8th, at Château-Thierry on the 9th, and completed the bridges there on the 10th.

On the 9th it came out, from accounts from the Grand Army, that Prince Schwarzenberg had preferred operating against Napoleon's right wing, leaving few troops in front of him. Count Wittgenstein's corps remained on the Aube in front of the enemy's centre. It was found too weak for this charge. The Emperor of Russia wished therefore that Kleist's corps should strengthen Wittgenstein's, and he, instead, placed Winzingerode's corps under the Field-Marshal's orders.

Prince Schwarzenberg assumed, that Napoleon had indicated by his retreat upon Nogent his intention to concentrate his forces ; and therefore it would be expedient for the Silesian Army to draw near

---

* A chaussée from Montmirail to Château-Thierry is marked down on Cassini's map, which did not really exist, as the road from Montmirail to Viffort (nearly half way) is quite impassable in spring.

Nogent. The Field-Marshal accordingly directed the corps of Kleist and Capczewitsch upon Fère Champenoise, then to remain the following day at Sezanne, united with General Olsuview. But in the night of the 9th to 10th, news came that Bonaparte was marching with his Guards by Villenoxe. If his intention was to hinder the farther pursuit of Marshal Macdonald by marching on La Ferté Gaucher, he probably came too late. If Napoleon marched upon Fère Champenoise, the Field Marshal would move round the Marais de St. Gond, to unite with General von Sacken; but if Napoleon marched upon La Ferté Gaucher, he would follow him by Sezanne. It happened unfortunately that Kleist's corps had but one regiment of cavalry, and two Cuirassier regiments belonging to this corps could not arrive for some days.

Towards noon, intelligence arrived from General von Sacken that, with the conviction that the enemy's movement by Sezanne was not meant in earnest, he had commenced his march towards La Ferté-sous-Jouarre, to intercept Marshal Macdonald there, who was still between Château-Thierry and La Ferté-sous-Jouarre on the 10th. Although this intelligence could not be welcome to the Field-Marshal, still he calculated that Sacken might at all events cross the Marne at La Ferté, and join General York at Château-Thierry. About noon he learnt that Bonaparte had slept at Sezanne on the 9th, and that neither Count Wittgenstein nor Count Pahlen were between Fère Champenoise and the Aube.

Thereupon the Field-Marshal himself repaired to Fère Champenoise. However, before he arrived there, he heard that General Olsuview had been attacked and overpowered by superior forces. On receiving this account he led back the corps of Kleist and Capczewitsch the same night, to the position of Bergères not far from Vertus.

On the 11th the remains of Olsuview's corps were collected at Bergères, and it appeared that his loss amounted to 1500 men and nine guns. Olsuview had been taken prisoner, after defending himself obstinately.* In the opinion of all present in this affair, the enemy had developed considerable strength, especially in cavalry.

The light cavalry which had been detached towards Sezanne reported that they had seen on the 10th troops continually marching from thence to Baye, so that it was natural to conclude that the whole French army was opposed to us. According to accounts previously received, Count Wittgenstein had caused a bridge to be constructed over the Aube in the vicinity of Plancy ; we therefore naturally supposed that the Grand Army would either follow Bonaparte, and march upon Sezanne, crossing the bridge for that purpose, or proceed straight to Paris, from whence they were still four long marches distant. In both cases (whether Bonaparte turned on the 11th against us or against General Sacken) such a march

* General Olsuview had not taken up the position best adapted for his defence; but it is necessary to mention the following particulars in his justification. In the affair at Brienne, as above mentioned, one outlet of the town was left unguarded, and the enemy penetrated into the place. General Sacken was very near being taken prisoner in consequence, and Olsuview was not only reproached with it, but Field-Marshal Blücher, in order to settle matters, was even obliged to call him to account on the subject. This had the effect of making him apprehensive about his responsibility ; and when, on the 10th, several officers of rank advised him to change his position, and to take up one by the wood of Etoges in the rear, (where he would have had a much better one,) he replied, " I was called to account about Brienne ; I cannot retreat."

of the Grand Army could not but be decisive. The Field-Marshal resolved, in case Bonaparte advanced with his forces against Bergères, to retire himself upon Epernay, avoiding a battle.

The enemy remained on the 11th quietly at Etoges, where he established a bivouac, and this seemed to prove that Napoleon had turned towards Montmirail.

Towards noon on the 11th a warm cannonade was heard from the camp at Bergères, in the direction of Montmirail, which seemed however to be receding. The Field-Marshal would gladly have attacked the enemy at Etoges at once, if he had had any cavalry. Some 800 horse of Kleist's corps would not arrive till the 12th or 13th, and the attack must be deferred until then, as he could not know what forces might be at Etoges.* Meanwhile accounts arrived from General York which spoke of his having assembled his corps at Viffort on the 11th, and formed a junction with General Sacken. Two bridges at Château-Thierry were completed.

General von Sacken sent word that he had found on the 10th troops near La Ferté-sous-Jouarre, placed by Marshal Macdonald to cover his retreat by La Ferté; that these troops had been attacked and defeated, and three guns taken, and Macdonald's corps pursued to Trillport, where he had destroyed the bridge.†

---

* It must be observed, that however well Blücher's *espionage* was organised in Germany, here in France he could succeed but little in procuring intelligence by means of spies. The French, indeed, liked well enough the money offered them, but they were too much afraid of Napoleon's severe measures, if, after the close of the war, anything should be discovered.

† Had General Sacken, after separating Bonaparte from Macdonald by the destruction of this bridge, constructed others at La Ferté, in the night of the 9th and 10th, Bonaparte would have

When General von Sacken learned from the posts that he had left behind him at Montmirail, that the enemy was advancing on that place, he resolved on going to meet him and attacking him there, and summoned General York to his support.

So far the reports. General York was not inclined to engage in an attack against his instructions, but he was desirous that General von Sacken should draw near him on his left, to cross the Marne at Château-Thierry in concert. From Viffort to Château-Thierry there was a chaussée; but the road from Viffort to Montmirail was reported to be so bad, that General York did not think he could get over it with his twelve-pounders. After dispatching his report to the Field-Marshal, he sent to Vieux-maisons to represent all this to General von Sacken.

Still this report threw no light on the cannonade heard on the 11th. On the arrival, therefore, on the morning of the 13th, of the two Cuirassier regiments of Kleist's corps he had been waiting for, the Field Marshal immediately attacked the enemy at Etoges. The enemy showed few troops; he soon retreated by Champaubert, and was pursued to Fromentières.

Early on the 14th (about 7) the Field-Marshal set out for Montmirail, and found the enemy at Vauchamp, where he defended himself obstinately. We had committed the error of moving the advanced guard commanded by General von Zieten too far from the rest of the corps, so that it could not be supported at the right time.

reaped no advantage whatever from his march to Sezanne. If he moved towards La Ferté, then Sacken's Corps could go on the right bank· of the Marne, and the fire of its batteries would have rendered it quite impossible for Napoleon to march on the chaussée to La Ferté on the left bank.

The whole number of troops collected here by the Field-Marshal amounted to about 15,000 men. The remains of Olsuview's division, under General Udom, about 1,800 men, with fifteen guns, had remained behind at Etoges on the 13th, to refresh and reorganize themselves. They had orders to advance to Champaubert on the 14th, and there to await farther directions. By this movement they would cover our rear on the side of Sezanne, in case any other hostile force should come from thence.

General Zieten attacked Vauchamp in earnest. The first Silesian regiment carried the village, and made many prisoners. But behind this place considerable bodies of the enemy's troops formed in line, who turned to good account the circumstance of the corps being still too distant to support its advanced guard properly. The enemy's cavalry trotted round the village, ruined a battery (which, however, managed to get off after all the gunners were wounded), and cut into the first Silesian regiment which was coming in open ranks from the village with the prisoners. After this unfavourable beginning, the Field-Marshal's little corps formed, and was instantly attacked on the left by a very superior force of cavalry, which overthrew ours, and then fell upon the squares of infantry, but was forced to retire without breaking into them. The briskness of the attack led us to conclude that Bonaparte was present. This was confirmed by a captain of the guard whom we took prisoner, who deposed that Bonaparte had had affairs on the 11th and 12th with Sacken and York, and had driven both across the Marne at Château-Thierry, from whence the French army had now come by a forced march through the night.

Several prisoners made the same statement, and reports came from the right wing that a strong body of cavalry, 6,000 at least, was moving (beyond the reach of cannon-shot) round our right wing.

The Field-Marshal's object of disengaging Generals von Sacken and York was attained ; the whole of his cavalry consisted of about 1,100 horse : it was therefore hardly possible for him to accept battle, while on the other hand it was almost impossible to avoid it.

The position in which the corps would have had to deploy to take up the advanced guard, was a very bad one ; the left wing might rest on wooded heights, but then the troops did not extend farther than to the chaussée, which could on no account be given up. A farm, put down in the chart as La Ville Neuve, which lay in front of the right wing, was occupied by Kleist's corps, but this did not hinder the hostile cavalry from turning us.

The Field-Marshal decided on the retreat. The whole of our cavalry which was on the left wing, was moved to the right, and both corps (Kleist's and Capczewitsch's) were instructed to keep the chaussée in the middle. The retreat proceeded with the utmost order. Meanwhile Lieutenant-General von Diebitsch sent word from Sezanne that he had pursued the enemy with the light cavalry of the Guards, and would advance this day, the 14th of February, from Sezanne to Montmirail. This support would have been of the greatest importance to us had not the Petit Morain divided us. It was, however, a useful diversion for us, as it held out a prospect of the enemy's attention and strength being divided.

The enemy committed the mistake of not pushing

enough in front. The column of cavalry, which was turning us, continued its march uninterruptedly in the same direction; and when we came to Fromentières, it appeared that this direction was the plain of Champaubert. Fortunately for us, General Udom must (as we supposed) be there; and if he occupied the wood of Etoges, no mischief could befall him, and the retreating troops might get back unharmed. An aide-de-camp was dispatched to charge General Udom to occupy the wood. The ground was pretty well saturated; the enemy's cavalry proceeded at a foot-pace, so that General Kleist's infantry not only advanced as fast, but even gained a start upon it. But General Capczewitsch loitered, and marched *en échequier*, as on parade*. The Field-Marshal, who was with the Russian troops, praised their order and composure, and replied to the messages from the right wing recommending speed to reach the wood of Etoges, that "nothing must be hurried." At last General Kleist had orders to halt. He instantly obeyed; but as he *only* could overlook the movement of the enemy's cavalry, he made remonstrances. It was too late. When we reached the plain between Champaubert and the wood of Etoges, the enemy's cavalry quickened its pace, overthrew our cavalry, drove it entirely off the field, and surrounded us on all sides. But it was a great mistake on the enemy's part to surround us thus, for it weakened him and prevented the unity of his attacks.

General Udom was not in the wood of Etoges. We learned afterwards that General Capczewitsch,

* If troops retreat *en échequier*, i. e., forming two divisions, whereof one constantly stands still till the other has moved through, it requires double time to get over a given distance.

being apprehensive about him, as he was without cavalry, had sent him orders to march back to Etoges.

We were still about 1500 paces from the wood, and in half an hour it became dark. The masses were pressed closely together; the enemy attacked them on all sides, but was repelled everywhere. His attacks had no *ensemble*. What we most feared was his penetrating by a gap between the masses, and causing these to fire on each other. This would have occasioned great confusion, and opened a wide field to the enemy's cavalry*. Meanwhile the guns of some Russian horse artillery drove off the cavalry that was between us and the wood.

The march proceeded. The battalions were kept together by beat of drum. Thus we reached the wood. But two Prussian battalions at the extreme rear were lost,—they did not pay attention enough; when it grew dark, and while they were defending themselves on the right flank, the cavalry broke in upon them on the left.

At the entrance of the wood (which extends to Etoges) the fighting seemed ended; it was now, too, quite dark; but some hostile infantry, who had remained the previous day at Etoges, knew of a footpath to the town, and got there sooner than our rearguard, and fell upon it from a side-street. This caused us again considerable loss. It was ten o'clock at night. We marched on to the position of Bergères, where we all assembled. We had lost between 3000 and 4000 men of Kleist's corps, and 2000 of Capczewitch's corps, killed, wounded, and missing. Kleist's corps had lost besides seven pieces

* General Capczewitsch had three battalions of recruits with him, who had never yet seen an enemy. They behaved very well.

of artillery, partly dismounted, partly broken. Sword in hand, the enemy had taken nothing.

We were not pursued beyond Étoges, but we had to expect the next morning a continuation of the fight ; and in this case the position of Bergères, with no obstacles of ground in front, was ill adapted to our reduced corps. The Field-Marshal resolved to retreat to Chalons, where in case of attack he could hold the Marne until he obtained reinforcements. We set out accordingly before daybreak, leaving only some light cavalry behind to watch the enemy's movements. Towards noon on the 15th, we all entered Chalons, and it was seen that the enemy did *not* follow. Here too accounts now arrived from Generals York and Sacken.

When General Sacken arrived at Vieux Maisons on the 11th, and found Montmirail strongly occupied by the enemy's infantry, he proceeded at once to attack it. He thought that he could not fail to crush the enemy at Montmirail, and therefore extended his right wing out as far as the Petit Morain ; his left wing held the chaussée of Vieux Maisons. The right wing attacked and took the village of Marchais. The enemy received reinforcements, and there began such long and eager fighting for this village, that by four o'clock in the evening the greatest portion of Sacken's corps had moved towards this right wing.

When General von York heard this warm cannon-nade, he made Pirch's brigade and one of cavalry advance by Fontenelle, and the rest of his corps remained drawn up in the position of Viffort. These brigades encountered so many difficulties, that it was only with the greatest trouble they could get a 6-pounder battery through the bad roads.

About four o'clock, when Sacken was in possession of the village of Marchais, Bonaparte made his Guards advance in close column on the chaussée against the left wing. Sacken had no troops left to meet the hostile Guards. This movement was a decisive one. If Bonaparte succeeded in separating Generals York and Sacken, the latter would be driven into the Petit Morain.

At this critical moment, when Sacken had no resource but to give up the advantages of his right wing, and to draw it back quickly on the chaussée, (which, indeed, was hardly any longer possible,) General von Pirch attacked Bonaparte from Preles on his right flank, and thereby gave General von Sacken time to retreat, which he achieved in the night with great exertions.*

On the 12th the enemy pursued Sacken's corps. General von York commenced his retreat as soon as Sacken had moved past him. The enemy's cavalry manœuvred so skilfully that both corps again suffered considerably before they crossed the Marne at Château-Thierry. General von Sacken lost seven guns, and was obliged to leave behind the three he had taken from the enemy on the 10th; General von York lost three guns, that could not be brought away on account of the heavy roads. The two corps had lost about 7,000 killed, wounded, and missing; of these 5,000 belonged to Sacken's corps.

This disaster might have been avoided had General von Sacken, as before mentioned, constructed

* Sacken's line of retreat was necessarily upon Château-Thierry; and to get there, he had only a heavy forest road in which all the batteries stuck. But the Russian cavalry attached their horses with their forage cords to the carriages, and dragged the artillery through.

bridges at La Ferté-sous-Jouarre, or had he not assumed the offensive on the 11th of February. At any rate it was an error on his part to attack with his right wing, thus separating himself totally from General von York. He should have attacked with his left wing, as he would then have had it in his power to retreat on General York when he wished. The strategical point of attack happened also to be the tactical one best adapted to the ground. Between Montmirail and Verdelot some little brooks fall into the Petit Morain, all of which have their sources between Vieux Maisons and Fontenelles. Had General Sacken, on leaving Vieux Maisons, taken the left wing, he would have gone round the sources, and gained the flat commanding heights; instead of which, by the movements that were executed, just the contrary took place.

This affair generated ill-humour between the generals in command of the two corps. They did not agree in their views. But who could censure General von York for not liking to deviate from his instructions, when there was no sufficient reason for doing so? Although his remonstrances were un-heeded by General von Sacken, he did not assist him the less on that account; he ordered General von Pirch to attack, and sacrificed 2,000 men to extricate General Sacken from his embarrassment.

Field-Marshal Blücher, who was accurately informed of everything, made no reproaches to General Sacken, and took all upon himself in the reports he drew up. General von Sacken had rendered too many important services, and given too many proofs of his unshakeable courage, to expose him to varying judgments for a mistaken view. He might have erred, but his error was that of a hero who trusts too much to his own strength. We had not many such men, and only such were capable of conquering Bonaparte.

Had there not been a partial alteration of measures at royal head-quarters, and had the Silesian Army not been informed of it too late, this misfortune would not have befallen us.

The two generals, Sacken and York, marched by Oulschy, Fismes, and Rheims, and joined Field-Marshal Blücher at Chalons on the 16th and 17th of February.

The enemy did not pursue us. This was a clear proof that he had turned against the Grand Army. Officer after officer was dispatched to give notice of this, and to recommend precaution. Meanwhile this movement of the enemy required our immedate reappearance on the stage, and it was therefore decided to give the army only two days' rest at Chalons, for reorganization, and then to move by forced marches towards the enemy. Under these circumstances orders were sent to Count Langeron to resign the blockade of Mainz to the Duke of Coburg, and to come on with the rest of his corps by forced marches.

A large convoy of shoes arrived just at the right moment for York's and Sacken's corps. This article was not to be procured in Champagne, where wooden shoes are almost universally worn.

The Emperor of Russia, who foresaw the consequences of Bonaparte's march upon Sezanne, had done his utmost to infuse activity into the Grand Army, and to undertake offensive operations on Bonaparte's rear. But the Grand Army lost time behind the Seine, being too much scattered. In addition to this, the Austrian army, in the neighbourhood of

Lyons desired reinforcements, and it was resolved to send Colloredo's corps there.

Immediately after the affair at Vauchamp, Bonaparte marched off with his *Gros* by Rozoy, leaving the cavalry to follow by forced marches; and on the 17th he fell upon Lieutenant-General Count Pahlen in the vicinity of Nangis. The latter retreated, after losing nine guns and some battalions of infantry, towards Provins, on General Count Wittgenstein, who took up a position at Nogent. On the 18th the Crown Prince of Würtemberg was attacked at Monterau, but got out of the affair tolerably, after having completely repelled an attack in the morning.

It was thereupon decided in the Grand Army, to concentrate retrograding near Troyes, and to accept a battle in the position of St. Parre, if Field-Marshal Blücher could make his appearance there on the 22nd or 23rd with 30,000 men. To this invitation Blücher replied, "I will be at Méry ready for battle, with 53,000 men and 300 guns, on the 21st."

After a loss of 14,000 men and twenty-seven guns, six days before, this seemed hardly possible; however according to the above-mentioned organization of the departure of Langeron's corps from Mainz and of the successive arrivals of Kleist's corps, in a few days there arrived Generals Rudczewitsch and von Corff, the first with six regiments of infantry, the second with a considerable force of cavalry, to join the army. These were followed at intervals of a few days by General von Röder, with a brigade of cavalry, and General Klüx with one of infantry and several batteries, together with ammunition. Then after a similar interval came General von Lobenthal, with a reinforcement of 2000 Prussians. He again was followed by General Count Langeron with about 1000 horse and half a battery ; then followed in succession, Count St. Priest with three regiments of infantry and one of cavalry, and Lieutenant-General Pantschoulizew with seven regiments of infantry and five of cavalry and thirty guns; and lastly General von Jagow with seven battalions of infantry and two batteries.

SECTION VII.

The Silesian Army crosses the Aube at Arcis.—Combat at Méry. —The Grand Army avoids a Battle.—The Silesian Army re-crosses the Aube, and advances towards Paris, to draw off Napoleon from the pursuit of the Grand Army.—Field-Marshal Blücher receives the command of the three corps of the Army of the North.—The Silesian Army crosses the Marne at La Ferté-sous-Jouarre.—Junction of the Silesian Army with two corps of the Army of the North.—Defence of Soissons.—Battle of Craonne.—Battle of Laon.—Action at Rheims under General Count St. Priest.—New plan of operations.

On the 19th of February the army marched to Sommesous, where Generals von Corff and Rudczewitsch joined it. On the 20th to Arcis, where General von Röder joined it. The 21st, the army entered Méry, where General Count Wittgenstein was stationed with his corps, which however had orders to move the next day on the right bank of the Seine towards Troyes.

Night closing in, it was no longer possible on the 21st to relieve General Count Wittgenstein in his position. General Count Pahlen was attacked in the afternoon in the district of St. Hilaire, and driven back towards Chartres, where Prince Eugene of

Würtemberg was posted with a division. A cause-way runs from Chartres to Méry, which is very easy to defend. If therefore offensive operations were to be attempted on the side of Méry, it would be necessary to hold Chartres or the heights beyond as a *tête du pont*. Early on the 22nd Prince Scherbatow was to relieve the Prince of Würtemberg; but as it happened, before the former could establish himself regularly, the enemy penetrated into Chartres, and advanced as far as Méry. The Seine divides the town into two parts, and is crossed by a wooden bridge. An attempt was made to pull this bridge down, and as this failed, to burn it, which was also impossible. During this time a conflagration sprung up on the east side of Méry, from the bivouac fires, which Wittgenstein's corps had left burning in all the courts, having departed without first extinguishing them.

Prince Scherbatow's troops occupied the houses on the Seine, and defended the access to the bridge: but these houses also caught fire by degrees, and the heat became so intense that towards noon the town was abandoned with the Field-Marshal's consent. The French tirailleurs made use of this, to seek a passage through singly, and about two o'clock in the afternoon a considerable number of them made their appearance on this side Méry, opposite General von York. He was charged to drive them back, which was immediately effected. He then threw two Jäger companies into the burning town by the bridge, who soon inspired such respect with their rifles that the enemy drew back his advanced posts and did not fire another shot, and in the night the bridge was thrown down.

Field-Marshal Blücher waited the whole of the

22nd for the disposition for the promised battle. But
now great was his astonishment, when he learnt in
the evening that application for a truce had been made
to Bonaparte, and that the Austrian Colonel Prince
Wenceslas Lichtenstein had returned with a direct refusal! The Field-Marshal immediately dispatched one
of his confidential officers to Troyes, to conjure Prince
Schwarzenberg to give battle, and not to allow himself to be led astray. He offered to give battle alone,
and believed that his army would be strong enough,
if the Grand Army would only form a reserve.

It was too late. When the officer arrived the
retreat was determined upon and prepared—a retreat
with which the Sovereigns themselves were dissatisfied,
as they, with their heroic feelings, would have much
preferred giving battle. A general disposition for
the retreat had also been already sent to the Field-
Marshal. The confidential officer, seeing that there
was no longer any possibility of a change of measures
in the Grand Army, represented that, with his well-
known character, Blücher would hardly resolve on
commencing a retreat, which was entirely contrary to
his views, and, as he believed, quite unnecessary.
He inquired whether the Sovereigns, whose armies
the Field-Marshal commanded, had *expressly ordered*
that the Silesian Army should retreat with the Grand
Army, and whether they had sent him orders to this
effect; and when he heard that such *was not the case,*
he returned to the Field-Marshal in the forenoon.
The Field-Marshal had heard in the interim, with
what a high tone Bonaparte had addressed Prince
Lichtenstein, and had received the disposition for the
retreat; and it is easy to infer that all this accorded
very ill with his views. It cannot be denied that many
of his suite, and many superior officers of the Silesian

Army, regarded all that had occurred since the battle of Brienne as intrigues of the peace party. They believed that the Field-Marshal had been intentionally left in the lurch in the affairs of Champaubert and Montmirail, in order to weaken him, so that he should not be able to form any opposition against peace, and that he had now been summoned to a battle, only to involve him in a retreat, the end of which must be a peace.

On what a footing did we stand on the 22nd of February compared to the 2nd! Fugitives, avoiding a battle with Bonaparte, who was probably only *half* as strong as ourselves;* disunited, without confidence in ourselves, we had to commence a retreat which, should Bonaparte leave us no time to recover ourselves, and restore harmony, would very probably lead us to the Rhine.†

---

* Assuming that the Grand Army consisted of—

Wrede's Corps	20,000	men
The Crown Prince of Würtemberg's	10,000	„
Count Wittgenstein's	12,000	„
Count Giulay's	9,000	„
Guards	20,000	„

This makes altogether 71,000 men. The Silesian Army, under Field-Marshal Blücher, had 53,000 combatants: consequently we had 124,000 men.

It is not likely that Bonaparte had more than 62,000 at Troyes, for Marmont and Mortier were both detached; consequently there only remained the five corps of Gérard, Oudinot, Macdonald, Victor, and the Guards.

On the 17th, General Treilhaud, with the Dragoons of the Spanish Army, entered Nangis.

† In the French public reports the Austrians were spared. The *Moniteur* of the 21st of February states, that the preservation of Fontainebleau was owing to the Austrian General, Hardegg. The *Moniteur* of the 24th states, that the Emperor Alexander had his head-quarters at Bray on the 17th, and wished to remove to Fontainebleau on the following day; and that the Emperor of Austria had not left Troyes.

Field-Marshal Blücher was firmly resolved not to follow the Grand Army in its retreat. His position allowed him to take this resolve. He had the option of three plans :—

1. To wait for the above-mentioned reinforcements, which would bring the numbers of the Silesian Army to 80,000, and then give battle to Bonaparte. Until their arrival he might manœuvre on the Aube at Arcis ; or, in case Napoleon found means of crossing the Aube, he might manœuvre between Châlons and Vitry to form a junction with the Army of the North.

2. General Winzingerode had reached Rheims with a corps of 30,000 men. His advanced guard under General Czernitscheff had taken Soissons by storm in the first half of February, but had given it up again, whereupon the enemy had re-occupied it ;—the Field-Marshal, by taking the direction of Epernay, might form an immediate junction with General Winzingerode, and afterwards with General von Bülow, who was expected with about 20,000 men at Laon, from the Netherlands ; he would then be able to operate along the Oise or the Marne upon Paris, or :—

3. He might construct a pontoon bridge at Auglure (he had fifty Russian canvas pontoons with him), and march straight in the direction of Paris, to draw off Bonaparte speedily from the pursuit of the Grand Army.

Against plan No. 1 there arose the question : Where could they procure provisions ? and might not the interval of ten to twelve days (and it might be as long as that before the reinforcements could arrive) be too distant a prospect for the Grand Army ? No. 2 was an operation sanctioned by all the rules of war. But if Bonaparte allowed us to march and continued in pursuit of the Grand

Army, then came the consideration that Rheims was farther from Paris than Méry, and we should consequently make a circuit of four or five days, which would be highly advantageous to Bonaparte. The 3rd plan was bold, but it was the surest for drawing Bonaparte away from the Grand Army. It could not be undertaken without pontoon bridges; but now we could turn by Sezanne upon Meaux or La Ferté-sous-Jouarre, and form a junction with the corps of Winzingerode and Bülow. Then the Field-Marshal would be in a condition to accept a battle with the entire French army. These two corps however were under the orders of the Crown Prince of Sweden, who was marching with his Swedes (forming about a fifth of his army) from the Elbe towards France. If the Sovereigns placed these two corps under the Field-Marshal's order, he could attain the double object of freeing the Grand Army from Bonaparte's pursuit, and striking a blow to terminate the war.

On the return of his officer from Troyes, he wrote with his own hand to the Sovereigns, whose armies he commanded, laid his project before them, and begged them to entrust him with the command of the two corps of the Army of the North; and to let the Grand Army turn round as soon as they observed that Bonaparte gave up the pursuit, in order to turn against the Silesian Army.

Paris was just the same distance from the crossing point, Auglure, as Langres from Troyes. By calculating at what successive hours Napoleon could hear of the Silesian Army's advance upon Paris, it was probable that his pursuit of the Grand Army would in no case extend beyond Bar-sur-Aube.

The Field-Marshal sent off a courier with his

letter to the Sovereigns, and proceeded to the execution of plan No. 3. In the night of the 23rd, the army marched off, and crossed the Aube at Auglure on the 24th. Here we learned that Marshal Marmont was posted with a corps at Sezanne. As it was not likely to be a strong one, the Field-Marshal determined on attacking it so as to surround it. For this purpose two wings of cavalry were formed, which were intended to turn the enemy, while the centre attacked and held him fast. Marshal Marmont retreated skilfully by the bridge at Esternay, but the Field-Marshal was not satisfied with the movements of his cavalry.

General von Klüx joined the army with his brigade this day. The Field-Marshal took up his head-quarters at Esternay. A courier was sent to meet General Count St. Priest, and deliver to him detailed instructions* for forming one whole out of all

---

* These instructions give so much insight into the Field-Marshal's intentions, that I will give them here word for word as an historical document :—

" *To his Excellency the Russian Imperial Lieutenant-General, Count St. Priest.*

" The Emperor Napoleon has thrown himself, with all his forces, on the Grand Army which occupied the Seine, from Port-sur-Seine to Monteraux. A few days before, intelligence reached it, that Marshal Augereau had been reinforced at Lyons up to 30,000 men, and had begun to operate against the left wing. General Bianchi had accordingly been sent off to reinforce Count Bubna, and he reached Dijon the $\frac{14}{23}$th. These operations were the occasion of my being moved with the Silesian Army to the right wing of the Grand Army, so that on the $\frac{19}{27}$th of February, the armies occupied the following positions :

" The Grand Army at Troyes; the Silesian at Méry; Winzingerode's corps at Rheims and Epernay; and Bülow and the Duke of Weimar on their march upon Soissons, which they might enter on the 26th or 27th.

the troops that were to follow. By these he was directed to take up a position at Vitry until further orders, or till Bonaparte crossed the Marne, in which case he was to endeavour to join the Silesian Army.

" The Emperor Napoleon displayed intentions of giving battle, but it was decided to avoid it for the present.

" On the 23rd, the main body of the Grand Army began to retreat on Bar-sur-Aube and Bar-sur-Seine; the rear-guards were to follow on the 24th, from the Seine. Count Wittgenstein's corps moved from Villacerf, by Piney and Dienville, towards Bar-sur-Aube, and broke up the bridge over the Aube at Lesmont. I caused the bridge at Arcis to be destroyed, and crossed with the Silesian Army by three pontoon bridges from Méry to Baudemont on the right bank of the Aube, the morning of the $\frac{12}{14}$th of February. The enemy, who had moved his forces to Troyes, leaving only an insignificant force at Méry, did not disturb us at all in this march. I was aware that Marshal Marmont was posted at Sezanne with a corps of about 8000 men. I have this day marched against him, and driven him on La Ferté Gaucher.

" To-morrow I continue my march. I will construct bridges at La Ferté-sous-Jouarre or Meaux, secure my communications with the Army of the North; and, if I cannot beat Marshal Marmont, I will disengage the Grand Army by operations on Paris.

" After this explanation of circumstances, I proceed to state what the enemy can do against me; from whence I deduce the instructions, which I have to give your Excellency in the present situation of affairs.

" The Emperor Napoleon cannot possibly follow the Grand Army with all his forces and allow us to march to Paris.

" He can do one of these things :—

" 1. Detach a corps to proceed by forced marches along the Seine to the support of Marshal Marmont, and for the protection of Paris; or,

" 2. March with considerable forces by Nogent to Provins against me; or,

" 3. Endeavour to check my operations, and relieve his fortresses, by interrupting my communications with the Rhine.

" I have therefore resolved that your Excellency should assemble a corps at Vitry from the troops under your orders, and a Prussian brigade of about 6000 men under General von

An officer was dispatched to Lieutenant-General von Winzingerode, who was then between the Marne and Aisne, to explain to him verbally the situation of the army, and to invite him to proceed towards

Jagow. You will collect all the Prussian and Russian troops that may follow, and carry out the following instructions :—

" A. Keep up the communication with the Grand Army, in case it should retreat even beyond Langres.

" B. Watch the passages over the Aube, at Arcis, Rameru, Lesmont, and Dienville.

" C. Keep up the connection with General von Winzingerode at Rheims, and through him (by Epernay or Rheims) with me..

" D. Under pretext that a place must be made for all the wounded and prisoners at Vitry and farther in the rear, cause all the lazarettos (as far as the diseases permit it) to be taken back to Nancy.

" E. Find out which of the three above-mentioned plans the enemy has adopted; and,

" F. In case he has adopted the 1st and 2nd, advance by forced marches by Châlons, Rheims, and Fismes, towards me; in the 3rd case, prevent the enemy from doing us injury by interrupting our communication; and give the earliest information to General Joussefowitsch in front of Metz. The means of executing this commission are:

" a. To give out that you have an army of 25,000 to 30,000 men. As the enemy has spies everywhere, and does not know our means of reinforcement, he may be easily deceived.

" b. To print a proclamation at Vitry, in which your Excellency will exhort the Department of the Marne not to be seduced, as you are arrived with a strong army to preserve tranquillity and order, and therefore you would instantly punish all villages in a state of revolt by fire. The inhabitants must not allow themselves to be deceived by false reports of the Emperor Napoleon having gained advantages. He was under the necessity of marching by Troyes, while our army, which he pretended was annihilated, was directed upon Paris, &c.

" c. As no intelligence whatever can be procured in the country of the enemy's movements, you must station your cavalry at St. Ouen and Montirender, and push it forward to the Aube. Individuals must not ride singly in villages, as many

Meaux, in the direction of Paris, to form a junction there with the Silesian Army.

On the 26th of February, the enemy was pursued from La Ferté Gaucher to La Ferté-sous-Jouarre by the corps of York and Kleist.

Sacken's corps, and the portion of Langeron's which was with the army, marched upon Coulommiers. General von Corff, with 4000 horse, formed the rear-guard, and had left some Cossack outposts on the Aube. He was commissioned to watch the country, especially towards Villenoxe and Provins, to secure the army's flanks from any unexpected attack from that quarter. Head-quarters were at Rebais.

Marshal Marmont's march from Sezanne to La Ferté-sous-Jouarre, whereby he abandoned the shortest line to Meaux and Paris, was inexplicable. He could march from Coulommiers to Meaux, and cross the bridge over the Marne there; but what

of our people have already been shot, beaten to death, wounded, or disarmed.

" *d.* You will forward convoys of ammunition and provisions with an escort to the army by Châlons and Rheims.

" At Châlons there is a small garrison and a Commandant, who has orders to defend the bridge, destroyed by the enemy and again restored, from a *coup de main.*

" I feel confident that your Excellency will fulfil these instructions perfectly, and that in case Napoleon turns against me with superior forces, you will procure timely intelligence thereof, and also join the army, by forced marches, in time for the battle.

" I beg that you will instantly transmit by courier a copy of these instructions to His Majesty the Emperor Alexander and to Prince Schwarzenberg, and give notice, at the same time, of the moment of your arrival, your strength, and other measures.

" The enclosed order places the Prussian General, Von Jagow, under your command.

" Head-quarters, Esternay, 1½th of February, 1814.
(Signed) " VON BLUCHER."

did he want at La Ferté ? Cross there and defend
the bank ? Then we should march by Meaux. Or
did he intend to march from La Ferté-sous-Jouarre
upon Trillport, where, according to the reports of
the country-people, a bridge of boats was constructed near the one that had been destroyed. But
then it was dangerous for Marshal Marmont to remain at La Ferté, as we were nearer to St. Jean
and Trillport by Signy and Signets, than by La
Ferté. A prisoner cleared up the mystery ; Marshals Marmont and Mortier had formed a junction
at La Ferté-sous-Jouarre. Both together were not
strong enough to attack us, or to wait for us in a
position at La Ferté. Marshal Mortier came from
the right bank of the Marne. It was therefore
clear that the enemy would march upon Trillport,
and the necessary orders were given accordingly.

The tirailleur fire at Jouarre, occupied by the
enemy, lasted till it grew dark. If the troops had
not been so weary, the Field-Marshal would have
ordered them to make a night march on the cross
road to Trillport, and then the situation of both
Marshals would have been perilous. But all these
accounts arrived so late, that the troops had already
arranged their bivouacs and fetched provisions from
the villages, and this reason alone made it impossible. The Prussian outposts did not observe the
enemy's night march until next morning, when he
had already passed the bridges at Trillport, and
broken them up after him.

February 27th, the Field-Marshal's object, to
free the Grand Army from pursuit, must now have
been attained or not, according to the accounts
Bonaparte must have received up to the 26th. The
Silesian Army had to proceed to the second part of

its task, *i.e.* to join the Army of the North. A pontoon bridge was immediately constructed over the Marne, not far from La Ferté, which was ready in the afternoon. Some troops, and all the superfluous baggage were sent across.

General von Sacken advanced towards Meaux. The troops of Langeron's corps stood on the road from La Ferté to Meaux. York's corps at Jouarre, and Kleist's at head-quarters in La Ferté-sous-Jouarre. Now that we had means of crossing the Marne, the danger of the march from the Aube to Paris was removed. If we obtained our object, of drawing off Bonaparte from the Grand Army, and he marched in our rear, we had only to cross the Marne, to gain a considerable start towards a junction with the corps of Winzingerode and Bülow.

Bonaparte might march by Epernay to Rheims. This would have been an extremely hazardous undertaking, as the Field-Marshal had more than 100,000 men, including the corps of Winzingerode and von Bülow. Bonaparte would besides, in this case, separate himself entirely from his two Marshals, Marmont and Mortier, who however could hardly have, together, 12,000 men; consequently, this march upon Rheims would not have been at all dangerous for the Field-Marshal, as, in case of the worst, he would have the connection with General von Bülow and the Netherlands at the command of the Silesian Army. It would be more dangerous to him, if Bonaparte sought a passage between Trillport and La Ferté-sous-Jouarre, to force the Field-Marshal to a battle before his junction with the Army of the North. His crossing at La Ferté (if we did not wish to defend the bank) or at Meaux, in order to unite with his Marshals, would not be dangerous to

us, as it would give us time, which was what we
wanted, to unite our forces and be able to use them
with advantage.

In order to force back the Marshals by manœuvring from Meaux, General von Sacken was
commissioned to attack and bombard Meaux from
the right bank of the Marne, and to draw the
enemy's attention to that point. During this time
General Kleist was to cross the Ourcq at Lizy, and
General York was to make a flank march to the
right to support him, to cross the Marne at Sameron,
and move on as far as Lizy. The troops of Lange-
geron's corps were to follow General von Sacken,
and York's corps only was to remain on the left bank
of the Marne, to take up General von Corff's
cavalry.

When Sacken ordered the attack on the suburb
of Meaux, on the left bank of the Marne, the enemy
destroyed a little bridge at the gate, and defended
the wall, which was not very easy to take without a
regular attack. General von Sacken marched, conformably to the disposition; meanwhile General von
Kleist crossed the Ourcq at Lizy, and advanced
towards Meaux, as far as the Therouanne. But
here he was suddenly attacked towards evening by
Marshals Marmont and Mortier.

Kleist had scarcely 10,000 men. In accordance
with his instructions, he would not engage in a decisive action, until Sacken had approached. The
enemy turned his left wing and got possession of
Lizy. General Kleist expected Sacken to arrive and
retake Lizy; but when the latter reached Lizy as
night was closing in, the bridge was already destroyed
by the troops who were posted near it. General
Sacken remained at Lizy. General Kleist retreated

a league as far as May, on the road from Meaux to Soissons, and took possession of the stone bridge between Mareuil and Fulaines, by which means he recovered his communication with the Grand Army.

This enterprise of the hostile generals is one of their finest in the whole campaign. Their correct judgment of Blücher's intentions, as well as the rapidity and boldness of the attack at the Therouanne, do them the greatest honour. They might, indeed, have received orders from Bonaparte to attack, but in any case it was not easy, with such small numbers, to press in between an enemy four times as strong, and to place it in such a situation that the little party was able to hold out against it a day and a half.*

On the 26th of February the Field-Marshal had already received accounts through Prince Schwarzenberg from the royal head-quarters at Bar-sur-Aube. His letter to the Sovereigns had occasioned a grand council of war. All had acquiesced in his views, the Sovereigns granted him full powers, and in conformity to his wishes, placed under his orders not only the corps of Winzingerode and Bülow, but also the Duke of Saxe Weimar's, which was in the Netherlands, and was to be relieved by the Crown Prince of Sweden.

* The French army had for nine years gained all its successes by great masses, which moved on rapidly to battles, and knew how to make the proper use afterwards of their victories. Manœuvring was little thought of, or rather not at all. The modern system of subsistence allows of no extensive manœuvres. When afterwards, in the Spanish war, Bonaparte required Generals who must understand how to manœuvre, he saw himself obliged to change continually, and to try all in succession. We did not see any great things there. Generally speaking, the French army possessed, in its Generals, tacticians merely, and no strategists. It is all the more surprising to see here, for once, a manœuvre well conceived and admirably executed.

The official brevet from the Allied Sovereigns did not however arrive till the 28th. Proper orders had been instantly expedited to General von Winzingerode and the Duke of Saxe Weimar ; the order for General von Bülow was transmitted to the Field-Marshal to forward. On the 28th the Field-Marshal sent out one of his aides-de-camp with fifty Cossacks from La Ferté to seek for General Bülow, find out his situation and prepare him for a junction, and also to procure intelligence of Winzingerode. The Field-Marshal expected at all events to find both generals so placed on the Aisne as to be able to form a junction with them in *one* day's march, if they came to meet him. He reserved further arrangements until he should have heard the accounts the aide-de-camp would bring him. General Bülow was only generally instructed to take the direction of Villers Cotteret to Paris.

Late on the 28th came the very welcome tidings, by the Russian General, Tettenborn, that Bonaparte was in full march towards the Field-Marshal. General von Tettenborn, who was stationed with a strong division of Cossacks at Epernay, had had an affair on the 28th at Fère Champenoise with Bonaparte's column marching upon Sezanne. Some prisoners had been taken, who had with one voice declared that Bonaparte was with the column and was coming by Arcis from Troyes. General von Tettenborn, who had observed his march very narrowly, computed the troops he had with him at about 30,000 men. He thought that Bonaparte must have marched as far as Sezanne on the 28th. This intelligence enabled the Field-Marshal to take all his measures. General von Tettenborn rendered him thereby a great service. At the same time news arrived from General von Winzingerode, dated Rheims the 26th, which stated that, conformably to the verbal instructions of the officer who had been sent to him, he would take the direction by Fismes to Meaux, the appointed place of rendezvous.

The Field-Marshal sent a courier to Nancy with orders, now that the successive reinforcements coming to the army from Mainz (which kept the fortresses in respect) must all have passed through Nancy, to form a detachment of all the levies which were to follow, in order to keep the fortresses in check, in conjunction with General Jouseffowitsch, until the Elector of Hesse's forces were strong enough and sufficiently well organized to keep the garrisons at least in check, if he could not undertake anything decisive against them. General Count St. Priest received by the same courier notice of what the Field-Marshal had resolved to do, namely, to go to meet both Winzingerode and Bülow, to unite with them, and to draw Bonaparte across the Marne, in order to give the Grand Army time to develop its measures.

Blücher would gladly have struck a passing blow at the united Marshals, Marmont and Mortier; for this purpose, he repaired early on the 1st of March before Lizy-sur-Ourcq; however, he found the enemy's position too strong to attack it without preparation, and there was no time left for preparations, as Bonaparte might reach the Marne by noon. General von Corff therefore received orders to retreat, and, after crossing the Marne, to have the bridge broken up, for which purpose two battalions and half a battery was left behind. By 10 A.M., he had crossed the Marne with all his forces. Immediately afterwards the first hostile troops appeared, and the enemy began to construct a bridge as the rear-guard retreated.

From this report, the Field-Marshal drew the following conclusions :—After crossing the Marne, Bonaparte will throw himself to the left on the Ourcq, to form a junction with his Marshals ; and the Silesian Army cannot hinder his doing so, as it cannot accept battle before its junction with the Army of the North. Should he, however, march on the chaussée to Château-Thierry, with the idea that the Silesian Army was retreating from him precipitately, this would give us an opportunity of attacking and beating him singly, even if *one* corps only of the Army of the North could co-operate. It is therefore incumbent on us not to leave the Marshals on the left bank of the Ourcq, and to reserve to ourselves the power of forming a junction with the Army of the North at Oulchy-le-Château.

With this view the army marched on the 1st of March as far as the vicinity of La Ferté Milon. The rear-guard remained at Gandelu and Crouy, and General von Kleist between Mareuil and Neufchelles. This General was instructed to make such movements as to induce the enemy to believe that we had intentions of attacking him from Mareuil. However the enemy was not to be deceived, and he engaged on the 2nd in a warm action with Kleist.

Intelligence meanwhile reached us that Bonaparte was marching to Château-Thierry. It was now time to gain Oulchy-le-Château, where the Ourcq forms a section of ground offering a good position. Oulchy-le-Château is half way between Château-Thierry and Soissons. York and Sacken accordingly marched upon Oulchy-le-Château, and arrived there about midnight on the 2nd. Kleist's corps and the part of Langeron's which was with the army, were to form the rear-guard and to meet at Neuilly, as the one came from La Ferté Milon, and the other from Gandelu. This movement was well executed, so that the enemy found no weak points when he attacked this rear-guard on the 3rd. On the 2nd, the Aide-de-camp sent to General Bülow returned with the news that Generals von Winzingerode and Von Bülow had formed a junction to take Soissons. Bülow stood on the right bank of the Aisne, Winzingerode on the left. The communicating bridge was to be constructed at Vailly.

All this gave no means of judging whether General von Winzingerode could reach Oulchy-le-Château with his whole corps on the 3rd, for the battle to which he had been summoned by an officer who had been dispatched to him expressly for the purpose. In the night of the 2nd--3rd of March, he wrote word that he was in treaty with the Commandant of Soissons, and that he hoped a capitulation would be concluded the following morning.

The Field-Marshal could not depend on such chances, he therefore determined on forming a junction with the Army of the North on the right bank of the Aisne, whether Soissons fell into our hands or not. The favourable moment moreover for defeating Bonaparte separately was gone by, as he might still join his Marshals at Oulchy on the 3rd. York and Sacken had already made the march from Oulchy to Fismes, after the affair at Montmirail on the 13th and 14th of February.

The army received orders to commence the march about noon. Arrangements were made so that even during the march, the army might take from Busancy (whither the Field-Marshal preceded it, to examine the position thoroughly) the direction either to Fismes, Vailly, or Soissons. The baggage was sent forward to Fismes. This was the safest way, for on whichever line the army directed its march, it might find its baggage on the right bank of the Aisne, or recall it. On its departure, the rear-guard was vigorously attacked in the neighbourhood of Neuilly, and intelligence arrived of the capitulation of Soissons. In order, therefore, to relieve his wearied troops, the Field-Marshal directed the march upon Soissons. That of the baggage to Fismes had already commenced—so all remained as it was, that is to say, it was to cross the Aisne at Berry-au-Bac.

Fighting continued warmly, with the rear-guard retreating from Neuilly to the Ourcq, where it ended about three or four o'clock in a cannonade, and the enemy marched to the right towards Rocourt.

On the 3rd and 4th the army passed through Soissons undisturbed ; conformably to the disposition, the baggage was to march on the 4th of March from Fismes to Berry-au-Bac. The baggage of York's and Kleist's corps obeyed this order, and reached the army without difficulty ; a portion of Sacken's on the contrary, from some misunderstanding, remained at Fismes, and was captured that same afternoon.

Bonaparte reached Fismes on the evening of the 4th.* He must have, for some time past, perceived

---

* It is easy to see, from this narrative, that Bonaparte's reports, as well as the opinion (expressed even in the Allied Armies) that the surrender of Soissons saved Field-Marshal Blücher, are quite false. Even had it not surrendered, the army would have reached Fismes on the 3rd (according to the disposition), and crossed the Aisne at Berry-au-Bac on the 4th; which it would have done, probably, before Bonaparte entered Fismes with his Guards. But had this not been the case, still

that his armies were not strong enough to cope with the armies of all Europe, and therefore his last remaining hope was to make the war a national one.* All his public measures, publications in the newspapers, and bulletins, were intended to stir up the French nation, and to excite it to take up arms. At Fismes he took still more decided measures. He published a decree by which the mass of the French people were to be considered as soldiers ; and as the Allies had threatened to treat as traitors and to shoot the armed peasants gathering in their rear, this decree ordered reprisals. A second decree purported that all " Maires" who discouraged the people from taking up arms against the Allies, should be considered and treated as traitors. Since the affairs of Champaubert and Montmirail, indeed, a portion of the inhabitants of Champagne had taken up arms against us, abandoned their dwellings, and fled into the woods with all their property. The country right and left of the Marne, especially from Epernay to Château-Thierry, was quite in insurrection. Bonaparte had left General Vincent at Château-Thierry, to superintend the arming, but the affair had no great results. We left some partizans in this district, who checked it completely. Here and there Cossacks were shot, and they caught all such insurgents in return. But the whole thing was more a defensive proceeding on the part of the inhabitants, to save their few cattle and the stores of grain they had concealed in inaccessible woods.

On the other hand, there is no denying that our mode of warfare was such as to drive men at last to

the position, with Fismes in front, was so strong that it could not have been easily attacked in front.

* As he himself said later.

take up arms in desperation. The war had been carried on for a month in a small space, and the army had never stayed three days together in one spot. After laborious marches, we got late in the evening to a bivouac, and there the first half of the night had to be spent in ransacking the villages to procure provisions and all the necessaries of a camp. It was impossible to avoid taking from the inhabitants all they had,—it was impossible to prevent some cruelties being practised.

The Field-Marshal took inconceivable pains to create reserve magazines ; but from whence was he to take the supplies ? The reinforcements came from the rear; on the theatre of war there were no conveyances to be had, and in the great necessity of the troops, no security for convoys. One took away from the other. The commissariat, however, had collected considerable stores at Châlons; but here bad customs deprived us of the advantage this might have been to us. On the 16th of February, according to the magazine reports, 62,000 bushels of oats lay in Chalons, so that there was *ten days' fodder* for all the horses of the armies there assembled. It was given out to be received. The difference of language produced misunderstandings and disorder. Divisions of troops took forcible possession of the magazines. Guards were fetched. At last a whole battalion kept guard at the oat-magazine ; but from the want of time, the evil could no longer be checked ; so that by the 18th, thus in two days nearly, the whole of the 62,000 bushels of oats was forcibly carried off, and the magazines were emptied.

The Field-Marshal, as well as General von Sacken, personally took all the trouble imaginable to restore order, even by force ; but this was the more difficult, as Russians and Prussians were to receive from one and the same magazine, and harmony between the common soldiers was never more necessary to us than just at this moment. The Field-Marshal was therefore obliged to pass over many things, which he would perhaps have punished severely, had he commanded an army of one nation.*

But the discipline in both armies could not fail to suffer from this state of things. In the bivouacs at Sommesous, Arcis, and Méry, there was a total want of wood; and it was, moreover, very cold: houses were pulled down for the soldiers to cook and warm themselves. Thus a whole village often disappeared in a night. This could not be helped; but such situations make soldiers hard-hearted and cruel.

When the Silesian Army formed a junction at Soissons with the corps of Winzingerode and Bülow, the latter stared at seeing the tattered cloaks of the soldiers and the lean horses. Almost on every face we could read, "We too shall be like this in a month!" It would have been better if each had said, "That is the army which has essentially contributed to success by its great exertions, and which has extricated itself from many difficult situations by courage and constancy."

In a national defensive war, where every step produces consequences, and every sacrifice has its reward, it is easy to strain every nerve. But far away from their own country, where it even requires great intelligence to understand that so distant a war is nevertheless a national one, the spirit of the soldiers

---

* Considered from this point of view, it was not very likely that an army so composed should again perform so much that was great, *during two campaigns*, as the Silesian Army did in 1813 and 1814.

can be upheld only by the feeling of honour and military glory.

The Emperor Alexander had formed a sagacious judgment of Napoleon's situation and that of the Allies; and he had become the rock round which all gathered, to which every one clung who comprehended the necessity of continuing the war, and dethroning Bonaparte. To him we owe much, perhaps all. Without his firm will, his armies would not have borne what they did, and acted with readiness; for there were many superior and inferior officers belonging to them, who longed for peace. In the corps d'armée commanded by Bülow and Winzingerode a good spirit prevailed. The higher places were filled by distinguished officers; but neither corps had hardly ever bivouacked in 1813 or 1814, nor were they accustomed to the exertions of the Silesian Army. Under the Crown Prince of Sweden, they had carried on quite another kind of warfare, and were much more used—Winzingerode's corps especially—to a slow systematic mode of proceeding, than the Silesian Army.

The corps of York and Kleist together amounted to 23,000 men; Bülow had 17,000, without including 9,000 who were still in the Netherlands. These were the remains of 120,000 men, who had appeared in line after the armistice in 1813, and already once received considerable reinforcements since the battle of Leipsic.

In many officers the thought arose, whether the Prussian army could indeed continue to take the lead in battle, without dwindling away so that it could no longer have a voice at the peace. In the Russian army it was asked: Why should Russians and Prussians do it all?

It was feared that Austria might have other interests, and even adopt another system; rumours had spread that matters did not look very well at royal head-quarters as regarded harmony.

This short exposition of the general views entertained, and of circumstances, is necessary in order to understand the following occurrences till the 23rd of March. They do not bear the stamp of the great and extraordinary character to which one is accustomed in the Silesian Army. Thus the actions of an army often depend on circumstances, of which the General is not always the master.

On the 4th of March, when the army had crossed the Aisne, and formed a junction with the corps of the Army of the North, it was in an extraordinary situation, in a military point of view: 109,000 men (after Count Langeron and the Prussian Colonel Von Lobenthal had joined) stood in an extremely advantageous position; in front of the right wing, Soissons (which offered a safe passage by a stone bridge, and one of boats constructed below the works)—the town itself in such a condition that it could not be taken by a *coup de main*; in front of the army, in a deep valley, flowed the Aisne, which had no bridge till Berry-au-Bac, but two fords, which, as could be seen at once, did not endanger the position.

A limestone-hill lies between the Aisne and the Lette (which run parallel at a distance of two leagues), and its plateau lies near to the Lette. The brooks flow all at right angles to the Aisne, and their valleys are likewise deep. There is no access from the Aisne to the plateau but through the valleys; from the plateau the Aisne can be approached by narrow mountain tongues, ending abruptly at the river. A high road leads from L'Ange Gardien (an inn three leagues from Soissons on the road to Laon) quite across the plateau to Craonne. The plateau is in many places six hundred paces, and in others a thousand paces broad, but very narrow in the middle, between L'Ange Gardien and Craonne, especially at the Farm of Froidemont.

If the army took up a position on this plateau, it would be impossible to attack its right wing or front, without the enemy's running the risk of being annihilated before he could march up.

The left wing only was assailable from Berry-au-Bac. However, if the towns of Corbeny and Craonne, with the intervening wood, were occupied, so that the army could debouch from the plateau by Craonne, the position was likewise very strong in that quarter.

The Field-Marshal left the *ordre de bataille* as it was, and, for the sake of the communication of the two new corps with their depôts in the rear, he placed the one (Winzingerode's) on the left wing, and the other (Bülow's) on the right wing. Kleist's corps had suffered so much by numerous actions, and by forming constantly the rear-guard, that it needed some time to recover, and the more so as the newly-arrived recruits were to be drafted into it. It was therefore transferred to Anizy-le-Château, between Soissons and Laon, as a reserve for the army. The other corps were posted as follows:—Bülow, at Loissy and its environs, to watch the Aisne from Soissons to Compiègne; York, at Broye and its environs; Kleist, as reserve at Anizy; Count Langeron, at Soissons, with his cavalry in the villages near, to watch the Aisne from Soissons to Vailly; Sacken, at Vailly and Soupire, to watch the Aisne to Beaurieux; Winzingerode, at Beaurieux and Craonne, to watch the Aisne from Beaurieux to Berry-au-Bac.

All the corps were instructed that the real proper position was on the plateau, and therefore the roads must be reconnoitred, to be able to move there as soon as it was necessary.

On the 4th of March, intelligence reached us that the enemy had fallen on our baggage at Fismes. Already on the 3rd a courier had brought news of the Grand Army, of its advance, its recapture of Bar-sur-Aube, and its resolution to continue advancing. On the 4th couriers set off from Soissons to take dispatches to the Grand Army, but they were obliged to turn back, as Rheims was taken by the enemy on the morning of the 5th. At eight that morning, the enemy appeared before Soissons, raised batteries, and fired at the suburbs, which he afterwards attacked, but without any result, until he got possession of the Rheims suburb after three o'clock, and from the roofs fired at the ramparts till six in the evening; he also threw shells into the town, which set fire to the Town-hall. This fight cost Langeron's corps (by his report) 1000 killed and wounded, and the enemy lost as many.

On the 6th, at six in the morning, the enemy renewed his attack, but it soon appeared that he only did so to mask his retreat, which began at about seven, on the chaussée from Soissons to Fismes.

The Field-Marshal removed his head-quarters on the 5th to Chavignon on the road from Soissons to Laon.* He had written to General von Winzin-

* The map of the Department of the Aisne gives the chaussée from Soissons to Laon quite in a wrong direction.

gerode, requesting him to watch closely the point at Berry-au-Bac, in order that he (the Field-Marshal) might assemble the army on the plateau, as soon as the enemy crossed over there, while Winzingerode held the position at Craonne. General von Winzingerode sent the following answer to the Field-Marshal : "He might be quite easy; he would act just as the Field-Marshal wished in fulfilment of his object."

Late in the evening of the 5th, news came from Laon, that the enemy had arrived before the town, at the same time with some detachments of Cossacks. The Field-Marshal sent over there ; things had been exaggerated, the enemy had pursued a Cossack regiment out beyond Corbeny.

However unintelligible this was, it induced the Field-Marshal to assemble the army on the plateau on the morning of the 6th. General von Winzingerode had about 10,000 horse of light cavalry: that active officer Lieutenant-General von Czernitscheff, commanded his advanced guard; should it not have been stationed at Berry-au-Bac? and would it not have reported if Czernitscheff had been obliged to retreat ?

On the 6th, towards noon, General Winzingerode sent notice that the enemy was advancing with considerable columns from Berry-au-Bac upon Corbeny. The Field-Marshal gave immediate orders to the army to make a flank march to the left upon the plateau towards Craonne. Meanwhile reports came that the enemy was withdrawing his rear-guard also from its position opposite Soissons. The columns were seen from the plateau marching upon Fismes.

It was calculated that the hostile corps which had stood before Soissons could not arrive by way of Berry-au-Bac before night on the 7th ; so that the forces advancing upon Corbeny must be Bonaparte with 40,000 to 50,000 men. The Field-Marshal's intention was to go to meet the enemy by Craonne and Corbeny, and to force him to accept battle before the other corps following him could approach to his support. When the corps were in march, the Field-Marshal proceeded towards Craonne; but a league this side of it he fell in with Winzingerode's corps in its position. There it had remained, and General Czernitscheff only had occupied Craonne with some Jäger battalions. When the Field-Marshal arrived, Craonne and the Wood of Corbeny were already in the hands of the enemy. This explained the enemy's advance by Corbeny; on the 5th, the enemy also got possession of the passage over the Lette at St. Martin.

The Field-Marshal saw himself engaged with the enemy on very uneven ground, where he could not make much use of his cavalry and artillery. The plateau of Craonne was so narrow, that it could be defended by few troops against the greatest army. The same was the case with the plateau on which Winzingerode's corps stood, supported right and left by two valleys, which ran parallel with the front. These circumstances decided the Field-Marshal (now that the mistake had been made) to give up Craonne and Corbeny to the enemy, to renounce his whole plan at once, and to alter it according to the ground. All the corps received orders to keep on the plateau.

The Field-Marshal resolved to leave Winzingerode's corps in its position, with Sacken's corps behind for its support, to defend themselves the following day should they be attacked. He consigned 10,000 horse and forty pieces of horse-artillery (to which each corps contributed) to the cavalry General von Winzingerode, with instructions to march off instantly and cross the Lette, in order to reach the road leading from Laon to Berry-au-Bac by the shortest way. Next morning, if Bonaparte attacked the plateau, the General was to fall on his rear by Corbeny, with this mass of cavalry and artillery. General Bülow received orders to march off in the night on the road by Chavignon to Laon ; York, Kleist, and Count Langeron, to hold themselves in marching order for next morning.

The Field-Marshal took up his quarters at Bray, with the intention of taking the command himself on the plateau the following morning, and of determining the moment when they should assume the offensive, after General Winzingerode's arrival on Bonaparte's rear.

Early on the 7th of March, the enemy showed by his movements that he was preparing to attack. At 9 A.M., just as the Field-Marshal was intending to repair to the infantry of Winzingerode's corps, which Generals Count Strogonow and Count Woronzow commanded, supposing Winzingerode, with his cavalry, to be already arrived on the enemy's rear, notice was sent him that the whole of this cavalry was still in the valley of the Lette at Chevrigny in his rear. This intelligence destroyed all the hopes of the day.

The Field-Marshal immediately ordered Kleist's corps to take the direction of Fétieux, on the high road from Laon to Berry-au-Bac, and resolved to place himself at the head of the cavalry which had been consigned to General von Winzingerode. York's corps was ordered to take the direction of Bruyères ; the portion of Count Langeron's that was not at Soissons, was stationed at the farm of Froidemont. The Field-Marshal invited General von

Sacken to a conference at this farm (where the orders were drawn out), and he consigned to him the command of the troops upon the plateau, with orders to accept battle, as no harm could befall him, on account of the strong positions which recurred at every half-league. As Generals Count Strogonow and Count Woronzow already stood in four or five divisions, and Sacken's corps formed three more, half a league in their rear, and Count Langeron's another again, half a league further back, the enemy could only attack by attempting to turn the wings by the valleys. These movements would always be overlooked. The Field-Marshal directed General von Sacken, as soon as such movement became dangerous, to retreat to the nearest of the two valleys; since it was desirable to remove Bonaparte a little from Craonne, where he, the Field-Marshal, would be then able to turn his army more effectually. In case it were quite impossible to make up for the time the cavalry had lost, and still to get to the enemy's rear, the Field-Marshal promised to send immediate notice to General Sacken, who was then to retreat by Chavignon to Laon.

In order not to expose the troops in garrison at Soissons, as they had no provisions, it was arranged that General von Sacken should give them notice if he retreated, in which case they were to march by Coucy, La Fère*, and Crepy to Laon, after destroying every means of defence at Soissons that could be destroyed. Conformably to this agreement, the Field-Marshal followed General Winzingerode's cavalry; he found it at 11 o'clock in great part

---

* La Fère had been taken by General von Bülow at the end of February.

drawn up in regiments behind Chevrigny, and furnished with such dispositions that it was absolutely necessary for him to speak with General Winzingerode, if he wanted to make any alteration in them. Meanwhile a warm fight had commenced with General von Sacken, who had been attacked by Bonaparte about 10 o'clock.

In order to proceed more securely and undiscovered, General von Winzingerode had unluckily taken the direction of Laon, and the Field-Marshal did not overtake him till he reached Bruyères.

It was as if everything had combined to frustrate his intentions that day.

Instead of selecting Neuville as the point for crossing the Lette, Winzingerode fixed upon Chevrigny, which occasioned a circuit of at least three leagues.

Moreover, he would have been glad to make Lieutenant-General Czernitscheff with his Cossacks his advanced guard. But they had fought at Craonne, and the horses must be fed; consequently, they could not arrive at Chevrigny till past midnight. It was dark; no messengers were to be found; one knows what that is; when day broke the horses were fed, and time slipped away. Finally, General von Winzingerode, instead of remaining on the plateau and marching straight by Martigny to Corbeny, took the direction of Laon, and thus lost three hours. Had he given orders to this effect,—"The cavalry of all the corps must cross the Lette where and as they can; only they must all be at the rendezvous by midnight, feed there, and await my further orders,"— he might have reached Corbeny with the head of his column by five in the morning. Czernitscheff would not have failed with his Cossacks. He had no further to go from Craonne by Neuville to Martigny than from thence to Chevrigny.

The Field-Marshal was forced to give up the result he expected from turning the enemy. From Bruyères he sent General Sacken the order to retreat. We may easily imagine how hard it was to him to issue this order, when we consider that it entailed the giving up Soissons, which was of such great importance and of such decided influence on the theatre of war upon which the Field-Marshal was now engaged. However, a battle at Laon must decide the fate of both armies; and if it were lost, Soissons could not be held, as it was ill supplied with provisions, and a garrison of 10,000 men could not be sacrificed.

To fight so that, if the battle were lost, the garrison might still be able to retreat, the battle-field must be selected near L'Ange Gardien. On the other hand, there was this to be said in favour of the Field-Marshal's plan, that as he only sought a field to bring matters to a decision, he found one at Laon extraordinarily well adapted to the composition of his army;* he strengthened himself for the battle with the 10,000 men of the Soissons garrison, and if Bonaparte was but beaten, Soissons could easily be retaken by the artillery from La Fère, should Bonaparte leave a large garrison in this inconsiderable place. General von Sacken retreated conformably to the agreement, and the enemy did not pursue him beyond Froidemont. General Count Langeron crossed the Lette, and took up a position at Troucy.

General Count Kleist reached Fétieux at four

* He had about 20,000 horse.

o'clock; General von Winzingerode arrived there some hours later. The favourable moment was gone. The Field-Marshal thought he could no longer hinder Bonaparte from uniting with the corps following him (if such were his intentions), and this induced him to accept battle at Laon.

On the morning of the 8th of March, all the corps moved into their position. Unusual as the position was, it was hardly possible to find one better adapted to the Field-Marshal's army. The hills which intersect the valleys of the Aisne and Lette terminate a full league from Laon; there a plain begins, which extends to the Serre. On this plain a detached hill rises, which has on every side a fall of 12, 16, 20, even 30 degrees; and upon its not inconsiderable plateau stands the town of Laon, which occupies the crest with its walls, except on one spot to the south-west, and one to the west; on the former an old ruined castle and windmill, and on the latter a windmill outside the wall, stand on small projecting points of the hill. At the foot of the hill (which is from 300 to 400 feet in height) lie four villages as suburbs, St. Marcel and Vaux to the north, and Ardon and Semilly to the south.

Five roads run from Laon in various directions: 1 to La Fère by St. Marcel; 2 to Guise and Landrecy, by Vaux; 3 by Vervins and Maubeuge; 4 by Berry-au-Bac to Rheims; 5 to Chavignon and Soissons, by Semilly.

The corps of York and Kleist, each too weak to act singly, united to form one *corps d'armée*.

The army was now disposed as follows:—Bülow's corps occupied the hill of Laon, and the villages of Semilly and Ardon. Winzingerode's corps formed the right wing of the army, while his left wing rested on the hill of Laon. The corps of York and Kleist constituted the left wing, while they rested their right on the hill of Laon. Behind the hill, at the village of St. Marcel, stood Sacken's corps, along with Langeron's, both as reserve. The headquarters were at Laon. Both wings stood without support. Laon and its hill constituted the pivot, and the Field-Marshal determined to turn round the hill during the battle, until he could assume the offensive. Bonaparte facilitated matters for him, as we shall see.

On the 8th of March, after all had moved into the position, General Czernitscheff remained at Etouvelle with the advanced guard of Winzingerode's corps, and a Prussian advanced guard at Fétieux on the left wing. The combat at Craonne had occasioned great loss to Winzingerode's corps and Von Sacken's; but the enemy had also suffered very considerably. General von Sacken's cavalry, under Lieutenant-General Wasiltschikoff, had made an onslaught by which it overthrew one hostile line, which was forced to leave its artillery in the lurch. This attack would have produced great results, if, in accordance with the General's intention, his dragoons had remained in close column in reserve. But unluckily they got scattered in the action, and when a close body of French cavalry came on, he was obliged to give way.

The object for which this combat had been undertaken was missed, and this caused much dissatisfaction. The Russians thought it strange that they only had been engaged, and that no Prussian had joined in the fight this day; they imagined that General von Winzingerode had been charged to do what was impossible. The Prussian officers fancied some intention in General von Winzingerode's conduct; in short, instead of the hitherto untroubled harmony of the Silesian Army, there now existed the elements of general discord. On the 8th of March this spirit revealed itself in many quarters; and in addition to this the two corps of the Army of the North considered themselves as strangers.

The Field-Marshal had given up his line of communication by Nancy, and been obliged to throw himself upon that of these two corps. They had encountered no fighting on their march, and had always cantonned. Their waggons were filled, and they had established small magazines in their rear. The four corps of the Silesian Army had no provisions left. The corps of the Army of the North were to share with them; this struck them as unfair,—they were not used to live from day to day. It required great prudence and firmness on the Field-Marshal's part, to prevent the smouldering fire bursting into flame. Early on the 9th the garrison from Soissons joined the army.

By three in the morning General Czernitscheff had already been attacked, and drew back into the position. When day broke, the fog was so thick that we were unable to see a hundred paces before us. This lasted until 11 o'clock. During this time the enemy's infantry attacked the village of Semilly, and got momentary possession of it, but was immediately driven out again. When the fog dispersed, we saw the enemy in possession of the villages of Etouvelle and Chivy, and extending towards Leully; so few troops however showed themselves, that we were led to suppose this must be a false attack, and that the *real* one would come from the direction of Bruyères, or even Fétieux. We had already prepared for all these various cases.

About noon it was reported that a strong column was advancing on the chaussée from Berry-au-Bac by Fétieux, which confirmed the previous conjecture; meanwhile more hostile troops made their appearance at Etouvelle, and it seemed probable that this was the portion of the enemy's army which had fought at Craonne on the 7th, while the column advancing from Berry-au-Bac must be the same as had attacked Soissons, which, as we already knew, was under the orders of Marshals Mortier and Marmont.

The first and most important measure now was to hinder the junction of the two widely separated corps, and to interrupt, if possible, the connection and concert of measures between them. Near Chivy and Etouvelle the ground was cut up by narrow paths to the villages and bridges, and both villages were easy to defend; on our left wing, on the contrary, the ground was open and well adapted for battle. The Field-Marshal determined therefore to execute a grand stroke on this wing, for which he had besides another reason; namely, that the Prussian Army stood there, from which he always had the greatest expectations.

Lieutenant-General Wasiltschikoff was accordingly commissioned, with a corps of cavalry and some horse-artillery, to turn the enemy's left wing by Classy (which was occupied by some infantry to secure his retreat), and to draw the enemy's attention on himself in that direction. This succeeded perfectly, and we discovered with telescopes that the enemy, who had not hitherto at all extended his forces over the brook (which, running from Ardon flows into the Lette the other side of Chavignon), now dispatched troops and artillery against Lieutenant-General Wasiltschikoff, who had pushed on as far as Creulles. Lieutenant-General von Bülow was now ordered to take possession of Leully, and to prevent all communication between the two hostile corps. This was done by Lieutenant-General von Oppen; and the enemy's infantry, being unsupported, retreated behind Chivy.

Now (it might have been 4 P.M.) it was perceived that the enemy's left wing, or Bonaparte's army, could no longer make any decisive attack that day; and therefore Lieutenant-General Wasiltschikoff received orders to retire slowly into the position, so as to reach it as it grew dark. The corps of Count Langeron and Von Sacken, together with 6000 Russian horse, who all stood concealed behind the heights of Laon, received instructions to make a flank march to the left, and to place themselves in reserve behind York and Kleist. The latter received orders to attack the enemy, as soon as these reserves arrived, whether it were day or night.

At 3 P.M., the fight on the left wing had commenced. The enemy brought up about thirty pieces of artillery, with which he set Athies on fire, and he attacked it with infantry, while he prolonged his right wing to outflank our left. It seems that the enemy had intended to make his real attack the next day, and that on this day he only wanted to gain the points from whence he could open the battle with advantage; for, as it grew dark, he suspended the firing on both wings. Just about this time the reserves reached their points, and Generals von York and Kleist advanced to the attack. Orders were given that all should remain in masses, and that not a shot should be fired.

Lieutenant-General Prince William of Prussia

was at the head of the attacking column on the left wing; Lieutenant-General von Kleist at the head of that on the right; Lieutenant-General von Zieten went round with the cavalry. The enemy was taken completely by surprise, just at the moment he was arranging his bivouac. There was very little resistance, and the discomfiture was general. This night combat only cost us between 100 and 200 killed and wounded. By midnight the corps were at Fétieux, after having captured the whole of the enemy's artillery except four pieces (some fifty guns), and the ammunition-waggons. Many prisoners were made; but as nobody would trouble himself about transporting them, most of them escaped in the night, so that only 2,000 were brought in next morning. The discomfiture was so great, that Marshal Marmont, who commanded here, could not bring his troops to a halt before reaching Fismes.

Here, for the first time, the National Guard fought against us. We learned that Bonaparte was with the left wing, and that he had his head-quarters at Chavignon. By this stroke he was now quite isolated with this wing; and as we might assume that he had but 40,000 men at most, we might expect that on the news of Marmont's disaster, he would immediately break up, and endeavour to reach Soissons. However, it was probable that the news might not reach him before eight o'clock in the morning of the 10th, and consequently we should have time to attack him before he set out.

The corps of Count Langeron and Von Sacken had remained stationary on the heights of Laon, as the battle had been so quickly decided. Some 70,000 men, therefore, were ready for the attack on Classy. But General Wasiltschikoff had been

obliged in the evening to give up Classy to the
enemy; and if the latter defended this village, as
well as Chivy, in earnest, he would have great advantage.   On the other hand, it seemed much more
advantageous for us to cut him off from his retreat,
which was now become necessary.   Generals Winzingerode and Bülow had together about 40,000
men, and stood in an almost impregnable position.
United they could bid the enemy defiance, if he remained stationary or attacked us, in case he had not
heard of Marmont's misfortune; and if he retreated,
they could pursue and endeavour to detain him while
the corps surrounded him.   Upon these grounds,
the disposition for the 10th (which was given out at
midnight) was based, the essential points being the
following :—

The corps of York and Kleist were to follow the
beaten enemy by Berry-au-Bac to Fismes.

The corps of Count Langeron and Von Sacken
were to march to Bruyères and St. Martin (where
they were to cross the Lette) upon the plateau of
Craonne to L'Ange Gardien, in order to cut off the
enemy if he still loitered at Chivy.

The corps of Winzingerode and Von Bülow were
to remain stationary, and to watch the enemy closely,
in order to follow him immediately if he retreated.

All set themselves in motion accordingly.   The
previous day had produced a great alteration in the
temper of the army.   The Russians, who know how
to value bravery in other nations, because they are
themselves brave, did full justice to the Prussian
army, and to Generals York and Kleist for their
ability and skill.   The Prussians rejoiced that the
fair lot had fallen to them, to avenge the loss of so
many of their brave comrades who had fallen at

Craonne, by a defeat which must essentially contribute to the termination of the war. All were once more contented and joyful, and the discord of previous days was forgotten.

Bonaparte still remained in his position on the morning of the 10th of March. The Field-Marshal, who had been far from well on the 9th, was attacked in the night with fever and a complaint in his eyes, which prevented his leaving his room. A number of officers of rank came to him in the morning, partly to congratulate him on his victory, and partly to enquire after his health. Many who were not accurately acquainted with all the circumstances respecting the strength, position, and state of the defeated army, considered the disposition that had been issued a hazardous undertaking; others had heard from deserters and prisoners that the 10th was the day properly intended by Bonaparte for his attack; and others were of opinion that his forces could not be calculated, now that the National Guards had joined him. To all this was added the consideration that if Bonaparte were really to attack us, the Field-Marshal would not be able to take part in the fight. In short, the four corps who had set out received orders to halt; and when, at about nine o'clock, Bonaparte made some movements as if he were going to attack us, they were even ordered to come back to Laon.

Thus the Field-Marshal's illness served to save Napoleon. The day passed with a tirailleur fire, totally devoid of object. Bonaparte was perhaps apprehensive that we might form the project of surrounding him in the night. He therefore attacked, an hour before it grew dark, the village of Semilly with three battalions, but was naturally soon repulsed, and he then commenced his retreat. It was reported, even before midnight, that the fires were diminishing; but he was only slightly pursued the following morning, and reached Soissons with no other loss than that of the stragglers and the sick and wounded, who were taken prisoners by the Cossacks.

On the 11th, the different corps had orders to march : Sacken's corps towards Soissons ; York's and Kleist's towards Berry-au-Bac ; Bülow's corps across the Oise towards Noyon; and Count Langeron marched out by La Fère, and on the 13th to Coucy-le-Château. Only Winzingerode's corps remained at Laon, where it was no longer possible to find provisions for the army.

The famine which must inevitably fall on the army if it advanced in such strength on the direct road from Laon to Paris, occasioned a new plan of operations, which involved the dispersion of the army. General von Bülow, as we have already mentioned, had still 9,000 men in the Netherlands. These were left with the Duke of Saxe Weimar, in order that he might be able to defend the Netherlands against General Maison, who, with a moveable corps, had made Lille the central point of his operations.

It was given out that General Maison could place 15,000 men in the field, leaving weak garrisons in his fortresses. The Duke of Saxe Weimar had 9,000 Saxons, and expected 9,000 more under General Thielmann. Until the arrival of the latter, the above-mentioned portion of Bülow's corps was to remain in the Netherlands, and afterwards to join General Bülow. Furthermore, the Duke of Saxe Weimar was to leave the Netherlands with his

18,000 men, as soon as the Crown Prince of Sweden arrived with his Swedes. It was the intention of the Sovereigns that the Crown Prince should then form a new army of Swedes, Danes, Belgians, Hanoverians, and other North German troops.

Lieutenant-General Thielmann arrived with his 9,000 men, but they were new levies of Saxon Landwehr, very ill supplied with arms; so that the Duke of Saxe Weimar could not undertake to defend the Netherlands with these troops, and therefore detained General von Borstel with the 9,000 men of Bülow's corps. It would certainly have been a great disadvantage to the Allies if General Maison had succeeded in gaining possession of Brussels, and had thereby cut us off from all means of communication with Germany; therefore the prolonged stay of the troops of Bülow's corps in the Netherlands was allowed; however, as the Duke of Weimar's forces now amounted to 27,000 men, and only 12,000 or at most 15,000 could act against him, Field-Marshal Blücher commissioned this corps to make an attack on the fortress of Maubeuge, while waiting for the coming of the Crown Prince of Sweden. This place was an extraordinary impediment to our communication from Laon to Brussels; as from Avesnes, which was in our hands, to Mons, we were obliged to go round by very bad roads by Solre-le-Château and Beaumont. Besides, by all accounts Maubeuge had only a garrison of 2000 men.

The Duke of Saxe Weimar borrowed siege-artillery from the English General Graham (who was before Antwerp), and bombarded Maubeuge; but he had too little ammunition to continue this bombardment properly, and was therefore obliged to give up the project. The Crown Prince of Sweden approached the Meuse, and the Field-Marshal sent instructions to the Duke of Saxe Weimar to put himself in motion with the 27,000 men under him, to join the army as soon as he was relieved by the Crown Prince. This corps, after uniting with Bülow's, (and according to circumstances with Count Langeron's and Sacken's,) was then to advance towards Paris on the right bank of the Oise.

This new plan, however, very soon underwent an alteration, in consequence of the accounts that came from the Netherlands. Notice was sent that the Crown Prince with the Swedish troops had made a halt at Liege, and would proceed no further. Moreover, the monarchs had agreed amongst themselves that the provinces situated on the left bank of the Rhine, Cleves, Guelders, &c., which had formerly belonged to Prussia, should be restored to her; and General von Bülow had therefore sent officers to Cleves to receive volunteers, and to establish the Landwehr as in the other re-conquered Prussian provinces. But the Crown Prince of Sweden had, on his arrival on the left bank of the Rhine, interdicted all armaments, declaring — "that it was contrary to former treaties with France, and especially the one ceding the left bank of the Rhine."

These indications, together with some others, awakened old recollections in the Field-Marshal, and excited his apprehensions that the policy of Sweden might be different from that of the other Allies. As the communication with royal headquarters was interrupted, and he had been for some time without news of the Grand Army, he thought himself bound to use the greater precaution, and to hold himself prepared for any event that might occur. These peculiar circumstances will explain why the Silesian Army continued for nine days after the battle of Laon in a state of inactivity, which could in no way be reconciled with its former conduct.

When, however, the Field-Marshal was able to discern how matters stood in this quarter, he resolved to leave the Duke of Weimar with his considerable and increasing forces in the Netherlands, between General Maison and the Crown Prince of Sweden, and to give up altogether the operations on the right bank of the Oise. The increasing exhaustion and diminution of Bonaparte's army afforded indeed prospects of crushing it in other ways.

On the 12th of March General Count St. Priest, who had had no accounts of the Field-Marshal, directed Rheims to be stormed, and in this operation he captured eight pieces of artillery and made some prisoners. General von Jagow was instructed to make a false attack with the Prussian troops on the side of the Soissons road, while the real attack was made by five regiments on the side of Rhétel. The columns were to be before the gates at five o'clock in the morning. General von Jagow was at his post as the hour struck, and began to mount the gates. General St. Priest approached from the east side. He had previously attacked Rheims on the 7th, but with much fewer troops, as General Pantschoulizeff, coming from Mainz, did not join him till the 11th; he brought with him all the troops of Langeron's corps that had been left behind at Mainz, except two regiments of infantry and one of dragoons. These three regiments, under Generals Davidoff and Wasiltschikoff III., threw themselves subsequently into Vitry. The sequel will show what good service they did there. General Count St. Priest heard of the victory of Laon at Rheims, and remained stationary there on the 13th of March.

Bonaparte saw what impression his retreat from Laon made on the army, and he had the more reason to dread the impression it would make on the people, as it was only by means of the latter that he could still hope to be extricated from his present difficulties. It was therefore of the utmost consequence to him to reinstate himself in public opinion, and with this view the approach of Count St. Priest, who could not be strong enough to cope with him, was very welcome to him.

Bonaparte could no longer expect any considerable reinforcements from the Loire ; on the other hand, the garrisons in the fortresses of Lorraine and the Ardennes must have pretty well drilled their recruits by this time, and must be in a condition to give up a portion of their troops for field service. It was therefore necessary for the French army to approach the above-mentioned fortresses near enough to draw reinforcements from them. When Soissons fell back again into French hands on the 8th of March, Bonaparte immediately ordered from Paris a number of field-pieces to arm the place, and it was also victualled. But it became subsequently necessary to consign this artillery to Marshal Marmont, to replace what he had lost at Laon. Soissons was garrisoned by National Guards and some regular troops.

After these preparations had been made, Bonaparte set out to attack Count St. Priest, who fancied himself quite secure at Rheims,* and had

* Count St. Priest had ordered a feast at Rheims on the 13th, and when news was brought that Bonaparte was coming to attack him, he would not believe it.

distributed his troops in cantonments. It fell to General von Jagow's lot to be removed towards Fismes; he expostulated, but Count St. Priest insisted on his moving into the cantonments designated.

Of his seven battalions General von Jagow placed two in advance towards Fismes, and kept the other five near the town of Rheims. The two in advance were taken prisoners at noon on the 13th, after retreating into a churchyard.

Towards evening Bonaparte came before Rheims. General St. Priest went through the suburb and over a long causeway to meet him, but was forced to retire before superior numbers, and lost on this occasion twelve pieces of artillery and a multitude of prisoners. He was himself struck by a cannon-ball, and died on the sixteenth day after. The remains of his corps arrived at Berry-au-Bac on the morning of the 14th, in detached troops, having continued to fight bravely.

Bonaparte entered Rheims, and wrote a high-flown account of the affair, in which he designated the battery by which Count St. Priest was wounded, the last judgment, as it was the same that had wounded Moreau at Dresden; from hence he communicated with the uninvested fortress of Mézières, which sent him reinforcements, and expedited orders to the other fortresses.

On the 14th, Marshal Marmont retook Berry-au-Bac, and made preparations for blowing up the bridges, to secure himself at Rheims. He sent Marshal Ney, with about 10,000 men, to Châlons, and, as soon as his reinforcements arrived, he marched to Epernay on the 17th, to Fère Champenoise on the 18th, to Plancy on the 19th, where he caused bridges to be constructed over the Aube, and to Arcis on the 20th, where he found the Grand Army facing him. Field-Marshal Blücher meanwhile had (since the 12th) received very imperfect accounts of Bonaparte's proceedings.*

General von Bülow received instructions to make an attempt on Compiègne, which Count Langeron was to support from the left bank of the Oise. The town was summoned on the 12th and 13th, and bombarded with some pieces from the right bank of the Oise, but without result.

General von Sacken found a hostile rear-guard before Soissons, attacked it on the 13th, and after a long fight, which cost him some hundred men, he drove it back into the town.

The capture of St. Quentin (in which we found a quantity of heavy artillery, that the enemy had been unable to drag on with him) furnished us some means of subsistence. When the remains of Count St. Priest's troops arrived on the 14th, they were sent to be drafted into their several corps, which were reorganized on the 15th and 16th.

After the bridge of Berry-au-Bac fell into the enemy's hands on the 14th, it was for a moment believed that Bonaparte had dispatched the corps which had stood opposed to the Grand Army, by Epernay to Rheims, in order to make another attempt to beat the Field-Marshal. The thing was possible, for it was a natural question to ask, " What will he do next ? "

---

* General Benkendorff had turned Bonaparte's left wing with his intelligent Cossacks, and observed his entrance into Soissons. He made some prisoners, and intercepted some baggage, couriers, and posts.

SECTION VIII.

The Silesian Army moves across the Aisne, and drives Marshal Marmont back by Château Thierry.—March by Rheims and Châlons.—Junction with the Grand Army for the march in concert to Paris.—Combat at Fère Champenoise, at Meaux, at Claye.—Battle before Paris.—March towards the Essonne. —Peace of Paris.

On the 15th of March the detached corps were recalled to Laon, to be prepared for all Bonaparte's measures. On the 16th and 17th all came in. On the 17th and 18th the army marched off to construct bridges over the Aisne, and to blockade Soissons; the latter task fell to the share of Bülow's corps.

The enemy stood opposite Berry-au-Bac. Lieutenant-General Czernitscheff crossed the Aisne at Neufchatel, and turned the enemy's right wing; while the corps of York and Kleist attempted to construct a bridge at Pennavaire, and the Russian corps one at Berry-au-Bac, for the enemy had destroyed the bridge there. The cavalry found fords. By this movement of General Czernitscheff, the enemy was rolled up; he retreated by Roncy (where Marshal Marmont had his quarters) back to Fismes.*

* As provisions and forage became every day scarcer, we had to send out farther and farther to procure them. From the Ardennes empty sacks were brought back, for all was in insurrection there. There had been proofs for some time past that the insurrectionary measures were supported and guided by the fortresses on the Meuse; but the Field-Marshal was obliged first to bring great affairs into order before he could think of the lesser ones. Meanwhile things continued to grow worse.

2 K

The bridges were completed on the 19th. General von Winzingerode marched to Rheims on the 20th. This caused the enemy to retreat on the 21st from Fismes by Fère-en-Tardenois. On the 22nd Generals von York and Kleist drove Marshal Marmont across the Marne at Château Thierry.

The Field-Marshal charged General Winzingerode to follow Bonaparte on the 21st with 8,000 horse of his corps, and to procure intelligence of his movements. On the 22nd the Cossacks took a courier prisoner who was conveying a letter from Bonaparte to his wife,* in which the Field-Marshal found all he wanted to know, namely, that on the 20th and 21st, he (Bonaparte) had fought with the Grand Army, and that he was drawing near the fortresses, with the hope of getting the enemy, by manœuvring,

The peasants kept watch in the villages, and no longer allowed any couriers to pass through, but took them prisoners, and brought them to Mezières; in short, the decrees of Fismes had done their work. At last, Major von Lutzow, who, with his Free Corps (about 150 horse), roamed about that district, was attacked everywhere. Signals for assembling were given in every village, and there was reason to conclude that all was regularly organized. Thereupon, General Count Witt, with four regiments of Cossacks, two of infantry, and four cannons, was dispatched to Réthel on the 20th, to disarm the insurgents, and to secure the army from similar insurrectionary measures in future; and he met with complete success.

* The Field-Marshal forwarded this letter to the Empress Marie Louise, and promised, since he had cut off the Emperor's communication, to transmit to her in future all correspondence relating to herself. Bonaparte's letter spoke of drawing the enemy from Paris. We could not at that time discover what was his reason for wishing this, for the vicinity of Paris and its resources constituted his military strength. We understood it all later, when we intercepted a report from Savary, the Minister of Police, in which he stated that he must repeat, that he could not answer for Paris, unless the theatre of war was removed farther from the capital.

away from the vicinity of Paris. He intended to be that night at St. Diziers. Many papers taken at the same time contained official and private accounts of the battle of Arcis, from whence it appeared that Bonaparte had totally failed in his object.

The Field-Marshal had previously decided on the 22nd that the army should march on the 23rd, and waited hour after hour for accounts from General Winzingerode, which were to determine the direction of the march. On the receipt of the papers taken with this courier, the following general plan was sketched out :—

Bülow's Corps was to remain before Soissons, and to take it ; but how ?—that was left entirely to General von Bülow.

The corps of York and Kleist were to follow Marshal Marmont.

With the corps of Winzingerode, Sacken, and Count Langeron, the Field-Marshal marched on the 23rd to Rheims, and on the 24th to Chalons.

Before he got there, news had already arrived from the Grand Army ; the connection with it was completely restored. General von Winzingerode had acted conformably to his instructions, and effected a junction with the Grand Army ; he received directions from the Emperor Alexander to follow Bonaparte to St. Diziers. The general news were, that the Grand Army had made a rapid retreat to Arcis on Bonaparte's moving against it on the 17th and 18th ; and that he had advanced against it on the 20th, after being joined by the detached corps of Gérard, Oudinot, and Macdonald ; but that, after a warm fight on the 21st, he had given up the attack and marched against Vitry. On the march the column in which his reserve artillery advanced was attacked, and a considerable number of guns and ammunition-waggons were taken. Instead of retreating towards Langres, as Bonaparte expected, the Grand Army followed him to Vitry, and on the 23rd its head-quarters were at Dampierre.

The Emperor of Austria, with his diplomatic corps, had gone from Bar-sur-Aube to Dijon, to be in the centre of operations. The operations around Lyons were of the greatest importance to Austria, on account of the connection with Italy.

March the 24th.—The Field-Marshal had his head-quarters at Chalons, and the corps of Count Langeron, Von Sacken, and Von Winzingerode bivouacked near the town. An aide-de-camp of the Emperor of Russia brought the news here that it was decided, if Bonaparte marched off, to let Winzingerode alone follow him, and to advance with the whole army to Paris. The head-quarters of the Sovereigns and Prince Schwarzenberg were at Vitry. It is impossible to describe the delight which this resolution produced in the Field-Marshal's head-quarters and in the army.

At seven in the evening some prisoners were brought in, captured by the Cossacks in the district of Sommesous. Similar convoys arrived at all hours of the day, and were sent to an officer whose business it was to examine them. They belonged to Marmont's corps; from them we learned that after crossing at Château Thierry, Marmont had marched by Montmirail and Sezanne, and had passed the village of Sommesous in the direction of Vitry in the evening of the 24th. On closer investigation, it came out that our patrols had seen this column march, and had taken it for one of ours. It was probable that Marmont intended to join Bonaparte, and came

upon our army in doing so ; but it was also probable, that he might discover the Grand Army on
the other side of Sommesous, and turn back the
same night.

The Field-Marshal sent immediate notice of this
to royal head-quarters, and as the Silesian Army
was to proceed in the direction of Etoges and Montmirail, he undertook to prevent Marmont from returning by Etoges.   He believed that Marmont
would be forced to lay down his arms if the Grand
Army could rapidly gain the Sezanne Pass.

On this intelligence directions were sent from
royal head-quarters on the 25th, just as the army
was marching off at six o'clock in the morning, for
the remaining portion of Winzingerode's corps, under
General Count von Woronzow, to proceed on the
chaussée from Chalons to Sommesous, as it was
possible that Marshal Marmont might turn upon
Châlons to join Bonaparte.

To march through a town and over a bridge like
the badly restored one at Châlons, always causes
delay ; it was almost noon before the advanced
guard of the Silesian Army passed the Soude brook
at Bierges.   The left flank patrol reported that a
hostile column with many waggons was marching in
the direction from Trecon to Ville Seneaux.   General
von Corff rode off instantly in that direction, with
some regiments of cavalry and two batteries of horse-
artillery.   He fell upon the hostile column, which
quitted the road, formed upon the height, and fired
on him with fifteen pieces of artillery.   General von
Corff captured on this occasion a number of bread,
flour, and ammunition waggons, and learned from
the prisoners, that this column was a division which
had departed that morning from Bergères, and had

orders to bring this convoy after Bonaparte. It did not belong to Marmont's corps. General von Corff kept up the cannonade to gain time, and to draw more troops there : five hostile battalions with fifteen pieces of artillery retreated across the country upon Fère Champenoise.

The Grand Army found Marshal Marmont in the morning at Sommesous, on his retreat to Sezanne. He had passed the night at Soude St. Croix. Conformably to the disposition, the Grand Army instantly attacked him warmly, and the fire moved pretty quickly towards Fère Champenoise. The Field-Marshal had ordered that the column of infantry should pursue its march to Etoges, and directed the cavalry of Sacken's corps, under General von Wasiltschikoff, to trot on beyond Bierges. The latter crossed the heights of Bergères by Petit Morain, at which place he found the hostile division just in a hollow, in full march upon Fère Champenoise, and in very good order. General von Corff followed beyond the range of cannon-shot.

Wasiltschikoff turned the enemy with his four regiments of cavalry, to detain him and to bring up some artillery ; but as the enemy continued his march, he attacked him. The hostile infantry defended itself so well, that he could not succeed in breaking in upon it : he was obliged to wait for his artillery. Before it arrived, the enemy had nearly reached Fère Champenoise ; and in front of this place was formed a line of twenty-four to thirty pieces of artillery, whether friends or foes no one knew. Just when the hostile infantry was in a hollow, this artillery began (firing above the enemy) to fire on General Wasiltschikoff, who answered the fire, his artillery having just arrived.

Luckily it was soon discovered that we were by mistake firing on one another; and on this discovery the whole artillery was directed on the five hostile battalions; two of these, wanting to escape from the cannon fire, separated from the others, and were attacked by the cavalry and taken prisoners. The fifteen guns fell one by one into our hands. The *three* remaining battalions threw themselves into *one*; and though they were fired at on two sides with case-shot, and attacked on three by cavalry, they repelled all attacks, proceeding on their march towards Banne.

The Sovereigns had come to the fight from the direction of Fère Champenoise,* and the greatest part of the Russian Horse Guards also came; but only the Uhlans joined in the fight. A Jäger regiment of horse from Count Langeron's corps penetrated at last into the compact mass, whereupon it was all captured.

The division consisted entirely of National Guards; ten days before they had joined the army from Melun, 10,000 strong; they had made some long marches, and had not yet seen an enemy. When they were taken, they still amounted to 5,200. The rest had deserted their colours, were left in lazarettos, or were marauding.

The Grand Army had gained great advantages over Marshal Marmont, and taken a number of guns from him. He remained stationary at Sezanne, and was not attacked there again.

* The King of Prussia sent an officer of his suite to the General in command of the hostile division, and summoned him to lay down his arms. General Pactod (who commanded the division) was disposed to negociate, as he saw no means of saving himself; but as he was attacked at the same moment by the Silesian Army, which knew nothing of the parley, he had no time for it.

In the afternoon a communication was opened between the Silesian Army and the corps of York and Kleist. General von Zieten, with the greater part of the cavalry of both corps, had reached Etoges in his pursuit of Marshal Marmont; he heard the firing at Fère Champenoise, turned to the right and came to Broyes. In the morning of the 26th, he sent forward a small advanced guard, which saw some hostile cavalry retreating through Sezanne, followed it, found the place unoccupied, and sent notice thereof to General von Zieten. He pursued the enemy with two regiments of cavalry, found some hostile infantry on the other side of the town, and saw unexpectedly behind him a great column of cavalry coming through Sezanne. It was Marshal Marmont's cavalry which had stood in front of Sezanne, and was now retreating. General von Zieten had no resource but to fight his way through, in which he succeeded indeed, but suffered some loss. The enemy pursued somewhat eagerly, until he came upon the reserve of two regiments of cavalry which General von Zieten had left, along with the horse-artillery, stationed behind the hill. This occasioned as great a loss to the enemy as General von Zieten had suffered.

On the 25th the Field-Marshal had his head-quarters at Etoges. Generals von York and Kleist were at Montmirail, and marched to La Ferté Gaucher on the 26th. At 4 p.m. just as they had taken up their position there, Marshal Marmont's column arrived on the chaussée from Esternay to La Ferté Gaucher. Unfortunately neither General had any cavalry, for the few horse that remained to them, had already been sent after the fugitives to Coulommiers. However they made 600 more prisoners.

The hostile column was received with the fire of

a 12-pounder battery, on which it immediately turned off to the left. Had there been any disposable cavalry, or had the pursuit been more active on the part of the Grand Army, Marmont must have lost all his infantry here. It escaped under cover of the night.

March 26th, the Field-Marshal, with the corps of Von Sacken, Count Langeron, and the remainder of Winzingerode's, was at Montmirail, and Prince Schwarzenberg at Treffaux. On the 27th, Blücher was at La Ferté-sous-Jouarre, the Sovereigns at Coulommiers. Generals von York and Kleist were that day at Trilport. Hostile troops (supposed to be 10,000 men) made their appearance opposite Trilport, on the right bank of the Marne; they wanted to hinder the construction of a bridge, and fired on the workmen with heavy artillery. Towards evening however the bridge was ready, and four grenadier battalions, under Lieutenant-Colonel von Hiller, pushed on to the suburbs of Meaux, after some warm fighting, which lasted till night. The enemy marched off in the night towards Paris, and at three o'clock in the morning blew up his powder-magazine on the hill behind Meaux.

On the 28th, the Silesian Army crossed the Marne. The corps of York and Kleist advanced by Claye; and from Claye to Montseigle, not far from Ville Parisis, they had some hot fighting, in which some companies of infantry allowed themselves to be surprised by hostile cavalry in the town of Claye.

The capture of the farm of Montseigle occasioned a still more considerable loss, as the French troops, though cut off, defended it obstinately. The Field-Marshal caused the bridge at Meaux to be immediately restored for the passage of the Grand Army.

The same evening a part of its staff arrived at Meaux.

On the 29th, the Silesian Army spread itself to the right, to make room for the Grand Army. Royal head-quarters were at Claye, Field-Marshal Blücher's at Aunay. The enemy had retreated from Livry to Pantin. By circuitous ways, Marshal Marmont reached the bridge of Charenton, and arrived at Charonne at five o'clock in the evening of the 29th. In the night he placed troops in the position of Belleville and Romainville, with Pantin in front.

Montmartre was provided with some entrenchments, and guarded by thirty pieces of artillery from the arsenal at Paris. Montmartre and the heights of Belleville formed, in a certain measure, two bastions. The villages of La Vilette and La Chapelle lay in the curtain. By means of the Ourcq canal, which goes from Pantin to La Vilette, and from thence to St. Denys, the whole polygon had a wet ditch in front. St. Denys had ramparts and walls, and was guarded against a *coup-de-main*. The Ourcq canal however was not completed, and was consequently filled with water only from Pantin to La Vilette. Between La Vilette and St. Denys there were several places left uncut for waggons to pass over.

In this position Marshal Marmont had collected from 30,000 to 35,000 men, including General Vincent's troops, the garrison of Paris, and the depôts of the army. We had committed the great mistake of allowing him to get to Paris, for we could have prevented it, if, when he was forced to turn off to the left from La Ferté Gaucher, we had taken pains to cut him off from Paris. But no one considered his corps of any importance after we had captured all his artillery. This corps indeed was no longer of importance in the open field, but it still had the gunners of the lost artillery, and in the Paris arsenals there must still be stores enough to enable it to replace its losses on arriving at Paris. Joseph Bonaparte, nominated by his brother, his lieutenant, Commander-in-Chief, and defender of Paris, was used indeed to command armies, but not to fight with them; he therefore fled in the morning of the 30th.

It had been already settled, on the 29th, to leave the corps of Von Wrede and Sacken at Meaux, in order to dispute the passage of the Marne with Bonaparte, in case he followed us. That we must attack Paris without loss of time was certain; for should Bonaparte get there, the National Guard must either fight us, or break out into formal rebellion against him. If he were not present, it might be expected that no one could demand or carry through anything. But it made an essential difference whether the National Guard came out against us or not, for by all accounts they were 30,000 men, though not all armed.

For the attack on the 30th, we had the corps of the Crown Prince of Würtemberg, Count Wittgenstein, and the reserve of Grenadiers and Guards of the Grand Army; and the corps of York, Kleist, Count Langeron, and Winzingerode's infantry, of the Silesian Army; in all about 90,000 men.

The Field-Marshal dispatched an officer to Claye, on the 29th, to procure the disposition for the following day; the officer did not return till a quarter past 7, A.M., on the 30th, bringing back the disposition, according to which the attack was to begin at 5 o'clock. The firing of the Grand Army was already heard, which was, according to the disposition, to attack the heights of Belleville and Romainville, while the Silesian Army was intended to carry Montmartre. It was probable that Montmartre, which formed the left wing of the enemy's position, was more fortified on its left side than on the side turned towards the position. With this view the disposition planned that the villages of La Vilette and La Chapelle, situated within the curtain, should be taken, and the ascent of Montmartre attempted from thence. This was also partly based on the circumstance of the heights of Montmartre and Belleville being so far apart that no cross-fire, even with 24-pounders, could take place in front of the curtain. In this disposition no attention was paid to the Ourcq canal, for it was not marked on any map, and the accounts of its direction and completion were extremely imperfect.

After 9 o'clock the advanced guard of York and Kleist's corps arrived between Pantin and the chaussée from Bourges to Paris; it found Pantin half occupied by us; but sharp fighting was still going on upon the heights behind.

The enemy occupied the Farm of Le Rouvroy, and had placed a battery of sixteen pieces of artillery in an excellent position behind it. In order to render some service to the Grand Army, General von Katzlar, who commanded the advanced guard, immediately opened fire with the half battery he had with him, but he fought with great disadvantages in point of position as well as numbers. When the corps arrived, the artillery of the brigades became by degrees engaged with the enemy's battery placed between Rouvroy and La Vilette; but the enemy silenced a great many guns, and in the haste of departure the reserve artillery had to be left behind in the rear of Winzingerode's corps. This is why the enemy retained the superiority in artillery the greater part of the day.

Count Langeron's corps had occupied Auber-viellers the previous evening, and found the enemy at St. Denys. A brigade was left between Pantin and the chaussée from Bourges to Paris, to support the advanced guard (which had in the interim attacked the Farm of Rouvroy and dislodged the enemy from thence); the rest marched off to the right to attack Montmartre and La Chapelle. The corps of York-Kleist rested its left wing on the chaussée from Bourges to Paris; Count Langeron had orders to mask St. Denys with one brigade, and to march by the plain of St. Denys to the attack of Montmartre.

While all this was was going on, the Grand Army pushed forward on the Belleville heights. The Guards stood in reserve behind Pantin. Some regiments of them followed, to be more à portée. At last the Prussian Guards received orders to support the attack. They did so, and even proceeded to attack, and took, a hostile battery. The Grand Duke Constantine, who commanded the Guards, would not allow any more of his troops to engage, and therefore came himself to the brigade which had been left behind Pantin, calling upon it to advance; upon which Prince William of Prussia, who commanded it, immediately traversed Pantin, and succeeded in driving back the hostile troops placed on this side, between the canal and the heights, into the barriers of Paris or La Vilette. The battery near Rouvroy alone still held out. But when the reserve artillery of York and Kleist arrived, and fifteen six-pounders were levelled against it on its left flank, it retreated. The infantry of Winzingerode's corps under General Count von Woronzow, had now arrived also, and formed into line on both sides of the chaussée from Bourges to La Vilette.

The tirailleurs of the Prussian advance-guard were quite close to La Vilette, when French troops of all arms broke out of this place, and drove back our troops towards the farm of Rouvroy. The 2nd regiment of Prussian Hussars of the body-guard went to meet the enemy's cavalry, threw it back upon the artillery and infantry, and captured a battery. General von Woronzow now advanced against La Vilette at the head of four battalions, carried it, took eight more guns, and drove the enemy within the barriers of Paris. All firing now ceased on the left wing as far as La Vilette, and soon after news reached this point that the Sovereigns had granted the city two hours' armistice, to enable it in that time to negotiate a capitulation.

On the right wing Count Langeron had just come far enough to turn Montmartre, and to draw up his troops in the avenue from St. Denys to the Bois-de-Boulogne, for the attack on Montmartre. Ten regiments of Russian infantry advanced from hence straight towards the hill, and ascended it under a considerable fire without flinching a moment. Luckily the enemy fired so high that the loss was not considerable. When the troops had advanced half-way up the hill, intelligence of the armistice reached them.

It was impossible to stop here or to turn back, they were obliged to finish the ascent of the hill. Twenty-nine guns were taken on Montmartre. The Grand Army had taken about forty. This day, therefore again cost the French army eighty guns, and a number of new powder-waggons.

The corps of York-Kleist had taken the village of La Chapelle at the same time as the attack was made on Montmartre. The Russian General Emanuel was detached to the right, and had the charge of guarding the bridges of Neuilly, St. Cloud, and Sèvres. Thus Paris was tolerably well invested on the right bank of the Seine.

On hearing that the capitulation was not yet arranged, and that in case of its failing we must hold ourselves prepared to bombard the city, the Field-Marshal transferred his quarters to Montmartre, and brought up all his heavy artillery, eighty-four pieces, against Paris.

Meanwhile the city capitulated, and on the 31st of March the Sovereigns made their entry. This day, St. Denys, which had been summoned in vain on the 30th, likewise capitulated. The garrison desired a written capitulation, but as threats had been held out on the 30th that if it did not surrender then no capitulation would be granted, these were now fulfilled, and it was obliged to yield at discretion.

The transactions in Paris, the establishment of the Provisional Government and its declaration of the dethronement of Bonaparte, are too well known to make it necessary to narrate them here ; but there remains to be told what Bonaparte had been doing all this time. On the 22nd and 23rd of March, on his way from Arcis, he invested Vitry, and summoned it to surrender. The commandant, the Prussian Colonel von Schwichow, had (as we have already mentioned) acquired a very strong garrison by the arrival of Generals Davidoff and Wasiltschikow III. The works being also in good condition, and the palisading completed, he declined all negotiation. Marshal Ney sent to request him to come on the glacis ;

the commandant did so, and here Marshal Ney in person called upon him to surrender,—a sign that the place was of importance to Bonaparte. On the 24th General Wasiltschikow III. made a sally and drove back the enemy towards St. Diziers. General Winzingerode pursued Bonaparte that day to St. Diziers, conformably to his instructions. He had about 8000 horse, 1000 Jägers, and proportionate artillery.

There is no doubt Bonaparte imagined, that if he manœuvred in the rear of the Grand Army, it would retreat, from apprehension for its line of communication. His movements show that this was his first thought. The orders expedited from Rheims to the fortresses in Lorraine also testify that he had an intention of strengthening himself with drilled soldiers from these fortresses, in the idea that strong garrisons would not be necessary, since the war must be decided in open field, and the fortresses were not likely to be besieged.

If, then, Bonaparte could still succeed in stirring up the people, and by that means delaying the Grand Army, or perhaps rendering it impossible for it to advance again, his operations had a very natural connection, namely :—

1. To make the Grand Army turn back by manœuvring.

2. To excite a general insurrection.

3. To strengthen himself from the fortresses in Lorraine.

4. To march back and form a junction with Marshal Marmont, in order to operate against the Silesian Army.

It has been previously mentioned that Field-Marshal Blücher sent on the 28th February, from La

Ferté-sous-Jouarre, directions to Nancy for collecting all the troops that might come there later, convalescents, recruits, &c., and for forming a body which was to be under the orders of Major-General Prince Biron of Courland. While this was going on, and Prussian as well as Russian troops were forming into a corps at Nancy, Monsieur (Comte d'Artois) repaired thither, and wishes were expressed that he should remain there, in order to accustom France to the thought that another rule was impending.

The Crown Prince of Sweden had arrived at Nancy at the same time, in order to proceed to royal head-quarters; but the inhabitants of the country round the town, which was from its hills and woods well adapted for guerilla warfare, were incited by Bonapartist officers to take up arms, and to seize upon couriers and convoys. The booty, and the small degree of danger attached to such attempts, perhaps also revenge for past excesses committed on them, soon increased the bodies of armed people to such an extent that the Allies were not safe outside the town without an escort, and the French partizans grew bolder and bolder in their undertakings.

The Crown Prince of Sweden travelled back to Liège, and the danger in which the Comte d'Artois stood of being attacked in Nancy itself, was concealed from him. Had he gone back, too, fear and terror would have spread, and the Bonapartist party would have quite got the upper hand.

The garrisons of the fortresses began to make sallies. General Jouseffowitsch was attacked on the 22nd in front of Metz. When, however, the garrison of Nancy became stronger, detachments were sent out to suppress the insurrections. When Bonaparte pushed detachments towards the Meuse, Prince Biron of Courland even went out to meet them.

Bonaparte's advanced guard proceeded from St. Diziers to Bar-sur-Aube, and even to Chaumont. Diplomatists of the Allies, baggage, couriers, and pontoons, were captured by it; but on all sides he received information that the Grand Army was not retreating towards Langres. As this was contrary to his calculations, it now became necessary to alter his plan. General von Winzingerode continued the pursuit, pretending to be the advanced guard of the Grand Army. It is not known whether Bonaparte was deceived by this, but he suddenly turned round on the 27th of March, and fell upon Winzingerode, who engaged in a combat in which he was beaten, and lost his artillery and a number of prisoners. He retreated in haste from St. Diziers, first towards Bar-le-Duc, then towards Châlons. On the 28th Bonaparte's advanced guard marched to Bar-le-Duc, the head of it had even a fight with the Prince of Courland. Here, as it appears, Bonaparte got information of the Grand Army's march to Paris, and he now resolved on marching rapidly to Paris by Troyes and Fontainebleau. No one impeded this march. Bonaparte arrived in person on the Essonne on the 30th, during the battle of Paris. It seems that he considered Paris quite lost, for he did not enter the city, and went back to Fontainebleau to wait for his army, which arrived there on the 4th and 5th of April.

On our side, when we heard of this march, and expected to be attacked by Bonaparte, the corps of Bülow, Sacken and Wrede were summoned to Paris. It was now a question whether we should attack

Bonaparte or await his attack. In a military point of view it was for us to attack him, for we were much the strongest, and had rested some days, while his army was arriving wearied and exhausted, after forced marches. But on the other hand it might be expected that the resolutions of the Provisional Government would produce a great impression on the army. Viewing it in this light, therefore, it seemed better to precipitate nothing, but to await the result of political negotiations and their effect on the army. For this purpose it was only necessary to secure the city of Paris from all Bonaparte's attempts and his influence. This could be done if the army held itself prepared for three different cases :

1. Bonaparte's advancing from Fontainebleau straight against Paris.

2. His pushing forward between the Seine and Marne.

3. His making a flank march to the left, to turn our right wing.

The first was the most probable for many reasons, and a position was found which would be advantageous, whether the enemy came from Corbeil, from Arpagon, or from Limours. This position was on the plain between Palaisau and the Seine. In front there was a tolerably deep valley, in which flows the Ivette and Orge, which runs into the Seine not far from Athis. On the plain, half a league from the Ivette and Orge, a brook rises at Vissous, which runs towards Paris, consequently at right angles to the Ivette, from whence commences a valley which separates the two roads from Fontainebleau to Paris, and from Longjumeau to Paris.

The village of Vissous was the centre of the army ; that is to say, the Silesian Army rested its left wing, and the Grand Army its right wing on it. This village was at the same time to be the pivot, if Bonaparte attacked; namely, when the advanced guard had defended the valley of the Ivette, and drawn every possible advantage from the ground to weary and weaken the enemy, it was then to retire ; in that case Bonaparte would have to decide which of the two armies to attack ; for he was too weak to fall on both at the same time : the one attacked would then remain on the defensive, and the other would assume the offensive, and take him in flank and rear. The garden-wall of Morengis had been battlemented for this purpose, and turned into an independent work ; 30,000 horse which we had at our disposition were to facilitate the movement. A route was reconnoitred, by which we could always remain on the heights between Versailles and Chevreuse, in case Bonaparte should turn our right wing. Bridges of boats were kept in readiness at Charenton, by which the army would be able to cross should Bonaparte advance between the Seine and the Marne.

All these preparations were unnecessary. Marshal Marmont, obedient to the call of the Provisional Government, separated with his corps from Bonaparte, who had been deposed ; the other marshals advised Bonaparte to capitulate ; and the end of it all was, as every one knows, the peace of Paris, and his retirement to the island of Elba.

Since the battle of Laon, the Field-Marshal had not so far recovered from the inflammation of his eyes as to be able to go through a whole battle on horseback. He attended to the business of the army ; but at the battle of Paris he was only able to appear on horseback for a short time, with a shade over his eyes. After the taking of Paris he laid down his command. He could not have chosen a better moment. To his constancy, and the almost unparalleled activity of his army, the Sovereigns chiefly owed the great result. Austria was most indebted to him, for she gained Italy without a battle, as a consequence of the capture of Paris. If, however, by his resolution at Mery, the Field-Marshal saved the Allied Armies from a ruinous retreat and the loss of the entire campaign,—if, at Laon, he broke Bonaparte's power, physically and morally,—still to the Sovereigns and to Prince Schwarzenberg (who, in the absence of his Monarch, represented the Austrian States) is due the lasting renown of having ended the campaign, and decided the fortune of Europe, by the grand resolution to march upon Paris.

Such will be the judgment of posterity and history. In our times, when events are so rapidly developed, it has already been often forestalled. Generals who wished to mystify public opinion, and, under its protection, wanted to place themselves high above others, have been judged by this same public opinion, and thrust back into the obscure insignificance to which they belong. The actions of the modest General were not overlooked by the multitude; the spirit of the age has proclaimed them with loud rejoicings; and if it is censured and abused by many as a bad spirit, it is truly not the worst point about it, that it thus permits every one to read his own epitaph.